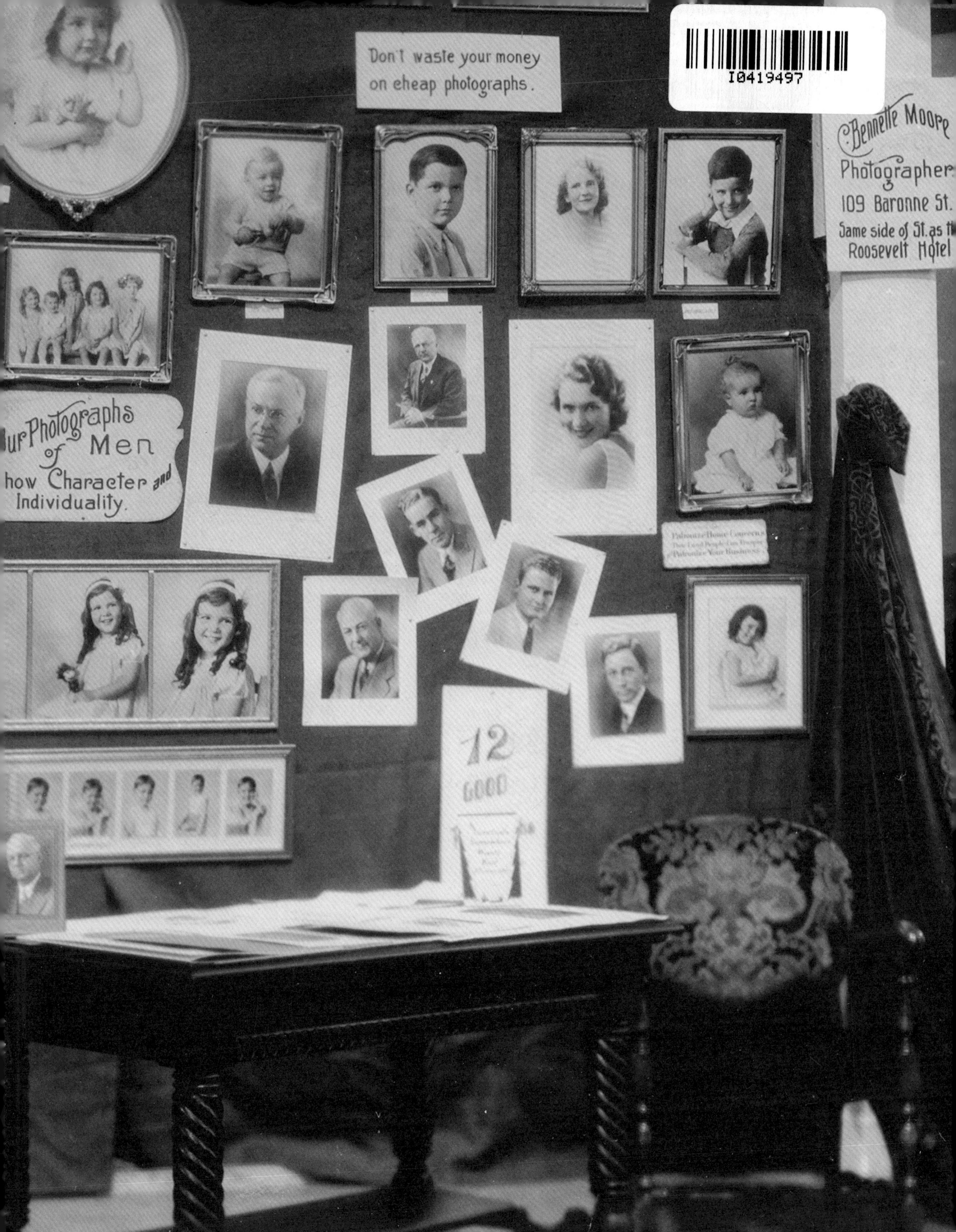

Louisiana Lens

Louisiana Lens

Photographs from The Historic New Orleans Collection

John H. Lawrence

Foreword by Jeff L. Rosenheim

The Historic New Orleans Collection

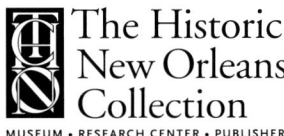
The Historic
New Orleans
Collection
MUSEUM · RESEARCH CENTER · PUBLISHER

The Historic New Orleans Collection is
a nonprofit institution dedicated to the
stewardship of the history and culture of
New Orleans and the Gulf South. Founded in
1966 through the Kemper and Leila Williams
Foundation, The Collection operates as a
museum, research center, and publisher in
the heart of the French Quarter.

© 2023 The Historic New Orleans Collection
533 Royal Street
New Orleans, Louisiana 70130
www.hnoc.org

EDITORS: Dorothy Ball and Cathe Mizell-
Nelson, with Margit Longbrake and Siobhán
McKiernan
DIRECTOR OF PUBLICATIONS: Jessica Dorman
PRESIDENT AND CEO: Daniel Hammer
DESIGN: Alison Cody

First edition. 2,500 copies.
All rights reserved.
Printed in Florence, Italy, by Conti Tipocolor
Distributed by the University of Virginia Press

27 26 25 24 23   1 2 3 4 5

ISBN: 978-0-917860-91-1

Library of Congress Control Number:
9780917860911

Louisiana Lens is dedicated to all photographers—past, present, and future—for their zeal in exploring and revealing this fascinating place, Louisiana, and to Priscilla Lawrence for tangible and intangible gifts too numerous to list.

Contents

FROM THE COLLECTION
Daniel Hammer   9

FOREWORD   11
Jeff L. Rosenheim

INTRODUCTION   15
John H. Lawrence

METAL, PAPER, AND GLASS   25
1843–1860

PRINTS ON PAPER   45
1861–1889

FROM PROFESSIONALS TO AMATEURS   65
1890–1935

EXPRESSION AND DOCUMENTATION   119
1936–1999

A DIGITAL EXPLOSION   249
2000–PRESENT

ACKNOWLEDGMENTS   281

INDEX   285

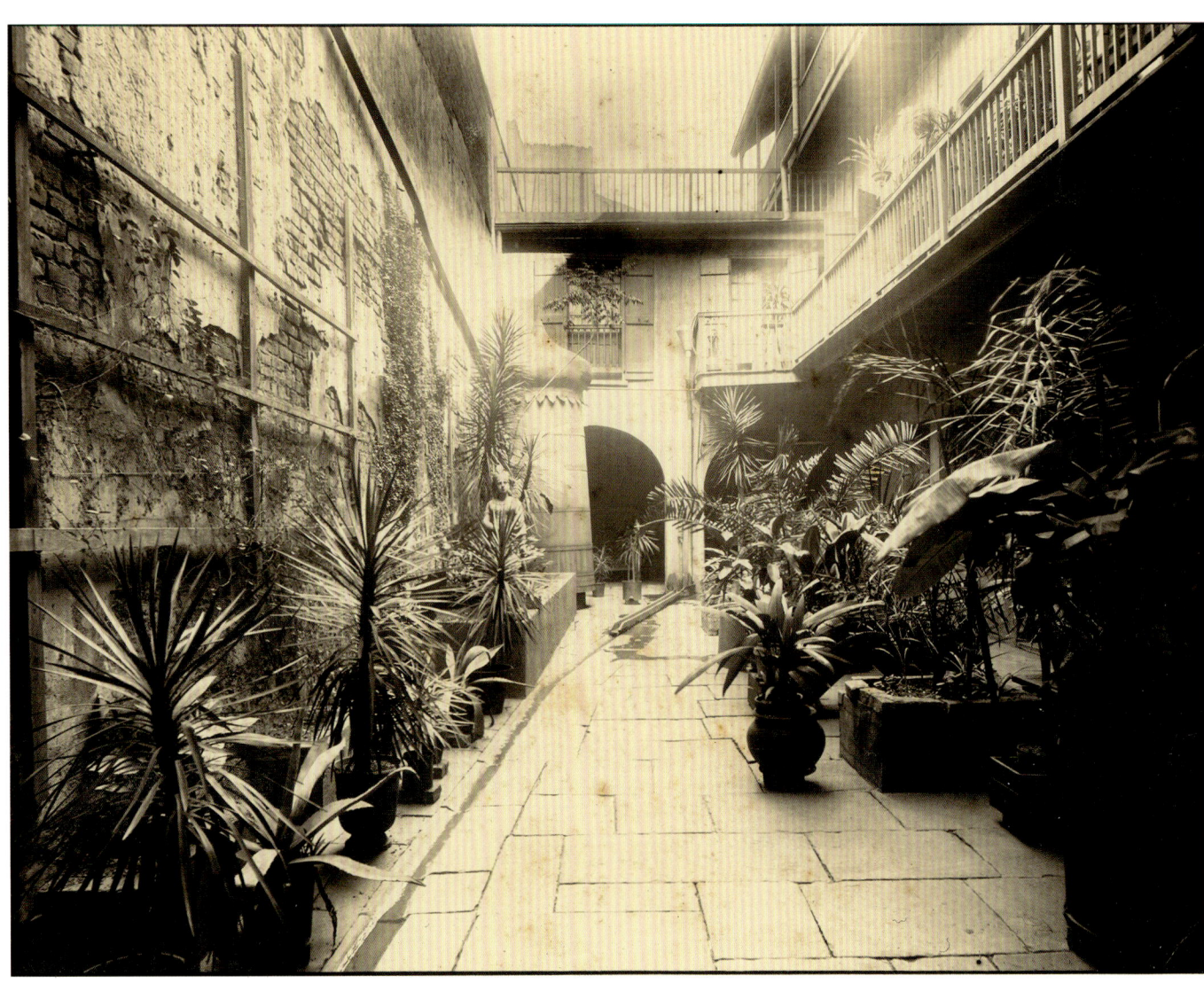

French Quarter courtyard with cistern, circa 1925

by Ernest J. Bellocq
gelatin silver print, 7¼ × 9⅛ in.
1997.32.1

FROM THE COLLECTION

It is my privilege and honor to dedicate myself to a singular and very important task: to ensure every reader of this book knows of The Historic New Orleans Collection's deep gratitude to John H. Lawrence. John's curiosity, intelligence, thoughtfulness, creativity, kindness, and warmth join the vision, passion, and resources of our founders in forming the basis upon which our institution is built. These values are second only to the public interest in the stewardship of our communal history and culture in defining what our institution is all about.

Of John's many roles in the development of THNOC, the most tangible is in the growth of our collections, where for over forty years John had a central and eventually leading part. This book describes some of those collections—the photographs—but, as Jeff Rosenheim points out in his introduction, those of us who know John realize that he is more than just a curator of photographs. At the same time, we recognize that if he were only the great curator of photographs that he is, that alone would make him remarkable.

During John's tenure at THNOC, the institution's holdings grew into the single largest collection of materials documenting the history and culture of New Orleans and the region. It is a collection that continues to grow through ever-developing methods and perspectives. And just as with taking a photograph, whatever the original purpose of adding any object to our collections, new meanings will be revealed by future observers. John's decades of leadership have helped us become what we strive to be—a museum dedicated to the stewardship of our community's history and culture, a resource for everyone who has something to learn or say about the people and history of New Orleans.

So, to John, thank you, and to all readers, welcome and enjoy!

Daniel Hammer
President and CEO

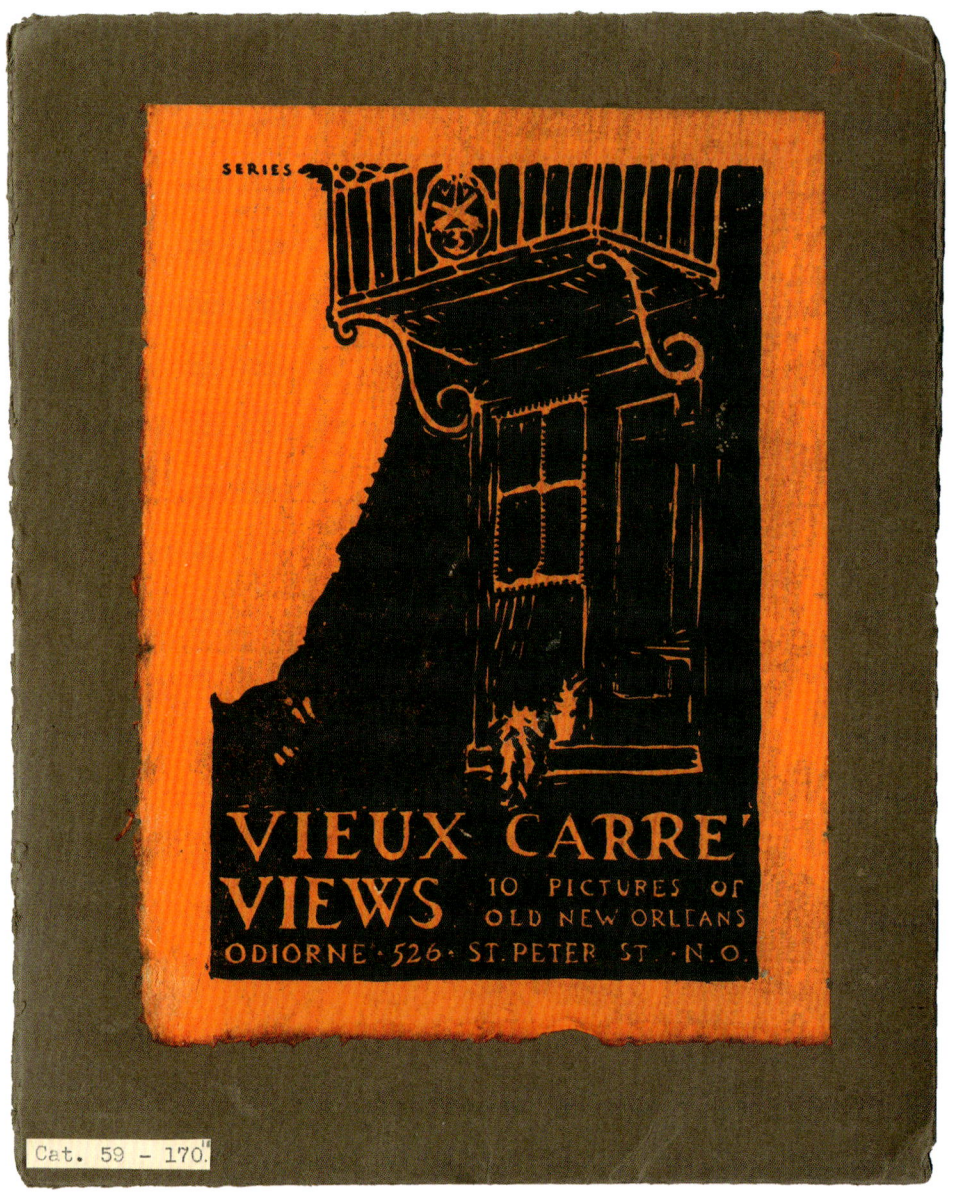

Cat. 59 - 170.

**Folder enclosure for a set of souvenir images of
New Orleans's Vieux Carré, ca. 1922**

by William C. Odiorne
paper folder with woodcut print, 9 × 7⅛ in.
gift of Boyd Cruise and Harold Schilke, 1959.170.11

FOREWORD

Stare. It is the only way to educate your eye, and more. Stare, pry, listen, eavesdrop. Die knowing something. You are not here long. —*Walker Evans, circa 1960*

Some cities live as much in the imagination as in reality: Athens, Jerusalem, Luxor, Varanasi, and Rome, to cite just a few. These age-old metropoli are still inhabited today and continue to lure travelers by name alone. We go to Kyoto to explore its temples, shrines, and gardens. We travel to Cuzco to experience its ancient Incan stonework architecture and to see firsthand the beauty of its elegant weaving tradition. In all these places, we immerse ourselves in the lives of the contemporary inhabitants and celebrate their unique customs, cuisines, and histories.

The city of New Orleans is just as beguiling and revered worldwide. Founded in 1718 (after Havana, Santa Fe, and New York), it is not an ancient city, and yet it has always lived in my mind's eye as much as Timbuktu. From my perspective—I'm a child of the Mississippi River, born in St. Louis, 700 miles north—New Orleans is without any question the nation's most exceptional and distinctive city and the first I called home after setting out on my own in 1983. I could hardly wait to move to the French Quarter, which I did forty years ago, to a tiny apartment in an 1852 building just two blocks from the main site of The Historic New Orleans Collection. The Xiques House, at 521 Dauphine Street, can even be seen in the background of a photograph by Peter Sekaer included in this book (p. 121).

John H. Lawrence has been a most generous and trusted guide to New Orleans to generations of captivated transplants, including me. Until his decampment to a farmhouse in Mississippi just a year ago, he lived in the city all his life. New Orleans and its complex and beautiful history sustained and stimulated Lawrence; and he in turn liberally shared his hunger for collecting and interpreting its past and present through his almost half century of service as a photography curator, director of museum programs, and master collection builder at The Historic New Orleans Collection.

Lawrence's knowledge of New Orleans culture is encyclopedic. His memory for fascinating if obscure facts is remarkable, his passion for visual culture intoxicating. In aggregate, his understanding of the city is the essential subject of this new publication. Lawrence's specialty is the era beginning with the birth of photography in 1839 and ending with the death of the medium . . . sometime in the far-distant future. In more ways than can be expressed, Lawrence became a benevolent caretaker for the city in his various roles at The Historic New Orleans Collection. This book, more than any of the others in his storied career, is a tremendous gift which he has bequeathed to us all and to New Orleans itself after his recent retirement. He is the city's modern-day Milton, its vanguard Vasari.

Leave it to Lawrence to construct a publication as dynamic and eccentric as the city itself: while it is arranged chronologically, the book is not wholly intended to be an encyclopedia of photographic treasures from The Historic New Orleans Collection. It fully accomplishes this noteworthy goal, but it does so while artfully serving as a portrait of New Orleans itself and as a partial sketch of its able servant who acquired for the museum almost every photograph and album featured. As the publication explores the minutiae of local history and culture, Lawrence slyly weaves into his writing enchanting details about photography's technological advancements and its many movements and schools of practice over a 180-plus-year history.

In its physical form, *Louisiana Lens: Photographs from The Historic New Orleans Collection* echoes a landmark book, *Looking at Photographs: 100 Pictures from the Collection of the Museum of Modern Art* (1973) by John Szarkowski, the lauded curator of MoMA's collection. Most of the texts in *Louisiana Lens* face the photographs to which they refer: they mirror the selected pictures and offer a literary reflection by the author on the matter at hand, whether it is a church organ, a portrait of a free person of color, or a hipped "umbrella roof." In his introduction to *Looking at Photographs*, Szarkowski writes: "As a way of beginning, one might compare the art of photography to the act of pointing. . . . It is not difficult to imagine a person—a mute Virgil of the corporeal world—who might elevate the act of pointing to a creative plane." Lawrence fully agrees with the clarity of this assessment of the medium of photography, as do I. And he has referenced his curatorial forebear and pointed the way for the next generations. Logjams on the Red River; the difficulty of documenting an illegal, bare-knuckle open-air boxing match swarmed by 5,000 spectators; and oystermen plying their trade atop a midden on Grand Isle are equally worthy of our attention. He, and we, become enthralled by the city's diverse commercial activity in the late 1880s, courtesy of the fantastic signage on the facades of dozens of businesses in the *Photographic Album of the City of New Orleans*, an exceptionally rare book of cyanotypes that serves as an early photographic Yellow Pages.

Lawrence examines with flair and passion: family snapshots made with one of the world's first hand-held cameras (a Kodak); elegant studio portraits from the Jim Crow era of early jazz musicians with their instruments; and an alluring nude study made by perhaps the city's most elusive artist, Ernest J. Bellocq, known for his unabashedly stylish photographs of women in Storyville, the infamous red-light district formerly located just a ten-minute amble from The Historic New Orleans Collection. Lawrence illuminates the performative dynamics of the city's now-famous jazz funerals, as well as the blood-red tonality of a NASA aerial photograph of the Bonnet Carré Spillway flowing into Lake Pontchartrain. Through a judicious presentation of photographs, he covers with panache and confidence the city's seemingly timeless love of football, politics, music, seafood, and sex.

It is no surprise that the book surveys in multiple examples the important role of Carnival in the city's past and present, notably with a droll autochrome portrait from 1921 depicting a masked krewe member in leather boots and medieval-style gauntlets wearing a saffron-colored suit and cape. It remains unclear whether this Mardi Gras knight has already ridden his noble steed or has yet to do so, or, for that matter, who made the photograph. This lack of certitude does not in any way disturb the reader, as is true for a good number of the most effective photographs in this fascinating anthology. It merely reflects Lawrence's acute, democratic vision.

Lawrence is a well-known expert on the achievement and legacy of Louisiana's native son Clarence John Laughlin, and thus it is appropriate to see not one but three superb examples of the photographer's work. The selections include the germinal *"Mother" Brown* from 1945, one of the first and only examples of camera art acquired by Kemper and Leila Williams, the founders of The Historic New Orleans Collection. As proposed by Lawrence in 1981, the museum acquired the negative and photographic print archive of the artist born in Lake Charles, the Baudelaire on the bayou, lauded for his idiosyncratic, surrealist photography, poetry, and prose.

The majority of Lawrence's selections are important works by nationally known makers including Jay Dearborn Edwards, Frances Benjamin Johnston, Doris Ulmann, Walker Evans, and two night-and-day-different artists each named Michael Smith. He also presents masterpieces created by lesser-known picture makers including Arthur P. Bedou, Mother Marie de la St. Croix, Jules Cahn, Christopher Porché West, Harold Baquet, and the still unheralded family of artists known collectively as "unknown photographer."

One must also note the pathos of the photographs Lawrence chose to commemorate the devastation caused by Hurricane Katrina in 2005. It's a body of work still being collected by The Historic New Orleans Collection from individuals and governmental sources such as the Federal Emergency Management Agency (FEMA). Some presented here are the works of first responders, including Chris E. Mickal, a chief of the New Orleans Fire Department; others are by photographers working for national media—like Robert Polidori, who grew up in the city's Gentilly neighborhood and who returned home to bear witness to the pain and destruction caused by the storm. His heart-rending portrait of an empty bedroom on North Miro Street, in the city's Lower Ninth Ward, presents the nightmare flooding in its most visceral architectural form. One wonders whether the residents survived the hurricane, and if so, did they return home and attempt to rebuild their lives?

In summary, *Louisiana Lens* is a delightful compendium of some 120 different photographers selected by Lawrence, who brings a passionate, resourceful, creative, and fearless eye (and hand) as a collection builder, historian, curator, and author. Lawrence's prose is delightfully readable, devoid of the arcane language that has become the lingua franca of contemporary scholarly discourse. It is thus a distinct pleasure to read the lyrical musings of a colleague so devoted to New Orleans and, simultaneously, so acutely aware of photography's visual and written history. The photographs and their careful analysis offer ample proof of Lawrence's humanity and erudition. Even for those well steeped in the city's unique traditions, the book offers a provocative study of New Orleans and the river region. What emerges from *Louisiana Lens*, and the collection on which it is based, is the construction of a new and elegant history of photography in the United States seen through the wide-angle lens of the Crescent City.

Jeff L. Rosenheim
New York, January 2, 2023

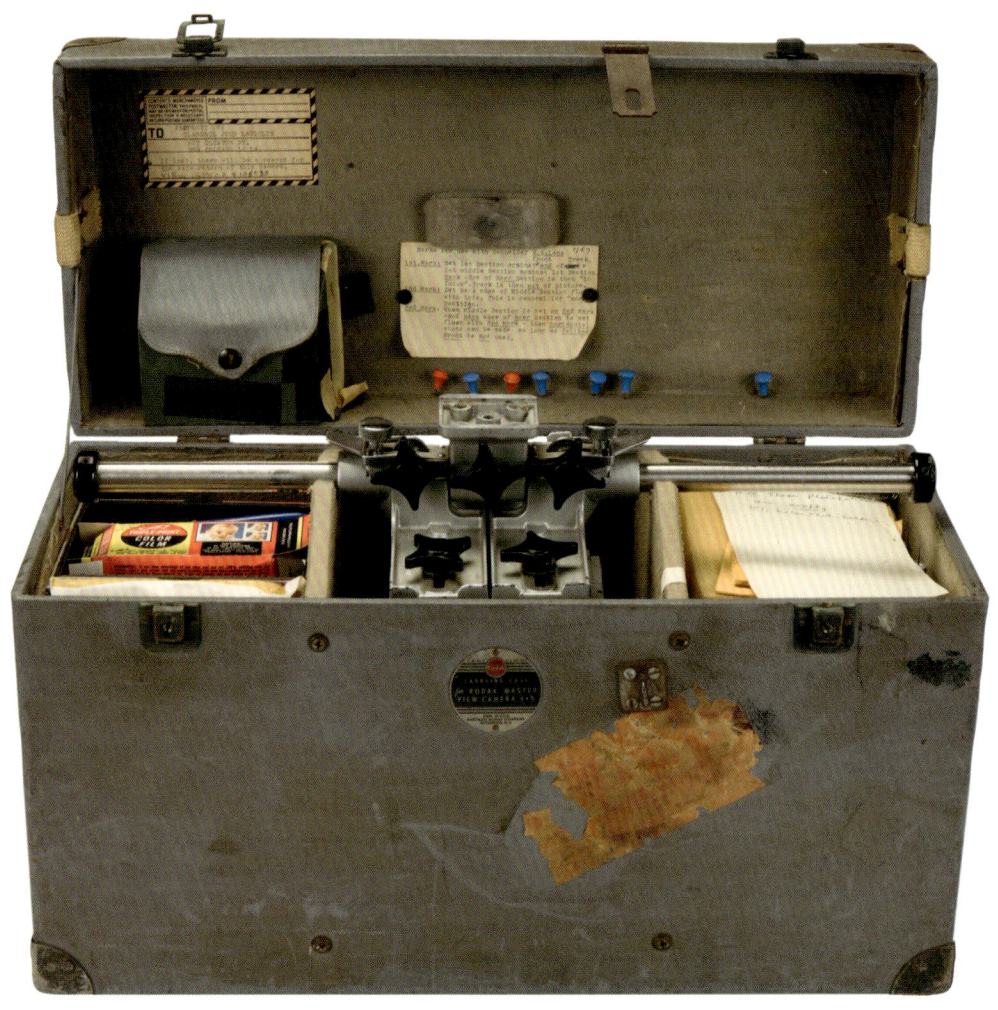

**Clarence John Laughlin's Kodak Master View Camera
in its original case**
late 1940s
1981.247.13.1

INTRODUCTION

How is it possible for an author to choose a very small group of pictures from among many hundreds of thousands and make a claim of being either objective or systematic in the process? It isn't. And so this book's approach to the subject of Louisiana photography is more representative than encyclopedic, and the ideas it engages are exploratory rather than conclusive. Representative because, in a practical sense, even a relatively small region like Louisiana is impossible to map exhaustively through photography; exploratory in anticipation of future scholarship that may well alter the factual data about these pictures while enlarging the context in which they may be understood. The static display contained within each photograph's borders is the constant in this dynamic situation, and it is hoped that the visual content of these images will continue to engage the interest of coming generations, regardless of other circumstances and interpretations.

Even a small museum photography collection has the attribute of being an "all-you-can-eat" buffet of image makers, symbols, and content. The person who tries to indulge in more than a sampling is confronted with a Sisyphean task of trying to consume it all. Like attempting to explain the origin of the universe (billions of years of history) in an executive summary, much must be left out. Such is the case even with objects in this collection numbering orders of magnitude fewer than billions. Including it all is not an option for this project. A collection can't be captured either physically or intellectually by throwing some large imaginary (and inadequate) net over it.

In putting an exhibition together, a curator mines the collection for items to include. If one assigns traditional products of mining to this effort, a curator may be looking for precious or base metals, gems, and ores among the collection, targeting whatever items are necessary to populate the exhibition. A book like this, however, differs from an exhibition

inasmuch as it is able to celebrate the entire range of a collection for its own sake, and can better suggest the collection's richness, rather than a narrow sampling of stunning examples devoted to a single practitioner, theme, or epoch. The selection of pictures in this book rests on a framework of defensible objectivity (a desire to include certain processes, makers, and eras) but the individual images are chosen more on instinct, which is to say a combination of experience and luck. The final result is a Venn diagram where the history of photography in Louisiana intersects the holdings of The Historic New Orleans Collection.

Acquiring photographs was not a priority for Lewis Kemper Williams (1887–1971) and his wife Leila Hardie Moore Williams (1901–1966) as they began, in the 1930s, to assemble the trove of Louisiana historical materials that, following their deaths, would form the cornerstone of The Historic New Orleans Collection (THNOC). The Williamses' interests lay, rather, in more traditional antiquarian materials: maps, rare books, prints, drawings, manuscripts, and paintings of different types, which served as elements in telling a story of Louisiana's (and especially New Orleans's) history. And the legacy they left was not only their collections and French Quarter properties but also an endowment that has permitted THNOC to grow far beyond its original idea.

In examining the founders' legacy holdings, two photographic acquisitions stand out: a portfolio of photographs by New Orleans–based Clarence John Laughlin, purchased from the artist in 1951; and a portfolio of French Quarter scenes by William C. Odiorne, acquired in 1959, that when produced in the early 1920s was primarily geared to the tourist market. Another notable early acquisition—a body of work relating to the post–Civil War New Orleans visits of popular illustrator Alfred R. Waud—included, alongside several hundred of the artist's sketches and finished drawings, a half-dozen full-plate tintypes (p. 48). Scattered among these early Williams acquisitions are a few historical photographic items, such as stereographs and cartes de visite, but most are those that marked personal milestones, family events, and Mardi Gras activities.

The Odiorne and Laughlin portfolios served as symbolic bookends of the region's expressive photography in the middle decades of the twentieth century. Odiorne's 1922 set was firmly rooted in the tenets of the latter-day pictorialist movement, emphasizing soft focus, warm tones, and picturesqueness of its subjects. Laughlin, a photographer whose approach to photography defies simple description, used the cold-toned, sharp, and glossy vocabulary of photographic modernism in his work, while accompanying his prints with commentary that was an integral element of the photograph's conception and presentation. Between these two points on a scale, THNOC's original holdings contained isolated examples of snapshots, documentary-style pictures, and studio portraits.

In 1974, the year THNOC hired its first full-time professional director, the acquisition of the Leonard V. Huber Collection (some 25,000 items across many types of media) ushered in the first major influx of photographic materials to The Collection's holdings following the deaths of the Williamses [xref]. This group included numerous vintage photographs—works printed at, or close to, the time the negative was made—as well as later prints from original negatives and prints that were copied from existing photographs. But this action did not signal a defined institutional intent to collect photographs as a medium. Photographs were one visual form of expressing historical data found in the Huber Collection, and those examples stressed the documentary or descriptive aspects of the medium rather than creative or expressive motives.

Among these was an 1859 salted-paper photograph by Jay Dearborn Edwards showing the newly constructed tomb of the New Lusitanos Benevolent Association in the Girod Street cemetery, a structure that had been demolished in the mid-1950s. The Edwards photograph represented a story not only of a tomb dedication but the full life cycle of the city's first Protestant cemetery. Wrapped around this photograph was an indisputable mantle of history. The photograph would also serve as a harbinger.

Over the years, beginning in 1981, more than forty additional photographs by Edwards were added to THNOC's holdings with the beachhead provided by the Huber prints. Today, as a group, these remain the earliest paper photographs of New Orleans that have come to light, giving a glimpse of the cityscape in the years just prior to the Civil War.

Edwards's photographic transcriptions of buildings, activities, and sites augment a robust assortment of printed views of New Orleans that were disseminated as single sheets, or that accompanied articles in the popular press. Prints such as those were avidly acquired by the Williamses. The photographic examples of subjects reproduced in other media are informative of the ways that artists and illustrators changed content, spatial relationships, and other elements in order to achieve a well-composed interpretation of what was actually present.

Photographs, sometimes in great numbers, sporadically entered THNOC's holdings in the 1970s and '80s. The year 1976 marked a start in collecting 35 mm negatives by New Orleans–based photographer Betsy Swanson. The bulk of her work at THNOC is a systematic documentation of historic architecture in the New Orleans metropolitan area, much of which was published in a landmark series of books issued by the Friends of the Cabildo organization. The many thousands of negatives by Swanson entered THNOC's holdings over a period of years, and what they show complements other collections and classes of objects at THNOC devoted to the history of the city's growth and neighborhood development.

In 1978, photographer Stuart M. Lynn donated several hundred prints and sheet-film negatives made during the 1940s and 1950s. In 1979, the acquisition of the Charles L. Franck archive solidified a conscious, systematic approach to collecting photographs that showed historical data from the early to mid-twentieth century. Again, the Huber Collection came into play, in the role of catalyst, because it contained significant subjects Leonard Huber selected from the Franck studio to illustrate multiple books that he authored. These selections suggested with relatively few examples the richness of Franck's archive and its suitability as a core collection. Though nearly five hundred vintage prints accompanied the Franck Collection, the bulk of the material was in the form of 8 × 10 sheet film negatives (some 7,100 in total) along with a quantity of panoramic photographs and their negatives. Over a period of a few years, The Collection engaged the services of Nancy Ewing Miner, a photographic printer, to create prints and allow easier access to the items acquired in negative form.

Soon after, the acquisition of the entire Clarence John Laughlin Archive followed in two separate transactions (1981 and 1983). The combined number of prints and negatives from these acquisitions was some thirty thousand items. Both were championed by Chief Curator (later Executive Director) Joanne "Dode" Platou, during whose tenure the photography holdings expanded greatly. Though Laughlin's stature as a Louisiana artist in the field of creative photography was a strong consideration in securing the work, the surface documentary character of his photographs underscored their use in the collections of a history museum.

Collecting contemporary photographs of documentary character by living and/or active practitioners took time to become a de facto policy, though an early instance of this occurred in 1976, when Josephine Sacabo was commissioned to create a portfolio about the city's markets and street vendors for an exhibition on that subject. After a point, the nature of historic photographs (their processes, subjects, and practitioners) and their use by scholars and the public in research projects helped to overcome the stigma initially attached to the "intrusion" of contemporary photographs into THNOC's holdings. This Rubicon was crossed when the acquisitions committee—responding to staff persistence and changing cultural attitudes about the role of photography in a historical institution—overcame their resistance to acquiring contemporary works, even those presented in a more "artistic" manner. The achievements of exceptional New Orleans–based photographers such as Michael P. Smith and Richard Sexton, who worked in a documentary style and made contemporary pictures deeply rooted in the city's history, culture, and neighborhoods, were in a large measure responsible for helping bring about this change.

For some decades, then, THNOC had been gradually moving in the direction of accommodating contemporary pictures in its permanent collection. Hurricane Katrina (2005) settled any remaining questions about the matter—sparking an explosion of both documentary and expressive photographs, and establishing both as essential to the creation of the historical record. For the last two decades, such work has regularly been added to the holdings through both gift and purchase. The Collection had achieved an important milestone, embracing a philosophy that photographs appropriate in the collection of an art museum could also support the collections and mission of a history museum.

Photographs in history museums often find themselves in the crowded ZIP code of "documentary photography," a form that seems to drive out portraiture, landscapes, and consciously created expressive (i.e., artistic) photographs. But are not these genres also a part of a place's history and its history of photography? *Louisiana Lens* includes examples of those.

Pictures made long ago can, of course, inform the viewer about the past as well as the present; what we can be assured of is that photographs augment our knowledge in direct proportion to the curiosity we bring to them. These are two of the reasons why museums collect them. But ill-considered links between past and present can create pitfalls. How photographs are used in the aftermath of their creation can amount to a gerrymandering of intent. Regardless of the timeless qualities inherent in some works, viewers who seek current meaning in historical photographs risk denying the creator's original intent. Such an approach can neuter the historical context of the picture, as well as dampen the pure pleasure of delectation. It is a challenge to see the original purpose of a photograph, whose durability as an object and an image may conjure a different meaning in the eyes of a present viewer. Looking at photographs can be an enjoyable and even whimsical experience, or can call up more sobering emotions, depending upon the subject matter. Optimally, a balance of original purpose and new meanings is revealed to the contemporary viewer.

The selection in this book is meant to acknowledge those poles and all of the nuanced latitudes that occur between them. THNOC's photography collection has not been designed as a comprehensive survey of the entire history of photography of the city or the state. That said, this book strives to cover the important movements of photographic practice (among them amateur, documentary, commercial, and expressive) as well as the major processes of photography of the last 175 years. The author's hope is that the pairing of image and words will help the reader construct a useful relationship to institutional holdings.

Any book that considers photographs made in Louisiana, especially in New Orleans, will need to contend with stereotypes of culture that have become, in some instances, commodified tropes: music, food, Mardi Gras, architecture, and the idea of "Creole-ness." The images chosen for this book acknowledge these tropes but suggest a broader definition of place: transportation, shipbuilding, heavy industry, religion, portraiture, building and infrastructure construction, family pictures and albums of different types, along with many other subjects and forms. New Orleans and Louisiana may be exceptional in some ways, but not all. Photographable "things" that happen around the world also happen in Louisiana, and photographs of things that might be considered routine are nonetheless important in describing a place's history and creating a portal to understanding it. Photographs are visual yardsticks: a means of measuring what people and places share, and what elements are specific (if not unique) to them.

Nonetheless, one will find that "Louisiana" photography is not limited to those items produced in the state or by those men and women practicing within its geography. THNOC's photography holdings offer insights into Louisiana histories of all types by photographs made as far away as France and Japan.

It has always been the author's contention that for a history museum, the acquisition of complete archives—or very large numbers of photographs from a single entity (business or individual) across an extended period of time—is preferable to the acquisition of singular, isolated visual points over the same time. It is the notion of critical mass that gives archives or large collections the ability to reveal, with greater accuracy and nuance, what has changed and what has remained static in any given epoch. This assumes that a goal of such a collection is to acknowledge how photographs have both shaped and recorded the events—quotidian, singular, and spectacular—that form a web of collective visual memories of a place and its populace. THNOC has over a dozen photographic archives of photographers or firms. Some are represented in this book by more than one example to demonstrate how pictures made by a single entity can differ across both time and subject matter. That said, selecting one or even a handful of examples from such rich practices has a way of skewing a viewer's perception and leaving many facets of individual careers unaddressed. For readers of this book, exploration of the archives, online or in person, is encouraged.

To the extent that a canon of photographic history exists, many if not most of the photographs and photographers presented here do not conform to its norms and values. Whether published between covers or existing online, canons are no sooner established than they are challenged by the ever-growing number of photographs and practitioners and the ever-shifting critical consensus about what constitutes a seminal work. Recent reevaluations have expanded the geographic boundaries of the canon, yet photographic practice and production have become so ubiquitous that any collation purporting to be a history of the medium must omit exponentially more work and workers than it includes. In some small way, this book seeks to establish both the richness and worth of photographs hitherto underappreciated due to their geographic specificity, their documentary purpose, and their limited or local audience.

In the photographic holdings of a history museum, one must both concede and accept the idea that photographs of important content and compositional elegance are made by all kinds of people, not only professional photographers and artists (whether self-identified or given that designation by acclaim and custom). What often separates the amateur from the professional isn't quality, then, but constancy of

application in making pictures, and consistency of a coherent and often innovative vision that produces a very high percentage of "good" ones. A photographic career—commercial, documentary, or artistic—is one that achieves and maintains a level of attention about describing the world in pictures.

The act of making a photograph contains within it a declaration (or at least a notion or hope) of future visibility. Stated alternatively, it is seen as a way of preserving some element of history, whether personal or communal. In considering historically oriented (or collected) photographs some thinking has gone so far as to posit the idea that the camera and photography are agents not only of self-representation, but self-determination. The ability to accomplish such things has changed dramatically in the last quarter century but is not a recent phenomenon.

For a very long time, photography and photographs have not required an intermediary to produce professionally acceptable results. This has been true since at least the rise of the mass-produced, handheld camera in the late 1880s and has only been made easier through the ubiquity and general technical excellence of digital methods in current use. Even before the rise of digital photography, Frank de Caro noted in his introduction to *Folklife in Louisiana Photography*, "Never before in history have people been able to achieve such a ready familiarity with images and to produce images for themselves with such ease, factors that have produced an incredible potential for self-depiction and for aiding personal and collective memory." Building on an extreme notion of this idea, the camera can serve the function of amanuensis, a characteristic spectacularly exploited by social media platforms. In the issue of quantity vs. quality, a nod is often given to the former, prompting the coinage of the term "phone-ography" by Metropolitan Museum of Art curator Jeff L. Rosenheim. The glut of imagery available to historians and curators is overwhelming not just in theory, but in fact.

What should be a defining attribute of a museum collection—whether consisting of artworks or historical materials—is assembling those items that rise above the background chatter of their forms, and in doing so provide a visual and historical clarity to their subject, as well as offering different approaches to viewing or appreciating the content. This clarity can take the shape of documenting the construction of a bridge, airport, or domed stadium; showing that a Natchitoches meat pie for sale at the annual New Orleans Jazz and Heritage Festival is an element of regional culinary culture; acknowledging personal milestones; or establishing that a finely designed building once stood at a certain intersection. Such photographs, when they exist in a critical mass that spans time, content, and authorship, begin to suggest that the medium is indispensable in creating a historical profile of a place, its inhabitants, and the activities that happen there.

Whatever else they may be, photographs are patient. Their content doesn't change, and the rewards they offer upon multiple viewings are cumulative rather than episodic. For the most part, the holdings of THNOC consist of dutifully made photographs aimed at describing particular people, places, and things (precisely because they are those particular people, places, and things) rather than consciously created works of artistic expression. One issue that curators are confronted with when collecting is the jumble of creative, technological, and content elements that are all drivers of producing a photographic image. Museums will emphasize these traits differently, and the justification for acquiring a particular type of photograph will vary from one institution to the next.

One must concede that art is part of any larger history of a region, and within the holdings of THNOC are photographs (and photographers) deemed significant by museums that consider artistic merit a primary attribute. But not every picture can be an artistic masterpiece, nor should that expectation exist in a history museum's collections. Photographs are often charged with showing nothing more than clearly described visual data that has the appearance of neutral documentation. Consequently, most photographs of interest to historical institutions are instructive more than exceptional. That a relatively small number of them are the result of masterful, even brilliant, decision making is a bonus.

Once created, physical objects and even their digital surrogates (including photographs) have a limited number of paths they can follow. They may be permanently discarded or otherwise destroyed, they may be awaiting discovery, or they may be kept and perhaps passed along. It is the latter category that allows the formation of "the historical record," whether the retention is fortuitous or deliberate. It's not quite accurate to say that the historical record consists of random survival of detritus, though to curators and historians it may seem that way. A photograph may have been born for a particular reason—but through the passage of time and/or a loss of context, that reason may be obscured or no longer relevant. What does that picture, bereft of those earlier qualities, mean now? Over time, the concept of photographer Henri Cartier-Bresson's "decisive moment" depicted in a photograph becomes more and more flexible intellectually, without ever changing what it is photographically.

The poet W. H. Auden noted in 1941 that "poetry might be defined as the clear expression of mixed feelings." This observation might also be applied to photographs, whose content, while usually clearly expressed, can be felt, experienced, or interpreted variably or even contradictorily. One might keep Auden's sentiment in mind when considering two basic approaches to looking at photographs: what does the photograph *show*, and what does it *mean*? There is a difference in seeing what the photograph shows and what we wish to see, and the size of that gap is proportional to our response, perhaps even helping to define our attraction to certain pictures. We must be aware of the notion that all photographs are on some level "bait and switch" enterprises, deluding the viewer into thinking that a photograph of a thing, person, place, or event is that thing (or person, or place, or event) itself. Indeed, one of photography's biggest deceptions is its surface appearance of avoiding deception.

In the preface to his *Tractatus Logico-Philosophicus* (1921), the philosopher Ludwig Wittgenstein observed, "What can be said at all can be said clearly, and whereof one cannot speak, thereof one must be silent." An avid photographer, he could have offered a corrective to this observation by adding, "Or one could take a picture." Any power that photographs have—historically or artistically—is in "saying" things that words alone (whether spoken or written) cannot express with the clarity or completeness of a photograph. Photography's particular history is part of the broader framework of events within which it occurs and by which it is influenced. Simultaneously, as Alan Trachtenberg has written, photographs shape the perception and understanding of history.

Just as there is more to playing the game of baseball than knowing the rules, so there is more to photography than simply pressing the shutter button. A level of skill, if not understanding, must be overlaid on the general structural knowledge for each subject. Photographs must engage not only our feelings (which is easy enough to do) but our intellect, which may require more work on our part. Yet on some level there is an expectation that a photograph bears some truthfulness to its subject. This tension between real and perceived qualities is almost an irritant as a viewer examines the picture. The irritation, or abrasion, occurring between photograph and subject (and photographer and subject) is a propulsive element in the interaction between the photograph and the viewer. When the photographs are referencing a generous, historically based universe, the mental irritant becomes the source of thinking about photographs in a way that transcends the simple subject. The photograph has become, as it were, a portmanteau—a container for other objects and ideas. We do photographs and photographers a disservice when we think of them and their creations as *truthful* rather than *factual*. The photographer can become a medium to another world, and the photograph can function as the séance.

Although a photograph is by its nature linked to a particular moment in time, its resonance extends beyond that moment. Like a tuning fork that is struck (the making of the photograph), the resulting picture continues to resonate, sending out signals (the viewing of the photograph) beyond its creation. At the moment a photograph is made, it both fixes that moment and embodies all previous moments that the subject has accumulated over its life that have brought the subject to its current configuration. A photograph showing a full-grown tree also includes, by assumption, the unseen moments when that tree was a seed, a seedling, a sapling, and a mature example of its species. A portrait of an elderly person contains the history of the subject's infancy, childhood, and adulthood, as well as the present old age of the photographed moment. Such readings may be seen as the backward-facing nature of photographs.

The forward-facing nature of photographs may be harder to untangle. When considering photographs that come to be seen as historical, assessing their future importance may be both premature and moot. While certain photographs—those of the first moon landing, for instance—may achieve immediate status as history-makers in their own right, relatively few works fall into this category. A future is long in its making, and the history of photography is still brief. It is difficult to say with certainty which photographs will achieve and maintain lasting importance. Yet the pictures we have are a backward-looking reference at how another future—our present day—has developed.

In ways that are different from paintings, prints, and drawings—all of which in some sense contain the expectation of artifice—photographs are *usually* grounded in a moment that actually occurred. After photography's introduction to the city of New Orleans by Jules Lion in the spring of 1840, it was not as if painting, drawing, engraving, and other forms of visual expression all disappeared. Arguably, all the visual and plastic arts became more vibrant, lively, and ubiquitous. Photography, both commercial and artistic, became a partner in the visual conversation of the area as its history unfolded.

As a result of the connection to reality, photographs that are not part of our personal histories can seemingly become part of our lives, corresponding to parallel or even desired experiences like the one depicted. Photographs help expand our historical bandwidth, allowing some vicarious exposure to an experience that we may never have or even be able to have. In addition to some ability to put flesh and muscle on the bony structures of historical timelines and facts, a photograph is akin to an inkblot—something whose interpretation and importance may vary with each viewer, and whose interpretation over time will vary.

One way of examining history is to look for watershed moments: bright lines that offer a clear distinction of how things were different before and after a particular event or circumstance. Photographs can help with that. Such episodes, however arbitrarily or perfectly they may be viewed, allow the past to be seen with greater clarity than a mere continuum of days, years, and decades provides: before and after emancipation, before and after women's suffrage, before and after Hurricane Katrina, to use a few examples. Photographs of these moments not only mark them but permit a visualization of them, offering another

tool for the student, historian, polymath, or other interested person to gather information using another sense.

What are some ways of understanding or evaluating photographs? A type of legibility or transparency is part of a historical photograph's profile, but not everything that is important can be measured or quantified. Photographs can become a memory, like a lucky coin or other pocketable talisman, to be touched for the comfort and understanding that they bring. Photographs can be considered moments of transience forever captured, which often efface the prosaic nature of their subjects with mystery or wonder. Indeed, as the mid-twentieth-century photographer Garry Winogrand noted, "There is nothing as mysterious as a fact clearly described."

The photographic frame and the camera can be likened to a cabinet of curiosities. Its displayed content is contained and finite, but within those limitations, it offers great possibilities of discovery. Historic photographs don't hide what they wish to say. They are direct—even guileless—in their stance and are for the most part without mystery, at least in what they purport to show. How a viewer perceives that, of course, is a matter of individual circumstance. But the decoder ring can usually be left at home. In looking at a photograph, we are observing something from the periphery, a vantage point that can assist us in understanding the essence of a work.

Life in the third decade of the twenty-first century can seem like a visual arms race, with proliferating images competing for meaning and attention. Photographs—often existing only as screen images rather than physical objects—have ceased to become solely pictorially representative. Many now exist primarily to attest to feelings or to state an emotional or intellectual position. Sometimes content other than the main subject is smuggled into the picture through specific context or juxtaposition. In such pictorial hitchhiking, the photographic frame is a place of entrapment as well as a place for exploration.

Photography is sometimes characterized as a visual common currency of understanding; nonetheless, everyone will assign the rate of exchange on a personal scale. Is a photograph an epigram, compact and totally contained? As much as we may wish for this, such is usually not the case. What is difficult about understanding photography is trying to explain why we find photographs compelling. It might well be easier to calculate the minute quantity of reduced silver in the prints by Clarence John Laughlin than to analyze their content or message. And should we ever want to "explain" photography? It might be akin to explaining a magic illusion, and with that, a path of inquiry would end.

It has been noted that the best time to plant a tree was twenty years ago, and the second-best time is today. We publish *Louisiana Lens* today with pride—but also with the hope that, twenty years hence, THNOC's collections will be richer still. Though a book such as this could have been written at any time in the past half-century (since the establishment of THNOC) earlier versions would have suffered from an insufficient number of photographic collections. Consequently, this compilation is as much a look forward as a look back. It offers a status check as well as a prospect (or even a promise) of an enhanced future condition. Within the realm of an authorial and curatorial context, this book showcases items at this moment in time, suggesting areas of depth and strength while implicitly identifying those that need bucking up. Filling such lacunae in collections is one thing that drives both curators and institutions to constantly examine holdings, and to augment them for the publics that the institution serves. The short essays accompanying the photographs in the following pages do not as a whole subscribe to a formula, though all include known essential information of subject, date, maker, and medium. The essays are discursive and at times speculative, for a thoughtfully made photograph is a spur to the imagination.

The structure of *Louisiana Lens* is based on themes of technological advancement and varying approaches to how photography has evolved in the nearly two centuries of its existence. The first chapter presents early models of photography on paper, metal, and glass that vied for prominence as the new technology searched for its social and commercial footing. Chapter 2 addresses the hegemony of paper photographs in mainstream culture, along with improvements—including the obsolescence of the wet plate process—that streamlined the act of making a photograph. Chapter 3 bridges the nineteenth and twentieth centuries, with pictures by both professional specialists and dedicated amateurs, whose motives were different but whose products could be indistinguishable. Chapter 4 includes pictures that are by turns concerned with exterior description and internal exploration. Finally, Chapter 5 must be considered a work in progress, as the role of digital imaging, and the efficiency in recording personal and public events continues to evolve. Ironically, the book concludes with a photograph whose technique hasn't been mainstream for over a century. Not every change in processes and materials was immediately or universally adopted, and some photographic trends have been continually practiced by photographers across many decades.

One purpose of this book is to enlarge an appreciation and understanding of people, places, and events that make up the history of Louisiana as presented through the medium of photography. Every selection in this book implicitly asks the question, "Why is this photograph part of a history museum's holdings?" The answers are as varied as the pictures themselves.

John H. Lawrence
The Historic New Orleans Collection

METAL, PAPER, AND GLASS

1843–1860

unknown photographer

Compared to drawing, painting, printmaking, or sculpting, the daguerreotype process presented the advantages of portability and speed of production. Moreover, daguerreotypes recorded objects with precision and detail.

The subject and provenance of this daguerreotype are established (something less common than might be imagined), though its authorship is not. Given the subject—the organ case for St. Patrick's Church in New Orleans—it is likely among the earliest photographs made in the Crescent City, and with more certainty, the oldest photographic object in the holdings of The Historic New Orleans Collection.

The design of the organ case, by James Gallier Sr., like the church building, represents the popular Gothic Revival style of the mid-nineteenth century. The instrument itself is the work of organ builder Henry Erben in New York and was played for the first time on April 16, 1843, having been delivered earlier that month. Until acquired by The Historic New Orleans Collection, the daguerreotype was among materials in the family-held archive of Gallier's descendants, and it is likely that the architect commissioned the picture or received it as a gift. The original organ served its purpose for nearly three quarters of a century and was replaced in 1914–15.

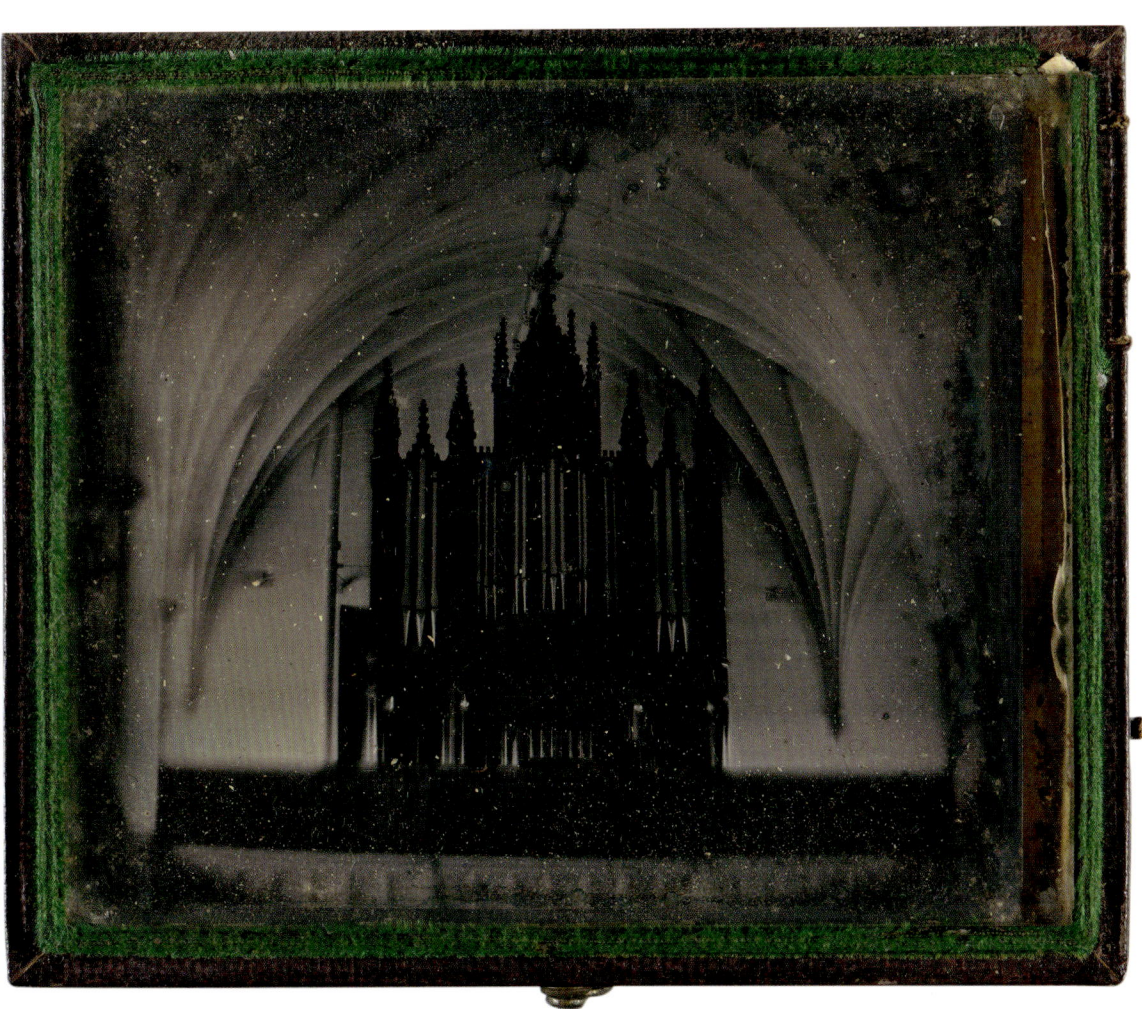

Organ case and organ, St. Patrick's Church, New Orleans, 1843?

by an unknown photographer
daguerreotype, 3 ⅛ × 3 ¾ × ¾ in. (cased dimensions)
acquisition made possible by Ann Masson, MSS 1059.3.3

unknown photographer

What is to be thought of this daguerreotype of a painting by James Guy Evans showing the second United States Custom House in New Orleans, erected in 1819 from a design by Benjamin Buisson? Like the daguerreotype of the Gallier-designed organ case its existence seems to be based on documenting an object, rather than making a photographic portrait or a scenic view. It is a credible (though hardly facsimile) likeness, differing in scale, dimensionality, and chroma from the original. The size of the painting is 30.7 × 38 inches, while the photograph has a surface area just shy of 24 square inches; the subtle silvery tones of the photograph, while beautiful, do not have the colorful hues of the oil painting. The daguerreotype may be held in the hands for close personal examination. The painting is meant for public viewing, and its ornate framing gives it a three-dimensional character not matched by the slim case of the daguerreotype.

Unlike the default reversal from left to right imparted by the daguerreotype process, the orientation of this picture is true to the original painting. It is possible that the photographer used a prism in front of the lens to permit the correct orientation. The same outcome could have been achieved by rephotographing a daguerreotype made without the reversing lens, though copies made by this method suffer a loss in quality compared to the original.

The estimated date of this painting raises a question of why it may have been made. The main subject of Evans's paintings were "portraits" of sailing ships involved in coastal or transoceanic trade. Some of these ships' cargoes likely cleared customs in this building, and perhaps a ship owner, captain, or broker commissioned the work. Perhaps the plans to replace this building with the much larger building that stands on the site today (and for which work commenced in 1848) may have already been leaked, and Evans wanted to paint the expendable structure before it was gone.

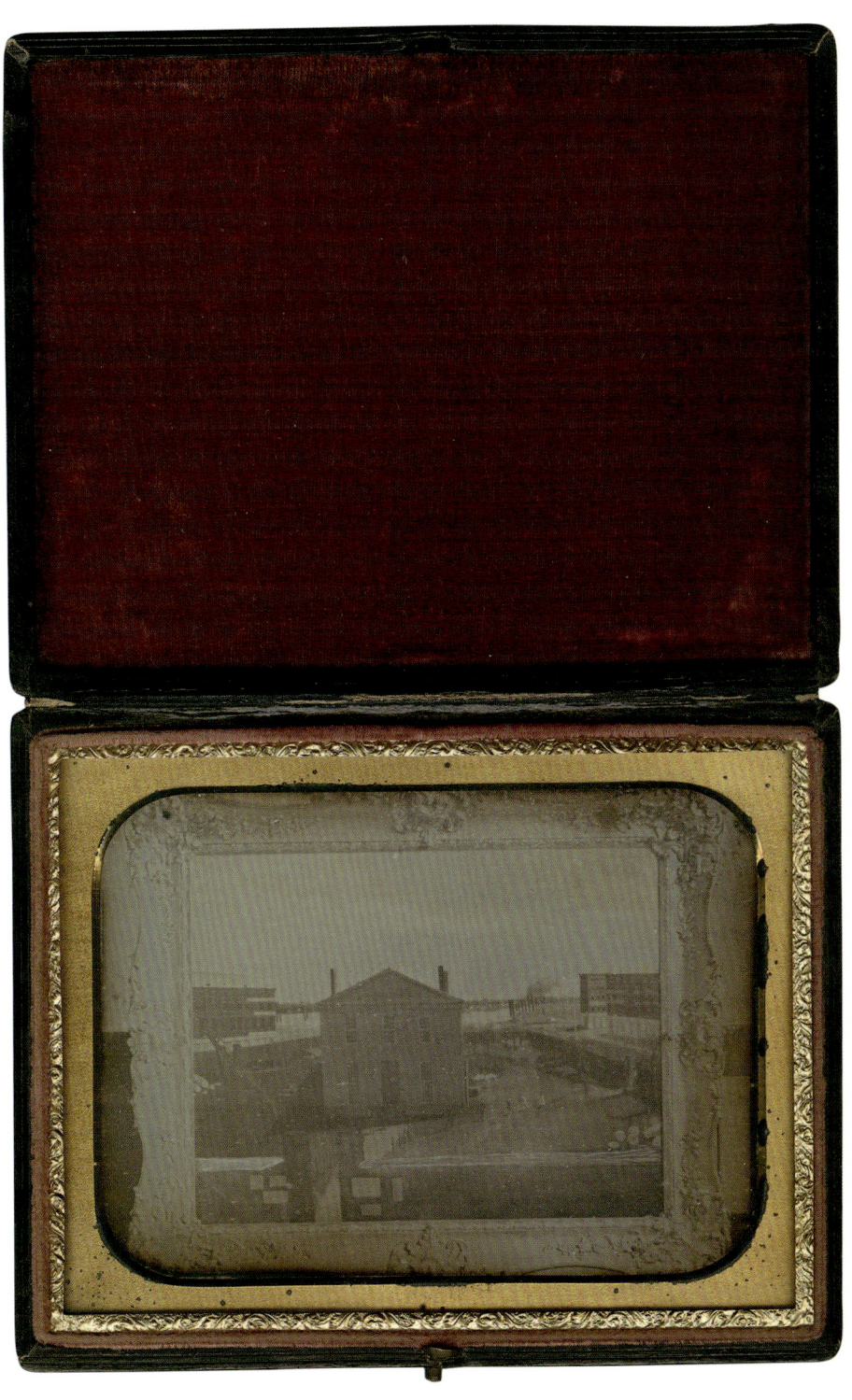

**Daguerreotype of a painting by James Guy Evans showing
the second United States customhouse, mid-1840s**

by an unknown photographer
daguerreotype, 5 × 6⅛ × ⅞ in. (cased dimensions)
1994.67

attributed to Jules Lion (1806–66)

It is said that every picture tells a story. But what story? Any story? A story we long to hear? A story that reinforces certain historical assertions? Furthermore, how can a mute object of barely a few square inches, whose known circumstances are more in the realm of fable than fact, tell a credible story? Some of those answers may be discovered in the image illustrated here.

This ninth-plate daguerreotype—about the same dimensions as a typical passport photograph—shows a young woman who is African American or of mixed race. Its location for the last several decades has been Louisiana. Those facts constitute the only established information about this item, along with an inferred date of 1850 to 1856.

The sitter presents herself with opposing forces in her posture: the slightly tilted torso and dropped shoulder balancing nicely with the nearly vertical position of the head and neck. Her positioning, along with her slightly downcast gaze, lends a sense of tenuousness to her pose. The set of her mouth suggests a serious demeanor. This bit of tension and balance makes for a far more interesting image than if a ramrod-straight pose had been struck. We see an individual, not just a woman.

French-born Jules Lion introduced the daguerreotype process—and photography—to New Orleans with an exhibition of local scenes presented at the St. Charles Museum on March 15, 1840. The search for Lion's daguerreotypes has long been a pursuit of those interested in the city's photographic history. Though many of Lion's lithographs are held in public and private collections—including more than a hundred at THNOC—his output as a photographer is, if not invisible, then maddeningly elusive. Since at least 1982, when it was first published, this portrait has been attributed to Lion. Its owner at the time was said to have acquired it in the mid-1960s from descendants of Lion living in New Orleans. The item was passed down in the family until The Historic New Orleans Collection acquired it in 2021.

The association with Lion is inferential. For the last few decades of the twentieth century, historians and art historians presented Lion as a free man of color, but art historian Sara M. Picard persuasively argued in a 2017 journal article that Jules Lion was a Jewish Frenchman. In Lion's thirty-year residence in New Orleans (from his arrival in 1836 until his death in 1866), only a few years of city directories (1850 to 1855) list his name along with the designation of "f.m.c.," or free man of color. In all other instances in the historical record, either Lion's heritage is not called out, or he is described as French. In numerous official and legal documents where his racial status, if other than white, would have been required, none is shown. Tellingly, Lion is not among those profiled in the 1911 work *Nos Hommes et Notre Histoire*, by Rodolphe Lucien Desdunes, lauding achievements by New Orleans's Black residents.

The directory listings for Lion as a free man of color coincide with his employment of Charlotte Armantine Broyard, a free woman of color who was fifteen when she entered his household. A year later, Broyard and Lion had a son together, and when she died, around the age of twenty, Lion's status in the directories as a free person of color disappears.

Is this tiny portrait (measuring just over 2 × 2 inches) of Broyard? If so, then is it by Lion, arguably the most likely person to have made it? The unknown answers to these questions do not make this picture less compelling. Perhaps they make it more so.

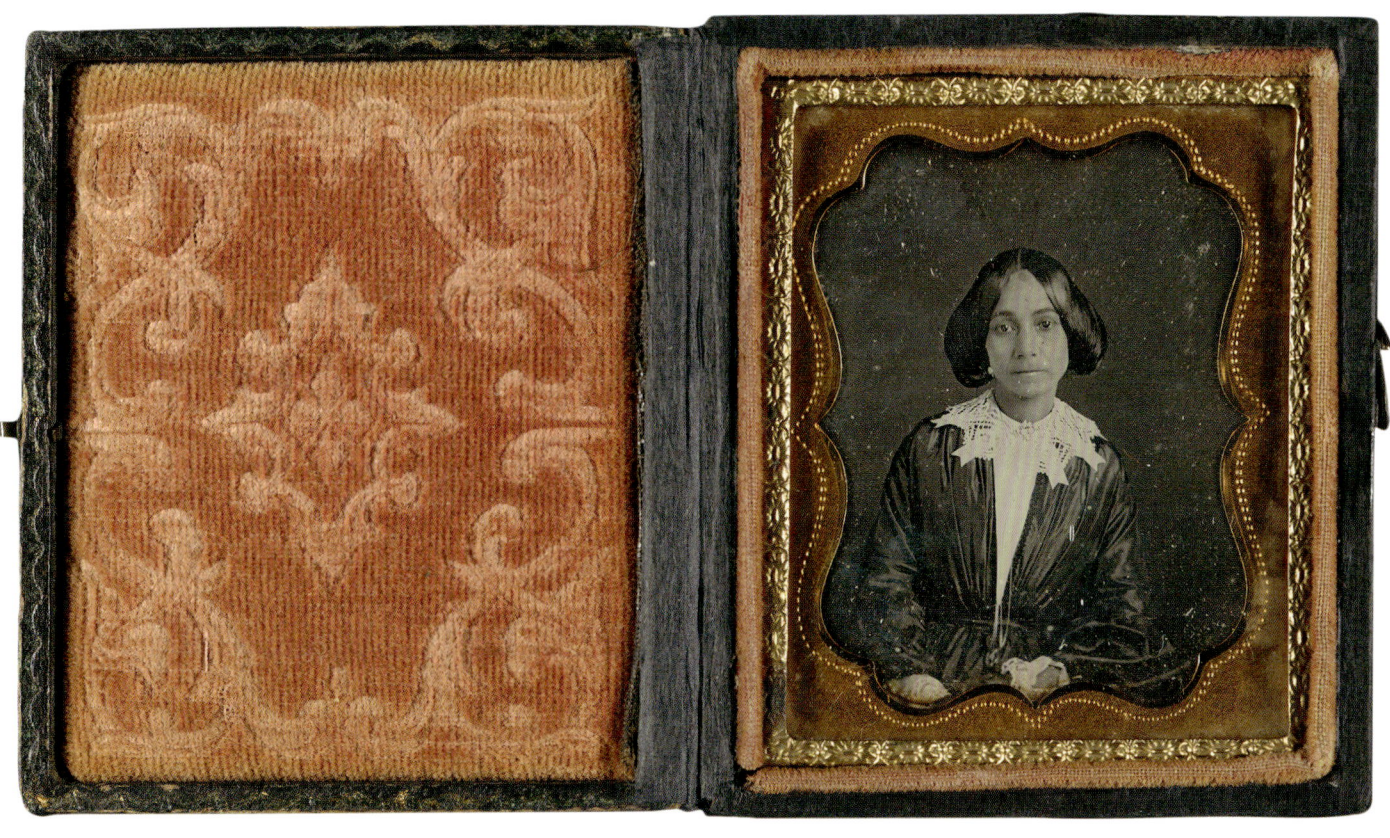

Portrait of a woman, circa 1850–56
attributed to Jules Lion
daguerreotype, 2⅞ × 2⅜ × ¾ in. (cased dimensions)
acquisition made possible by the Clarisse Claiborne Grima Fund,
2021.0080

Felix Moissenet (circa 1814–?)

Based on city directory listings, the French-born Felix Moissenet flourished as a daguerreotypist in New Orleans during the late 1840s and early 1850s. Moissenet's portraits are exquisite objects. The handful of examples in THNOC's holdings—most in the quarter-plate size—attest to his mastery of posing and lighting his subjects, as well as engaging their participation in the reciprocal contract that binds the artist and subject to each other. The adult in this portrait is Jeanne Roman de la Villebeuvre (1834–1889), daughter of Louisiana governor André Bienvenu Roman.

Set against the dark studio background, Villebeuvre is dressed in a high-necked garment; a nimbus of dark hair and a black bonnet, secured at her throat, surround her face, which floats, as if disembodied, in the pictorial space. The child—her daughter Anna Jeanne de la Villebeuvre (b. 1854)—is dressed in stark white, interrupted only by the arc of a pink ruffle on her cap. The tint, applied delicately by hand, is also evident in the faces of the child and mother, whose rings bear the faintest suggestion of gilding painted on the image.

This photograph could be read as expressing the circle of life. Jeanne Roman de la Villebeuvre's black clothing appears to indicate that she is in mourning, probably for her sister Aimée and brother Robert, who both died in late 1855. Her daughter, the deceased siblings' niece, is a physical fact as well as an emblem of a continuing female line of the family.

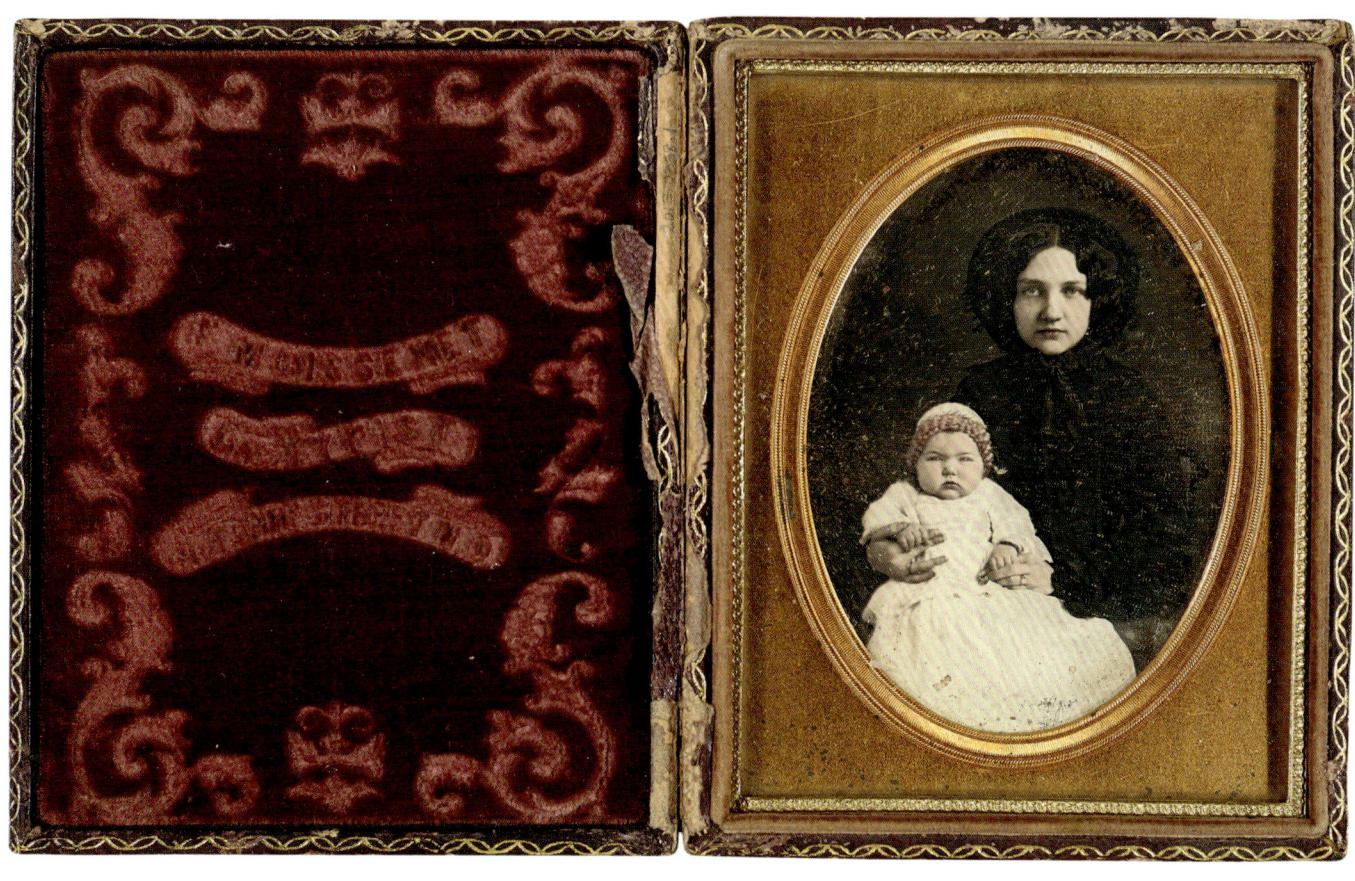

Jeanne Roman de la Villebeuvre and Anna Jeanne de la Villebeuvre, 1855–56

by Felix Moissenet
hand-tinted daguerreotype, 3⅝ × 4⅝ × ¾ in. (cased dimensions)
2013.0358.1

unknown photographer

The specifics of this plantation house—owner, architect/ builder, date of construction, and precise location—are unknown. It is also unclear whether the "Mississippi" inked on the mount refers to the river or the state. While the subject may in some fashion be emblematic of southern plantation architecture, it is likely a one-off example. The general proportions and key features of the house suggest antecedents from the eighteenth century, though this two-story model, with wraparound galleries on the ground and second floors, enjoyed popularity some decades into the nineteenth century. According to architectural historians Barbara SoRelle Bacot and Jessie Poesch, the perpetuation of older types and styles of such structures rested in part with later generations asking for a house "like my father's."

At the time this photograph was made, the building techniques of balloon framing and the later platform and stud construction were in their infancy, and this building would have likely been of timber frame construction. This method's reliable techniques had been perfected over centuries, but standardization was not part of its ethos. Though this structure resembles many others, virtually none of its parts would have been interchangeable with the elements of similar buildings. The heart of this substantial structure that does the real work of keeping the building aloft is the unseen timber frame, assembled with care and expertise, especially in the massive and complex truss that supports the roof.

The ground floor columns made of brick (which was likely produced on the property) are almost comically substantial when compared to the slender wooden colonnettes that support the entablature above them. Several attributes suggest a postcolonial date for this building. The symmetrical placement of the door and window openings is one. Earlier buildings of this type often displayed irregular spacing of such features due to the sizes and uses of the rooms.

Interior functionality trumped exterior symmetry in colonial times. Dormers are another feature often seen in houses of the American period, though they were not unknown during the colonial era. The hipped "umbrella" roof provided an ample space for dissipating heat, and habitable attic rooms (suggested by the dormers) were less common in colonial times.

By choosing an elevated camera postion (likely on the levee fronting the property) the photographer has rendered a full view of the house: the proportions of the building and completeness of the structure, trees, and fence are presented as a harmonious ensemble of landscape and architecture. A closer ground-level view, which would have presented more of the underside of the overhanging roof and gallery, while adding to the imposing nature of the building, would have taken away from its character as a dwelling.

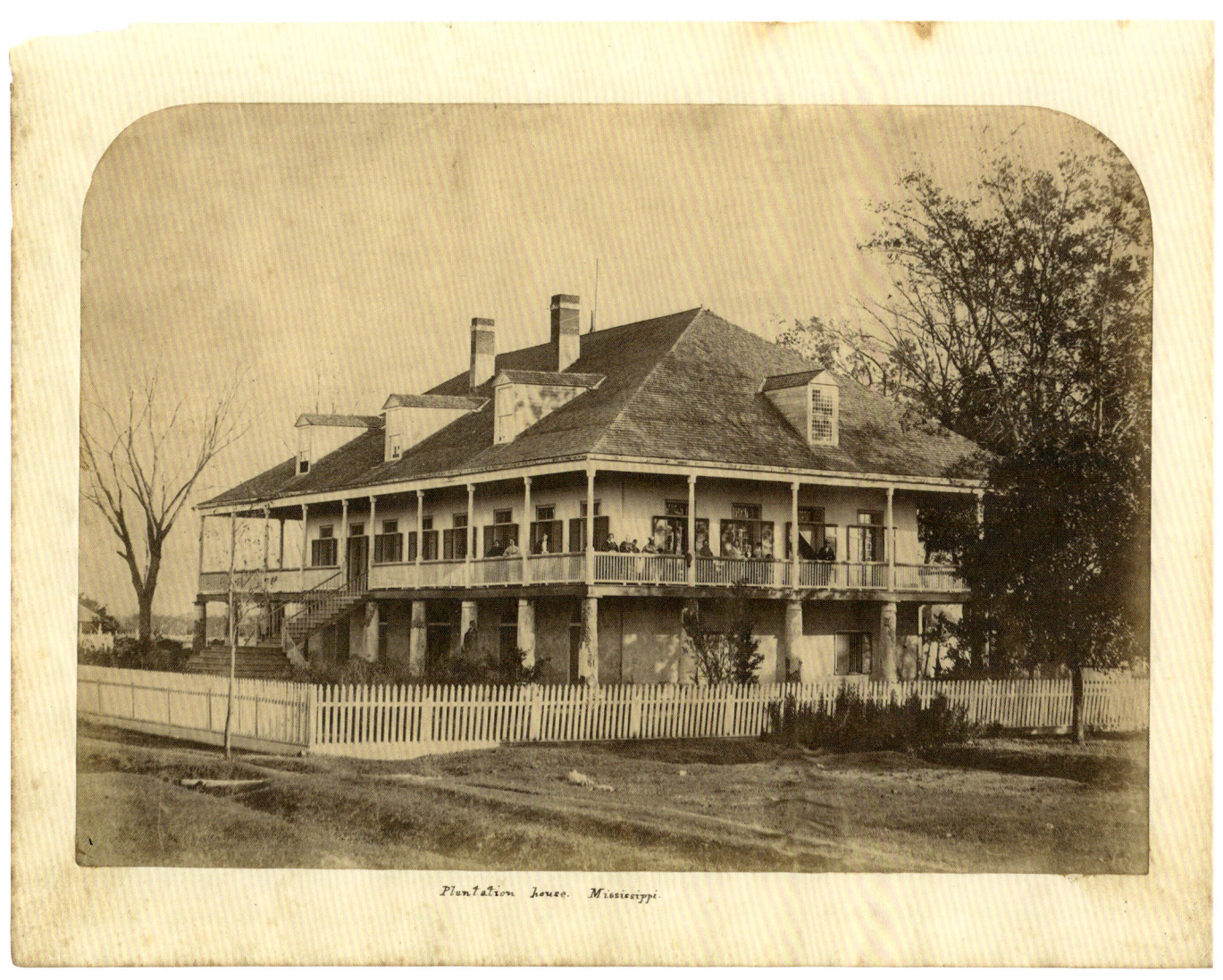

Plantation house. Mississippi.

Plantation House. Mississippi., 1850s
by an unknown photographer
salted paper print, mounted, 8⁷⁄₁₆ × 10⁹⁄₁₆ in.
2016.0026

unknown photographer

The subjects of this handsome portrait are Margaret Mary
Woods and her husband, New Orleans journalist and
publisher James Curtis Waldo. They were married in New
Orleans in 1856 and raised six children. J. C. Waldo—born in
Illinois—came to New Orleans in 1848. When he died in 1901,
Waldo's obituary in the *Daily Picayune* listed New Orleans as
his home for the "past fifty-two years." The *Times Democrat*
noted that his journalistic career included serving as a
"New Orleans correspondent for numerous American and
European newspapers." Waldo also published trade cards,
directories, and an 1879 visitors' guide to New Orleans; he
had a commercial engraving business as well. In addition to
his journalistic and publishing work, Waldo wrote popular
poetry under the pseudonym Tim Linkinwater. The obituary
also recalled Waldo's participation in the infamous Battle
of Liberty Place of September 14, 1874, an armed conflict
that pitted pro-integration forces against segregationists in
Lousiana's Reconstruction era. Waldo was a member of the
White League, insurrectionists who planned the attempted
coup.

The character of this double portrait suggests it may have
commemorated the couple's marriage, supporting a date of
1856, the waning years of the daguerreotype process. The half-
plate size of the picture and ornate frame, formal pose, and the
fine clothing and jewelry that the couple are wearing suggest
approaching or perhaps recently concluded nuptials. In 1840,
barely a decade and a half before the Waldos' wedding, Queen
Victoria in her white wedding attire began a trend of using that
color for the bride's gown. Nonetheless, brides in the United
States still commonly followed the earlier tradition of using a
favorite dress or a new dress in a favorite color.

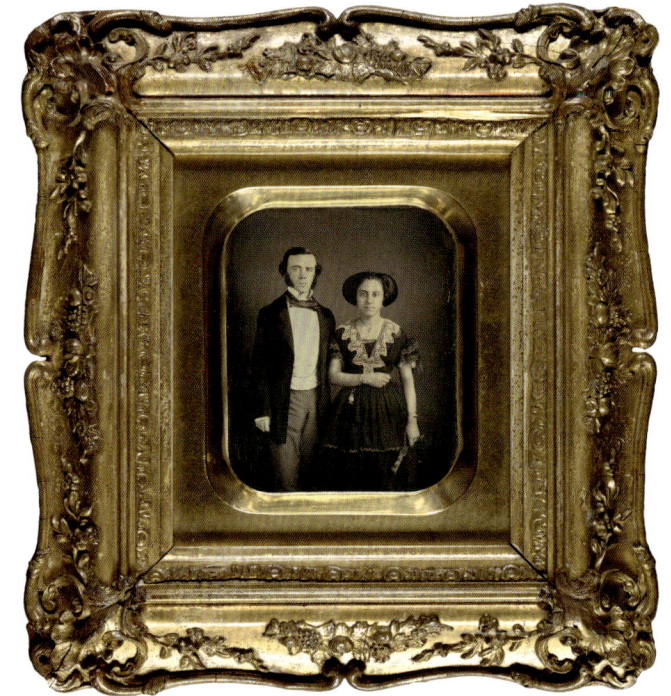

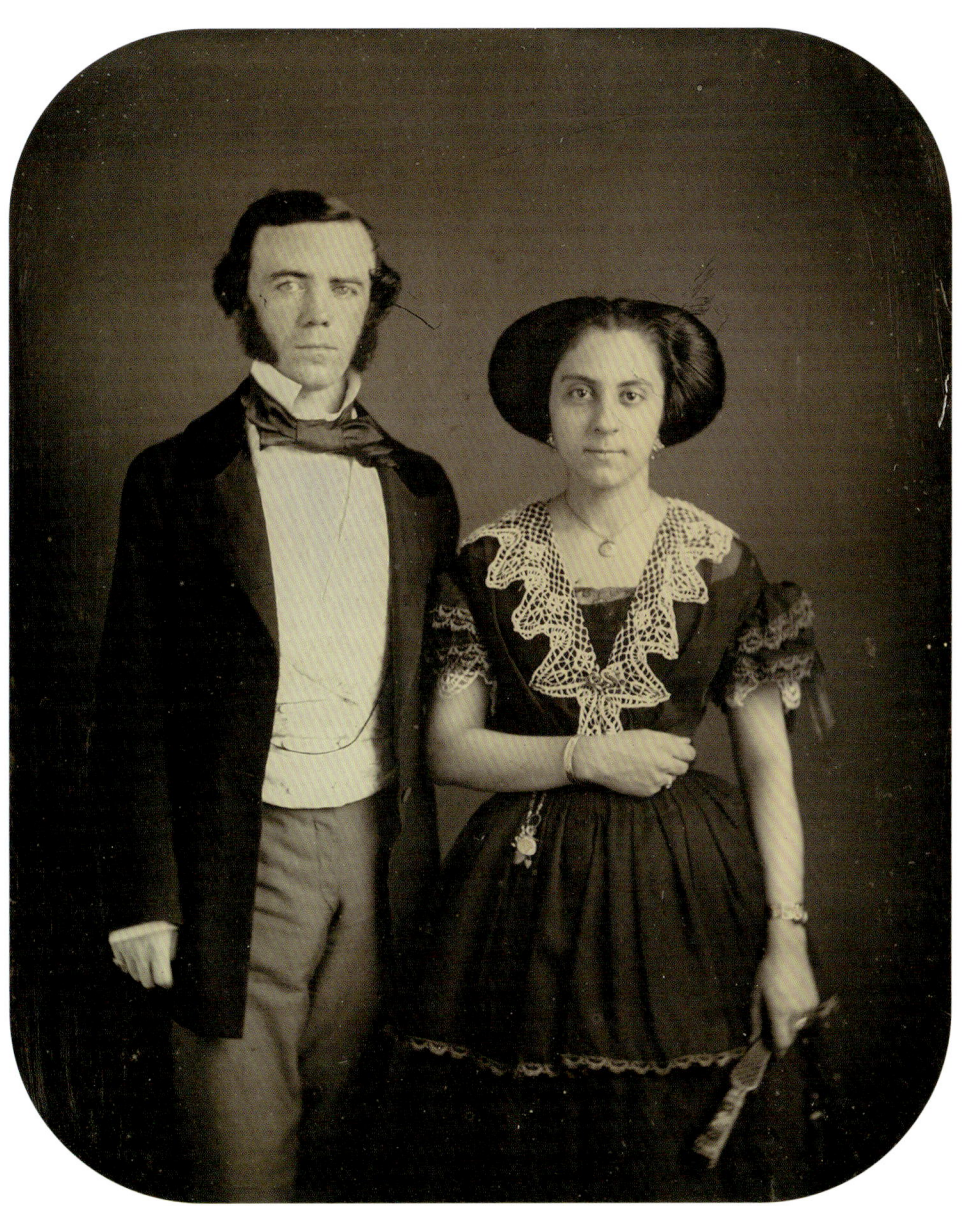

James Curtis Waldo and his wife, Margaret Mary Woods, 1856?

by an unknown photographer
daguerreotype, 11¾ × 10¾ × ¾ (framed dimensions)
1982.198

James Andrews (1829–1863)

A city thoroughfare since the early nineteenth century, Canal Street has played important roles in New Orleans's geography, culture, and transportation. It divided the old city from its first suburb, served as a boundary separating Creoles from "Americans," and provided ample room for traffic of all kinds. The broad neutral ground (or median), flanked by roadways, is among the widest in the city. Originally, plans called for a navigation canal running down this central portion, connecting the Mississippi River with Lake Pontchartrain, a tidal lake several miles away. This waterway would have supplanted a smaller canal in a nearby location that was built in the 1790s, the last decade of Spanish control of Louisiana. City officials ultimately abandoned the idea of a channel in the middle of Canal Street.

James Andrews's photograph of the downriver side of Canal Street shows the entire 800 block (between Bourbon and Dauphine Streets) flanked by portions of the 700 block to the right and 900 block to the left, including the landmark of Christ Church. The ambrotype is larger than the standard size full plate (6.5 × 8.5 inches), and as with other ambrotypes, the image is unique.

It is difficult to conjecture who the client for this photograph was. With the depiction of such a general scene, it doesn't seem likely the image was created for one of the recognizable businesses on the street. Perhaps Andrews made the ambrotype to display his trade and to exhibit in his place of business near the corner of Camp and Canal Streets (the vantage point for this view), impressing patrons with the full-plate possibilities of the process.

The existence of a wood engraving published in *Ballou's Pictorial Drawing-Room Companion* on August 1, 1857, crediting Andrews as the source for Samuel S. Kilburn Jr.'s engraving, suggests that the periodical commissioned the work. Kilburn took many liberties in transmuting the photographic image to

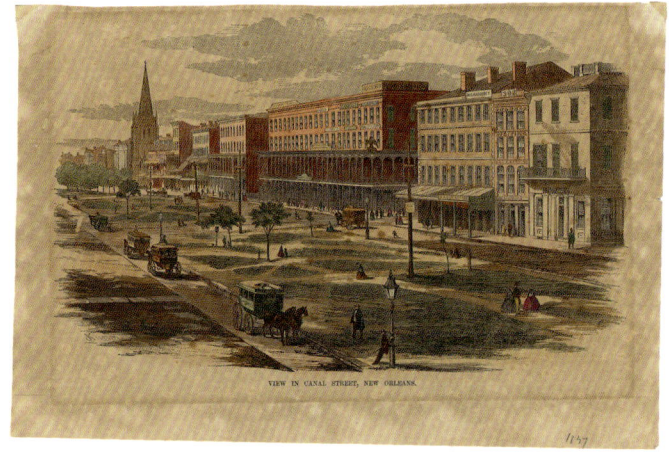

View in Canal Street, New Orleans; by Samuel S. Kilburn Jr., after an ambrotype by James Andrews; 7⅜ × 10⁹⁄₁₆ in.; from *Ballou's Pictorial Drawing-Room Companion*, August 1, 1857; *bequest of Boyd Cruise and Harold Schilke, 1989.79.16.2*

the engraving block. He expanded the field of view greatly, showing the entire 700 block of the street as well as the 1000 block, as the perspective recedes away from the camera position. The construction materials, scruffy ground cover, and general hubbub have been completely removed or restated in simpler form, presenting the promise, if not the reality, of a mid-1850s beautification project for the street. The serendipitous conversation between coach driver and the standing figure to the right in the photograph has been eliminated in the published view. Such adapations were common as source materials like photographs or drawings were sent to publishers to provide illustrations for articles.

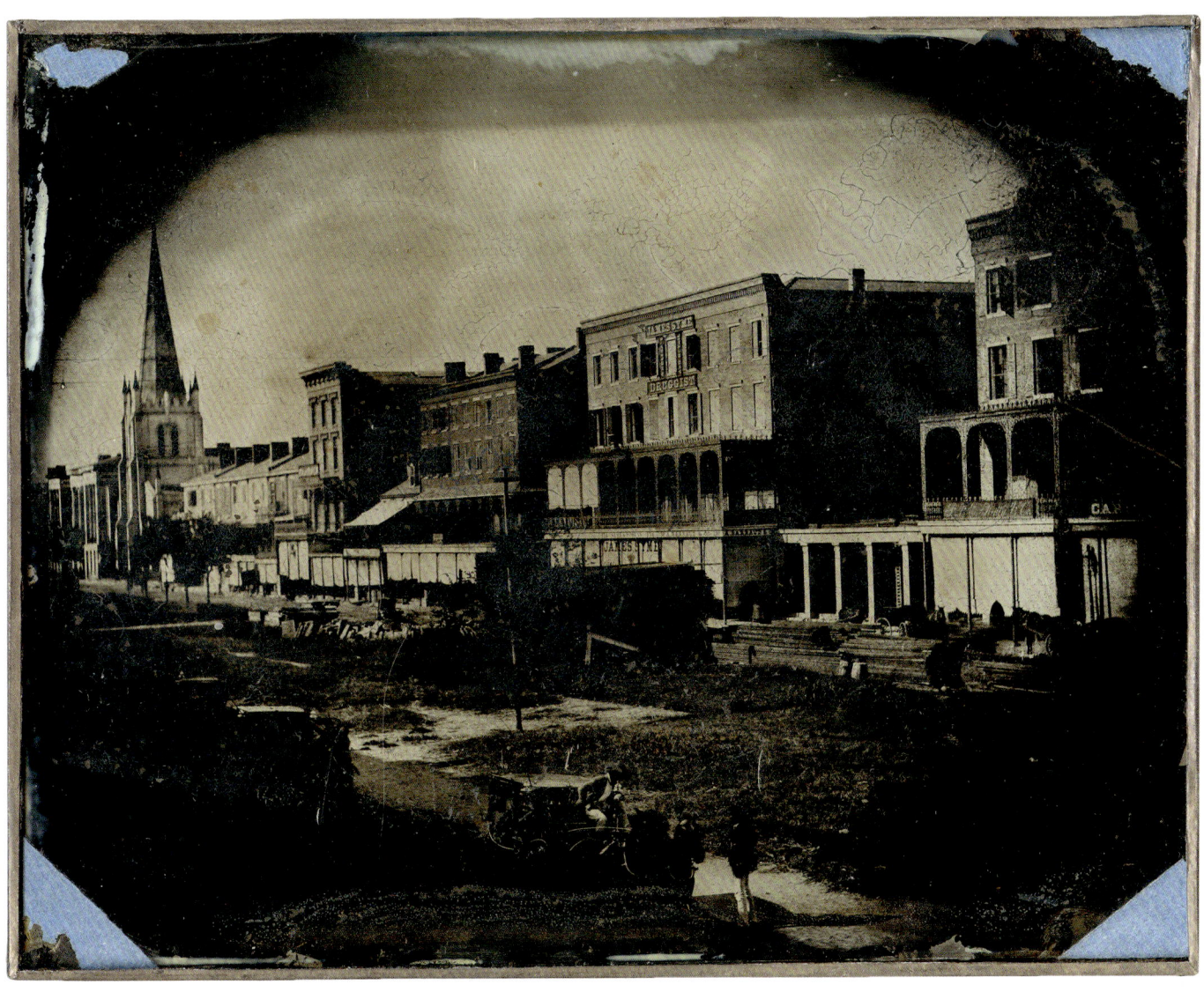

Canal Street, New Orleans, 1857

by James Andrews
ambrotype, 7⅜ × 10⁹⁄₁₆ × ¼ in.
2015.0465

unknown photographer

By the time this daguerreotype portrait of Dr. Louis Charles Roudanez was made in the late 1850s, photography's first successful commercial process was approaching its twentieth year and would not continue to be practiced as a mainstream form of photographic expression much beyond 1860. The process's ability to produce unique objects of exquisite beauty and allure was not enough to weather the onslaught of cheaper alternatives (offered by the also unique processes of ambrotype and tintype) and the rise of theoretically unlimited paper prints reproduced from a single negative. It is perhaps ironic that a process that was viewed as *retardataire* was employed to capture the likeness of a person who was so forward focused.

Dr. Roudanez's politics may have matured during the period of his medical education in France during the mid-nineteenth century (he reportedly took to the barricaded streets of Paris in the 1848 revolution) but they were formed by both his parents' experience of revolution in Saint Domingue and his early upbringing in New Orleans. As a free man of color, Roudanez inhabited a stratum of society and politics that offered far more liberties than enslaved people possessed, but not nearly as many as those enjoyed by whites. The focus on equality for all citizens, a through line in his life, is persistent.

Roudanez's message of equality for all citizens was trumpeted in two newspapers he helped found in New Orleans during the Civil War years: *L'Union* (1862), established with his brother Jean-Baptiste Roudanez and Paul Trévigne, and *La Tribune de la Nouvelle-Orléans* (1864), the United States's first Black daily newspaper. These trailblazing newspapers laid the groundwork for the modern civil rights movement in Louisiana.

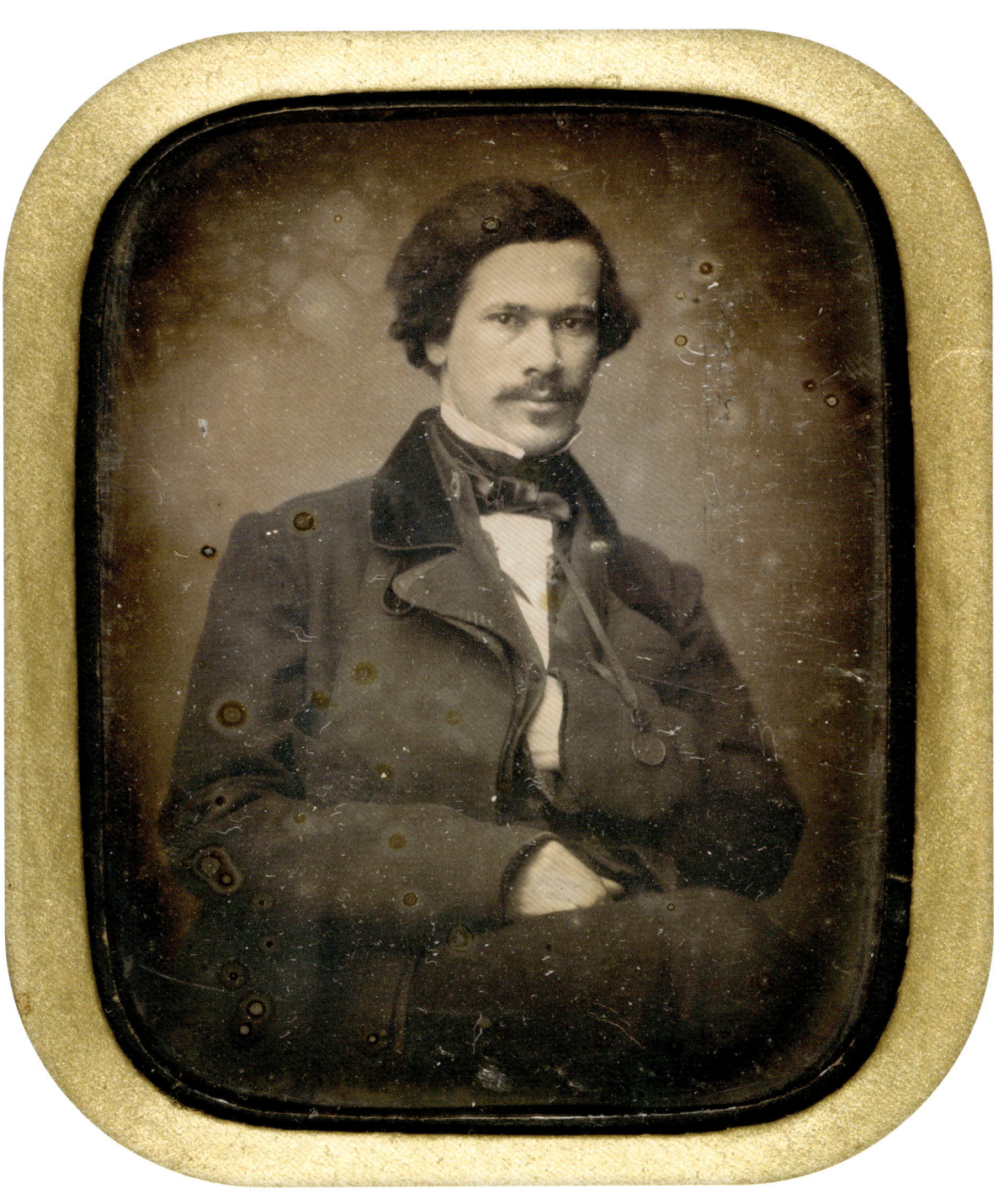

Dr. Louis Charles Roudanez, circa 1857
by an unknown photographer
daguerreotype, 6⅜ × 7⅝ × 1¼ in. (cased dimensions)
gift of Mark Charles Roudané, 2017.0201.1

Jay Dearborn Edwards (1831–1900)

A frontier is not an absolute concept. When we speak of a frontier, it is usually of a particular place and time, but not the only place and time where the definition might apply. By the time photography reached New Orleans, the frontier edge of the old southwest (New Orleans) was gone, having been pushed to Texas and points further west. Growth was still happening in New Orleans, but at a more refined pace. It is to such a place that Jay Dearborn Edwards came in the late 1850s.

A faint pencil inscription on the mount of this streetscape reads "Esplanade St. 2 rows of trees 2 miles long." Edwards's central camera position and the dramatic one-point perspective it offers certainly let the viewer buy into that declaration, though what the print describes with any clarity covers the distance of only a few blocks. The idea embodied in this photograph, if not the photograph itself, presents some notion of a designed and civilized landscape.

The photograph of the steamboat *Princess* has a hushed air, belying the noisy and boisterous activity it took to load and operate such vessels. These steamboats drove commerce in the city of New Orleans. The major cargoes of cotton and sugar that they deposited along the city's wharves for transshipment were the products of a slavery-based plantation system that would collapse after the Civil War.

Edwards arrived in New Orleans in late 1857 or early 1858, and—lasting until just before Union forces captured the city in the spring of 1862—his short-lived practice in the Crescent City offers the most comprehensive photographic record of New Orleans from the pre–Civil War era. Edwards advertised his gallery on Royal Street, which sold not only his own photographs of the city and region but subjects far beyond North America, presumably the work of others.

The several dozen known views of New Orleans identified as being by or attributed to Edwards (or the partnership of Edwards and E. H. Newton Jr.) complement printed (and often published) city views from that time executed in other media: lithography, steel engraving, and wood engraving. The nonphotographic representations often depict an idealized moment, created by an artist using elements that are visually effective but not "documentary" in the way that photographs can be. Photographs such as these show an unusually quiet moment on a bustling waterfront, and the unkempt grass, the irregularity of the boards protecting the tree trunks, and the intrusion of vegetation that obscures architectural detail and mass. Such "imperfections" were easily (and often) eradicated in a hand-drawn picture but had to be accepted and accommodated in a photograph.

Steamer *Princess*, between 1857 and 1859
by Jay Dearborn Edwards
salted paper print, mounted, 10¾ × 14⅛ in.
1982.32.1

Esplanade Street from Royal Street toward lake, between 1857 and 1860
by Jay Dearborn Edwards
salted paper print, mounted, 12½ × 14⅝ × ¼ in. (not cased)
1982.167.5

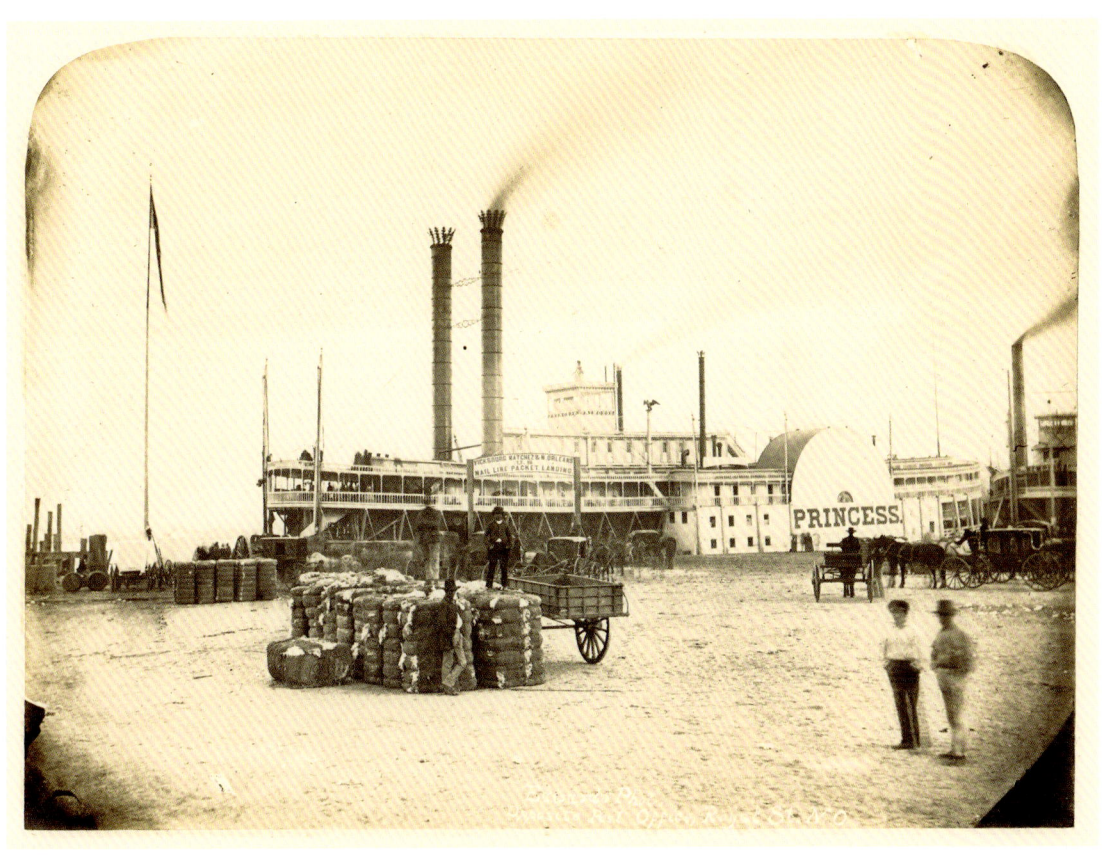

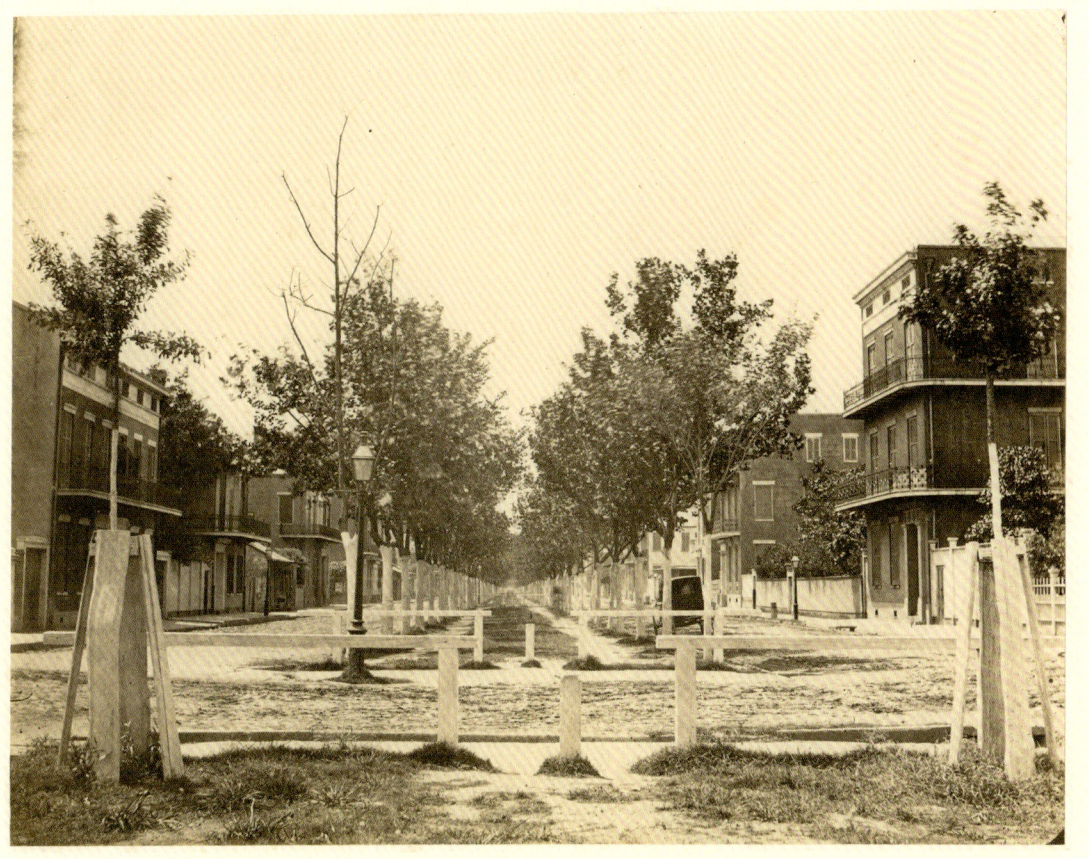

PRINTS ON PAPER

1861–1889

Theodore Lilienthal (1829–1894)

In the years immediately following the end of the Civil War, New Orleans looked to reestablish its former commercial status. Unlike other southern cities that had been heavily damaged by the fighting, New Orleans was captured by the United States Navy in the spring of 1862 without a shot being fired within the city limits. With the peace signed in the spring of 1865, the city wished to let the commercial world know that it was intact and ready to resume business.

New Orleans officials therefore commissioned Theodore Lilienthal to document the city's condition and institutions, and then present this photographic project at the 1867 Exposition Universelle in Paris. Napoleon III acquired the set of mammoth plate prints shown at the exposition. Dozens of the pictures were also issued in stereographic form for wide distribution.

Stereographs were made with a camera that mimicked human binocular vision, capturing a pair of images through its two lenses. The two nearly identical prints were mounted side by side on a single card. The stereograph was placed in a special viewer that could be focused by sliding the pictures back and forth along a rail connected to a pair of lenses through which the viewer looked. When the correct viewing distance was achieved, the reward of a single scene in three dimensions was the result. Stereographs offered both entertainment and education about places around the world, in a few square inches.

The Mechanics' Institute was built by the New Orleans Mechanics' Society, established as a philanthropic organization in 1806. New Orleans was one of many cities throughout the United States and Britain to have a branch. This building was relatively new, having replaced its predecessor, which burned in 1854. A few years after this photograph, in 1874, *Jewell's Crescent City Illustrated*, a boosterish publication designed to show postwar prosperity and normalcy in New Orleans, described the building:

The Mechanics' Institute is among the largest and most imposing of the public buildings of New Orleans. . . . The lower floor is occupied as the Library and Committee room of the New Orleans Mechanics' Society; two large rooms are occupied as the State Executive office; the Secretary of State has his office in another, and the Hall . . . is appropriated to the State Senate. The second story, reached by two broad staircases, is lofty, light and airy. It contains besides, two large apartments, the vast assembly room now employed as the Hall of the Louisiana House of Representatives. The third story is used now as committee rooms, the windows of which command a view of a large part of the city.

This glowing description does not mention the most notorious incident that occurred within the building's precincts, in late July of 1866. One contingent of Louisiana's Republican Party was about to convene a constitutional congress in the building. They intended to draft a new constitution granting voting rights to freedmen. A mob of police officers, firemen, and former Confederates, acting on the orders of New Orleans mayor John T. Monroe, attacked the assembly on the street and inside the Mechanics' Institute, killing some forty people and wounding almost two hundred others in what military governor Philip Sheridan described as "an absolute massacre." Such incidents plagued the Reconstruction efforts in Louisiana. Advancements for Black civil rights were significant but intermittent and short-lived.

In the mid-1880s, the Mechanics' Institute became part of the campus of Tulane University. The building housed the academic departments until the university moved to its present location in uptown New Orleans in 1894, and Tulane's law school took it over. In 1905, the building was torn down to make room for a thirteen-story annex to the Grunewald Hotel.

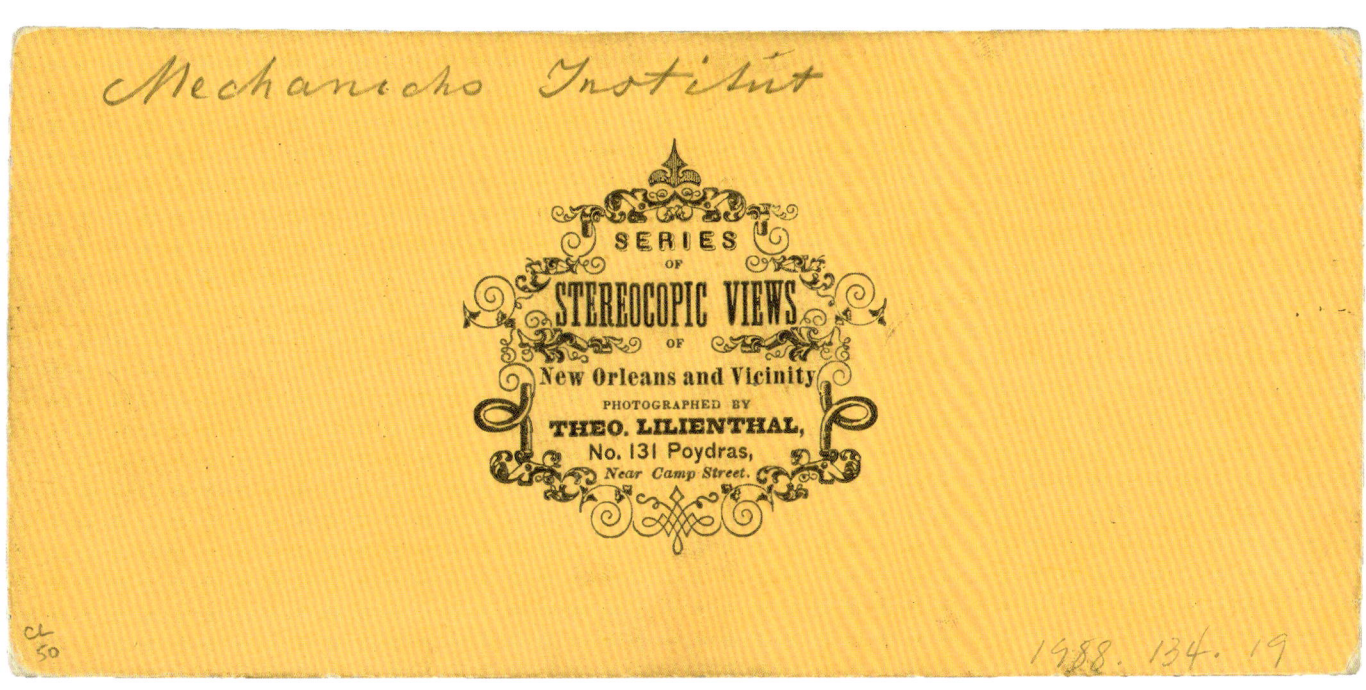

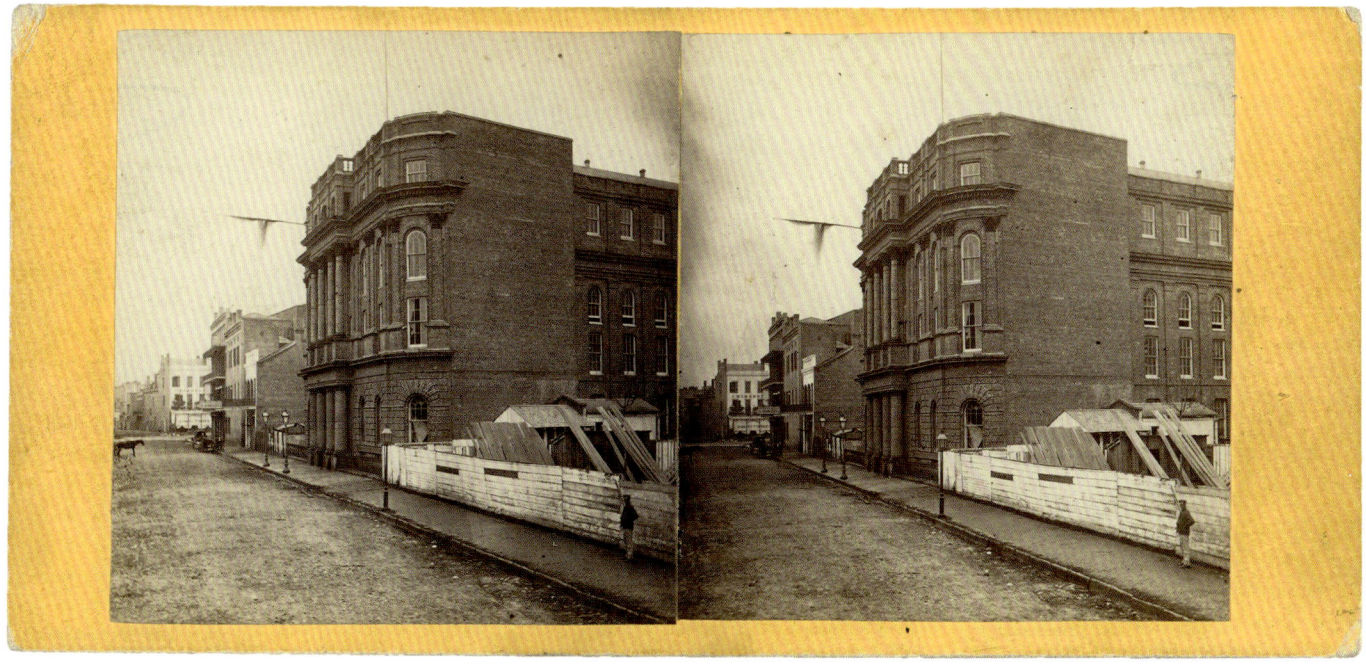

Mechanics' Institute, before 1867

by Theodore Lilienthal
albumen stereograph, 3¼ × 6¾ in.
1988.134.19 i,ii

unknown photographer

One of the great social changes photography instigated was to put a personal and portable visual history within the grasp of more people. The relatively small size of photographs allowed for easy transport and exchange, and they could be produced in multiple copies. Also, the economic threshold for acquiring a photograph was so much lower than the cost of commissioning a painting, miniature, or print. That being said, it is difficult to reconcile all of these circumstances with this portrait, a subject only identified by first name, scratched into the japanned surface of the tintype's verso (at right).

The tintype process, like the earlier daguerreotype and ambrotype, produced a single image directly on the plate. No negative was produced. Chemically, the process was more closely related to the collodion-based ambrotype. Though the tintype process lasted in very limited fashion into the early twentieth century, its heyday had passed by the time this picture was made. Along with the daguerreotype and ambrotype, the tintype was being driven out of fashion and practice by a model of photography that used a glass negative capable of producing as many paper prints as desired, and that could be enlarged to sizes greater than the standard tintype plates.

This tintype, in a less frequently found full-plate format (nearly 8 × 6 inches), deviates from the standard fractional plate dimensions that were far more common. Furthermore, because this image incorporated the entirety of the image-bearing surface, it did not make use of a multi-lensed camera that could project a grid of smaller images on the plate's surface, which would then be cut up into smaller, individual pictures after processing.

It is tempting to attribute this photograph to Alfred R. Waud, but it would be just that, an attribution. Waud was an accomplished draftsman and "special artist" for several nineteenth-century publications, but it is not known whether he made photographs as well. He was, however, often in the company of those men whose photographic work during the Civil War gave the American public its first real view of the battlefield. This particular image (along with a few other full-plate tintypes of New Orleans scenes) was among a group of Waud's drawings acquired by The Historic New Orleans Collection's founders in 1965.

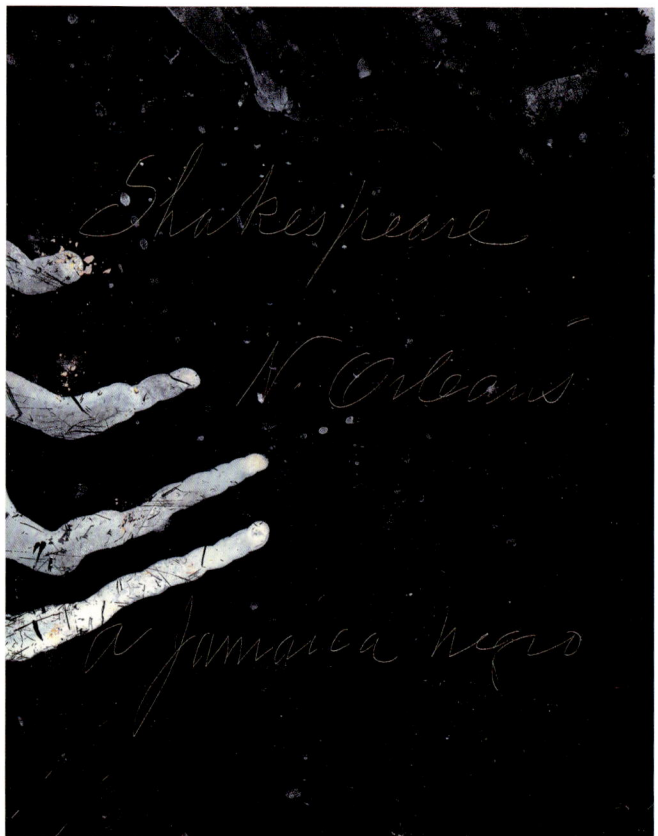

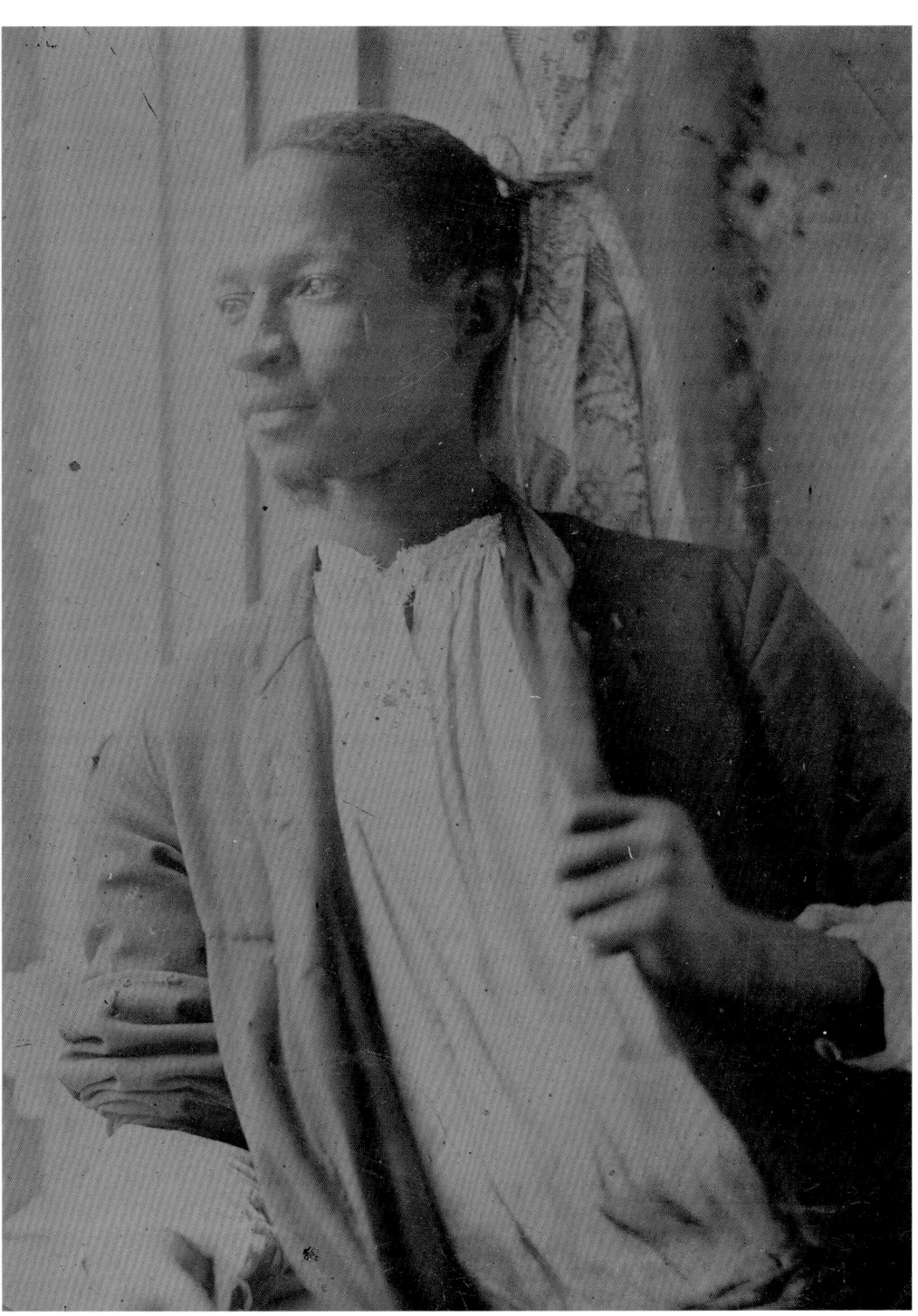

Shakespeare, New Orleans, a Jamaica Negro, 1871?
by an unknown photographer
tintype, 7⅝ × 5⅜ in.
The L. Kemper and Leila Moore Williams Founders Collection,
1965.90.268.3

Robert B. Talfor (1842–1905)

Photography, since its inception, has been used to record humankind's technological advances and its interaction with nature—from the pyramids of Egypt to the mountain ranges of the western United States, and from Niagara Falls to catalogs of steam engines, railroad apparatus, and ships. The pictures produced often either favored the technology or marveled in natural beauty. Robert B. Talfor's album of 113 hand-colored albumen prints combines the nature-technology binary with precise description as well as great delicacy and beauty.

Talfor's album documents the clearing of a thirty-mile logjam in the Red River. In the 1830s Henry Miller Shreve broke up the Great Raft, a centuries-old accumulation more than a hundred miles long. However, logs continued to clog the river over the next decades, requiring repeated efforts to maintain a navigable channel. The US Army Corps of Engineers, under the direction of Captain C. W. Howell and 1st Lieutenant E. A. Woodruff, finally managed to eradicate all logjams, allowing steamboats to travel to and from northwest Louisiana via the Red River's confluence with the Atchafalaya in east-central Louisiana, near Simmesport, and another branch that connects to the Mississippi a little farther to the north and east.

Talfor's pictures constitute a photographic essay as well as a documentary record. They permit the idea of altering and controlling nature to be, as it were, turned over and examined from different perspectives, through a period of two months rather than a single instant. Though this series includes many spectacularly realized photographs, it is safe to say that no one of them manages to tell the story that the combined group of pictures does.

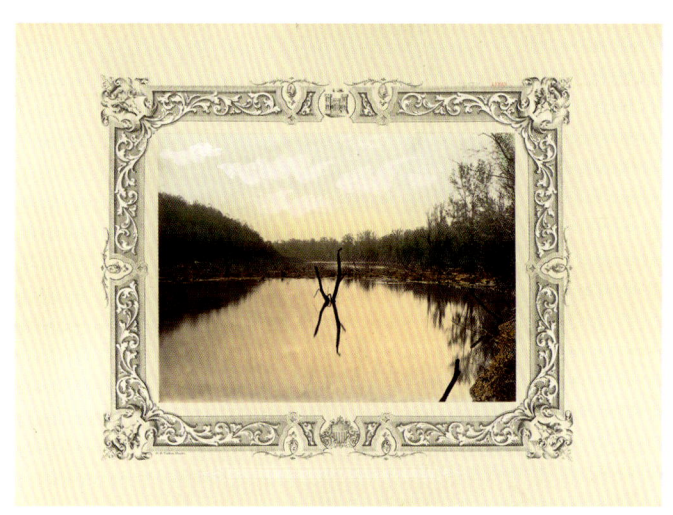

Images from *Photographic Views of Red River Raft*, 1873
by Robert B. Talfor
hand-colored albumen prints, mounted, 13 ⅜ × 18 in. (album page dimensions)
2018.0141.7, .10, .15, .88

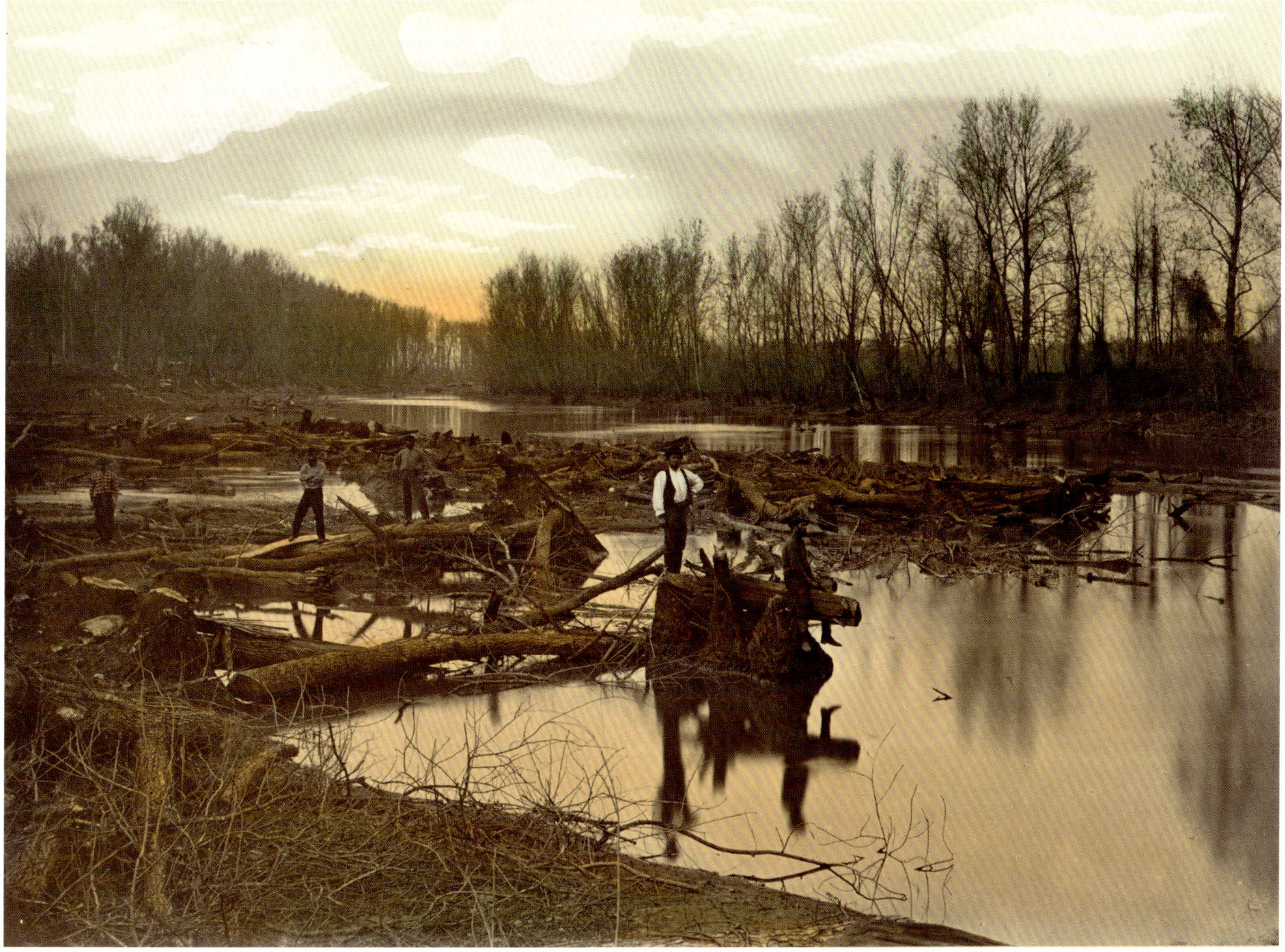

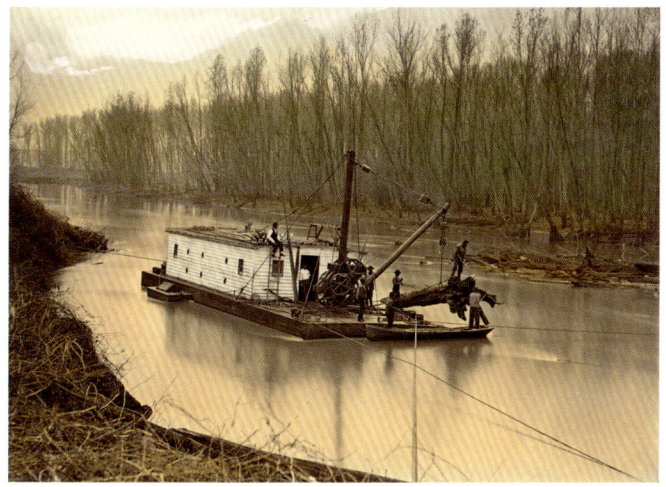

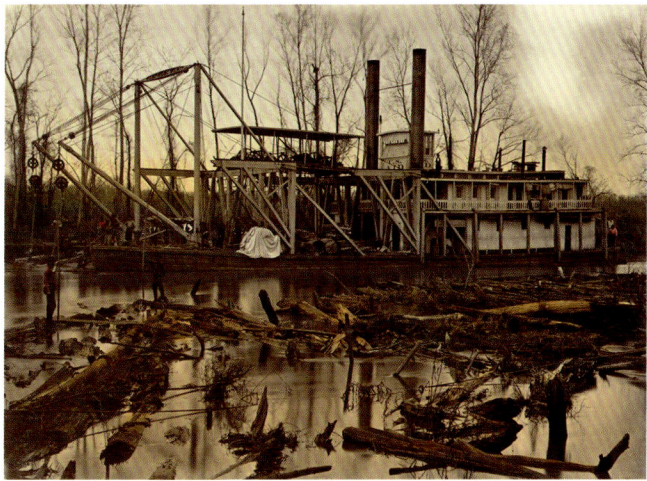

Gustave A. Moses (1836–1915)
Edward J. Souby (1844–1907)

New Orleans and the surrounding area was a major location for prizefighting at the end of the nineteenth century, and the sport remained popular at amateur and professional levels well past the mid-twentieth century. Local regulations sometimes prevented bouts within city limits, but promoters found ways to advertise and stage fights nearby, with high ticket sales and large purses. Some New Orleans–based bouts drew several thousand spectators. This pair of photographs captured the championship bout held at the Barnes Hotel near Gulfport, Mississippi, in which title holder Patrick "Paddy" Ryan was defeated by challenger John L. "The Strong Boy" Sullivan.

These pictures exemplify the gap that existed between photographic technology and public demand for prints. A boxing match is in one way an ideal event to be documented, since the dimensions of the ring (a square sixteen to twenty-four feet per side) limit the field of action, and the photographer can take advantage of zones of sharpness predetermined by the characteristics of the lens and the distance upon which it is focused.

But with the fast pace of a boxing match, shutter speed and emulsion sensitivity are more critical than focus for conveying the details of the bout. The large, tripod-mounted cameras used by Gustave A. Moses and Edward J. Souby were not equal to the task; in fact, few instruments of the day would have fared better in freezing the action of a fight without the use of supplemental lighting.

The "ghosting" of the pugilists caused by an exposure that was too long to record them clearly has been addressed by the negative being retouched to "draw" the figures into the composition, achieving an approximation of what the photographers and the crowd observed, and offering a lasting record to the public through this print. Even the motion of the crowd, cheering their preferred

fighter, is a little blurred. Those who wanted a likeness of the boxers, rather than this simulated action shot, would be better served by acquiring studio portraits of them, which due to their celebrity were readily available. Nonetheless, the picture attests to an event that was "from an instantaneous photograph taken on the spot."

Moses and Souby captured the fight from opposite directions. In the photograph below, the large platform holding the unwieldy camera is visible in the distance. Presumably, a similar instrument positioned close to the Barnes Hotel seen in the picture above would have been deployed as well. Though not easily identified in the hazy background, the second camera is likely positioned on the second level of the hotel, to the left of center.

The Sullivan-Ryan Prize Fight., **1882**
by Gustave A. Moses and Edward J. Souby
albumen prints, mounted, 14 ⅞ × 17 ⅞ in.
1978.85.1, .2

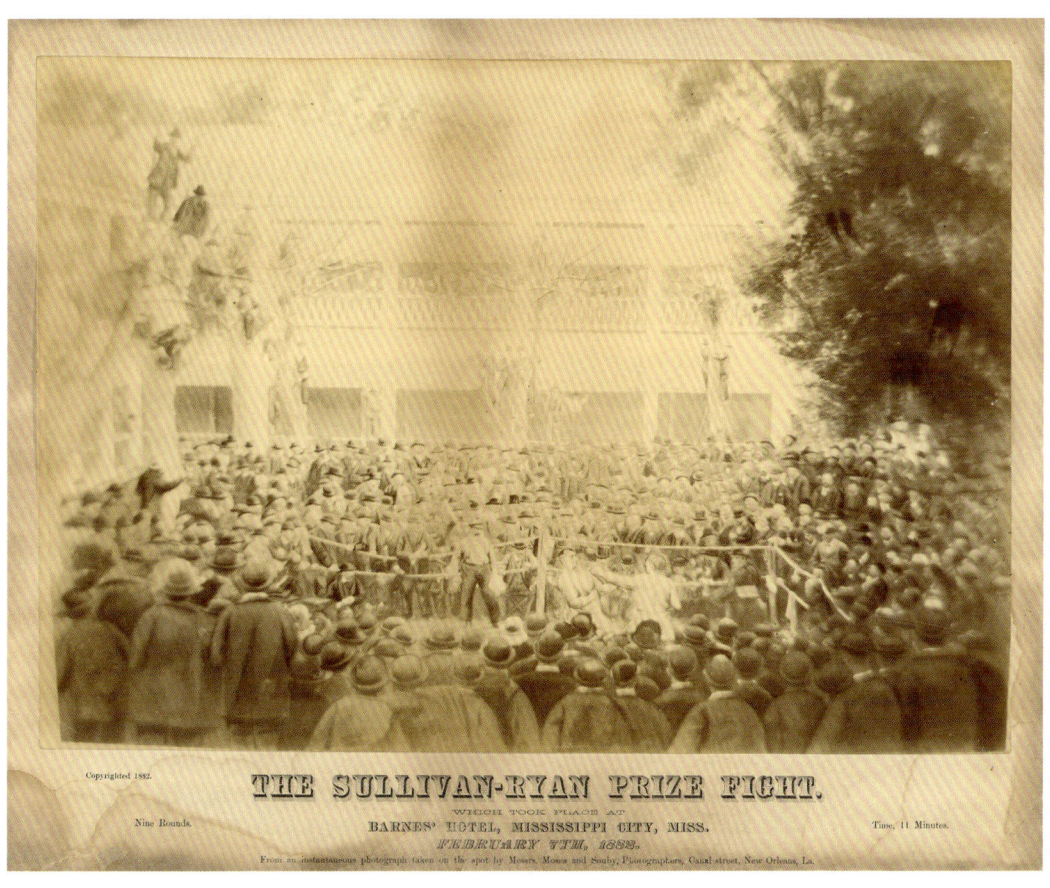

THE SULLIVAN-RYAN PRIZE FIGHT.

WHICH TOOK PLACE AT

BARNES' HOTEL, MISSISSIPPI CITY, MISS.

FEBRUARY 7TH, 1882.

Nine Rounds.   Time, 11 Minutes.

From an instantaneous photograph taken on the spot by Messrs. Moses and Souby, Photographers, Canal street, New Orleans, La.

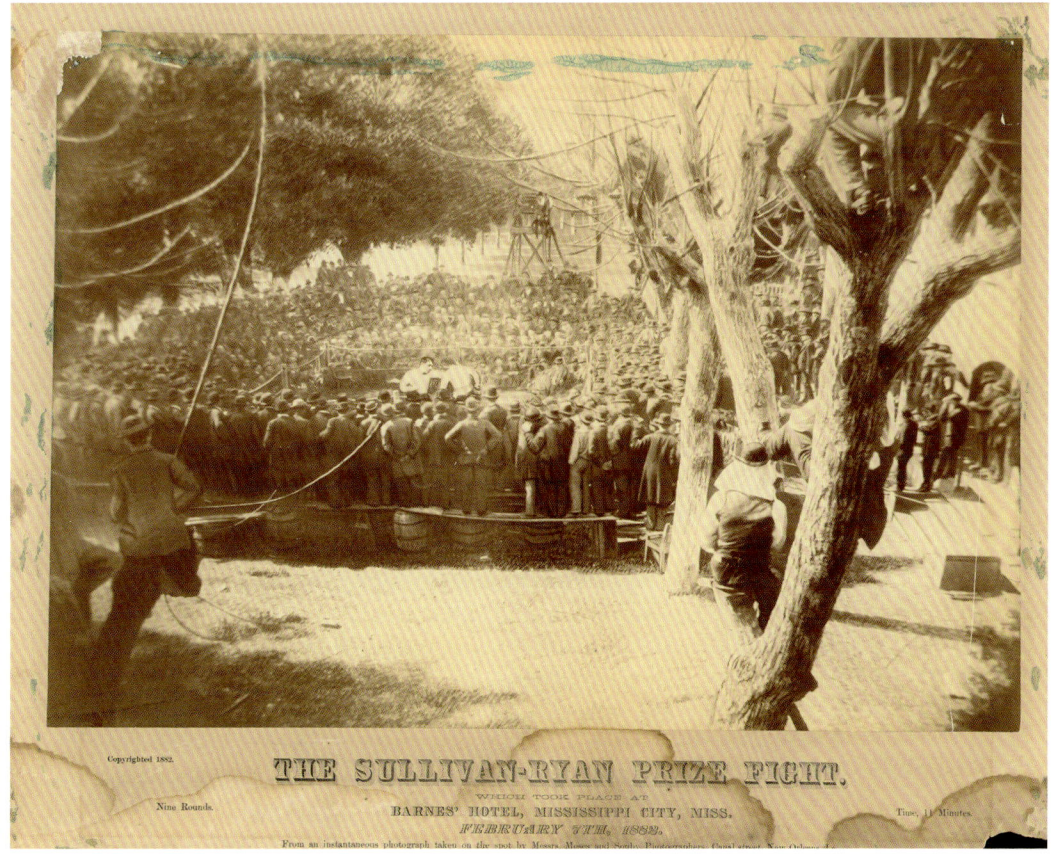

THE SULLIVAN-RYAN PRIZE FIGHT.

WHICH TOOK PLACE AT

BARNES' HOTEL, MISSISSIPPI CITY, MISS.

FEBRUARY 7TH, 1882.

Nine Rounds.   Time, 11 Minutes.

From an instantaneous photograph taken on the spot by Messrs. Moses and Souby, Photographers, Canal street, New Orleans, La.

Edward L. Wilson (1838–1903)

This picture presents a well-composed view that seemingly depicts a bowler-hatted figure contemplating the tranquility of nature. But nearly everything visible within the frame is a product of human design: the artificial lake, the landscaping and topography, the massive greenhouse, and the electric light tower behind it. An intriguing detail of the latter is the silhouette of a figure clinging to the structure.

This photograph was taken on the grounds of the World's Industrial and Cotton Centennial Exposition presented from December 1884 through June 1885 and later revived as the North, Central, and South American Exposition from November 1885, through April 1886. Note that the printed mount of the photograph scrambles the order of the words.

Edward L. Wilson of Philadelphia was the exposition's official photographer. He made hundreds of photographs of the exhibits and grounds, many of them produced in stereographic form. Wilson was an important figure of American photography in his day, associated with the practice and dissemination of the medium through lectures and sets of stereographic views.

The grounds, within the city limits of New Orleans, were the former site of the Pierre Foucher plantation. The site was acquired by the city of New Orleans in 1871 and designated Upper City Park. In 1886 it was renamed Audubon Park after the naturalist and artist John James Audubon, who lived in Louisiana (and briefly in New Orleans) during the 1820s.

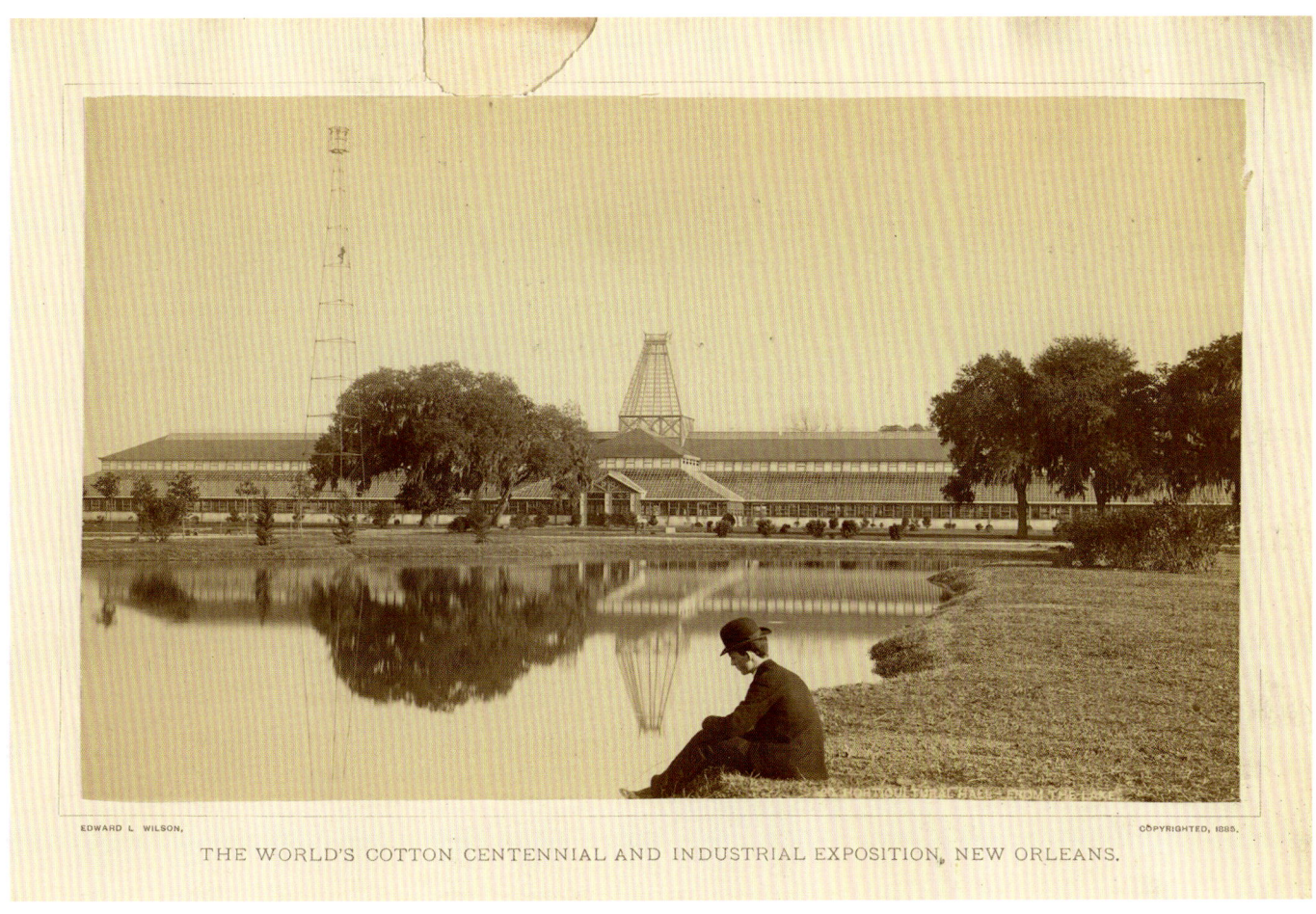

EDWARD L. WILSON,   COPYRIGHTED, 1885.

THE WORLD'S COTTON CENTENNIAL AND INDUSTRIAL EXPOSITION, NEW ORLEANS.

Horticultural Hall—From the Lake, 1885

by Edward L. Wilson
albumen print, 6 ³⁄₁₆ × 9 ¼ in.
1984.93   55

unknown photographer

The Creole Historic Exhibit was an influential feature within the World's Industrial and Cotton Centennial Exposition and its successor, the North, Central, and South American Exposition. In the exposition's first iteration, this collection of objects was part of the Women's Exhibit, but in the second fair, it was displayed as a separate entity. Direct descendants of Louisiana colonists, as well as people related to them by marriage, offered up relics of their heritage for public view, showcasing the region's past not only for locals, but for a national press and audience.

Simultaneous with the run of the exposition was the release of two cookbooks that exploited interest in Creole culture: *La Cuisine Creole*, by journalist Lafcadio Hearn (a resident of New Orleans for several years preceding its publication), and *The Creole Cookery Book*, published by the Christian Woman's Exchange in New Orleans. These publications are generally considered the first published record of what constitutes Creole cooking traditions and methods. The convergence of the expositions, with their special exhibits on local culture and increasing awareness of Creole heritage, contributed to New Orleans's aura of exceptionalism.

"Creole" has meant different things to different groups of people at different points in history, but the term embraces much more cultural diversity in the early twenty-first century than it did at the time of the exposition, when it often implied colonial ancestry of the white population.

Pictures can display, but they can't speak. Journalist Edward C. Wharton compiled an inventory of over four hundred items displayed in the Creole Historic Exhibit, and several dozen photographs visually corroborate the written record. C. F. Bragg of the *Illustrated Graphic News* of Cincinnati announced the intention to publish Wharton's list in a catalog of the Creole exhibit, but the work was never completed. The prospectus proclaims the great public interest in "the Creole race" shown by visitors to the exposition as the publication's impetus.

Pictures made of the exhibit's items were not themselves precious photographic artifacts but working documents. This role is amplified by the heavily annotated character of some prints, and the small brass grommets visible on others that were used to attach a larger card with additional data.

According to the notes on this photograph and elsewhere, the objects it presents were lent by Mademoiselle H. Leonie Pichot, daughter of Judge Adolphe Wenceslas Pichot (born in France) and his wife, the former Clementine de Morant (of New Orleans) and in some sense may be considered typical of those on display. Though Judge Pichot was technically "foreign French" and not a Creole, his wife's colonial connections constituted a strong basis for inclusion. The notes on the photograph offer some connection to other Louisiana Creole families associated with the loaned objects—the de Morant, Pontalba, and de Léry families—as well as to French monarchs Louis XIII and XVI. At least one of the items—the rosary made of amber having belonged to a daughter of Louis XVI, the duchesse d'Angoulême—was noted as a bequest to the Louisiana State Museum in its 1908–10 report.

Many of the loans to the exhibit indicate that a woman was the point of contact for the material. Examining the entirety of this exhibit, the vital role that women played in preserving (and sometimes promoting) family history is evident.

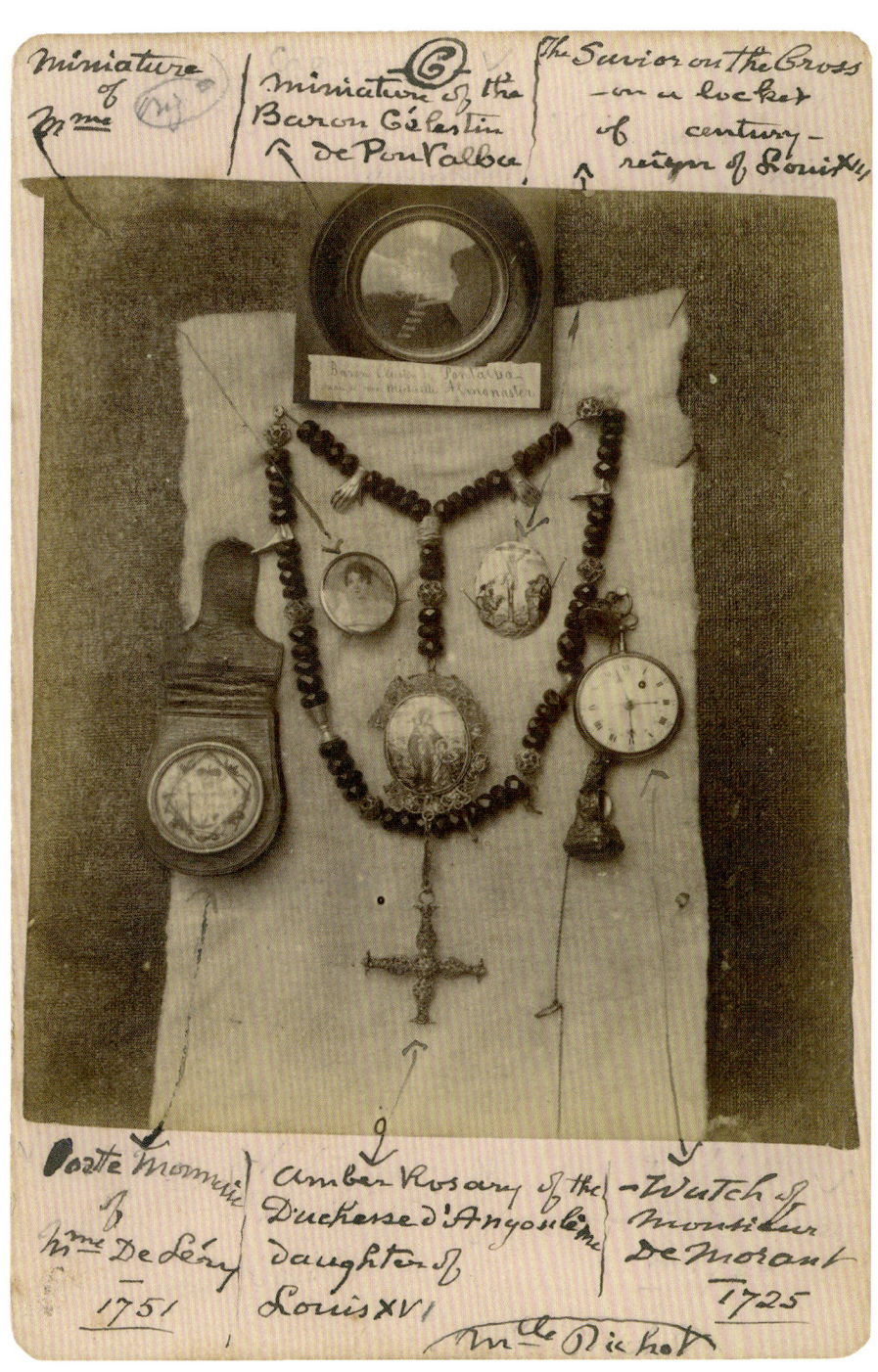

Photograph of display in the Creole Historic Exhibit, 1886?
by unknown photographer
albumen print, mounted, 5 × 3¼ in.
MSS 216.77; 58-101-L.3

Hofeline and Adams (active 1887)

There is no confusing the cyanotype with other photographic processes. Its brilliant blue color, formed by the action of light on salts of iron, is unique in the realm of photographic imagery. The process was introduced in 1841, resulting from experiments by British scientist Sir John Herschel, and for well over a century it was used for amateur, professional, and artistic photography. Until photocopiers and computer printers became dominant, cyanotype was the ubiquitous medium for architectural and engineering blueprints.

Paper coated with iron salts is used to this day in making cyanotype photograms—cameraless images produced by placing objects on the sensitized sheet, exposing it to sunlight, then developing the image in plain water—as a way of teaching some of the science of photography to children. In the late twentieth century, cyanotype, along with other antique processes like gum bichromate printing, kallitype, and platinum printing, enjoyed a revival. Photographic artists compounded the chemical solutions and painted them on printing paper themselves. The handmade character of these processes could be viewed as complementing the more rigid mechanics of traditional photography, emphasizing the personal agency and choices of the photographer.

The employment of the cyanotype process for the *Photographic Album of the City of New Orleans* is an interesting use of the medium. The bound volume (of which several copies are known to survive) consists of advertisements of selected businesses, with text shown on facing pages opposite a cyanotype print, usually of the business establishment being touted in the text.

The effort to make the individual prints and letterpress descriptions and bind them must have involved considerable expense. The directory's listings, illustrating a tiny fraction of New Orleans businesses, were selective and likely driven by

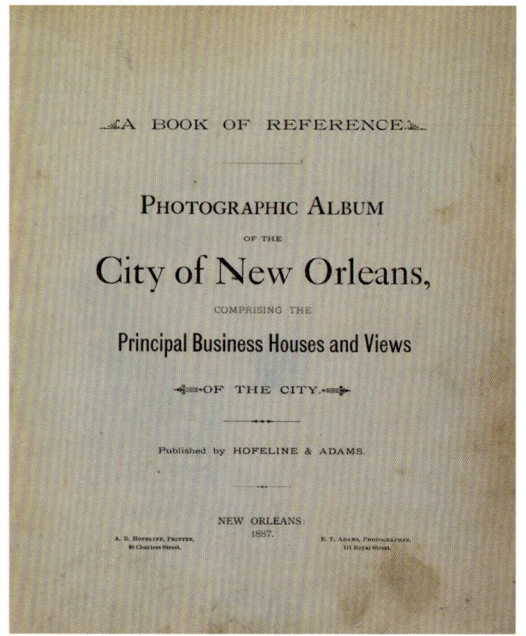

subscription. The publisher must have estimated the market for this book at a fairly low number or produced the volume for a targeted list of clients.

A decade and a half before Hofeline and Adams's enterprise, *Jewell's Crescent City Illustrated*, a much larger commercial directory, was published. Its illustrations of businesses, civic organizations, and leaders of New Orleans industry and politics took the form of wood engravings. Among its hundreds of illustrations (and some four hundred total pages), many were based on photographs by Theodore Lilienthal (p. 46). The repurposing of Lilienthal's albumen prints to wood engravings permitted a much more efficient form of reproduction for the relatively large run of *Jewell's Crescent City.*

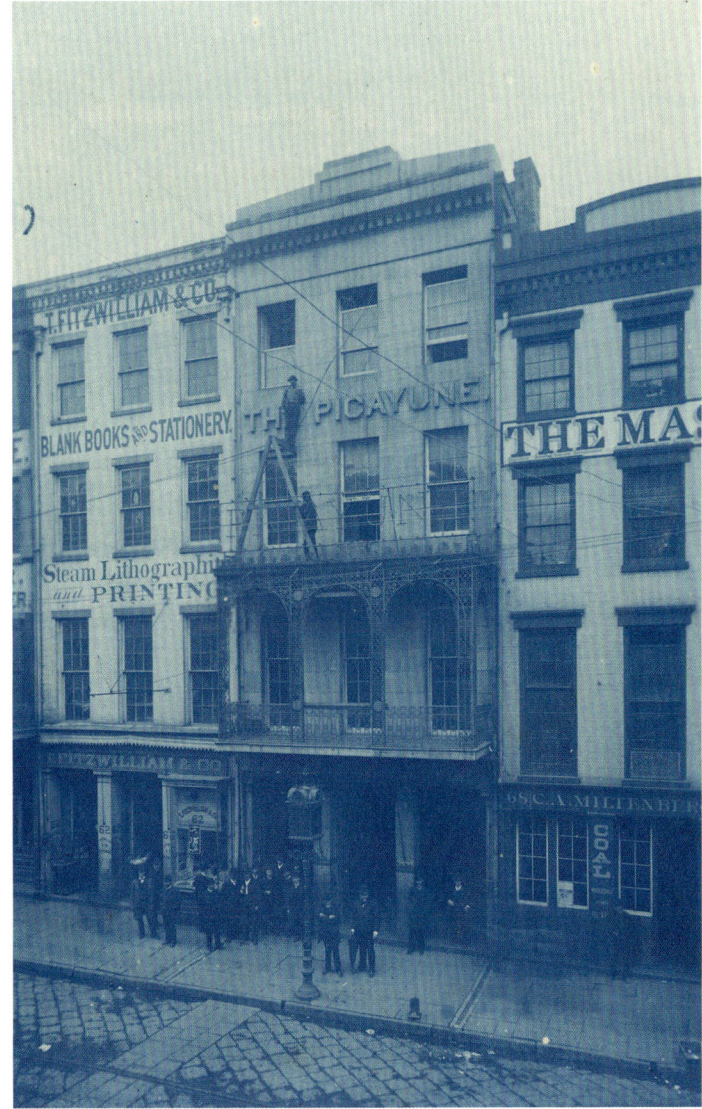
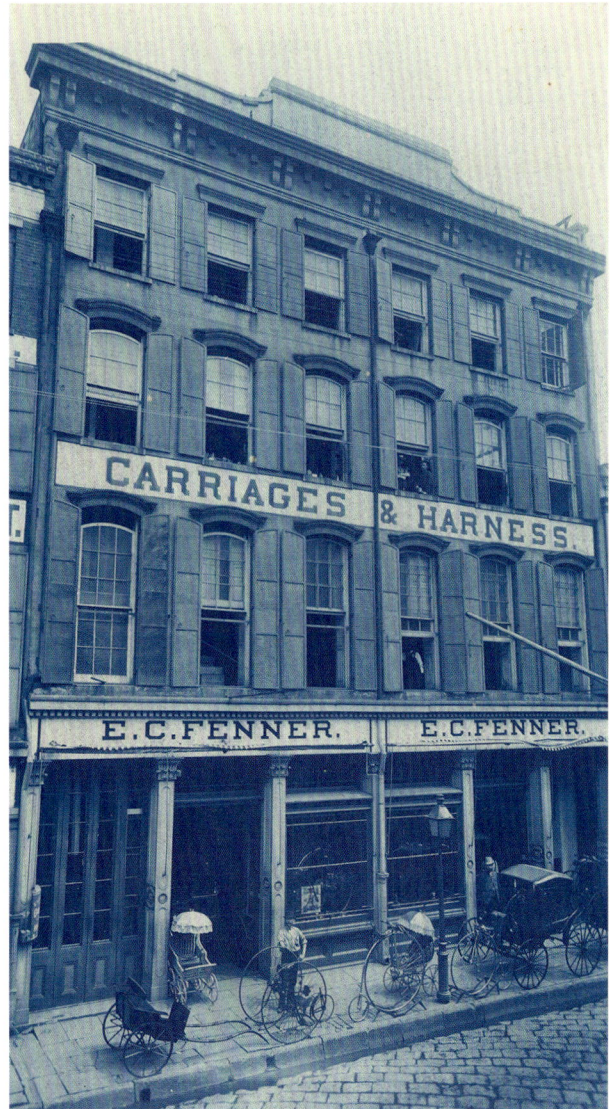

Photographic Album of the City of New Orleans, 1887
by Hofeline and Adams
cyanotype and letterpress, 11 × 9 × ½ in. (overall book dimensions)
77-224-RL

George François Mugnier (1855–1936)

George François Mugnier, a Swiss immigrant, established himself in New Orleans photography circles in the early 1880s, and evidence indicates that by the end of the decade, his formal career in that field was over. Among his early documentable works are stereographic views of New Orleans and the region that seem to have been marketed during the 1884–86 expositions in New Orleans—The World's Industrial and Cotton Centennial Exposition and the subsequent extension billed as the North, Central, and South American Exposition.

This large picture (the print is more than 17 × 21 inches) comprises a number of compositional elements. The overall complexity and "busy-ness" of the scene can be mentally cropped into more visually digestible vignettes: the two youngsters in the foreground (one on horseback, the other standing near a hay rake whose operators have their backs to Mugnier's lens); the loaded wagon emerging from the barn; the team of mules standing by, ready to do whatever work is required; a jumble of cattle and men in the middle distance; and the architectural complex that provides a backdrop and limit to the pictorial space. The barn's scalloped verge boards and slatted wall sections merit their own attention.

Barely visible where the left-hand slope of the barn roof ends stands a bell tower. A plantation's bells regulated the operations of labor and rest on these large complexes, and though the status of the labor force changed with the abolition of slavery, the work nonetheless remained arduous.

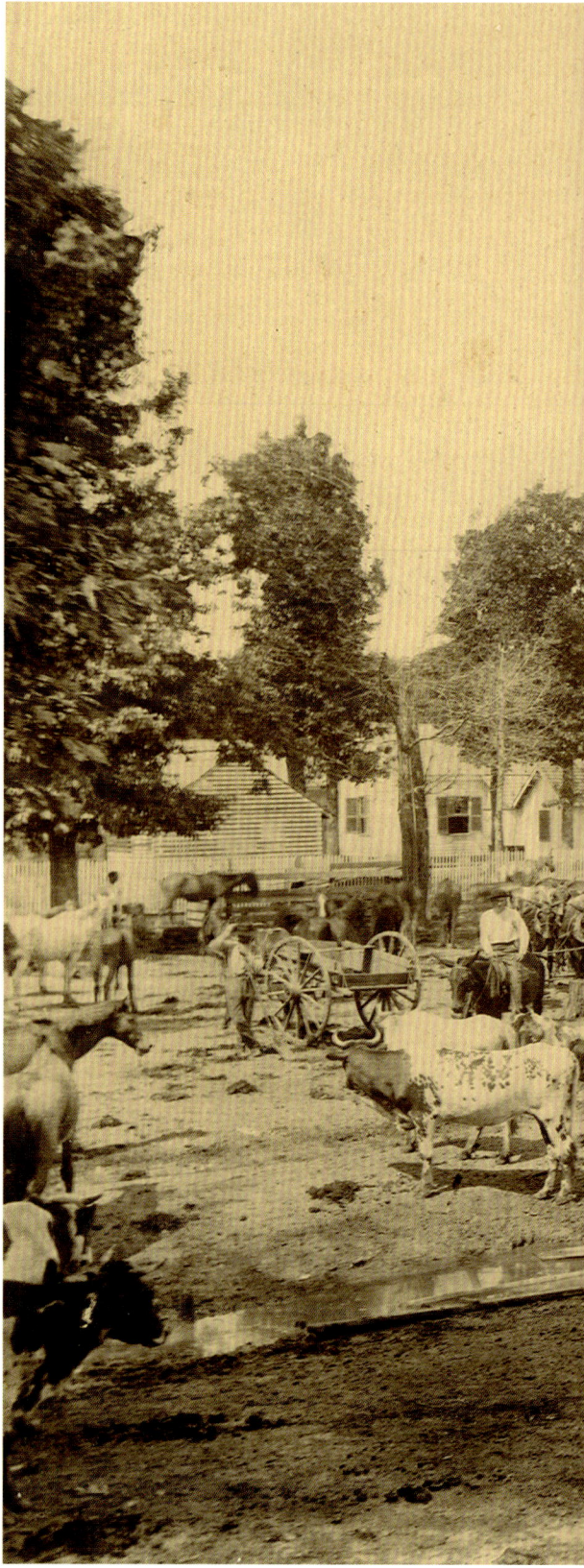

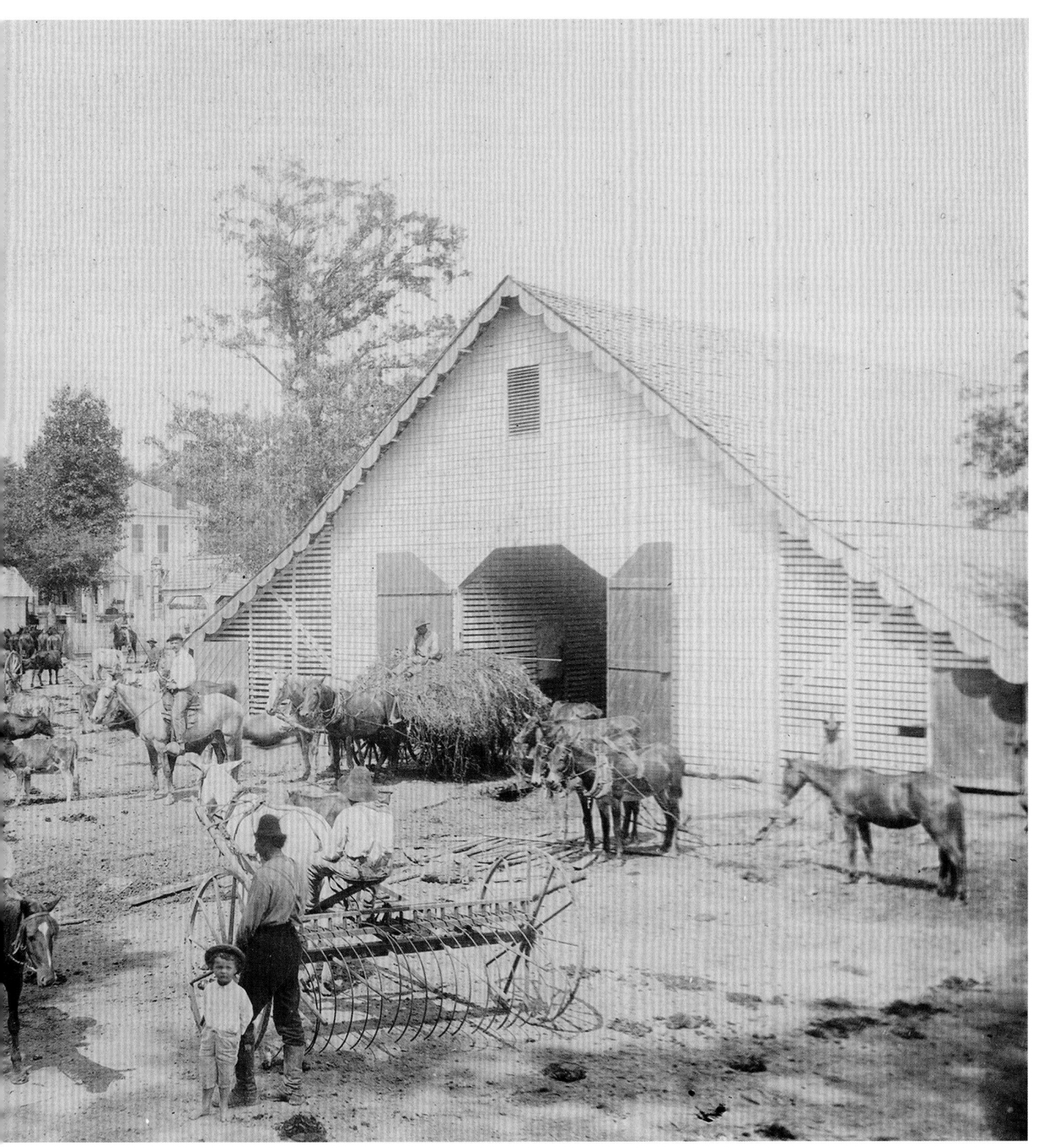

Early Morning on a Plantation, circa 1889
by George François Mugnier
albumen print, 17⅛ × 21¼ in.
gift of N. West Moss, 2016.0386.1.1.65

unknown photographer

The term *snapshot* dates from 1808 and originally referred to a shot that a hunter took without carefully aiming. Its use as a photographic term comes more than five decades later and wasn't in common usage for nearly another forty years beyond that. This picture embodies the snapshot aesthetic.

The ability to aim the camera and immediately make an exposure coincides, more or less, with the introduction in 1888 of the Kodak No. 1 camera. This instrument and its successors introduced over the next several years were revolutionary in many ways. Small by standards of the day, the camera could be held in the hands rather than needing to be mounted on a tripod. It used flexible film—a recent invention—in a roll or spool mounted inside the camera instead of relying on individual sheets of film or glass that needed to be carried separately and inserted into the camera for each exposure. The roll offered the user the ability to make one hundred pictures before it was exhausted. This capacity encouraged users to quickly consider and execute variations on a picture. The time between pictorial decision-making and execution was greatly reduced.

Once the roll was fully exposed, the user sent the camera to the Kodak factory, where the film was developed and printed, and a new roll was placed in the camera. The prints, negatives, and reloaded camera were sent back to the user. Convenience was what Kodak was offering a new type of amateur, expressed in its slogan, "You press the button, we do the rest."

The jumble of shadows cast by people and animals, both visible and unseen, are one element of this snapshot aesthetic, as well as the horse's head jutting in from the left and the somewhat tilted horizon line and architecture of the background. With all of these "faults," this snapshot is nonetheless a compelling photograph.

The setting for the photograph is Evan Hall plantation near Donaldsonville, Louisiana, several dozen miles upriver from New Orleans. At the time this picture was made, enslavement of the workers had ended some twenty-five years earlier, but the architectural vestige of the condition in the two rows of cabins that flank the central road remains.

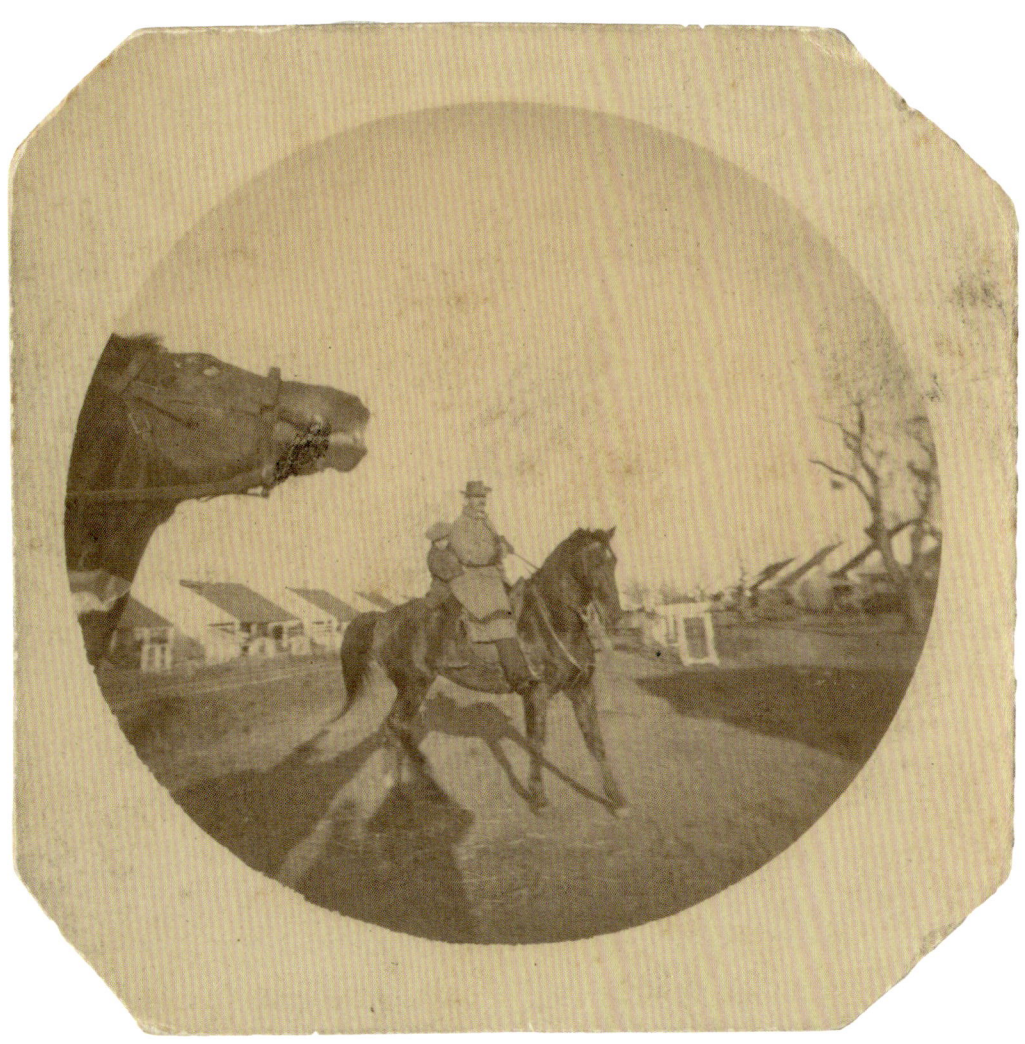

Alphonse and Mac, between 1888 and 1895
by an unknown photographer
gelatin silver print, 3⅛ × 2⅞ in.
gift of James L. McCall Jr., 1978.26.4

FROM PROFESSIONALS
TO AMATEURS

1890–1935

Mother Marie de la St. Croix (1854–1940)

When it comes to documenting an insular community such as a convent, a photographer with inside access to the operations and physical environment has a great advantage. Mother Marie de la St. Croix (born Marie Faureaud in 1854), one of the earliest known woman photographers in New Orleans, had just such an advantage: as part of the Ursuline community of nuns from 1873 until her death in 1940, she had a unique vantage point on the city's influential Ursuline Convent. With the support of the abbey's head, Mother St. Ignatius, and mentorship from optician Edward H. Claudel and Jesuit Father Albert H. Biever (who would eventually become the first president of Loyola College (now Loyola University New Orleans), St. Croix got to work photographing the boarding school-cum-convent that played significant roles in music, medicine, and women's education in the Gulf South. *Views of the Ursuline Convent*, an album containing thirty-seven original photographs, was assembled in 1894.

The order's presence in New Orleans is nearly as old as the city itself. The first nuns arrived in 1727, less than a decade after the city's founding, in 1718. In nearly three centuries since, the Ursulines built three substantial complexes to house the community and to offer education to young women. The campus depicted in St. Croix's photographs, which was in use from 1824 until 1912, is the only one of the three to have been demolished.

The apparatus used by St. Croix—a large, tripod-mounted view camera using glass negatives, some as large as 14 × 17 inches—required her to preconceptualize the pictures she made. The equipment could not capture fast or spontaneous action. When her lens was turned to the architecture and grounds of the campus, camera placement and lighting conditions were her main considerations. Those subjects were not going to move. When it came to depicting the students' activities, St. Croix acted as choreographer. She staged the girls in

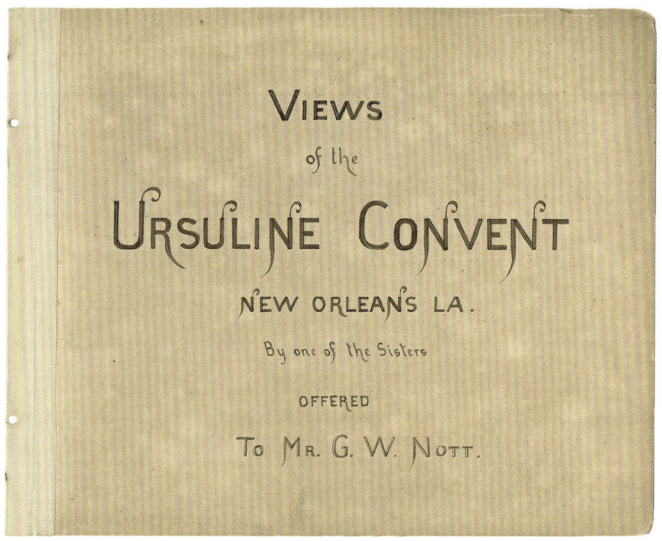

poses that would meaningfully depict their activities and could be maintained for the duration of the exposure, which could be several seconds long. In the photographs seen here, St. Croix's use of the static and linear architectural backgrounds as a counterpoint to the organic shapes of the students and teachers is a compositional tour de force.

THNOC's 2018 acquisition of the album was followed by the 2020 acquisition of the Mother St. Croix archive of glass negatives and photographic equipment from the Ursuline Sisters of New Orleans.

Images from *Views of the Ursuline Convent*, between 1888 and 1894
by Mother Marie de la St. Croix
albumen prints, mounted, 10 × 12 in. (album page dimensions)
2018.0242.20, .30

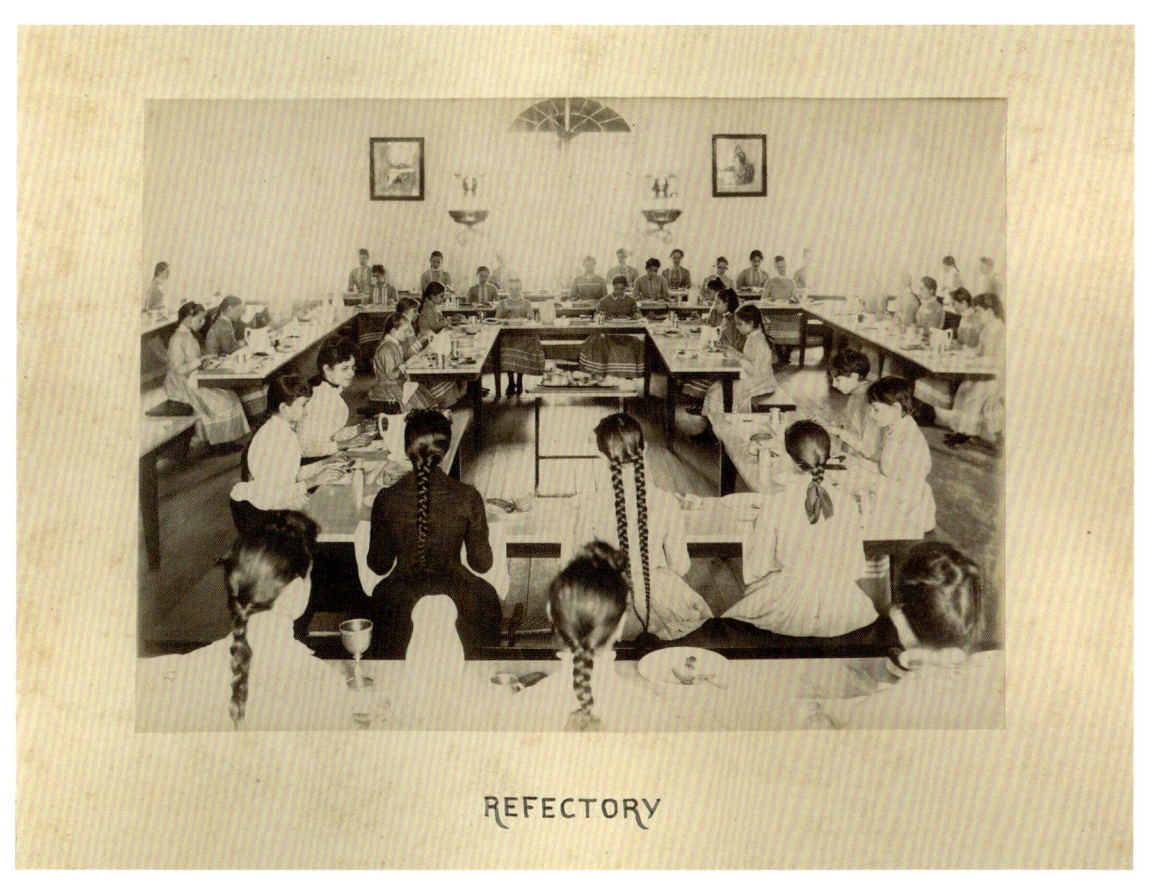

REFECTORY

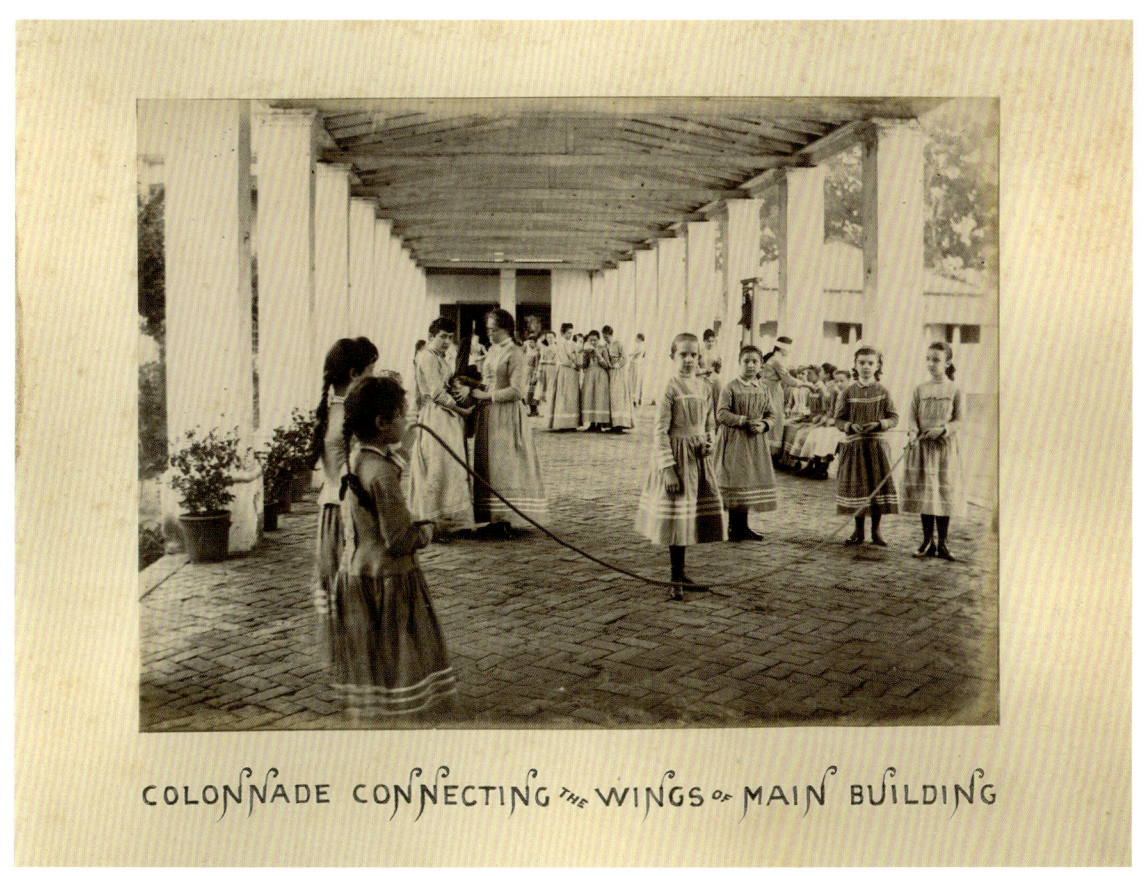

COLONNADE CONNECTING THE WINGS OF MAIN BUILDING

John Norris Teunisson (1869–1959)

The yellow fever epidemic that struck New Orleans in 1905 was the last significant outbreak of the disease in the city—and, in fact, in the United States—but citizens had no way of knowing that at the time. The often-fatal fever had plagued New Orleans almost annually for most of the nineteenth century, and some especially devastating outbreaks took thousands of lives in a single season. Seeking cures and scapegoats was a common pastime. For decades, New Orleans–bound ships arriving from overseas ports where yellow fever was endemic had been required to visit quarantine stations along the Gulf Coast before entering the city. Inspections and fumigation of cargoes were routine. By 1905, doctors in the US Army had confirmed that *Aedes aegypti* mosquitoes were responsible for transmitting the virus, and improvements in sanitation had lowered the death toll, but the new outbreak revived tension and suspicion directed at Central America and other supposed sources of the disease.

The United Fruit Company, which had been importing bananas to North American ports (including New Orleans) for the last quarter of the nineteenth century, became a suspected conduit of the disease. In the summer of 1905, the public became increasingly persuaded that the company's operations in Central and South America and the Caribbean islands were bringing fever to the city. To counter its detractors, the company organized a "quarantine tour" of its facilities and invited the press to go along. Photographer John Norris Teunisson of New Orleans documented the trip photographically and compiled the rather sumptuous album that visually summarized the rather sumptuous album that visually summarized the three-week tour.

In keeping with some typical aesthetics of photographic presentation of the era, the pictures are displayed on layered mounts of subdued tones. Letterpress titles and commentary, in colored ink on subtly tinted pages, provide the text. A day-by-day calendar lists ports of call where the company's steamship *Anselm* stopped. The pictures emphasize the clean and modern operations of the United Fruit Company in each location.

The Progressive Era investigative journalists, keen to expose the plight of exploited workers, would have been a source of pressure for the company. The photographs imply good working conditions while avoiding focusing explicitly on employees, instead concentrating on a legitimate concern for public health. The album describes the tour participants as "the health authorities of Texas, Louisiana, Mississippi, and Alabama, and of the Marine Hospital Service." Because the United Fruit Company sponsored the tour and had a strong hand in shaping the text that affirms "they found the health conditions at the majority of the various ports to be most satisfactory," the trip and the photo album can be characterized at least partly as propaganda. Ultimately, as far as the issue of yellow fever was concerned, the lack of later outbreaks in the United States made the public relations goals of this tour moot.

Teunisson was a native of Mississippi, born in the Pike County town of Summit in 1869. He is first listed as a photographer in the New Orleans city directory of 1901, though he moved to the Crescent City in 1892. Teunisson's long career included photographing aspects of Mardi Gras, as well as sites and scenes that were reproduced on postcards and in publications geared toward visitors to the city. He died in Washington, DC, in 1959.

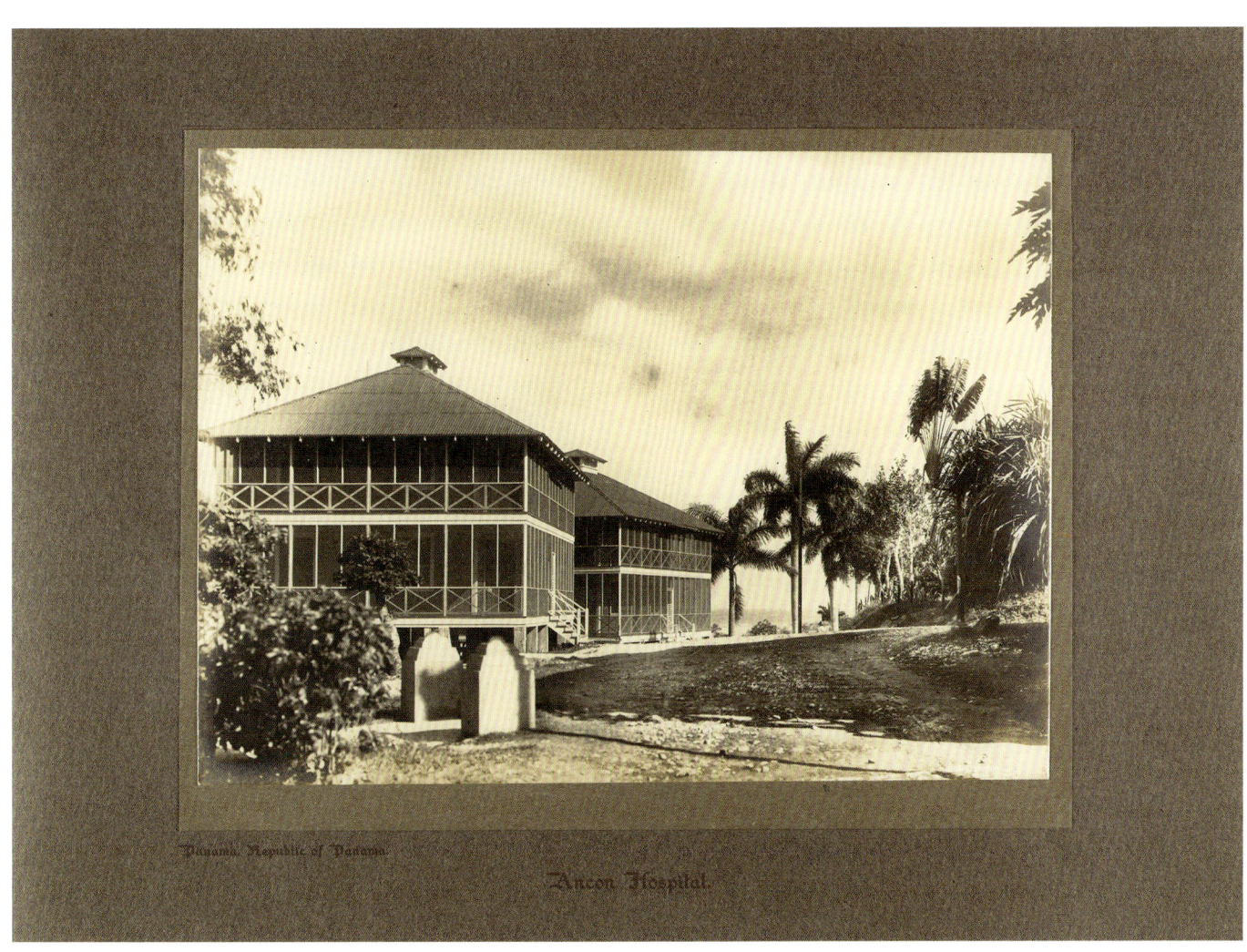

**Ancon Hospital [Panama City], from photograph album
produced by United Fruit Company, 1906**

by John Norris Teunisson
gelatin silver print, mounted, 11⅝ × 15½ in. (album page dimensions)
1996.14.27

John L. Haller (1874–1948)

In July 1906, the New Orleans Horticultural Society marked its twenty-first anniversary with a three-day excursion from New Orleans to Grand Isle, a barrier island on the Gulf of Mexico at the southern end of Jefferson Parish. In a neat bit of symmetry, the boat that carried the group (and a load of mail) was also named *Grand Isle*. Its captain was Michael McSweeney.

At least two copies of a photographic album commemorating the trip were made. The photographer has been identified as John L. Haller. His photographs (ten in all) capture subjects that, while commonplace in that day, have no real parallels in the twenty-first century. Oystermen no longer build palmetto shelters on shell middens; the shrimp-drying industry that flourished around Manila Village (a place name that gives a nod to the Filipino settlement there) is gone. And though one can still see the sun rise on Grand Lake (also known as Barataria Bay), that body of water has become more or less open to the Gulf—separated by wispy filaments of land—and not what we would consider a bay, lake, or other similarly defined aquatic feature.

Photographs, despite transcribing a "real" physical world, are—like maps—abstractions, in that they express qualities apart from their subjects, such as being two-dimensional, embodying distortions from lenses, and often being monochrome instead of in color. Photographs and maps each supply data. One could argue that a map, by nature and presentation, is more neutral than a photograph, though like photographs, maps are shaped by human priorities and decisions about what the viewer needs to see. In an object of a few hundred square inches, a map would offer a way to envision a large, complex arrangement of sea and land. The map would allow one to pinpoint where oyster reefs were, as well as the small hummocks of land that sustained the huts of the oystermen. In even fewer square inches, the photographs made at the outing

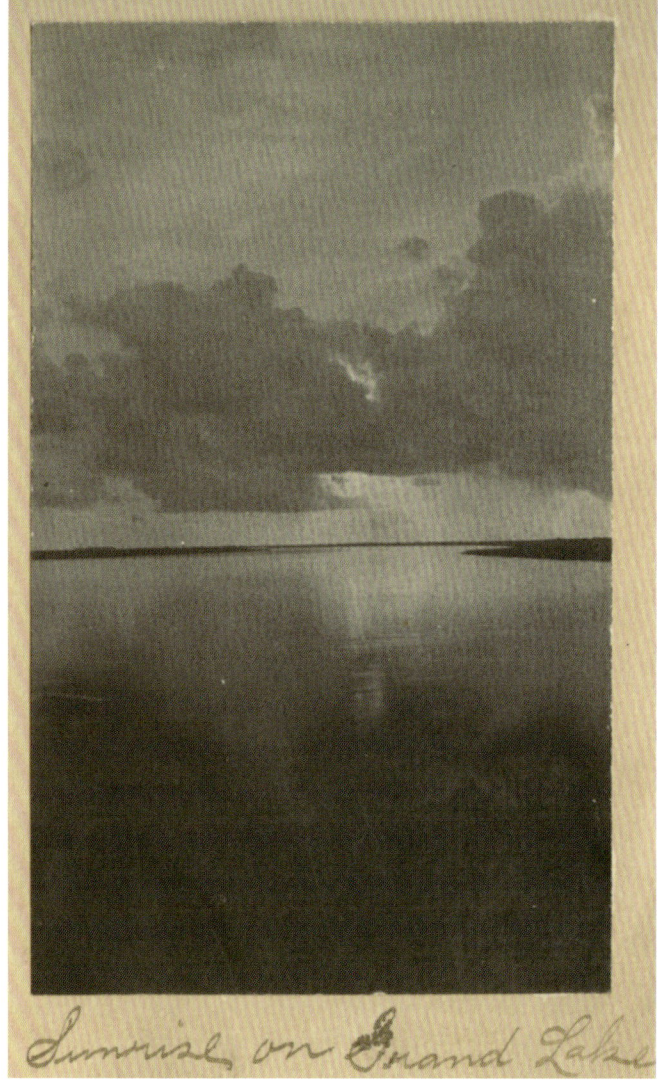

of the New Orleans Horticultural Society offer something different—namely, a glimpse at the industry, character, population, and routines of these communities. Though the photographs were made merely as a keepsake of the society's outing, they show how those ways of life from the last century are impossible today.

Images from album commemorating New Orleans Horticultural Society trip to Grand Isle, 1906
by John L. Haller
platinum prints, mounted, 5½ × 6⅝ in. (album page dimensions)
1991.22.6, .7, .8

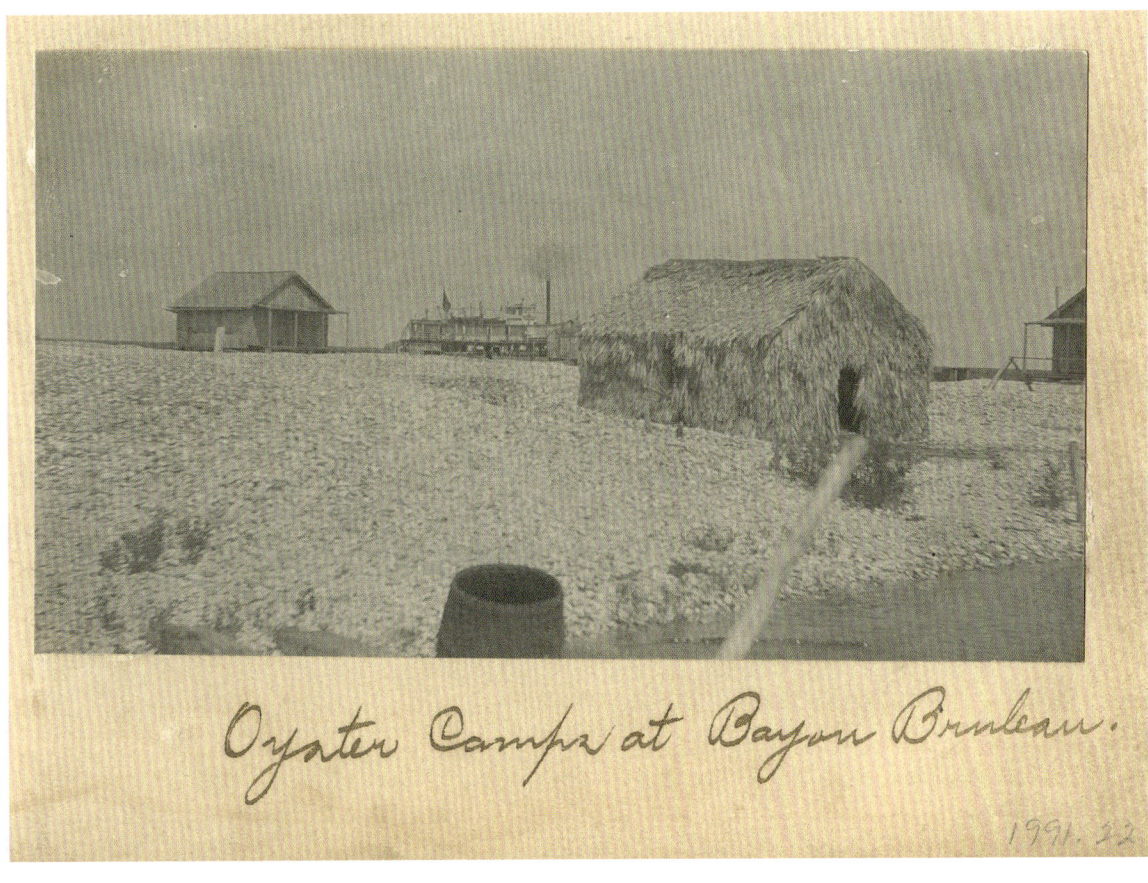

Oyster Camps at Bayou Brulean.

1991.22

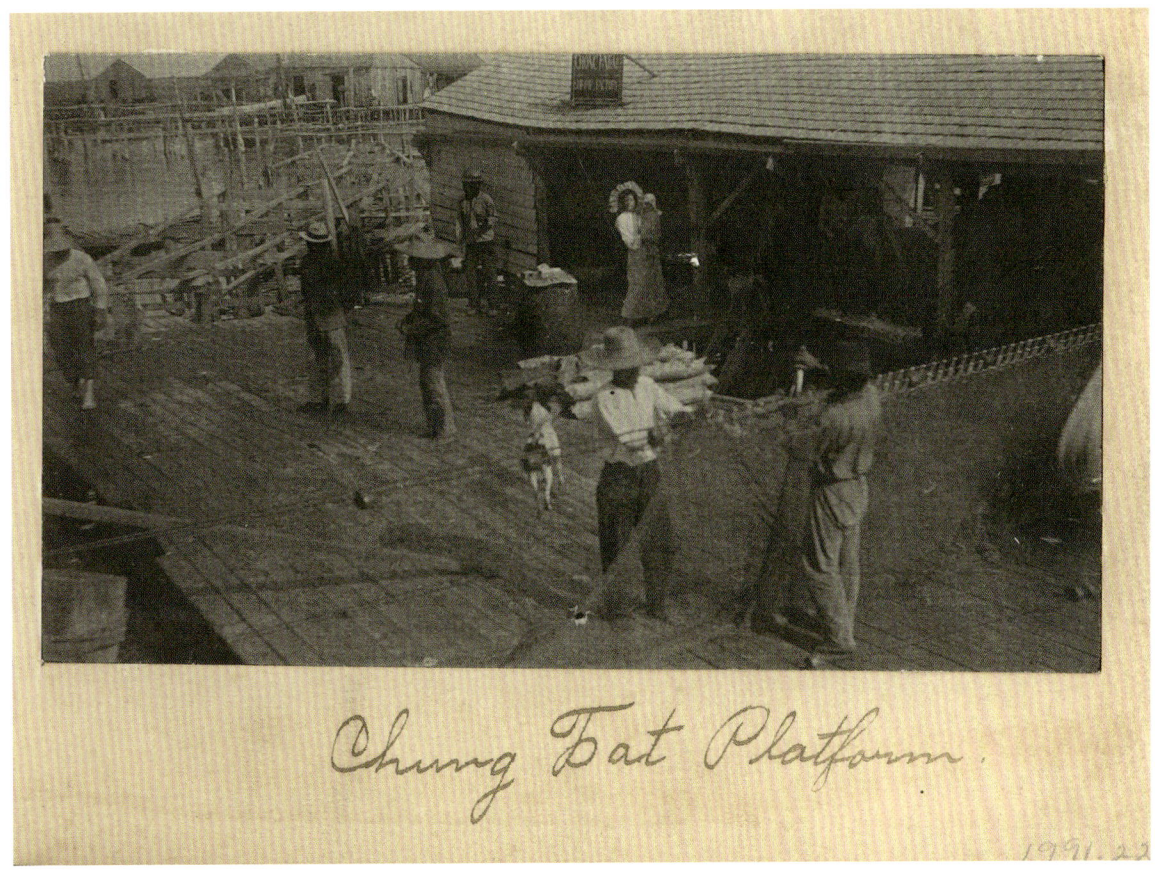

Chung Fat Platform.

1991.22

unknown photographer

Streetscapes in dense, mixed-use urban areas can present unusual juxtapositions of trades, services, and merchandise. This cyanotype of a portion of the 200 block of Chartres Street in New Orleans's oldest neighborhood, the French Quarter, is a good example. Chartres's history as a vibrant retail thoroughfare goes back to the early nineteenth century and endures to an extent today, though much of the retail activity in the city had shifted to Canal Street by the time this photograph was made. The slightly cocked presentation of the print on its mounting board, the absence of authorship, and the use of the cyanotype process suggest (but do not prove) that the unknown maker was not a professional. The simplicity of preparing cyanotype paper and developing the exposed sheet (only water was required) made the process appealing to amateurs who lacked either the disposition or the physical setup for more elaborate techniques. This print could, however, have been hastily prepared by a professional as a proof for a more carefully presented version, perhaps in a silver- or platinum-based medium.

From a subject standpoint, the picture is a tale of two showcases: a pet shop on the left (mostly out of the frame), and the offices of a fireworks manufactory and merchandise importer on the right. The George Washington Weingart named on the columns was "an importer and jobber of notions, toys, baskets, musical instruments and fancy goods," according to an 1879 price list for this enterprise. Examples of these wares may be discerned in the display of the showcase on the picture's right side. Lurking in the shadowy region between two columns and set back from the sidewalk is the sign for the other business that operates on Weingart's premises: the

Southern Fireworks Manufactory office, established in 1893.

William Bartels of New York, whose store appears at the left side of the photograph, was involved in the wild animal and pet trade. A newspaper article from 1900 describing his wildlife farm in New Jersey declares him the largest importer of wild animals in the United States. During this time he served as a procurement agent for animals destined for the National Zoo in Washington, DC. An entrepreneur, Bartels operated stores in New Orleans, New York, St. Louis, and San Francisco. According to city directory listings, the store in New Orleans remained active for fifty years (1883–1933), the bulk of that run being at the 231 Chartres Street location.

Elements of this picture visible in the foreground allude to the infrastructure of the French Quarter location. The large stone blocks are street pavers used in the Quarter prior to the ubiquity of asphalt and concrete, and defining the lower edge of the composition is a pipe for either water or gas, awaiting burial beneath the sidewalk or roadway.

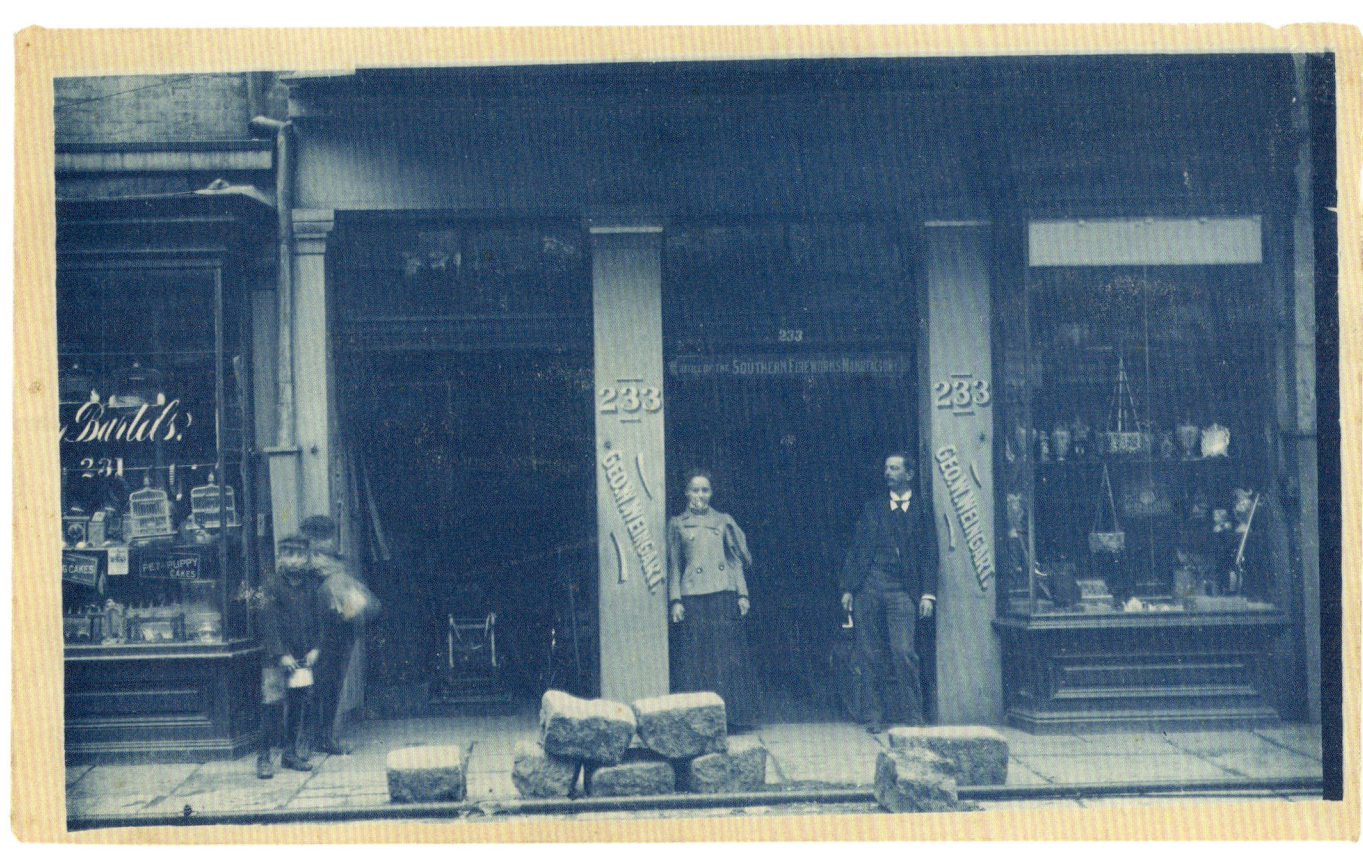

**Bartels' pet store and Weingart's office of the Southern
Fireworks Manufactory, Chartres Street, circa 1910**

by an unknown photographer
cyanotype, mounted, 5¹⁵⁄₁₆ × 10 in.
gift of Audrey Moulin Stier, 2003.0167.2

Morgan Whitney (1869–1913)

The photographs of Morgan Whitney display the variety of a dilettante's interests and include content many professional photographers would have overlooked. His photographic world could be as small as a tabletop flower arrangement or as wide as the Louisiana bayou landscape, and he found extensive interest in photographing architecture in the older sections of New Orleans and in the countryside. Whitney expressed his belle epoque vision in platinum prints from 5 × 7-inch negatives, over three hundred of which are in THNOC's collection. Though the composition of many of his photographs (especially the landscapes and certain architectural subjects) can seem formulaically picturesque, his still lifes, and the two surviving portraits he made, exhibit a flair for sophisticated composition.

Born into a wealthy family, Whitney supported, collected, and engaged in arts of all kinds. He studied music and painting in Paris, sang and acted in amateur productions and fundraisers, and exhibited paintings and drawings in local art shows. Within a week of his death in 1913 after a long illness, Whitney's bequest of more than a hundred Asian artworks, principally carved stone objects, to the Isaac Delgado Museum of Art (now New Orleans Museum of Art) was on display. His still life photographs, which consist mostly of flowers, occasionally feature some of these items from Asia.

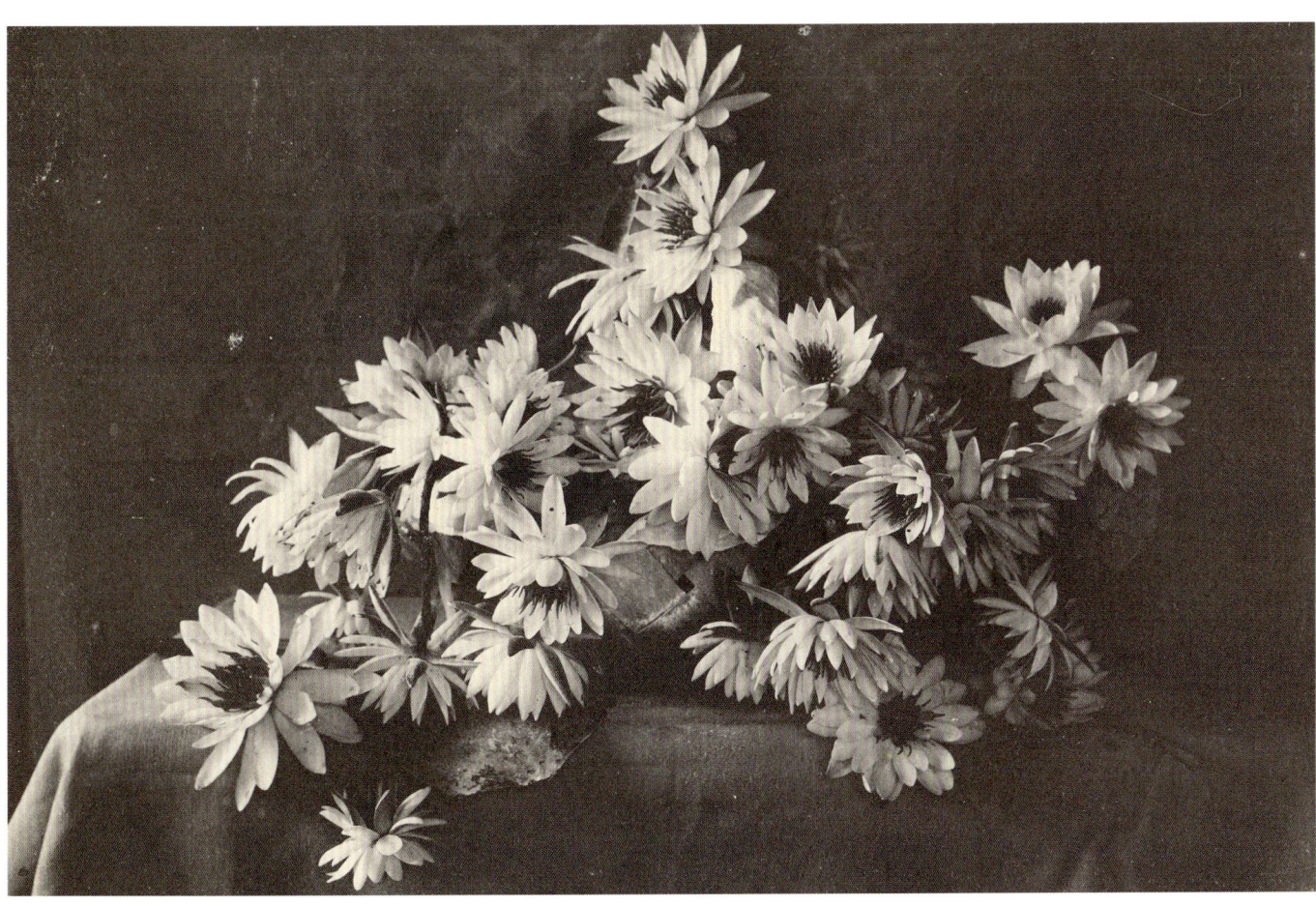

Water lilies, circa 1910

by Morgan Whitney
platinum print, 4⁹⁄₁₆ × 6⁹⁄₁₆ in.
gift of Mrs. Morgan Whitney, 1975.21.47

Ernest J. Bellocq (1873–1949)

The career of commercial photographer Ernest J. Bellocq will forever be defined by a small group of photographs he made that are detached from the studio portraits, architectural subjects, and other oddments that photographers for hire routinely undertake. Created in the early twentieth century, Bellocq's most famous photographs show women who are presumed to be sex workers in New Orleans's Progressive Era experiment with a legally defined district of prostitution. The trade thrived from 1897 until late 1917 in the twelve square blocks nicknamed Storyville, after the author of its enabling legislation, alderman Sidney Story. The experiment ended when the US Navy prohibited prostitution within five miles of naval bases, due to health concerns for men of the armed forces serving in World War I. Storyville was caught in this dragnet.

Bellocq's subjects appear before the camera in various poses and degrees of undress. Most seem at ease with him and with being photographed. The tone is not overtly erotic. While the pictures may have been commissioned to illustrate one of Storyville's so-called blue books (directories of sex workers and advertisements for establishments, products, and services) or for another commercial purpose, there is no evidence of their having been so used. Whether the photographer-subject relation was economic, artistic, or friendly is unclear. The series consists of about a hundred surviving examples.

The figure lying on a wicker chaise is a bit of an oddity in the Storyville group. She (her identity is unknown) is stiff, almost as if in rigor mortis, rather than comfortably facing the camera. She exhibits neither the playfulness shown in some subjects' faces, nor the serious demeanor of others.

Few prints from the Storyville series are securely identified as being produced by Bellocq's own hand. Most of what is known of this body of work comes from prints made by photographer Lee Friedlander (b. 1934), who began printing from Bellocq's 8 × 10-inch glass negatives in the late 1960s after acquiring the group from New Orleans art dealer Larry Borenstein. A smaller set of prints, slightly enlarged from Bellocq's negatives and printed in the late 1950s, predate Friedlander's work. These photographs (about thirty of them) and two by Friedlander are part of THNOC's holdings. Friedlander printed the one featured here.

In the half century between the creation of the negatives and Friedlander's acquisition of them, many sustained damage. In the modern printings, these defects (such as cracks in the plate, emulsion loss, and patterns produced by mold or fungus growth) have become part of the object and testify to a history of a thing rather than a history of what the thing depicts. In the example here, a crack from lower left to upper right diagonally bisects the picture. Mold growth has eradicated the gelatin-based image matrix, resulting in areas of pure black in the center of the picture and scattered throughout the top, middle, and bottom areas, where the exposure has been made through clear glass. At one point the negative must have been placed between or against corrugated cardboard, perhaps to ensure the cracked plate would suffer no more damage: a series of light parallel lines in the picture's upper-left quadrant attest to a reaction that imprinted the lines of corrugation on the negative, creating areas of differing optical density.

In the past fifty years, research into Bellocq's life, persona, and career as well as the people and operations of Storyville have resulted in a much greater contextualization of the series. But there is still much to learn about this photographer, these subjects, and the work made for reasons known, at least to this moment in time, only to themselves.

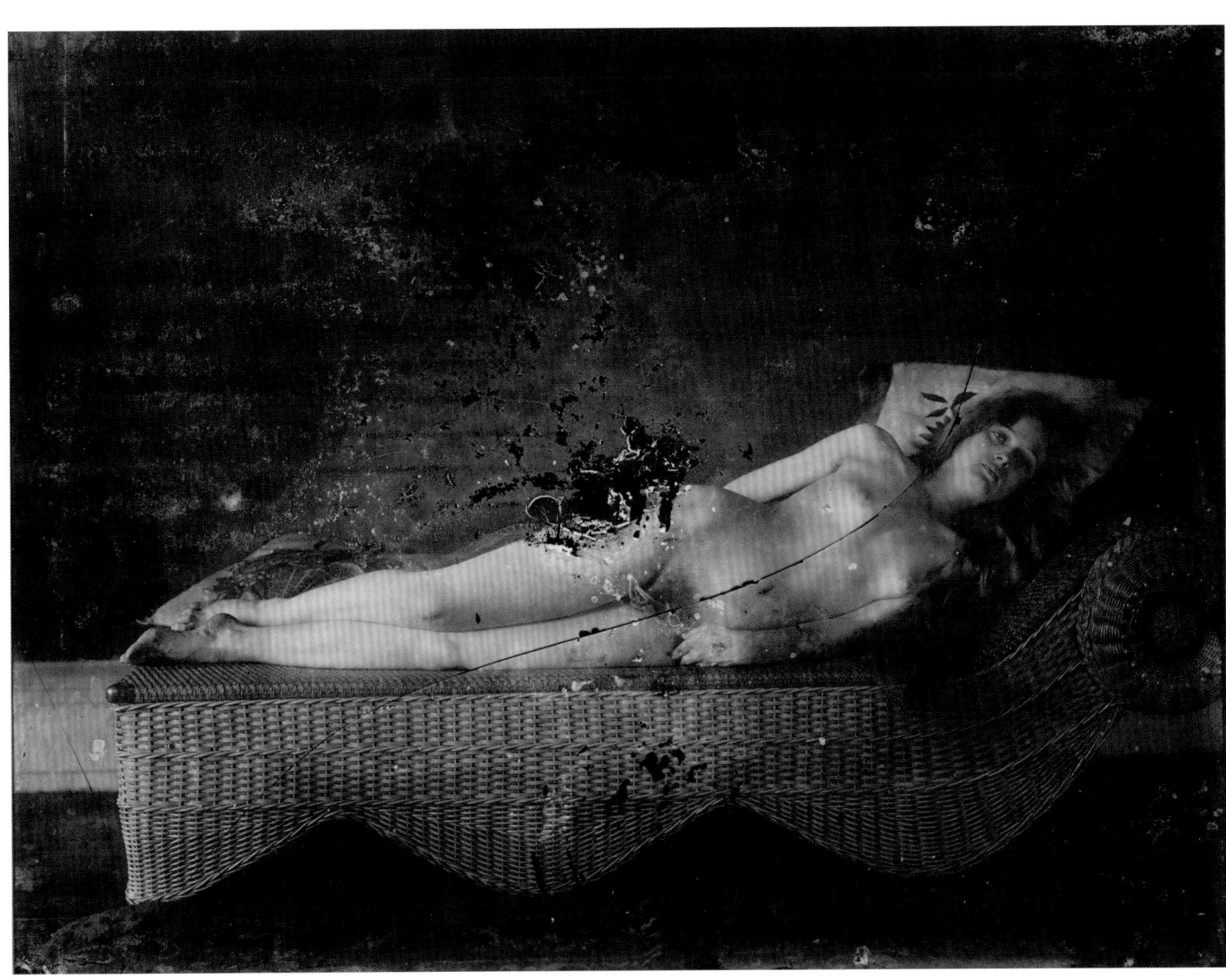

Storyville portrait, between 1911 and 1913
by Ernest J. Bellocq, printed by Lee Friedlander
gelatin silver print, 8 × 10 in.
gift of Gary Hendershott, 2015.0221.1, image by E. J. Bellocq
© Lee Friedlander, courtesy Fraenkel Gallery, San Francisco

The gelatin silver print was made between 1966 and 1970 by Lee Friedlander from
an original glass negative.

Arthur P. Bedou (1882–1966)

The relationship between Arthur P. Bedou, an African American photographer who operated a studio in New Orleans for decades, and civil rights pioneer Booker T. Washington was a special one: Bedou had been Washington's personal photographer at the Tuskegee Institute in Alabama. During his 1915 tour of Louisiana, nearly two decades after the US Supreme Court's *Plessy v. Ferguson* decision, Washington delivered speeches proposing that discrimination should be overcome through achievement and education, a message that enjoyed wide support from both Black and white audiences. From April 13 to 15, Washington toured the state, visiting New Orleans, New Iberia, Lafayette, Crowley, Lake Charles, and the state capital of Baton Rouge, where this photograph may have been made.

Bedou's photograph captures Washington in mid-gesture, conveying his dignity and forcefulness as a speaker. Some details of the picture suggest an impromptu nature to this event: the platform on which Washington stands seems to be a writing desk turned on its side, and the scattered papers at his feet perhaps notes discarded as the talk progressed, there being no podium to contain them. Washington died seven months after his tour in Louisiana, on November 14, 1915.

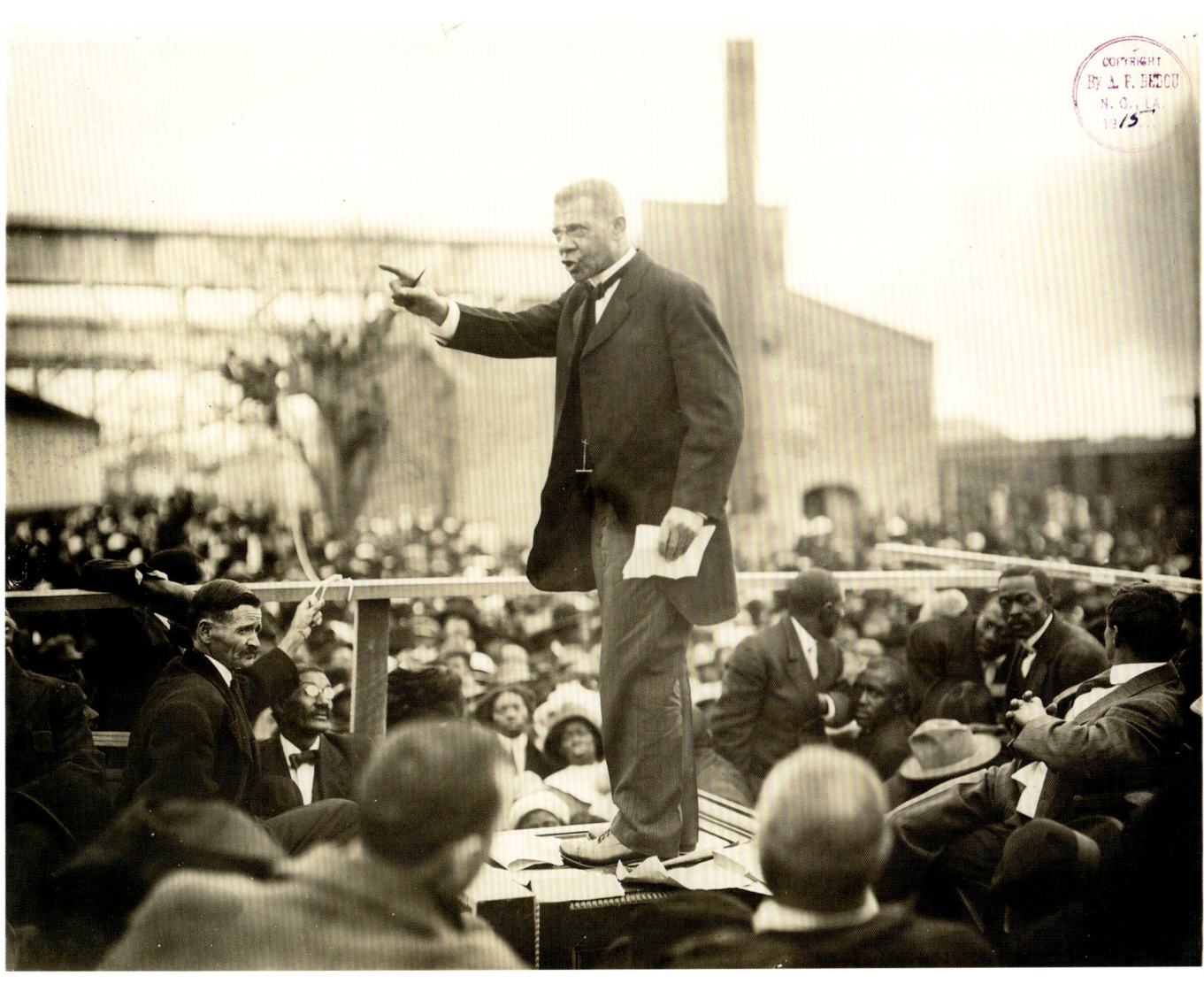

**[Booker T. Washington] Speaking during His Last
Educational Pilgrimage in Louisiana, 1915**

by Arthur P. Bedou
gelatin silver print, 8 × 10 in.
2010.0297

Lewis Wickes Hine (1874–1940)

Perhaps no other photographer influenced the movement for changing the conditions of child labor more than Lewis Wickes Hine. Working for the National Child Labor Committee from 1908 to 1924, Hine traveled to many parts of the United States, training his camera on workers in factories and other fields of commerce to call attention to the long hours, the often dreadful and unsafe working conditions, the debilitating effects of such employment, and the youth of the employees, some of whom were children less than ten years old.

The ages of the young workers in this 1913 photograph are not known. The picture was taken at Lane Cotton Mill, whose principal buildings occupied lands along the riverfront in the West Bouligny neighborhood, a few miles upriver from the center of New Orleans. At its peak, Lane Mill employed some 1,400 workers.

In 1874, *Jewell's Crescent City Illustrated* (a publication designed to boost New Orleans's post–Civil War economic rebirth) stated that

"Lane Cotton Mill, beautiful and commodious structures, situated on Tchoupitoulas Street, . . . in which yarns, ropes, osnaburgs, sheetings, shirtings and blankets, of the finest texture, are manufactured, . . . has introduced an era in this great industrial interest, for which not only New Orleans, but the whole Southern country is greatly indebted. . . . Not only men, but indigent boys and girls, clamoring for bread but willing to work, have been employed by [mill owner Henry Abraham] and rewarded for their labor."

The Louisiana Society for the Prevention of Cruelty to Children would be established in 1892. By this time, attitudes about teens and younger children in the work force had already changed dramatically, in New Orleans as throughout the nation, but child labor would not be effectively regulated by federal law for decades.

Hine's work was allied with the nationwide political Progressivism of the early twentieth century, a movement especially attuned to conditions of factory labor, worker safety, and compensation. His career as a socially concerned documentarian began in 1904, when he photographed immigrants arriving at New York's Ellis Island station. In Louisiana he visited New Orleans, Shreveport, and the coastal community of Dunbar, where oysters were harvested, shucked, and canned. Hine's comments on his urban Louisiana photographs mention that clerks, newsboys, messengers, and factory workers were not as young as other workers he found in his travels. But his notes on the oyster cannery state that children as young as four were working in some capacity.

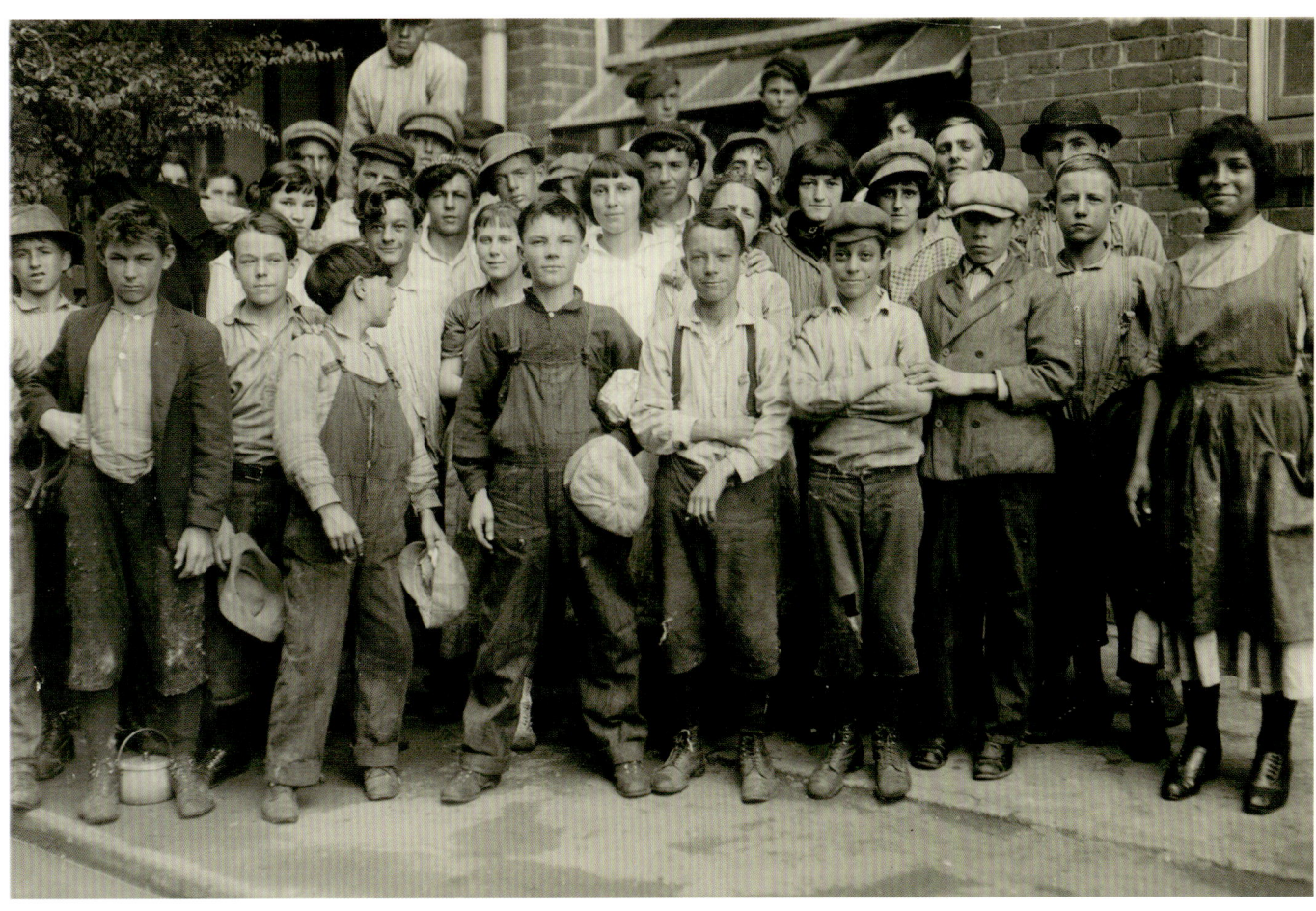

Group of workers in Lane Cotton Mill, New Orleans, 1913

by Lewis Wickes Hine
gelatin silver print, 5 × 7 in.
2001.92.2

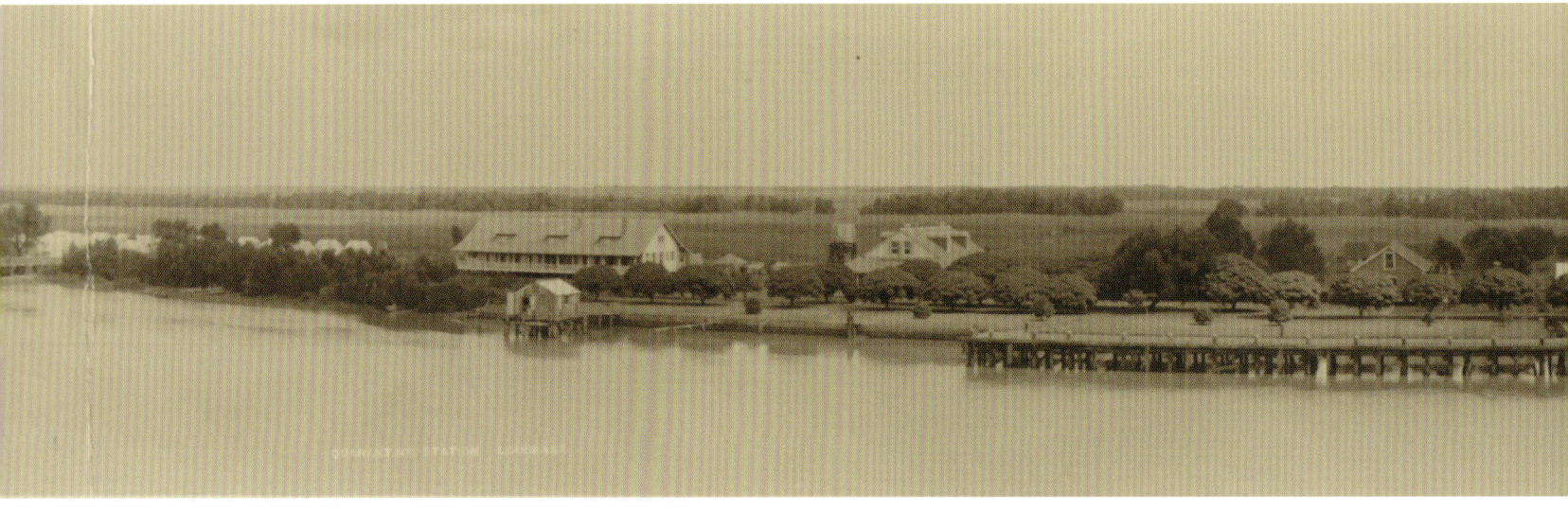

attributed to J. A. Stewart (life dates unknown)

The gentle curve of the scene in this photograph indicates it was made with a special type of panoramic instrument—the Cirkut camera. The device was mounted on a tripod, and a series of gears and spring-driven motors swept the entire camera through a predetermined arc—up to a full circle—while a long roll of film unwound past a moving slit that projected on it a slice of image. This operation exposed the image, a bit at a time, onto the entire roll of film. The composition's characteristic curved appearance was the result of the lens's being closer to the center of the scene than to its ends.

The Cirkut camera was used extensively to photograph large groups of people: the distortion of the arc could be avoided by arranging the group in a complementary formation, in which people at the edges were placed closer to the camera than were those in the middle. When done correctly, this arrangement produced a straight-line image of the assembly. Depending on the size of the camera used (there were five models, accommodating film widths from five to sixteen inches), a single Cirkut image could measure several feet long.

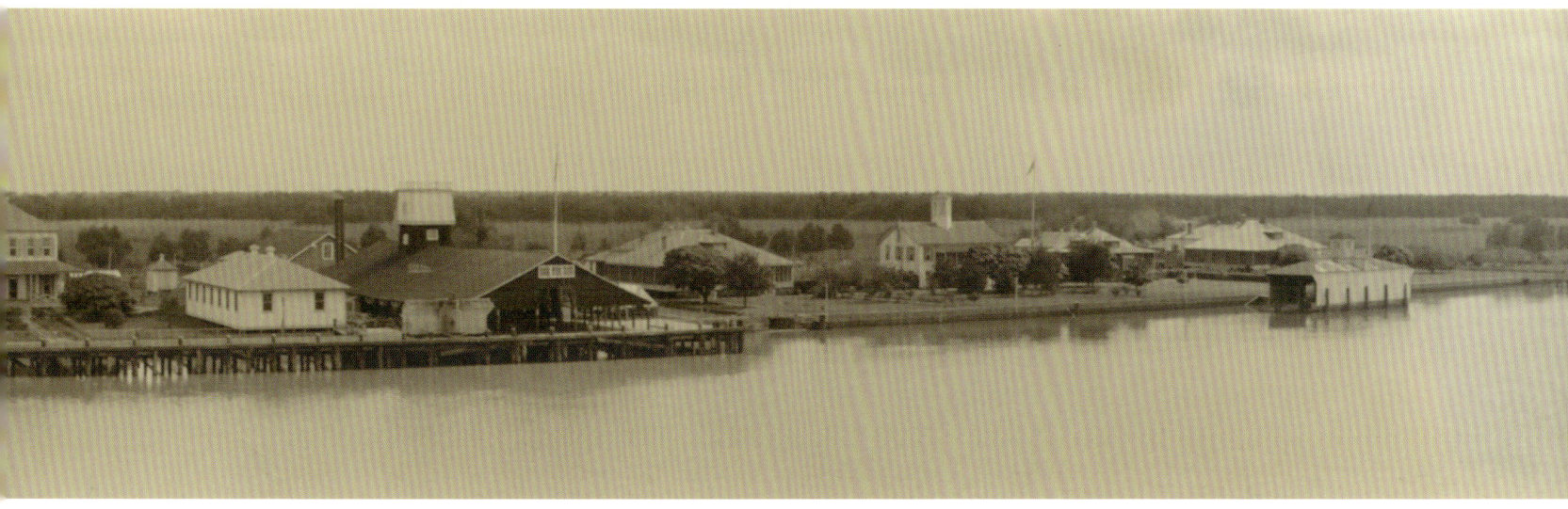

The complex pictured in this serene view is the United States quarantine station downriver from New Orleans, near the settlement of Pilottown. Quarantine functions included inspection of ships as well as fumigation of passengers and cargoes to prevent vermin or disease from entering New Orleans and other population centers on the Mississippi River.

The station began operations during what would turn out to be the final years of yellow fever epidemics in New Orleans; the last recorded one was 1905 (p. 68). An 1890 report on public health describes the complex thus: "The plant consists of five buildings exclusive of out-houses, viz., a disinfecting-shed and boiler-room, quarters and mess-hall for the disinfecting-crew, boat-house and boatmen's quarters, and two residences for the quarantine officer and his assistant." The picture seems to show more buildings than that, evidence of the station's expansion in its first decades.

The annual mosquito-borne scourge had been conquered by the time this picture was made. The quarantine station operated until 1931, when it was moved closer to the Algiers neighborhood of New Orleans.

Quarantine station, Plaquemines Parish, between 1908 and 1918
attributed to J. A. Stewart
gelatin silver print, 3½ × 21¹³⁄₁₆ in.
gift of the Louisiana Historical Society, 2019.0395.1

John Tibule Mendes (1888–1965)

Though this photograph has appeared in print with the title "Female Impersonator," that description doesn't seem accurate. There is no intent to impersonate a woman. It is just a guy in costume, presumably during Carnival season, an artifact of an era when lodges and fraternal organizations staged farces known as "womanless weddings," in which men played all roles, including that of the bride and female attendants. Role reversal was played as comedy at these events.

Photographs may be the result of a trained vision or simply a strong intuitive reaction; this picture leans toward the latter. The street theater of this composition is amazing. Frozen in time by the shutter, the masker forever teeters between balance and pratfall, poised in the center of multiple bodies in motion. Only one person in the picture appears to pay attention to the spectacle before Mendes's camera—we see a sideways glance from a man moving to the right. It is impossible to know if the soldier standing halfway in the left edge of the frame, adjusting his box camera, has taken or is preparing to take a picture of the masker, or whether some other sight, out of Mendes's range, has caught his attention.

Amateur photographer John Tibule Mendes spent years photographing New Orleans life in his free time. His cache of several hundred glass negatives, discovered and preserved by his neighbors and ultimately donated to The Historic New Orleans Collection, offers a glimpse of the city during the 1910s and 1920s through the window of one person's interests.

The Charles L. Franck photograph of the king of the Krewe of Proteus parade (p. 99), made at roughly the same time, makes a useful pairing with Mendes's photograph. Together they offer a look at the spectrum of Mardi Gras participation: the public spectacle of formal ceremony and parades at one end, and at the other, the intimacy of an individual embracing being someone else, even for just a day.

In 2009, decades after Mendes's death, a selection of his photographs appeared under the title *Dogs in My Life*. The book's title was the same as a memoir that Mendes published in 1964, recounting the several canine pets that he'd cared for over many decades. The 2009 publication was the first extensive presentation of his photographs.

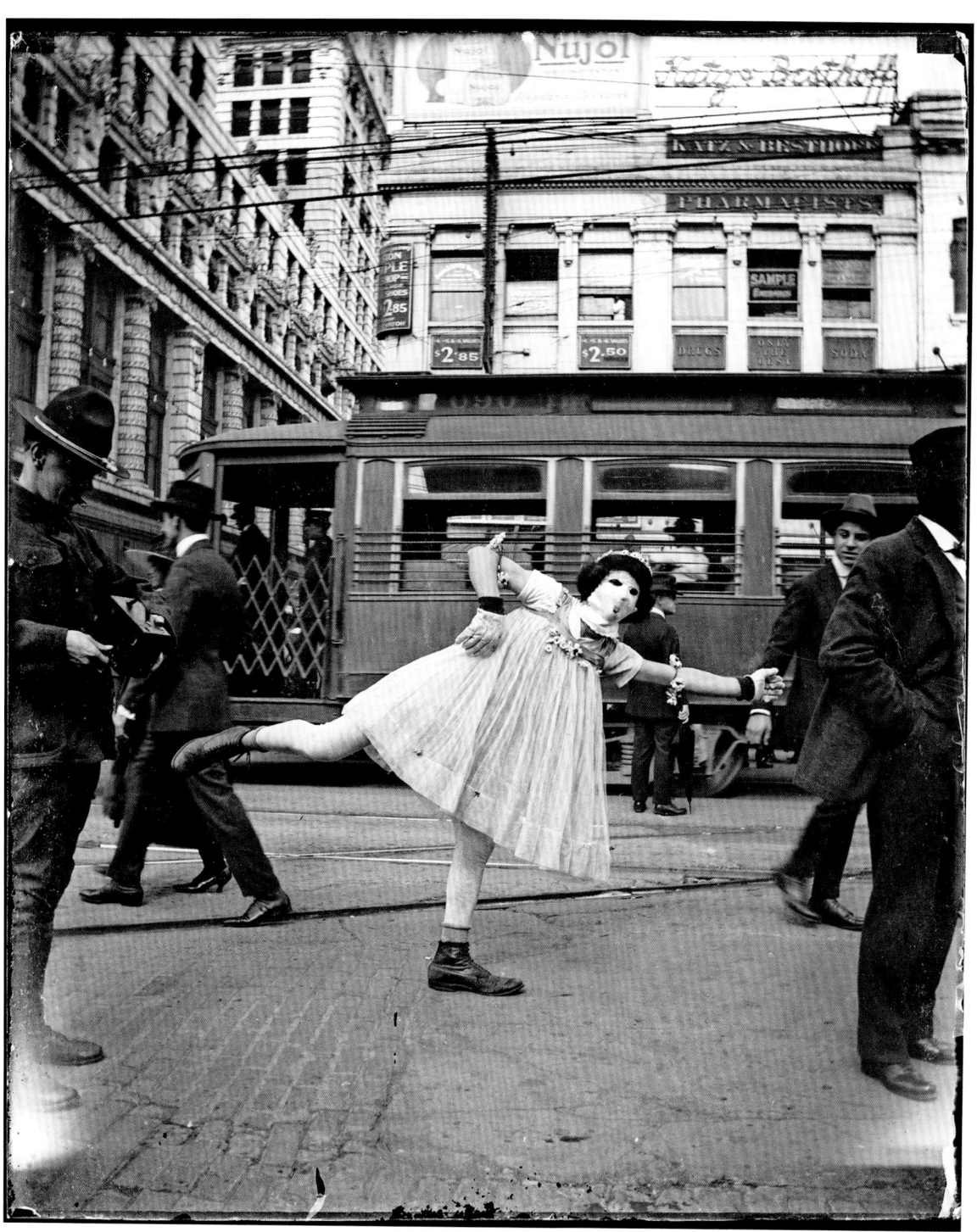

Carnival masker, 1919

by John Tibule Mendes
gelatin dry plate negative, 5 × 4 in.
gift of Waldemar S. Nelson, 2003.0182.159

Charles L. Franck Photographers (active 1905–1980s)

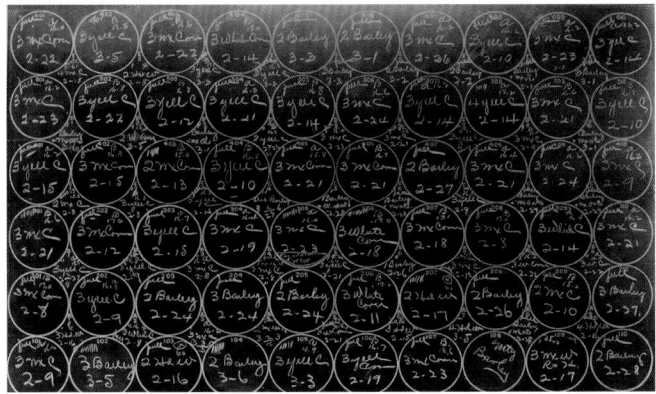

When transported in large quantities, small grains are a commodity best placed in railcars or on ships and barges that float the cargoes to their final destinations. Whether consisting of a single tower or groups of silos, grain elevators are impressive industrial structures, dotting prairie landscapes and waterfronts throughout the United States and the world. They are a critical element of the food distribution chain.

When it opened in 1917, the Public Grain Elevator in New Orleans consisted of nine reinforced concrete silos with a capacity of 2.7 million bushels of grain, which could be loaded on or off oceangoing ships or barges. By 1921, the capacity of the elevator permitted two additional rail carriers—Southern Pacific Company and the Louisville and Nashville Railroad—to transport grains, joining the Illinois Central and Texas and Pacific lines already operating in that role.

In 1989, barely seventy years after ths silos' construction, the Port of New Orleans deemed the Public Grain Elevator unnecessary and authorized its demolition, noting at the time that the elevator had been obsolete for nearly a quarter century and that ten more had been built between Baton Rouge and New Orleans.

The two photographs reproduced here are from a collection of thirty-three bound in an album produced by Charles L. Franck at the commencement of the facility's operations. One picture features the huge grain chutes that could be swiveled to various storage ports beneath the floor. A second photograph shows a blackboard diagram for tracking the content of each bin and the date the grain was deposited. Though Franck had been hired by the Board of Commissioners of the Port of New Orleans simply to document this facility as a matter of record, the images suggest he was also fascinated with the sculptural beauty of the building and its apparatus.

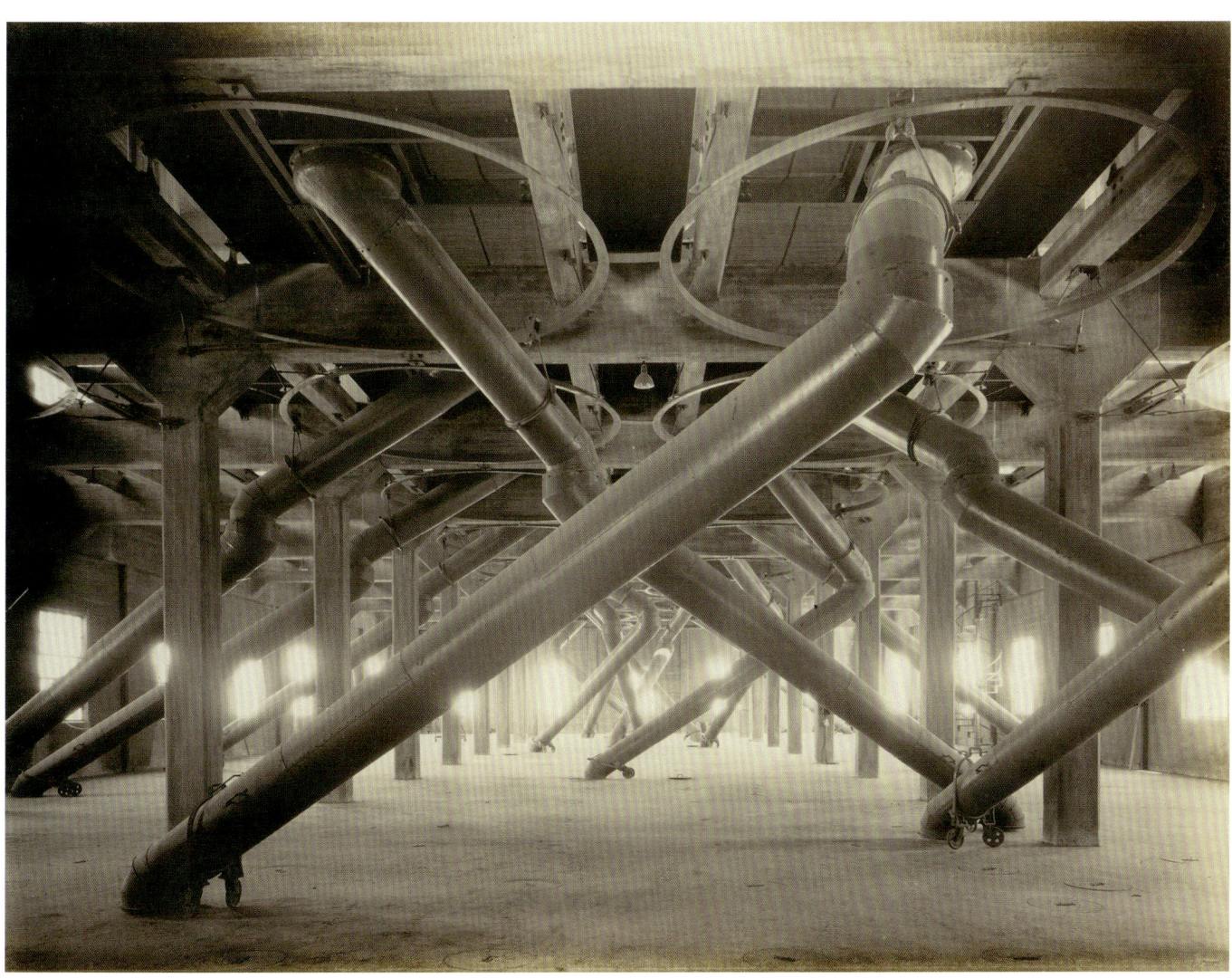

Images from Public Grain Elevator commemorative photo album, 1918?
by Charles L. Franck Photographers
gelatin silver prints, mounted, 7¼ × 10½ in.
The Charles L. Franck Studio Collection at THNOC, 1979.89.7579.14, .23

William C. Odiorne (1881–1978)

According to the typescript of his unpublished memoir in The Historic New Orleans Collection, William C. Odiorne arrived in the city at the dawn of 1919, traveling by train from New York, and soon began making a living as a photographer. Newspaper assignments focusing on the people who defined high society in the Crescent City became the mainstay of this early work. Odiorne's memoir serves as a key to under-standing his approach to the medium in New Orleans: he mentions the heavy atmosphere, timeworn buildings, and tranquility of the French Quarter at certain times of day, and his views of the city often reflect these observations. Odiorne's photograph of this cluttered corner of the lower Vieux Carré blends historic architecture with everyday life, characterized by the merchandise festooning the building. The soft focus and warm tones of the print help soften the contemporary intrusion of washtubs, brooms, sacks, and barrels. In his memoir he recalls someone saying, "Odiorne, you are an incurable romantic," to which he offers no written objection.

Originally from Chicago, by 1922 Odiorne was a bona fide member of a French Quarter bohemian demimonde, describing himself in this milieu as "an accepted colonist." Odiorne led a life of wanderlust and left Louisiana in 1924 for Paris, where he continued his photography and met William Faulkner. Odiorne is one of the several dozen men and women caricatured in *Sherwood Anderson and Other Famous Creoles* (1926), a playful project created by two other members of the circle, the artist William Spratling and the not-yet-famous Faulkner. Most of the book's subjects were, like Odiorne, neither Creole nor from New Orleans.

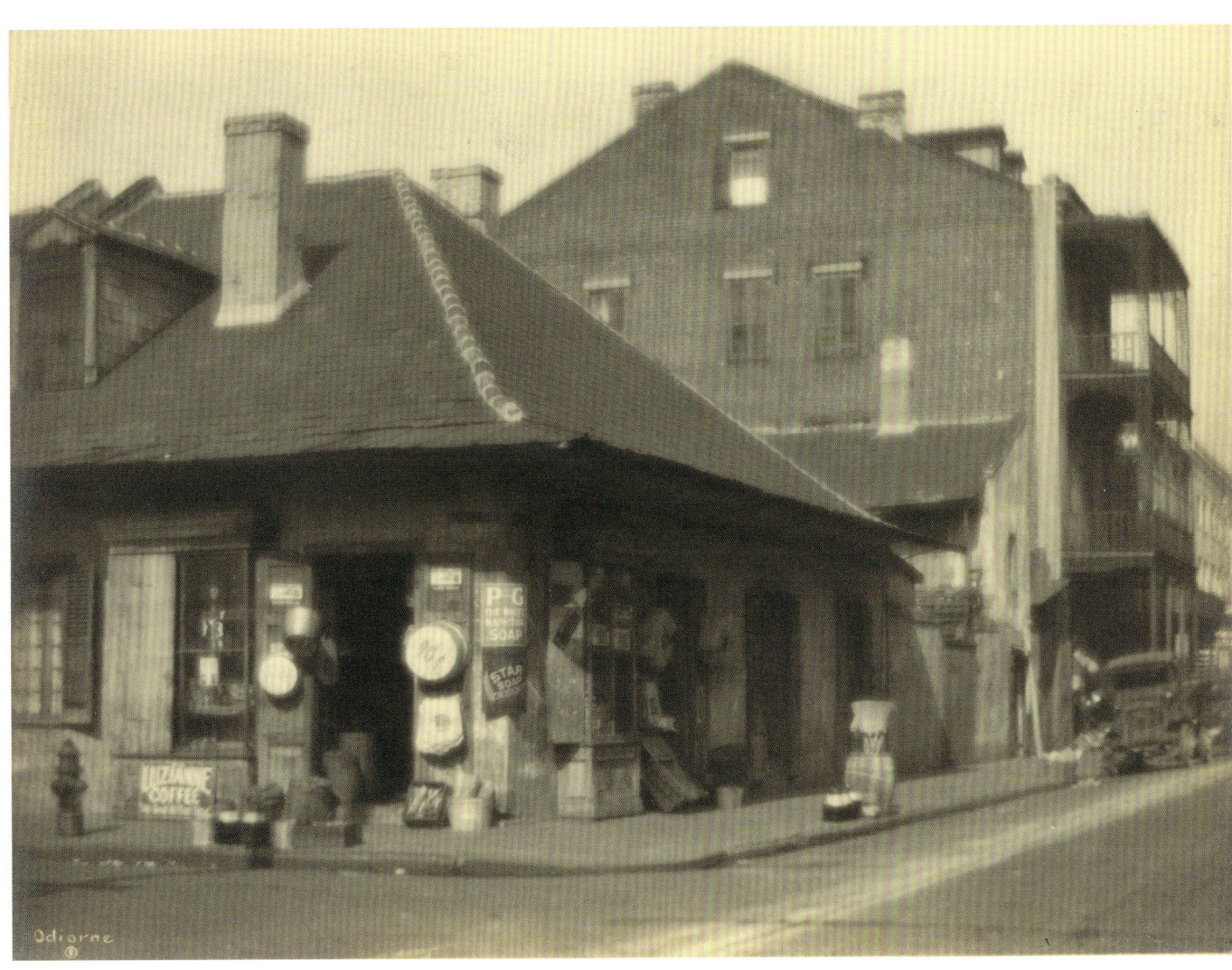

Souvenir view of Ursulines and Chartres Streets in the French Quarter, 1922
by William C. Odiorne
gelatin silver print, 6 ¼ × 8 ⅛ in.
gift of Boyd Cruise and Harold Schilke, 1959.170.10

Arthur P. Bedou (1882–1966)

This photograph brings together two important figures of New Orleans culture at moments of great achievement in their careers. Armand J. Piron was a successful and accomplished bandleader, composer, and recording artist, and Arthur P. Bedou a respected and much sought-after portrait photographer. That both were African Americans at a time when Jim Crow laws were rampant certainly affected how their considerable talents were perceived and consumed. About the same time this picture was made, Bedou created stunning portraits of Elinor Bright, a white woman who was Queen of Carnival in 1920, but it is not clear whether this represented a cross-racial clientele at large, or simply an anomaly.

Piron and his musical partner Clarence Williams had a big hit with the 1922 "I Wish I Could Shimmy Like My Sister Kate"; dozens of artists recorded it during the 1920s. Seeking to capitalize on the song's success, the orchestra went to New York in 1923, the same year this portrait was taken: it is possible that Bedou's photograph served as an official portrait, introducing Piron and his band to New York. Within a year, however, the homesick band returned to New Orleans, where they continued to be in demand for the remainder of the decade. Piron's success as a bandleader and the skill of his musicians made his orchestra a popular choice for white society functions.

It is difficult to know whether Piron's intensely serious air in this portrait is a momentary affectation or a habitual expression. The bold cropping of the subject and the angular composition created by the violin, its bow, and Piron's right arm reflect the aesthetics of modernism. In any event, the portrait is at odds with the campy, racist poses used in a photograph of Piron's band made a few years earlier, likely also by Bedou (a picture that, despite the stereotyping, is tightly composed and elegantly structured).

A portrait is a collaboration between subject and photographer, a transaction often primarily financial but always somewhat emotional. While the opinions of its participants are unknown, twenty-first-century viewers of this solo portrait may deem that contract a success.

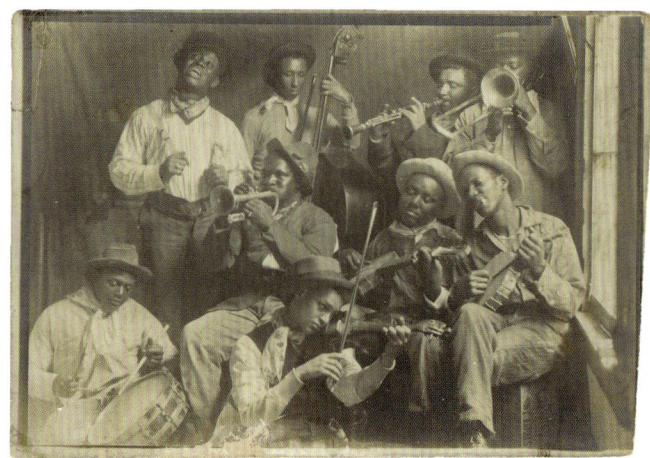

Clarence Williams and Armand J. Piron band, circa 1916;
attributed to Arthur P. Bedou; gelatin silver print, 5 × 7 in.; *The William Russell Jazz Collection at THNOC, acquisition made possible by the Clarisse Claiborne Grima Fund, 92-48-L.283*

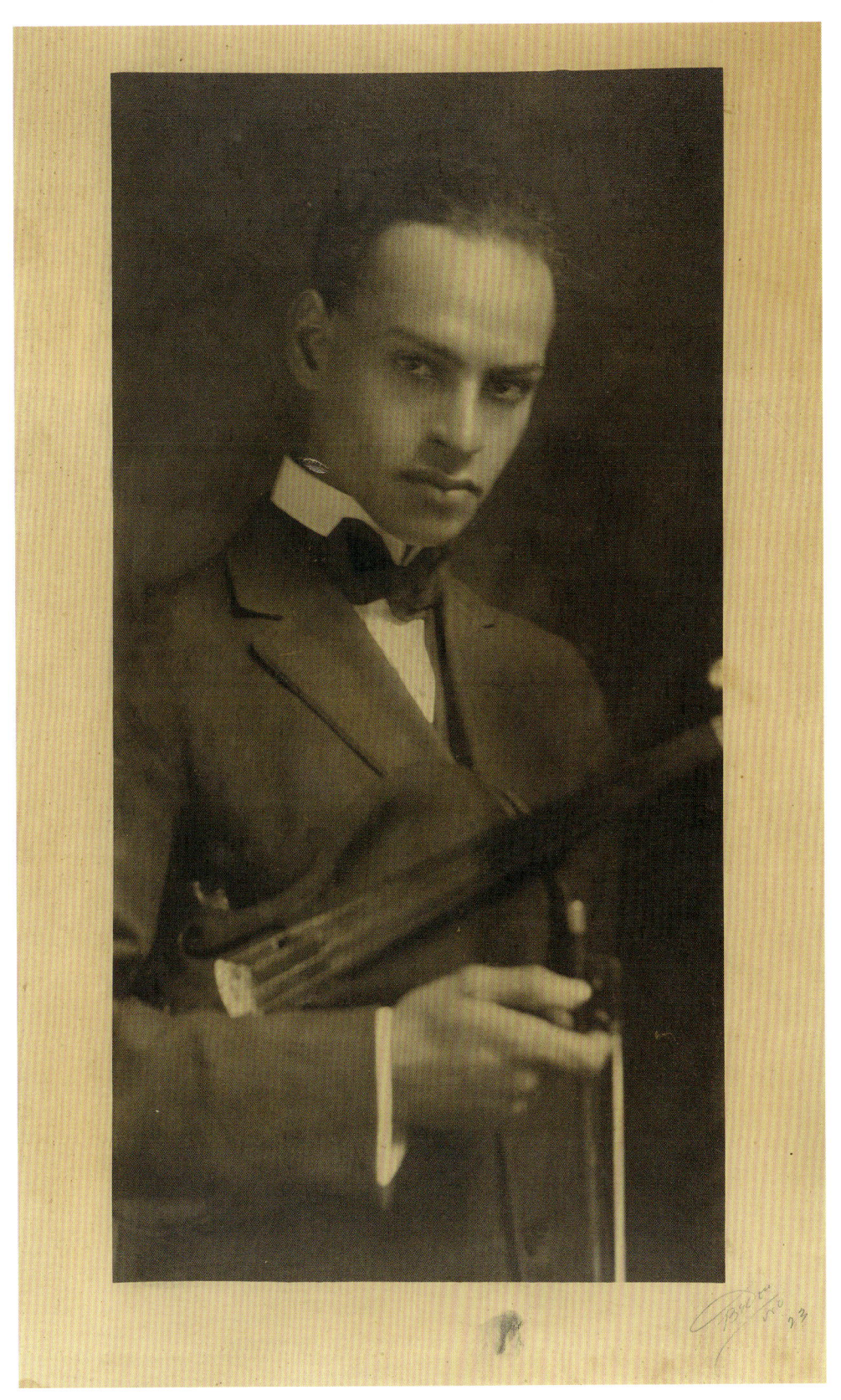

Armand J. Piron, 1923
by Arthur P. Bedou
gelatin silver print, 23⅞ × 14⅞ in.
partial gift of Priscilla and John Lawrence and Burt L. Barbre,
2009.0228

unknown photographer

Mardi Gras season in New Orleans has, from the outset, been described as colorful, not just metaphorically but literally. Surviving watercolor costume and float designs, along with late nineteenth-century chromolithographed parade bulletins, show the events brimming with rainbow hues. Yet from the time of New Orleans's first organized Carnival parades in 1857 until some half century later, capturing that vibrant aspect of the celebrations in a photograph was not possible. The first practical color process—the autochrome—changed that.

Autochromes were not paper photographs but pictures made as glass positives, designed to be viewed by transmitted rather than reflected light. An individual could hold the glass up against a light source to look at the picture, or the autochrome could be viewed through a special apparatus— the diascope—that used a mirror to create a projection of the image, enabling several people to view it simultaneously. To accommodate larger groups, autochromes could be projected on a screen, theater style.

The autochrome was an invention of Louis and Auguste Lumière, French brothers who had previously pioneered early motion picture photography. The brothers began the manufacture of autochrome plates in 1907. The emulsion of the autochrome consisted of a light-sensitive silver coating and a thin layer of potato starch, whose microscopic granules were dyed in red, green, and blue. Filling in spaces between the colored grains was powdered carbon. When the plate was exposed, light passed through the colored grains to the silver layer. When developed, the image on the plate became visible through the granules, whose filter effect produced a color image noted for its pastel character, sometimes described as luminous or dreamlike. The autochrome was favored by amateur photographers. Its limitations for manipulation made it less popular among professionals and photographic artists. Interest in the process lasted into the 1930s, with the last autochromes being made on a film support rather than glass. A paradigm shift—from the additive color of the autochrome to the subtractive color model Kodak introduced in 1935 as Kodachrome—marked its commercial demise.

When this picture was made, around 1921, Ernest Doty Ivy was a lieutenant in the Rex Organization and manager of the Otis Elevator Company office in New Orleans. The membership of Rex drew not only (or even primarily) from so-called old New Orleans families but from the business and commercial leaders of the city. The Rex parade's theme in 1921 was "Porcelain in Fact and Fancy." Ivy held memberships in other social and fraternal organizations, including the Masons, the Knights Templar, the Shriners, the Elks, the Louisiana Club, and the Chess, Checkers, and Whist Club.

The maker of Ivy's portrait is unknown. The blurred fluttering of his cape in the breeze suggests an exposure of at least a few seconds, accounting for the pose that is equal parts comfortable and jaunty. The high boots, with their crenellated tops, and the long black gloves indicate that his mount for the parade was probably a horse rather than a float, which in his era would have been drawn by mules. Today, select members of the Rex Organization still appear on horseback, though for decades, diesel-powered tractors have been the preferred source for pulling the floats.

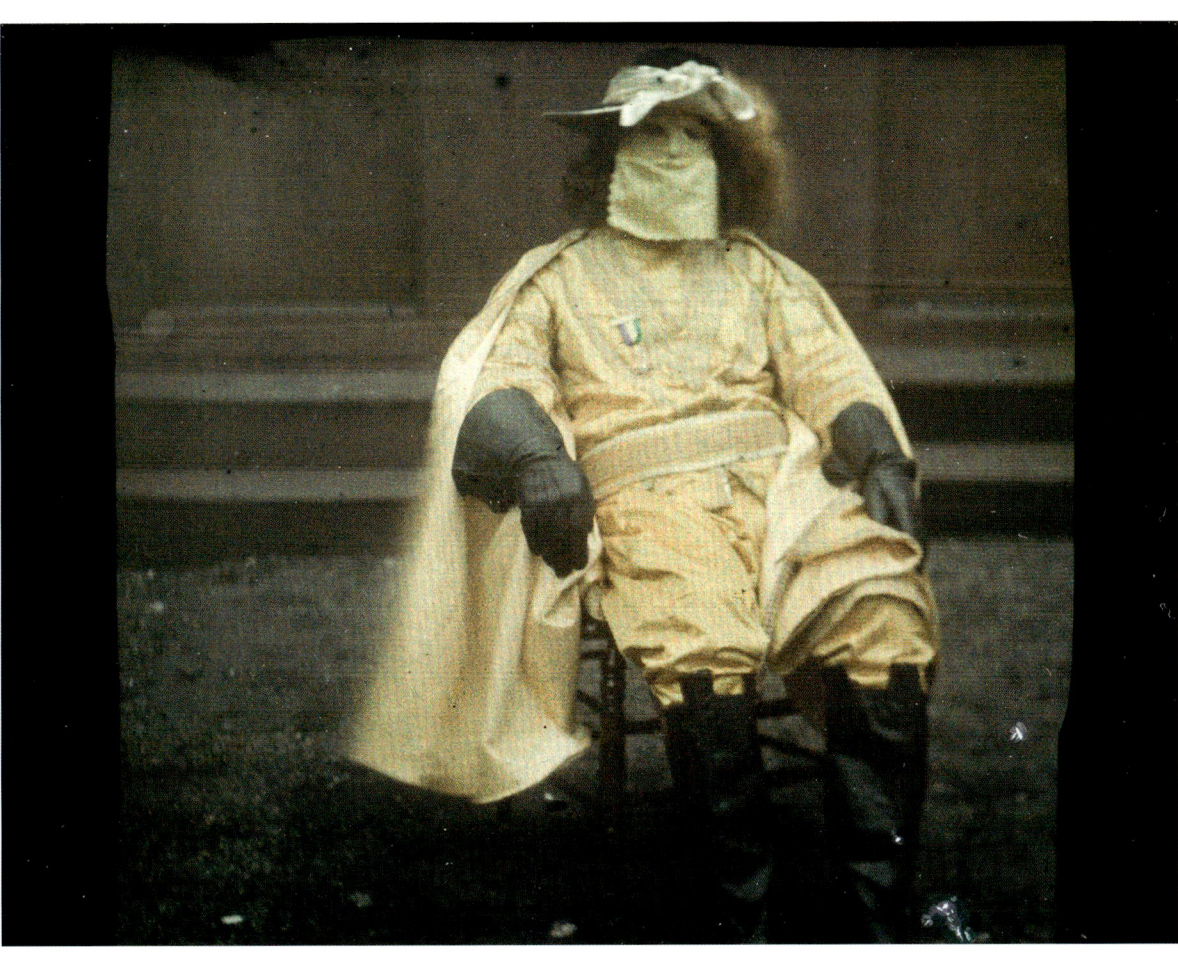

**Ernest Doty Ivy, lieutenant in the Rex Organization,
circa 1921**

by an unknown photographer
autochrome, 3¼ × 4
gift of Mrs. George Stahler Jr., 1980.45

Linnenkohl Photographs (active 1918–1928)

This room, clubby and comfortable within the dictates of its time, suggests something waiting to happen and simultaneously begs explanation of many things that have already happened. The photograph evokes an entire atmosphere: the smell of dust, fur, and maybe a whiff of arsenic, once commonly used to preserve animal pelts, permeates the scene. It looks like a setting that might be described in a mystery story, a room in which a crime has occurred, the only eyes to witness it the glass ones of the taxidermically preserved occupants. If explored in the dark of night, the room would give one the heebie-jeebies as a fur-obstructed, stumbling transit of its dimensions took place.

The McFadden Mansion sits on manicured and extensive grounds within the footprint of a public park. The house was built for businessman Fred Bertrand in 1909 on a tract of land then adjacent to City Park. A decade later, William Harding McFadden, a wealthy oilman from Texas, purchased the property as a vacation home, enlarging and remodeling Bertrand's dwelling. Benjamin Linnenkohl's series of photographs, of which this is one, dates from the early years of McFadden's ownership. Charles L. Franck's firm also photographed the house and grounds in 1923, as did noted photographer Joseph W. "Pops" Whitesell in the mid-1930s.

The more than four acres of land on which the house sat was heavily landscaped with lawns and terraces, a bamboo grove, a wisteria arbor, rose gardens, lagoons, a greenhouse, and a grotto. In 1943, McFadden sold the property to City Park. After the sale, the site had a brief stint as a federal government agricultural station until it was leased to a private boys' academy from about 1950 until 1959. The current tenant, Christian Brothers School, took up occupancy in 1960.

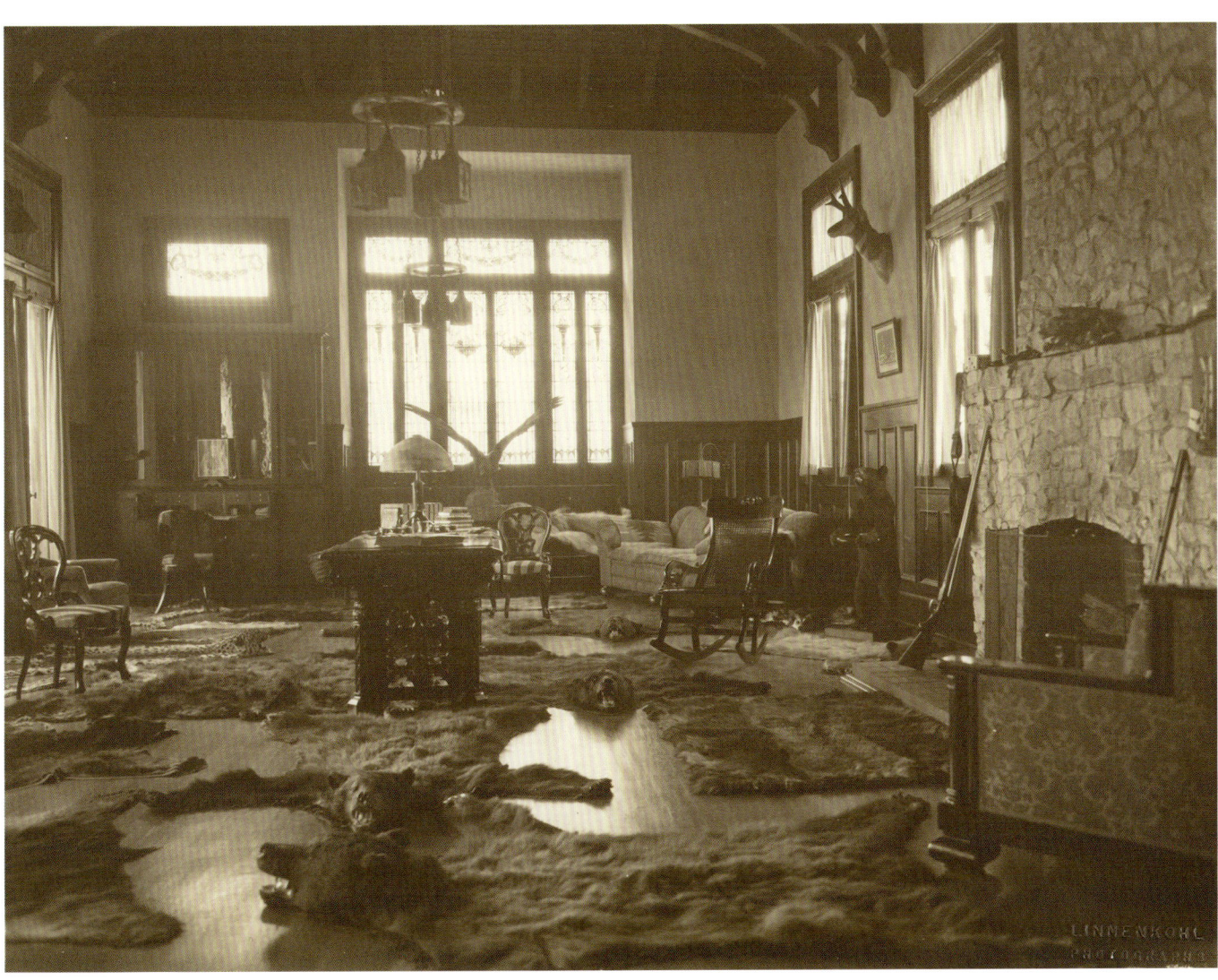

**Den in McFadden Mansion, 8 Friederichs Avenue, City Park,
New Orleans, circa 1923**

by Linnenkohl Photographs
gelatin silver print, 7⅝ × 9⅝ in.
gift of the Wichita-Sedgwick County Historical Museum, 2004.0034.5

Charles L. Franck Photographers (active 1905–1980s)

Charles L. Franck's business specialized in progress photography—that is, tracking stages of change at a construction site. But unlike wharves, roads, bridges, warehouses, and other commercial complexes covered in this type of work, which remained in place when construction was finished, much of what was built and photographed at this shipyard was floated away.

Numbers at the lower right-hand corner of each image in this series suggest that at least seventy-four photographs were part of the group. Marked on the negative, the ink blocked the light from exposing the white photographic paper. The negatives are glass plates, whose use for field work (that is, outside of the studio) was waning by the 1920s but not totally gone.

When compared to larger oceangoing vessels, those constructed at the Louisiana Shipbuilding Corporation on Bayou Bonfouca in Slidell, Louisiana, might be considered small, though the photographs here show these ships and their scaffolding dwarfing the human figures in the frame. The shipyard built steel vessels and also composite ships, which had planks of southern yellow pine bolted to a steel framework that formed the hull.

What these pictures depict can be described in a series of declarative sentences—"The water is still. The ships are large. The people are small. The scaffolding is complicated," and so forth. But more than merely conveying information, the pictures invite the viewer to wonder why the ships are being built, what cargoes and people they may carry and to what destinations, whether their launches into the canal went smoothly or were fraught with trouble, and more. It would be unfair to ask the pictures to do all of this, but our minds want those questions—and others—asked and answered.

Shipping has of course been essential to trade for millennia, even after the development of other modes of transportation; a mega-sized modern container ship can carry thousands of cargo jets. Though Louisiana ports continue to handle a large volume of freight coming from and going to points around the world, the state's last major shipbuilder, Avondale Shipyard, closed in 2014.

Vessels like the ones under construction in these photographs played key roles in international trade and the US entry into World War I. The manufacture of durable goods is not a sector typically associated with the New Orleans region, but ships must be built near a convenient loading and launch point, and thus the city, as a major port and entrepôt for international cargoes and trade, unsurprisingly attracted shipyards large and small. The Louisiana Shipbuilding Corporation specialized in producing "steel freighters up to 3,500 tons dead weight capacity," according to a 1919 article in the trade publication *Iron Age.*

Images of the Louisiana Shipbuilding Corporation, Slidell, Louisiana, between 1918 and 1924
by Charles L. Franck Photographers
gelatin silver prints, 8 × 10 in.
The Charles L. Franck Studio Collection at THNOC, 1979.325.3157, .3187

The gelatin silver prints were made between 1979 and 1983 by Nancy Ewing Miner.

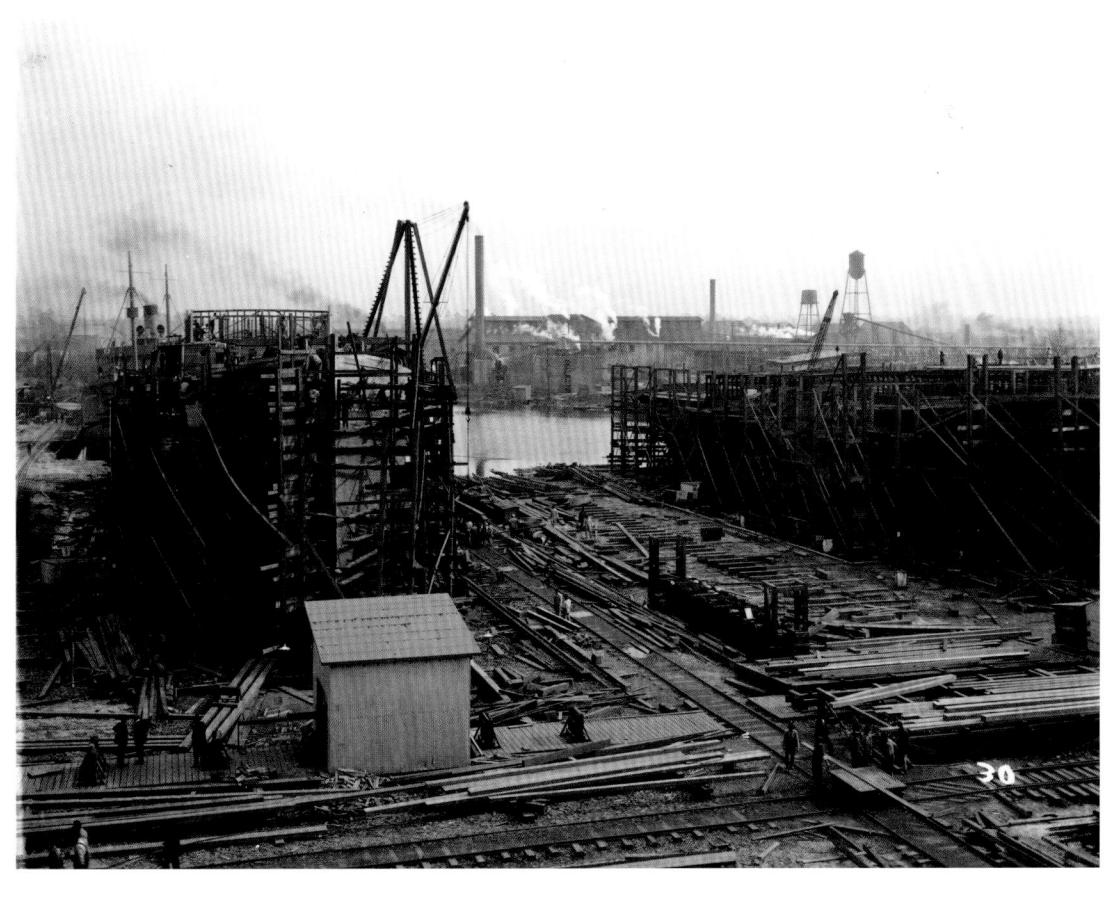

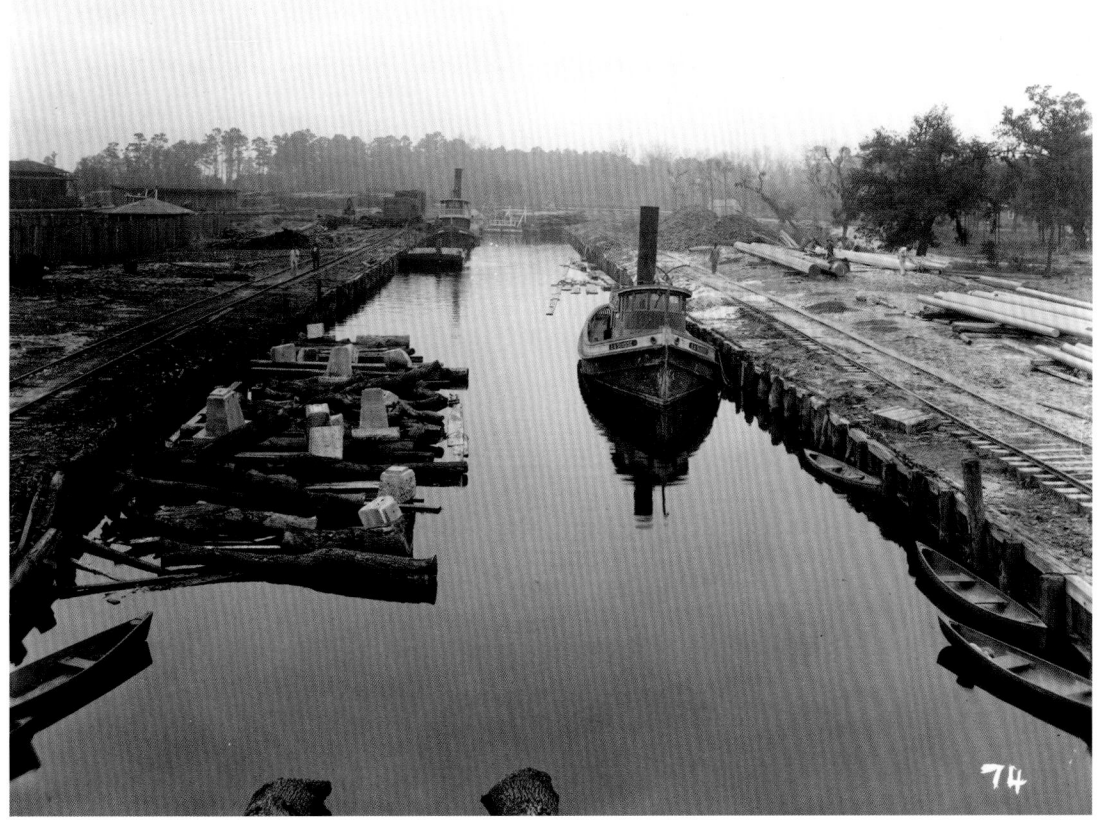

Charles L. Franck Photographers (active 1905–1980s)

If ever a subject was made for a photographic format, the celebratory ritual of Mardi Gras pictured here—a king toasting his court at a reviewing stand—is one. The photographer has used a panoramic view camera, sometimes referred to as a banquet camera because it was often employed to photograph large groups of people. These instruments came in various sizes—7 × 17 inches, 8 × 20 inches, and 12 × 20 inches were among the negative sizes customarily used. This scene was made with an 8 × 20-inch version. The oblong shape of the film, with its 1:2.5 ratio, captures the main participants, along with a good bit of contextual information.

The float, designed by Léda Hincks Plauché for the 1925 Krewe of Proteus parade's theme "Tales and Romances of Old Japan," is the central subject. (In 1981, Plauché's design would inspire the float representing 1925 in the Krewe of Proteus's one hundredth anniversary parade.) The monarch—whose identity is never publicly revealed—toasts his queen, the debutante Adele Dunbar. Strings of electric lights illuminating the grandstand are practical as well as decorative in this nighttime scene. The flambeaux carriers and their kerosene torches alongside the float, with white-hooded mules that pull it, inject a spectral character into the image. The scintillations coming from the float's gilded elements suggest that Franck used either flash or continuous-source artificial illumination to record the scene.

Charles L. Franck Photographers—and the successor firm that continued his business after his retirement in 1946—chronicled the length, breadth, and pace of New Orleans for much of the twentieth century. Franck began his eponymous studio activity in 1905, and its later incarnation, Franck-Bertacci Photographers, operated into the mid-1990s before closing its doors. As a major work-for-hire photographic studio that mostly eschewed the portrait trade—the firm advertised itself as "industrial photographers"—the collective operations

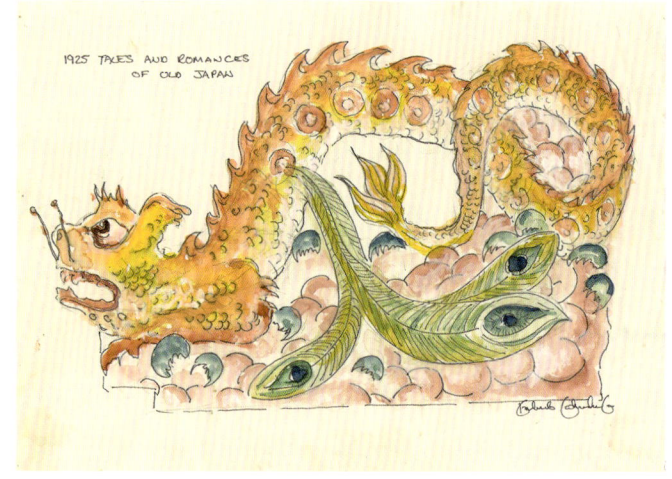

Float design for 1981 Krewe of Proteus 100th anniversary parade, referencing 1925 Proteus parade; by Herbert Grant Jahncke Jr.; ink drawing and watercolor, 8 ⅞ × 12 in.; *gift of the Crescent Club, 2010.0229.3.9*

included real estate photography (demolition, construction, and beauty shots of residential and commercial buildings); tracking the progress of large infrastructure projects (wharves, power plants, and bridges); business advertising (store openings and operations); and documenting Mardi Gras (both public and private aspects).

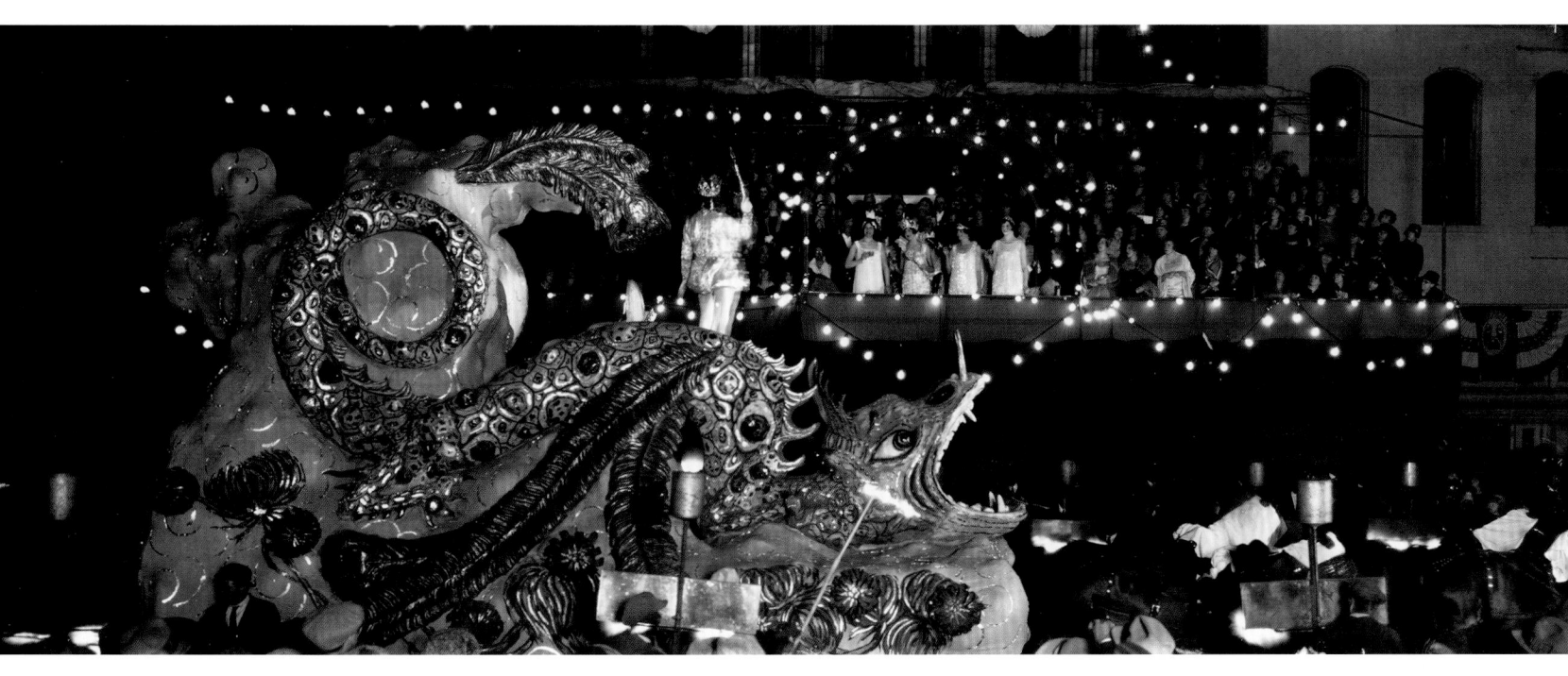

Proteus parade in front of reviewing stand, 1925
by Charles L. Franck Photographers
gelatin silver print, 8 × 19¾ in.
The Charles L. Franck Studio Collection at THNOC, 1979.325.6526

The gelatin silver print was made between 1979 and 1983 by Nancy Ewing Miner.

Arnold Genthe (1869–1942)

The work of Arnold Genthe embodies the idea that photographs, if they are to be of lasting interest, must be not only visually compelling and technically competent but also informed by a worldview or by life experience. From his early twentieth-century photographs of San Francisco—notably those taken in the city's Chinatown and following the destruction of the 1906 earthquake—to his portrait practice in New York and his highly personal take on the French Quarter of New Orleans in the early 1920s, Genthe's camera was an instrument of interrogation. His prints, on the other hand, could be instruments of deception.

In some sense, all photographs are time machines, taking the viewer back to a moment that has passed. In his New Orleans photographs, Genthe exploits that notion in spades. His photographs of the city, published in 1926 under the title *Impressions of Old New Orleans*, are meant to evoke a city he never experienced—one from an earlier century. His techniques sometimes involved subterfuge: he would often photograph at dawn or dusk, in order to hide the French Quarter's twentieth-century details, such as fire hydrants and electrical lines, in shadows or crepuscular illumination. When avoiding such intrusions was impossible, he would actively eradicate them by retouching prints and negatives.

Trained as a philologist, Genthe valued writers and literature, and their influence is evident in his work. The German native had considered photographing the city after reading descriptions by George Washington Cable and encountering Lafcadio Hearn's writings about 1870s and 1880s New Orleans. The idea would be revived by the New Orleans writer Grace King, a friend of Genthe's and the subject of one of his portraits. In the early twentieth century, as modernization gathered momentum, King and other artists had taken up the cause of preservation in New Orleans. William Woodward, for example, a painter and the founding director of the Tulane

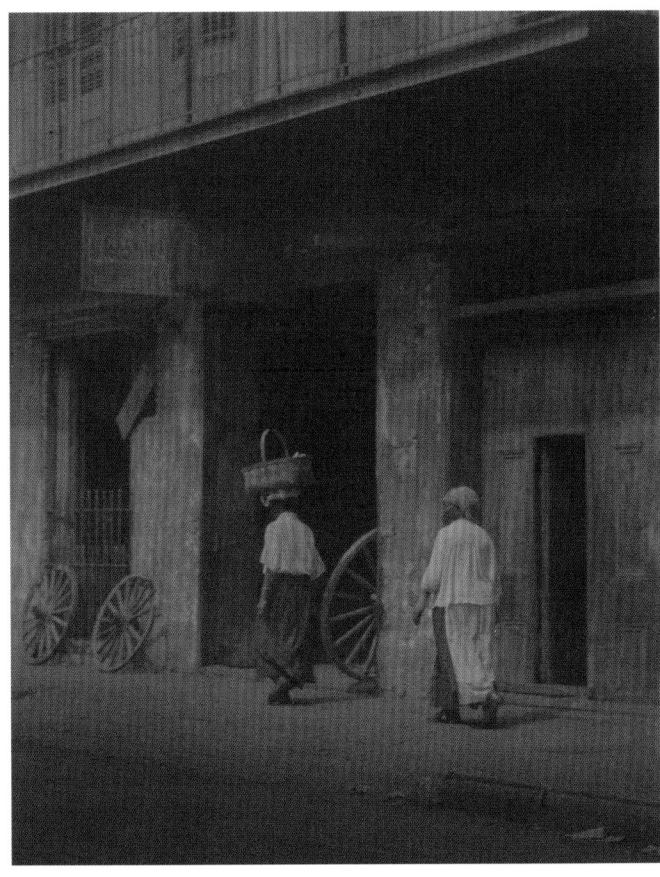

University School of Architecture, was feverishly documenting the buildings and tout ensemble of the city's oldest neighborhood in hundreds of paintings. King urged Genthe to visit the Crescent City and photograph its historic places before they were lost to redevelopment and other forces of change. If Genthe was leaning toward taking King's advice, what sold him on the project was reading Edward Larocque Tinker's dire description of the destruction of the Vieux Carré that had occurred in the previous two decades, along with his urgent assertion that there was still time to rescue it before the losses became irreversible.

Way to Market, 1925 or 1926
by Arnold Genthe
gelatin silver print, mounted, 10½ × 7⁹⁄₁₆ in.
1978.39.2

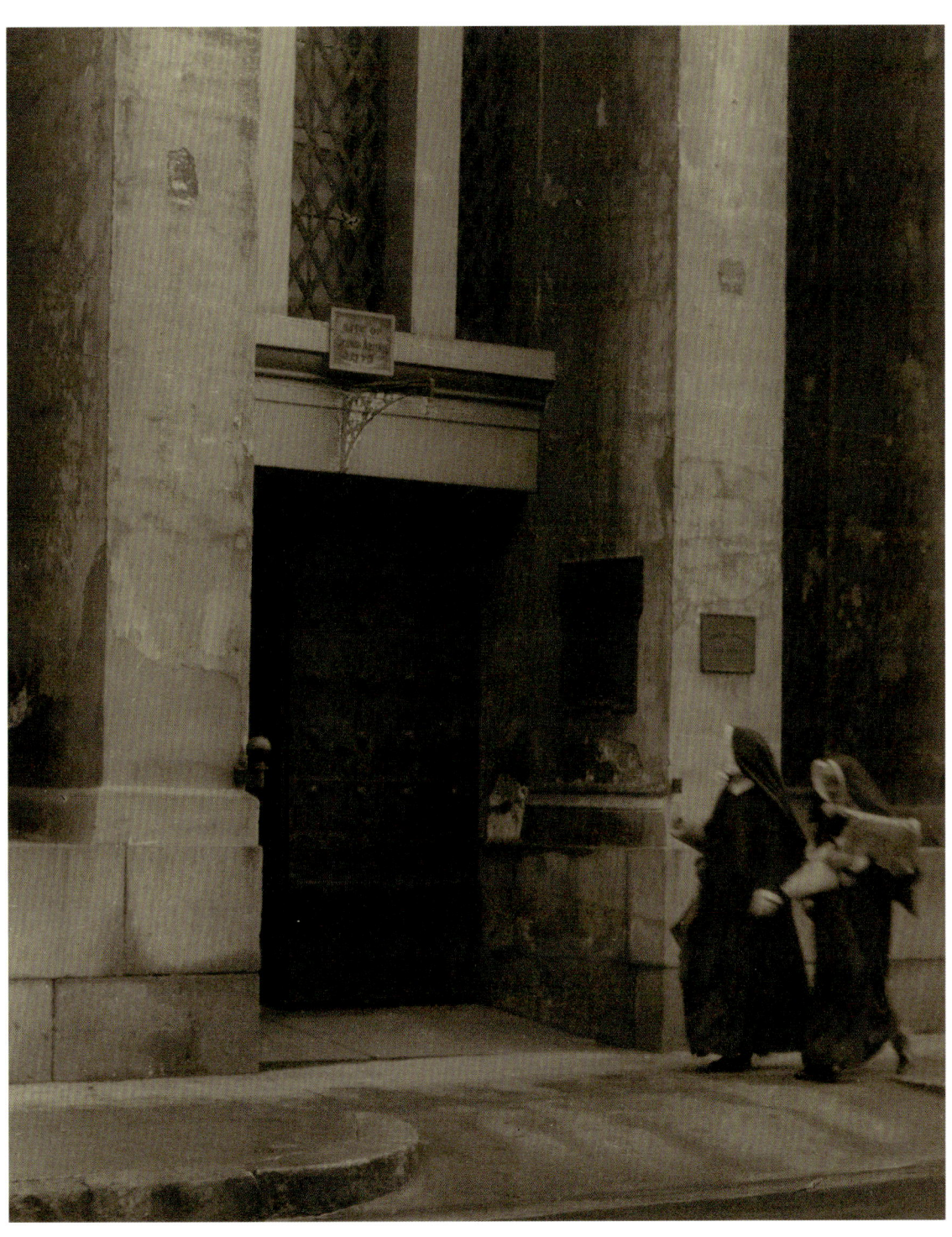

Nuns Walking in Front of the Arsenal, 1925 or 1926
by Arnold Genthe
gelatin silver print, mounted, 18 × 14 in.
1978.39.1

Robert W. Tebbs (1875–1945)

Photographs made by Robert W. Tebbs of a core cluster of timeworn buildings composing Columbia plantation on the Mississippi River between New Orleans and Baton Rouge show the hundred-year-old spatial relationships of the group unchanged. Structures with key functions are close to the main house: the brick kitchen immediately to the left of the house, and the pavilion-like brick *fournil* (a covered outdoor oven for baking bread) to the left of the kitchen, in the distance. Like the systematic Historic American Buildings Survey, which followed several years after Tebbs's Louisiana visit, the purpose of the project was to preserve in photographic form examples of regional colonial and US architecture. Tebbs had been engaged to make photographs for a planned series of books on US historic architecture, a project of the American Institute of Architects that was never realized beyond the first volume on Charleston, South Carolina, in 1927.

Guided by New Orleans architect Richard Koch, project director for the proposed volume on Louisiana and Mississippi buildings, Tebbs made some four hundred photographs during his 1926 visit. Many of those were associated with the plantation economy of Louisiana.

When active in the nineteenth century, Columbia plantation grew sugarcane and processed the crop into sugar. Nineteenth-century maps indicate that the acreage of the enterprise was considerable, and other plantations on the west bank of the Mississippi River as well as the bank opposite formed a nearly unbroken line of sugar production from below New Orleans to Baton Rouge. Plantations were also situated along smaller waterways. Site plans of Columbia's grounds show not only the cluster of buildings seen in the photograph but nearly forty cabins for the enslaved workers whose labors drove the cycle of cultivation, harvest, processing, and replanting.

Over the course of the twentieth century and into the twenty-first, development along the banks of the Mississippi River has transformed many former plantation tracts into petrochemical and other industrial manufacturing sites (p. 171). Some architectural remnants of the agricultural economy still survive, mostly in the form of the principal dwelling or manor house of the plantation and occasional acreage planted in sugarcane. In the early 2010s, the main house of Columbia plantation was moved to a location on the Mississippi River several miles from its original building site, where it stands in a restored condition as a private residence.

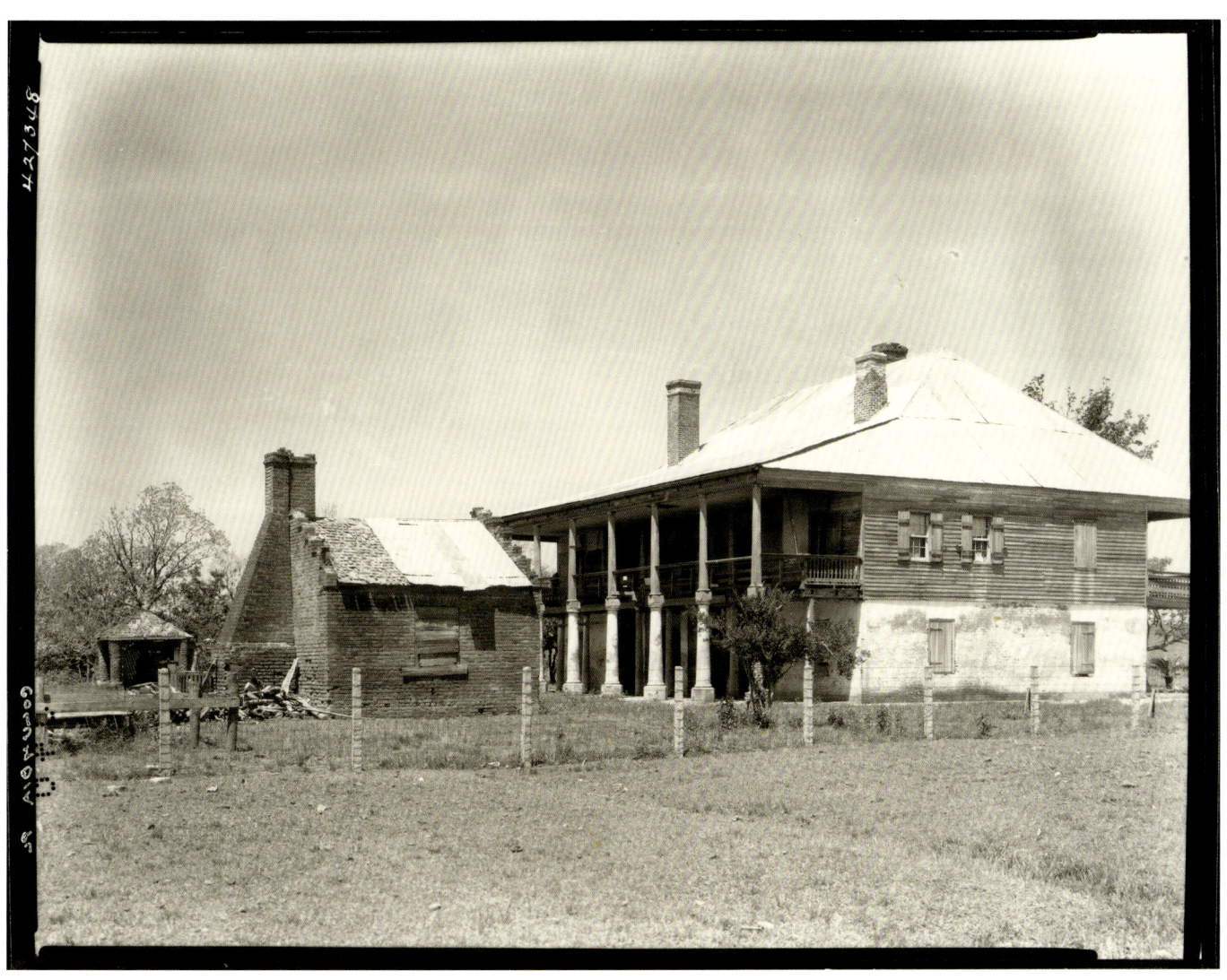

Columbia plantation, St. John the Baptist Parish, 1926

by Robert W. Tebbs
gelatin silver print, 8 × 10 in.
2000.79.58

N. M. Swinney (1891–1985)

Pierre Brulatour, a wine merchant and grocer during the 1870s, did not have a long or illustrious tenancy in the building at 520 Royal Street, yet it is his name that has steadfastly been identified with the property since the 1950s, and more specifically with its courtyard, a portion of which is seen in this photograph. For much of the twentieth century—especially during the years the Arts and Crafts Club of New Orleans had its galleries and classrooms on the site (1921 to 1926), around the time this picture was taken—the Brulatour courtyard was a favorite subject for artists to paint and to photograph. Whether artistic or commercial, images of the courtyard adorned prints, paintings, photographs, posters, postcards, and advertising through the middle of the twentieth century.

The courtyard has achieved an architectural stasis of sorts some two hundred years after the French furniture maker François Seignouret erected a fine townhouse and service buildings on the property, a site believed to have been among those severely damaged by the city's late eighteenth-century fires. The size and shape of the courtyard remained relatively constant over time, but the facades of the buildings that formed its walls underwent changes, especially in the early 1920s, when William Irby owned and remodeled the property. Plantings and other elements (notably a fountain) were part of the changing history of the space.

N. M. (Nellie May) Swinney's photograph, made about the time Irby's renovations had been concluded, documents a trend in Spanish-style architectural elements and landscaping popular in many parts of the country at the time. The Swinney Studio was located just a block away from the Brulatour house, at 429 Royal Street, and was known for atmospheric scenes of the Vieux Carré. Portraits of brides and bridal parties made by the Swinney Studio appeared on newspaper society pages throughout the late 1920s and the 1930s.

From the early 1950s until the mid-1990s, New Orleans's first television station, WDSU, centered its operations in the Brulatour building and adjacent ones, connecting the disparate pieces of architecture with labyrinthine hallways. The property was incorporated into the campus of The Historic New Orleans Collection in the early twenty-first century.

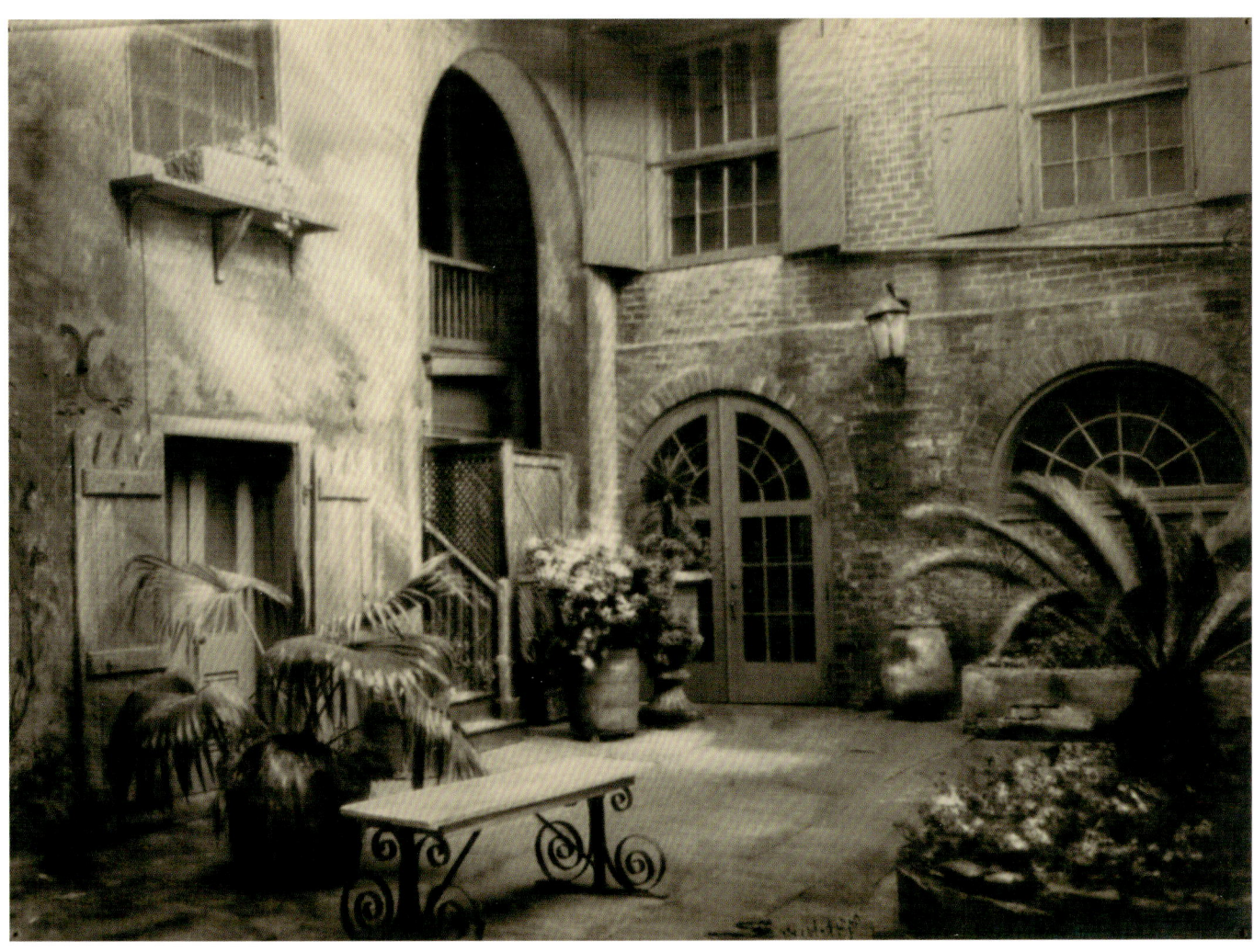

Brulatour courtyard, circa 1927
by N. M. Swinney
gelatin silver print, mounted, 8⅛ × 10⅝ in.
gift of Albert Wibergh, 2017.0128.2

C. Bennette Moore Studio (active 1904–1960s)

After serving in the Spanish-American War, Charles Bennette Moore (1879–1939) of Sauk Centre, Minnesota, moved to New Orleans in 1899, in the year of his twentieth birthday. Moore's brother, Frank B. Moore, was already operating a photography studio in the city, but C. Bennette chose employment in the Baronne Street studio of Julien Emile Rivoire. In 1904, three years after his marriage to Elise Wehrmann, Moore acquired Rivoire's business and started operating it under his own name.

The 1917 publication *Club Men of Louisiana, in Caricature* included Moore as one of its profiles, highlighting his portrait specialty: the photographer is depicted with a large studio camera mounted on a dolly, asking his customers to "watch the little bird." Moore's clients included prominent businesspeople, brides, and several Mardi Gras organizations, among them the krewes of Comus and Proteus and the Mystic Club. The slogans on the signs in this picture ("Don't waste your money on cheap photographs" and "Give good photographs for Xmas") track the content and sentiment of the studio's newspaper advertising. The assertion "Our photographs of men show character and individuality" appears front and center next to a portrait of Huey Long, then an influential Louisiana power broker on his way to becoming governor of the state and eventually US senator.

Moore's studio windows, initially at 109 Baronne Street and later at 314 Royal Street in the French Quarter, were used to promote products for sale, much as a department store displays clothes on mannequins in its windows. Examples of portraits in different sizes and with varying finishing techniques and framing demonstrated the firm's capabilities. Though the collection of portraits in the photograph seen here has that kind of quality, its crowded character, the bunting at the upper right, and the glimpse of passersby on the right, beyond the installation, suggest the image depicts not a window display but Moore's booth at a trade show or conference in New Orleans. The left-hand sign's explanation of the studio's location in relation to the Roosevelt Hotel, the "No. 61" (an exhibitor's number, perhaps), and misspelling of "Bennett" on the black placard add weight to its being an exhibit booth.

Moore's success as a photographer was not confined to portraiture: scenic photography would soon supply regular income as well, tapping into a tourism market for photographic images that included picture postcards as well as stereographs. Moore's views, with their hand coloring, set them apart from such mass-produced articles. The publication of *Impressions of Old New Orleans* (1926), by photographer Arnold Genthe, invited national interest in the unique look of the city. Seizing the opportunity, Moore documented New Orleans's subtropical setting and architecture in individual prints, which he sold in sizes convenient for framing and display. He eventually added to his offerings a series of French Quarter scenes reproduced as etchings. The souvenir images proved popular, and in the 1920s and 1930s the studio was producing them at a brisk pace, in sizes ranging from a calling card to an easel painting. The pictures, printed in black and white, often received hand coloring, applied by Moore's wife, Elise, or his daughters, Grace, Phyllis, Lisette, and Ruth. More than mere souvenirs, the hand-colored images can be considered products of artistic collaboration.

Moore was a major figure in his profession by the time of his death, having worked four decades behind the camera and in the darkroom. He died unexpectedly of a heart ailment while at work on December 8, 1939. The Moore Studio's legacy included not only the photographs of its founder but also the work of Moore's successors: his wife, daughters, and granddaughter, Eugenie Stoll Ragan, who operated the C. Bennette Moore Studio until the late 1960s.

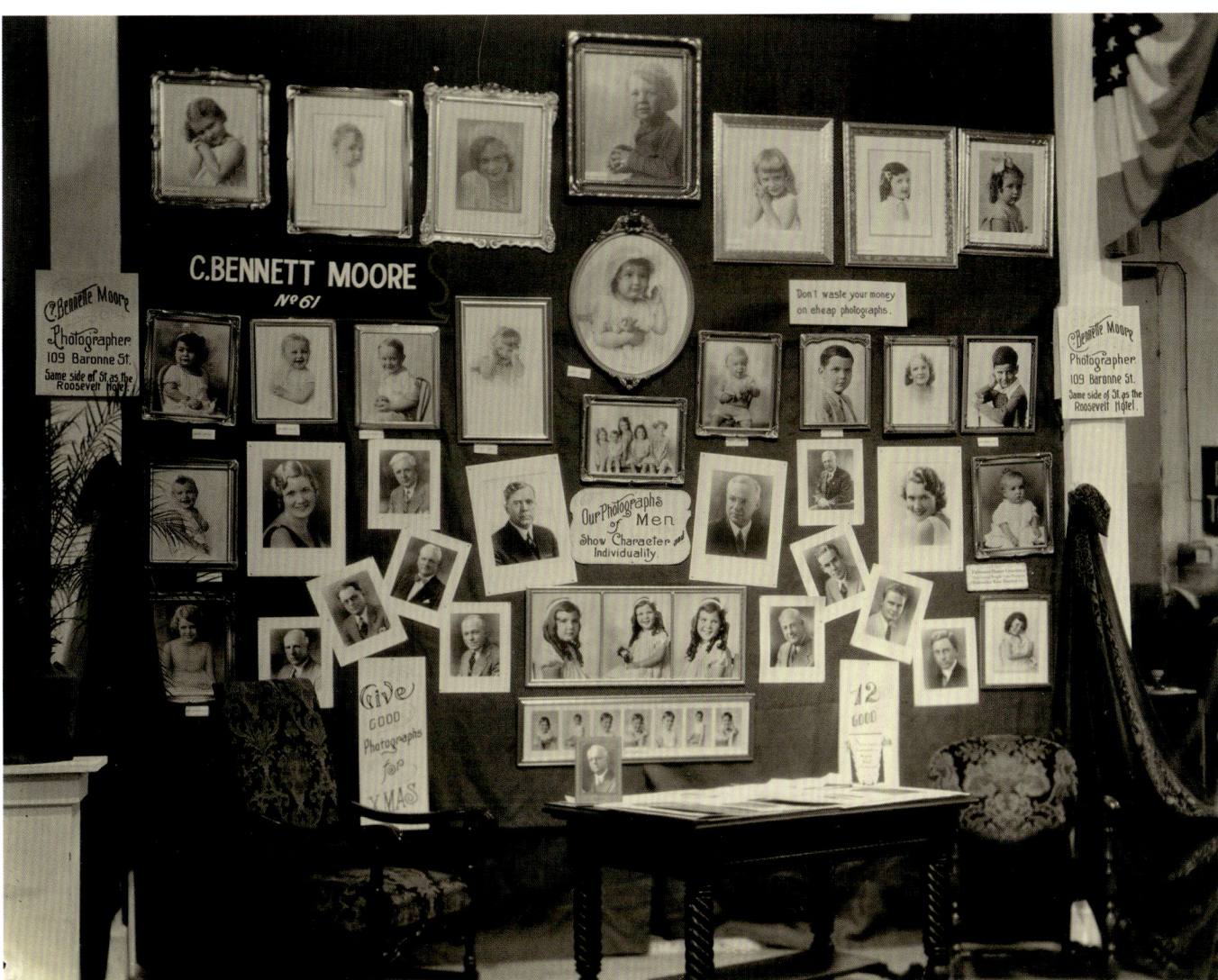

The Moores' associations with photography trade groups—notably the Professional Photographers of America (PPA)—helped define technical excellence in photographic practice as well as a type of photographic artistry for a photo-consuming public. The studio was active both nationally and regionally, participating in exhibition competitions, delivering lectures on everything from lighting and other studio techniques to the use of oils in coloring black-and-white prints, and teaching master classes at the PPA's headquarters in Indiana.

The business eventually closed in the late 1960s, and the archive came under the stewardship of Joseph Bergeron, who had joined the firm earlier in the decade. Bergeron operated the archive business for another four decades, until transferring the archive to The Historic New Orleans Collection in 2011.

C. Bennette Moore Studio advertising display, circa 1926
by C. Bennette Moore Studio
gelatin silver print, 7¾ × 9¹¹⁄₁₆ in.
acquisition made possible by the Laussat Society, 2011.0220.1.506

Doris Ulmann (1882–1934)

The portrait of Sister Mary Ann Sampson with her young charge is characteristic of the late-career work of photographer Doris Ulmann. From 1918 until about 1925, Ulmann operated a very successful portrait studio in New York City, catering to wealthy and prominent sitters, but her interests ultimately shifted to photographing rural communities and folkways that she and others saw vanishing. Artists with whom she collaborated included composer John Jacob Niles, who documented traditional music, and writer Julia Peterkin, whose 1933 book *Roll, Jordan, Roll* showcased Ulmann's photographs. Peterkin's text and Ulmann's images focused on the Gullah residents whose enslaved ancestors had worked the fields of Lang Syne plantation in South Carolina. Similarly invested in "lost" communities and work patterns, Allen H. Eaton's *Handicrafts of the Southern Highlands* (1937) features Ulmann's (posthumously published) photographs of craftspeople of the Appalachian Mountains.

Ulmann took photographs in Louisiana in the early 1930s, hosted at least part of the time by Cammie G. Henry, doyenne of Melrose plantation, near Natchitoches, in central Louisiana, who welcomed and housed writers and artists for extended stays. (The portrait here comes from a group of photographs acquired by the donors at an auction of the contents of Melrose plantation in 1970.) While in Louisiana, Ulmann produced two series of portraits of nuns: some were members of New Orleans's Ursuline order, and some, like the woman in this picture, belonged to the Sisters of the Holy Family. This New Orleans religious community dates back to 1837 and is the second-oldest order of Black nuns established in the United States.

Likely made at the order's school when it was situated in the French Quarter, this double portrait is formal in character and conveys a tenderness between the two subjects, though neither seems particularly engaged with Ulmann. Sister Mary Ann's gaze is far away from this earthly moment of photography, and the face of the young girl suggests she may be wondering when the photo session will end so that she can resume her studies, playtime, or lunch.

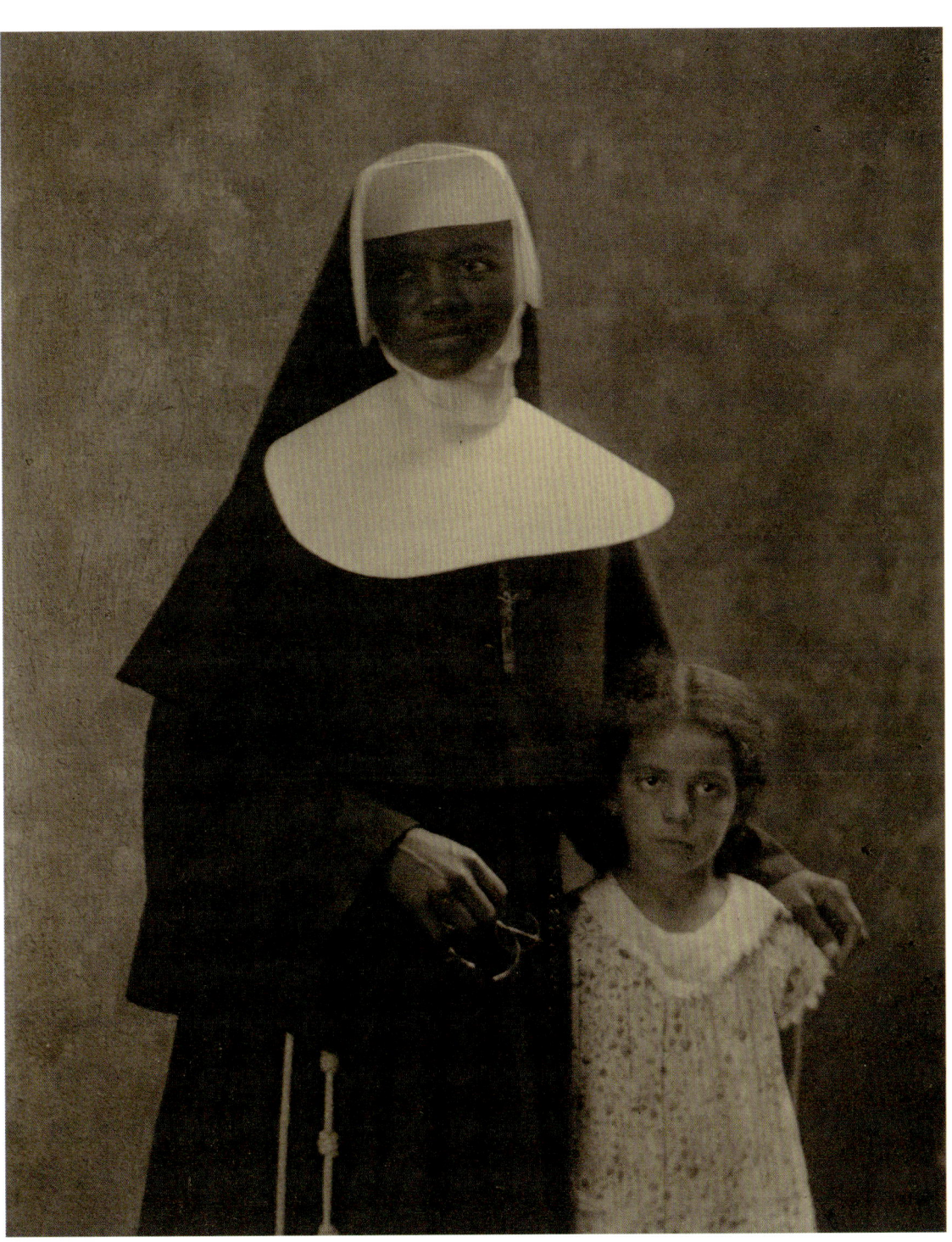

**Sister Mary Ann Sampson and unidentified young girl,
circa 1930**

by Doris Ulmann
platinum print, 7¾ × 6 in.
gift of Mr. and Mrs. L. Kent Nelson, 1981.329.42

Dan Leyrer (1898–1978)

Dan Leyrer practiced photography in New Orleans from the 1920s until his death. Initially his subjects and role varied: he photographed buildings, people, objects, and events, and one exceptional assignment in the early 1930s found him accompanying noted archaeologist Frans Blom to Mexico, to photograph temples and other structures in the Maya city Uxmal.

This photograph was made relatively early in Leyrer's career. Elmwood plantation, several miles upriver from New Orleans in Jefferson Parish on the Mississippi's east bank, no longer exists. When Leyrer's photograph was made, the building was about a century old, having replaced eighteenth-century structures on the site. Elmwood was built as a two-story house, but after a fire destroyed the upper story and roof in 1940, the property was rebuilt as a one-story structure, its appearance and proportions dramatically altered. In 1962, Elmwood began operating as a restaurant, still surrounded by some of the live oak trees seen in the photograph. Another fire destroyed the restaurant in 1978, and years of negotiations with the owners to have it restored were unsuccessful. The ruins were removed, and Elmwood was not rebuilt.

Work making prints of architect Richard Koch's photographs of Louisiana's historic structures gave Leyrer additional experience in architectural photography and better prepared him for the large-scale project he would undertake in the early 1960s. The city of New Orleans, through an advisory committee, hired him to take pictures of the buildings of the French Quarter in the first systematic photographic inventory of the historic district. Leyrer's workmanlike photographs, made on black-and-white film with a 5 × 7-inch view camera, form the visual basis of the important historical resource now available online as the Collins C. Diboll Vieux Carré Digital Survey. Leyrer's French Quarter studio locations (his last being in the 700 block of St. Peter Street) positioned him geographically and perhaps also dispositionally for the project. Since its inception, the survey has been updated two more times with new photography, once in 1979–80 (using 35 mm black-and-white film) and again in 2010–12, using digital color photography.

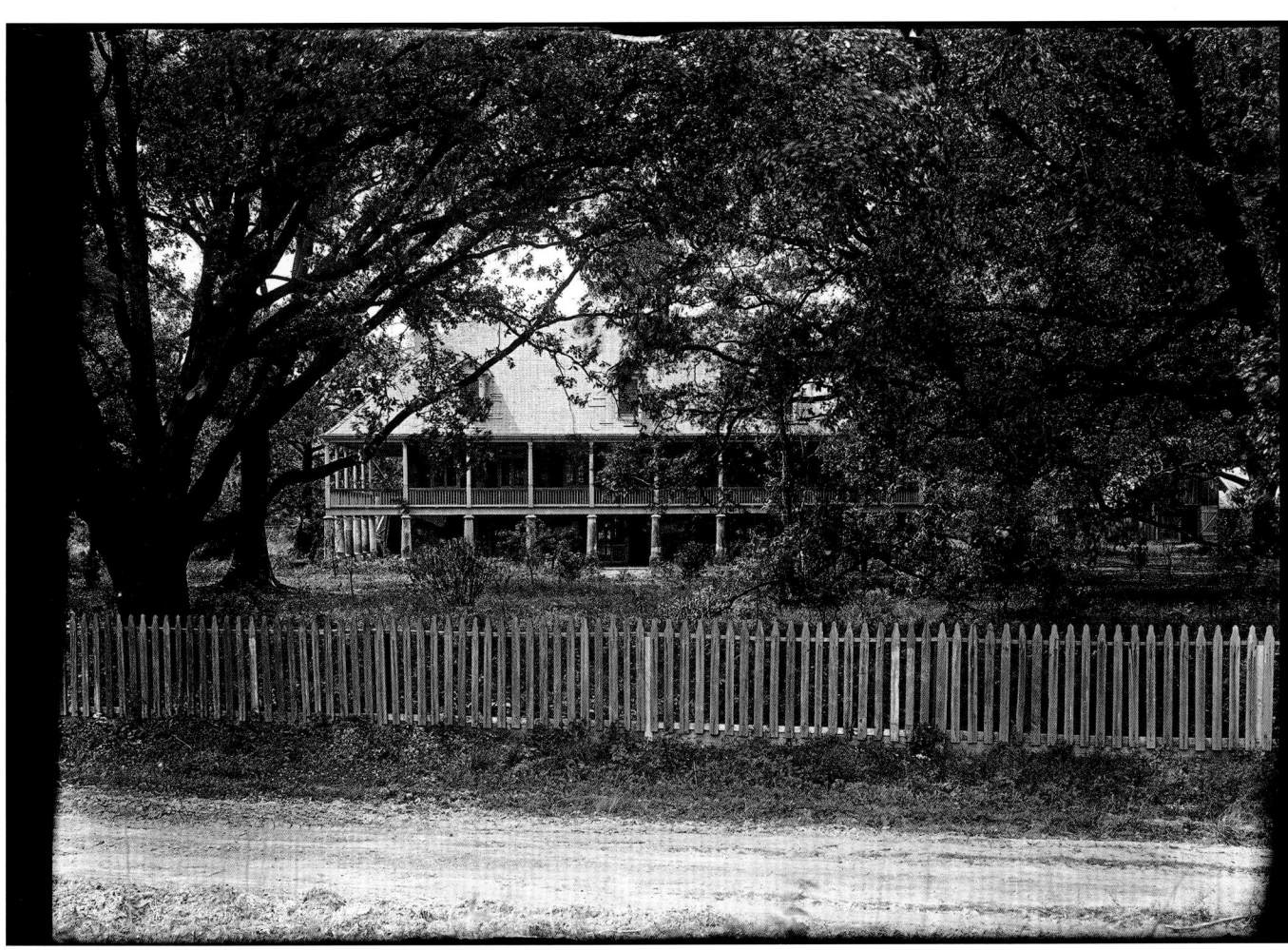

Elmwood plantation, between 1929 and 1940

by Dan Leyrer
gelatin dry plate negative, 5 × 7 in.
gift of Allan Phillip Jaffe, 1981.324.1.75

A contemporary gelatin silver print made from the original negative is
reproduced.

Walker Evans (1903–1975)

This image of the 500 block of Bourbon Street, created by Walker Evans, one of the giants of twentieth-century photographic expression, recalls a time when the famous strip was part of a residential, workaday neighborhood, rather than the entertainment district it has been since the 1940s. Taken during the years when Evans's preferred approach of directness and clarity, a "documentary" style, was crystalizing, the image offers a straightforward, sober look at its subject, three shop facades that address a variety of social and economic needs: a drugstore, a barbershop, and a Chinese merchants' association office. But one could argue that none of these compelled Evans to set up his bulky 8 × 10-inch camera and tripod. The stripes of the French Opera Barber Shop, in all their helter-skelter glory, are what visually define this picture.

Although Evans was born in St. Louis, his sojourns in Paris, the South Pacific, and New York, where he ultimately settled, shaped his life and aspirations as a writer and visual artist. At the time this particular picture was taken, his most prominent photographic publication was a series of pictures made principally in Havana that had appeared in Carleton Beals's *The Crime of Cuba* (1933). Evans's landmark book of images, the 1938 *American Photographs*, which included *Sidewalk and Shop Front*, was still a few years away, and his portfolio of Depression-era Hale County, Alabama, the visual counterweight to James Agee's prose in *Let Us Now Praise Famous Men* (1941), was further still from being realized. His 1935 visit to New Orleans, besides producing some career-defining photographs, put him in touch with a woman he would later marry, the artist Jane Smith Ninas.

Shortly after his New Orleans visit, Evans worked briefly taking pictures for the Resettlement Administration, recording New Deal projects designed to address the plight of out-of-work and displaced Americans, but his sense of how photographs should be visualized and made ultimately proved a bad fit for the structure of the program, and the relationship did not survive the 1930s. His career forged ahead, and his reputation—not only as a photographer with pictorial intelligence and sublime perception of his subjects' relationship to the photographic frame, but also as a picture editor and educator—was well established before his death in 1975.

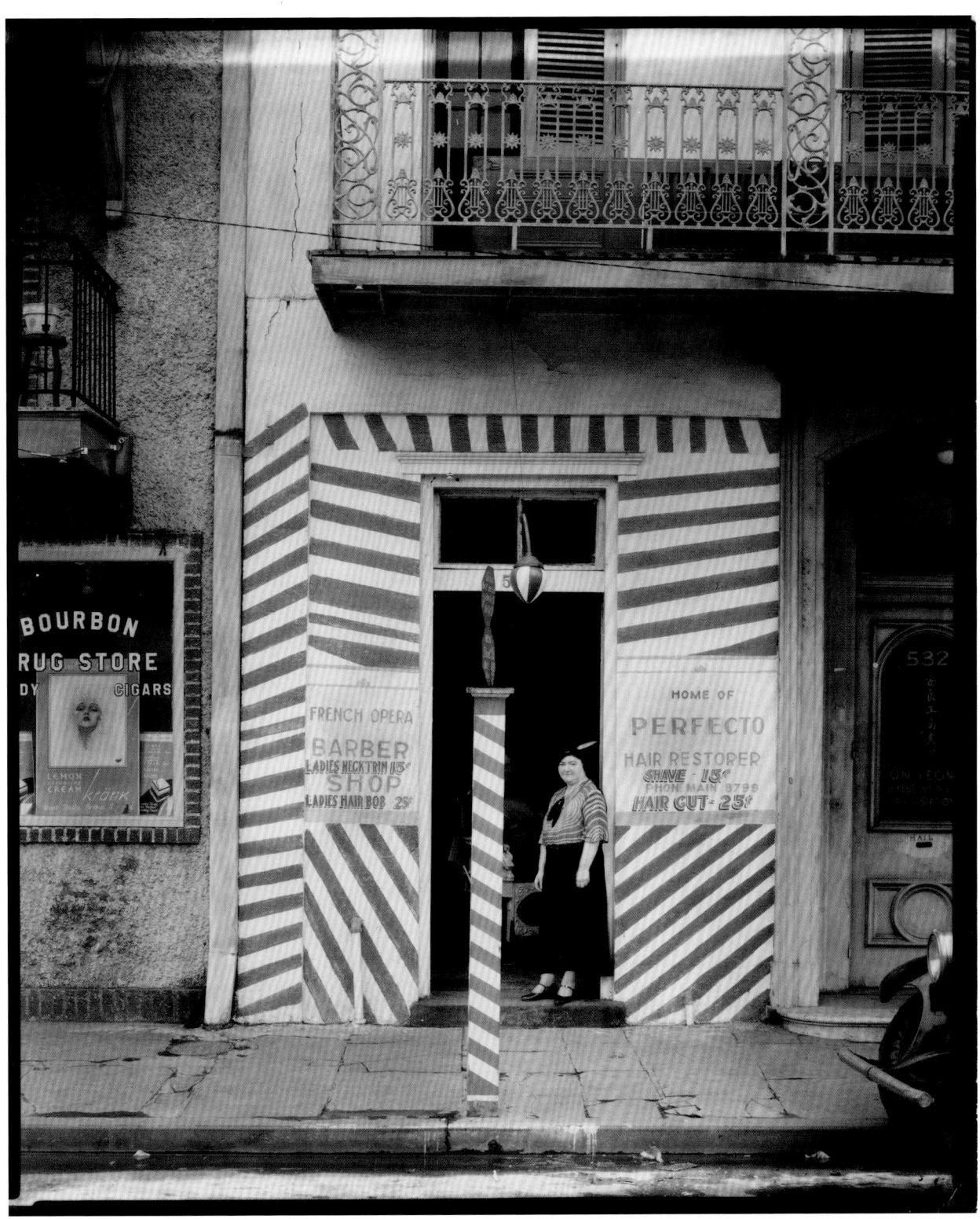

Sidewalk and Shop Front, New Orleans, 1935

by Walker Evans
gelatin silver print, 10 × 8 in.
1978.84.1, © Walker Evans Archive, The Metropolitan Museum of Art

Richard Koch (1889–1971)

In 1926, Louisiana architect Richard Koch served as the American Institute of Architects (AIA) contact for New York–based photographer Robert W. Tebbs on the latter's visit to Louisiana (p. 102). The AIA had embarked on a project to record nationally important architecture by region and style, and Tebbs's firm, then at the top of its game, had been selected to document Louisiana's plantation structures. Tebbs made hundreds of photographs during his visit, and though the AIA's grand scheme for a series of books on US architecture was not fulfilled, it is highly likely that Koch had this experience with Tebbs in mind when, in 1934, he became head of the Historic American Buildings Survey (HABS) in Louisiana. Koch served HABS while continuing his private architectural practice.

HABS was established as a national program that offered meaningful employment to architects, draftsmen, designers, photographers, and historians during the Great Depression. State coordinators assembled teams to identify and document historic architectural structures that were then measured, drawn, photographed, and examined as whole buildings and for their salient details. In addition to being Louisiana's coordinator for the project, Koch served as the principal photographer. When the US entered World War II in 1941, the program was suspended.

HABS (and its companion programs, the Historic American Engineering Record and the more recent Historic American Landscape Survey) continues today. Its rigorous rules and procedures for drawn and photographed documentation ensure that the visual characteristics of selected buildings are recorded in ways that are complete, accurate, and consistent.

Koch, a traditionalist in architectural design, often adopted a more modernist approach when photographing historic buildings, especially their details. This interior view of Madewood plantation on Bayou Lafourche (in Napoleonville,

Louisiana) is an example: the photograph's composition is as much about abstract shapes as about architecture, an effect enhanced by a printing technique that reveals some detail but that uses contrast and tone to highlight formal relationships.

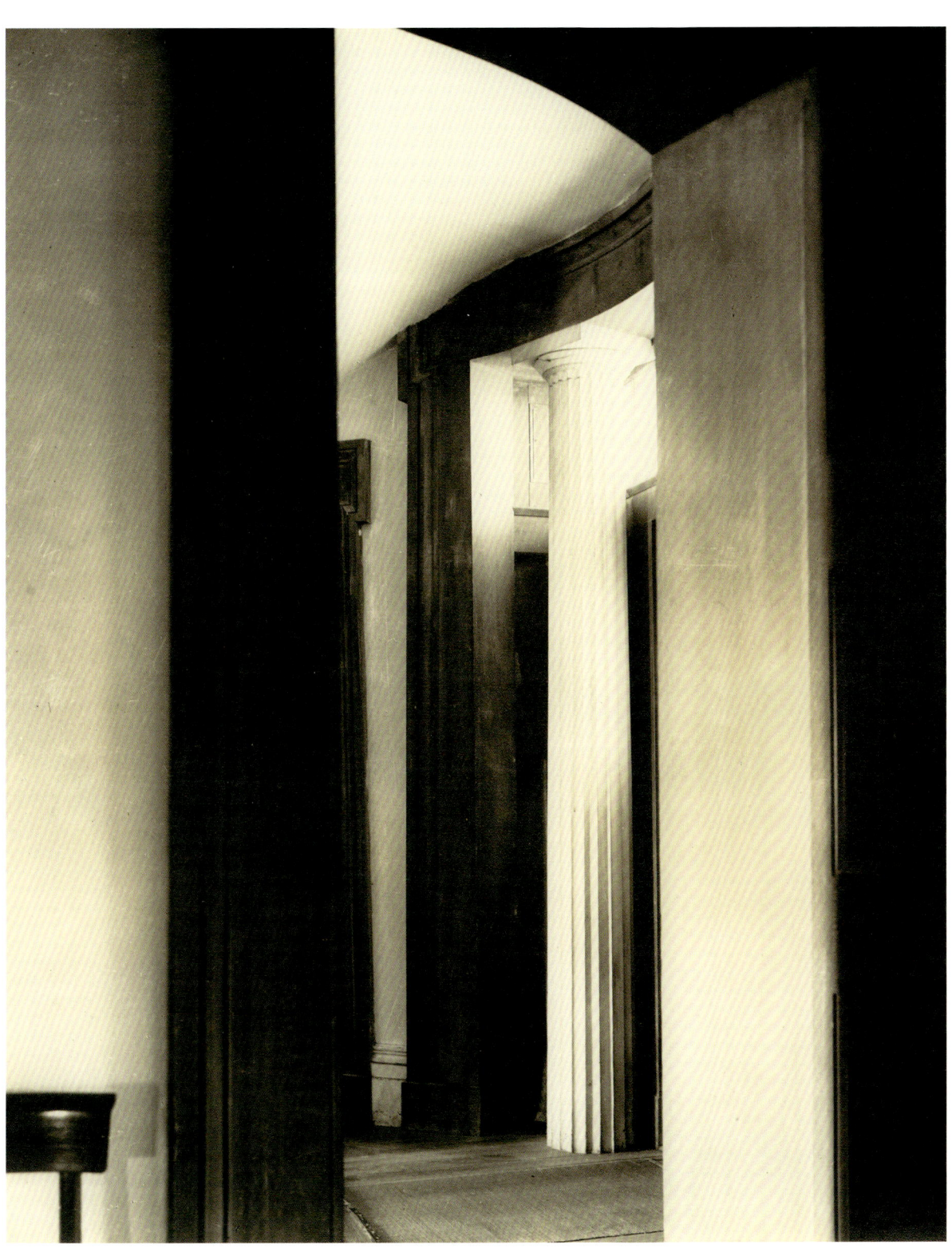

Madewood interior, 1930s
by Richard Koch
gelatin silver print, 14 × 10⅞ in.
gift of Mrs. Solis Seiferth, 1985.120.246

George Ernst Durr (1888–1957)

The photographs collected by a history museum are not limited to works by professional photographic artists, commercial photographers, and photojournalists. Amateur photographers, who may not share the professional's economic or expressive goals, continually mark historic moments, chart changing epochs, and document everyday life. Consciously or not, an amateur photographer who amasses images over time provides a visual equivalent to a written journal or series of letters. When a personal collection spans decades and reveals an investigative and documentary bent, it becomes a window not just on one person's way of life but on the history of a region. The photograph albums of George Ernst Durr constitute one such window.

The family album was originally a showcase for professionally produced studio portraits (usually of loved ones, friends, and celebrities) intended to appeal to a wide range of viewers. The rise of the handheld camera designed for recreational use transformed the idea of the album, making it a document the photographer compiled of experiences, people, and events that may have had little resonance beyond their intimate circle. Amateur photographers often produced their own prints as well, creating a seamless authorship that extended from making the picture and developing the negative to crafting the print and then mounting it in the album.

Durr, an engineer by education and profession, spent four decades taking photographs, printing them, and arranging them in six neatly labeled albums. These volumes chronicle aspects of a personal and professional life from the early to mid-twentieth century. Durr's works included portraits and candid photographs of family and friends; scenes from trips to New York, Havana, Mobile, and California, among other places; and pictures made during day trips to St. Tammany Parish and the Mississippi Gulf Coast.

Though the natural comparison of the album is to a book, a photo album is equally akin to a mass storage unit, collecting and preserving visual information of its day and presenting it in organized form to the viewer.

Pages from personal photo albums, 1915–30
by George Ernst Durr
gelatin silver prints, mounted, 10 × 12 in. (album page dimensions)
gift of Kris Pottharst, 2011.0299.1.69, 2011.0299.3.28, © George Ernst Durr

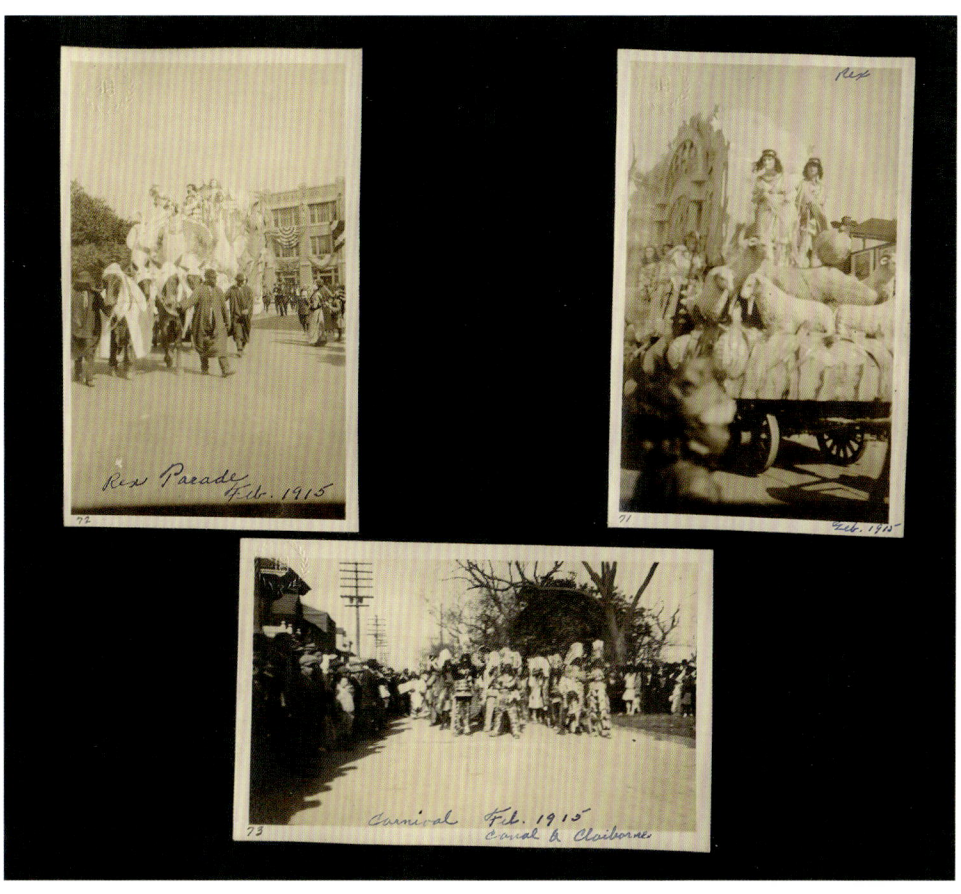

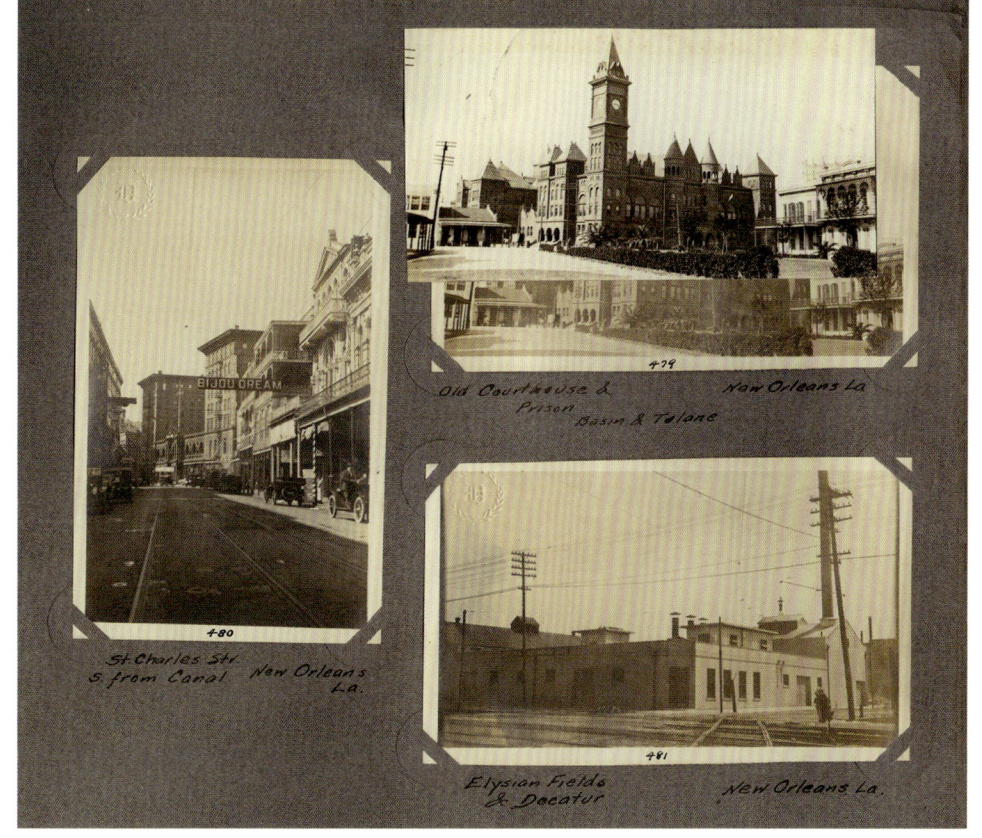

EXPRESSION AND DOCUMENTATION

1936–1999

Peter Sekaer (1901–1950)

Peter Sekaer was born in Denmark, and after coming to the United States in 1918, he was soon earning a living as a sign painter and poster maker. After taking up photography, he was one of the many practitioners who worked during the 1930s and early 1940s for various federal agencies associated with the New Deal. Like some of his colleagues—Walker Evans, for example—he worked in Louisiana.

The "alphabet soup" of federal programs during the New Deal of president Franklin D. Roosevelt employed dozens of photographers. Sekaer initially worked with photographer Walker Evans for the Resettlement Administration (RA), later renamed the Farm Security Administration (FSA). He photographed on his own for the Rural Electrification Administration (REA) and later the United States Housing Authority (USHA) and the Office of Indian Affairs (OIA). The early 1940s saw him making photographs for the OWI, or Office of War Information. Following World War II, Sekaer moved from Washington, DC, to New York's mid–Hudson Valley, where he was a freelance editorial and fashion photographer. A heart attack claimed his life at the relatively young age of forty-nine.

The date of this picture suggests it was made while Sekaer was with the REA, in the year before he became the head of that department. However, its subject, an animated corner of New Orleans's Vieux Carré, is neither rural nor especially descriptive of electrical infrastructure. It is rich in the language of signs, both hand-lettered and professionally produced, and shares that kinship with other Sekaer photographs of this era.

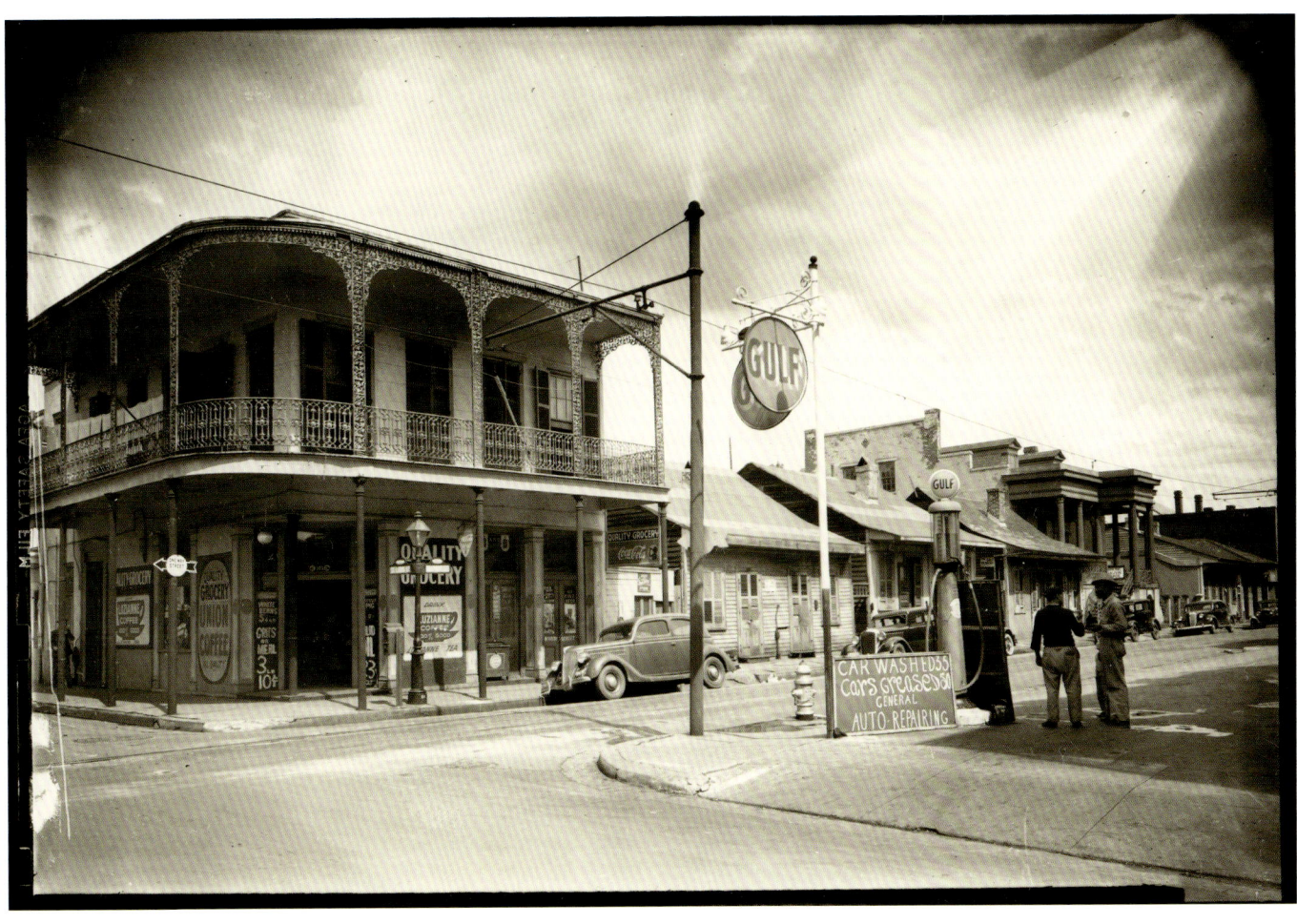

501 Dauphine Street, 1937

by Peter Sekaer
gelatin silver print, 5 × 8 in.
1981.311.12, © Peter Sekaer Estate

Fonville Winans (1911–1992)

Fonville Winans's connection to Louisiana of the 1920s was immediate and deep. His father's work as an engineer took the young Fonville (born in 1911) to Louisiana in 1928, when he was still in high school, a period when he also took up photography as a hobby. With southern coastal Louisiana as his new home, Winans began exploring its marshy landscape in a boat and meeting the inhabitants of the towns and villages scattered throughout it. He used both 16 mm movie film and still photography to record this, for him, strange world.

In 1934, he enrolled at Louisiana State University, and after studies in journalism, took a job with the state as a photographer, specializing in making pictures of Louisiana's industrial activities, from salt mining and oil drilling to oystering and moss ginning. Winans gained some notoriety for his portraits of the state's political figures of the mid-twentieth century. In 1940 he opened a studio in Baton Rouge whose main trade was weddings and portraits. In what may be a unique aspect of his career, he made aerial photographs of Baton Rouge in 1947. Winans continued to operate his studio business until his death in 1992.

The two pictures here from the 1930s show the gritty reality of the world away from the studio's pristine visages, poses, clothing, and lighting designed to flatter the subject. The prison photograph, based on the date and the subject, may have been related to Winans's work for the state. The farm at Angola Prison (which held both male and female inmates during this time) was part of the state's penal system. The hard work of manual agricultural labor comes through in this photograph, as well as the historical specter of prisons run as private labor camps. The mostly anonymous portrayals of the prisoners and guard underscore the dehumanizing effect of such a system. But personalizing the prison experience is not a role this picture was meant to fill.

The "Chickazola" (or, more traditionally, Chighizola) dwelling was on Grand Isle, where Jefferson Parish meets the Gulf of Mexico. The island and its surrounding network of waterways was a favorite spot for Winans. Louis Alcide Chighizola, or "Nez Coupé," was one of the Baratarians associated with Jean Laffite, and the name may have been part of the reason for Winans's interest in photographing the structure. The circumstances of the building and its residents seem meager, and undoubtedly the seasonal work of hunting, fishing, and trapping was hard. But unlike those shown laboring on the Angola farm, the people were free to choose their occupations and could work on a schedule of their own making.

Angola Hoers, **1938**
by Fonville Winans
gelatin silver print, 16 × 20 in.
2018.0513.9, © Fonville Winans Estate

Chickazola Shack, **1933**
by Fonville Winans
gelatin silver print, 16 × 19¾ in.
2020.0015.1.10, © Fonville Winans Estate

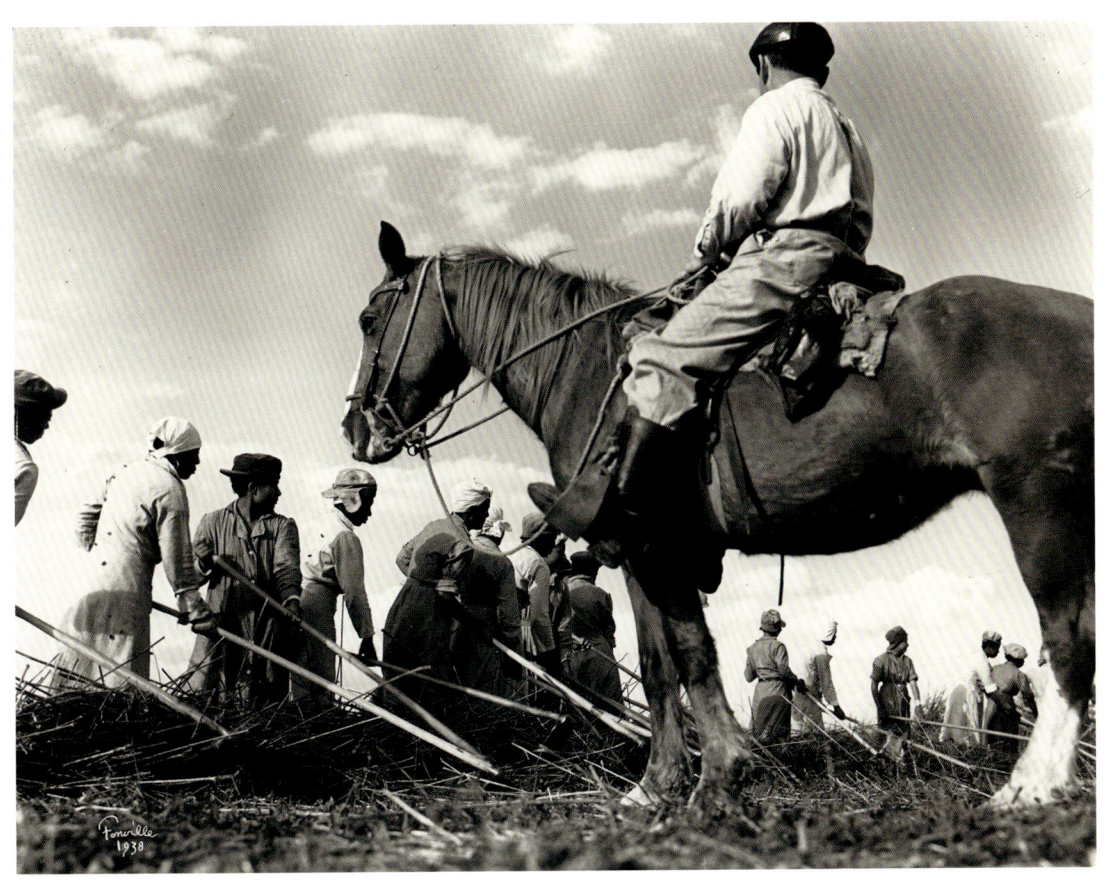

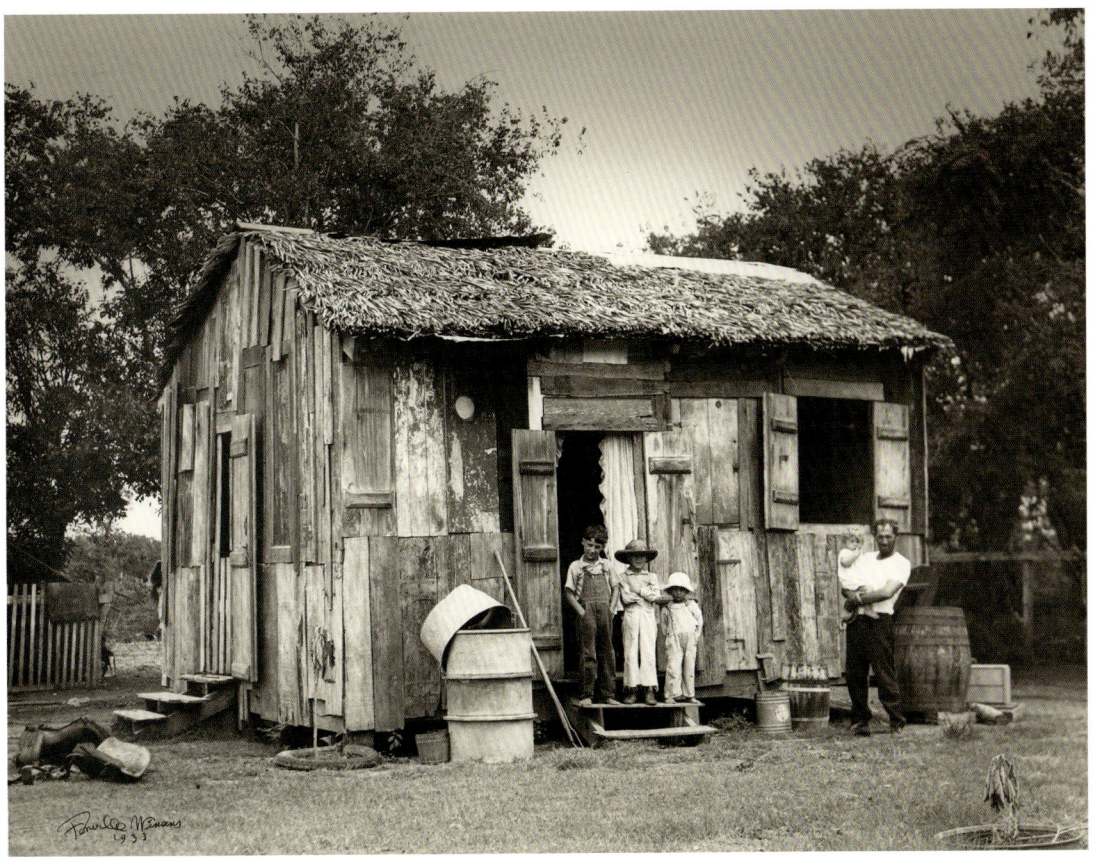

Frances Benjamin Johnston (1864–1952)

Frances Benjamin Johnston was born in the final years of Abraham Lincoln's presidency, began practicing photography when Benjamin Harrison held the office, and died on the eve of Dwight D. Eisenhower's first term. Johnston, who was based in the nation's capital during the first decades of her career, was especially active in photographing administrative activities of the Harrison, Cleveland, McKinley, and Theodore Roosevelt presidencies. Her 1899 photographs of Hampton University are a remarkable project commissioned by that institution for African Americans. Before and between the world wars, Johnston visited the lower South frequently on photographic assignments, and beginning in 1940 she lived in the French Quarter of New Orleans. By that time, she had been a photographer for over fifty years. In 1945 she purchased a house at 1130–32 Bourbon Street (between Ursulines and Governor Nicholls Streets), living there until her death in 1952.

The photograph reproduced here is of the Le Pretre Mansion, at the corner of Dauphine and Orleans streets in the French Quarter. The print dates from between 1937 and 1939, when Johnston used her sixth grant from the Carnegie Corporation to photograph in Louisiana, Mississippi, and Alabama.

The building in Johnston's picture dates from 1836, when Joseph Gardette commissioned it from builder Frederic Roy. Ownership soon passed to Jean Baptiste Le Pretre, who owned it from 1839 to 1878, and whose name is most often associated with it. The wraparound cast-iron galleries, supported by slender iron columns, date from approximately 1850, softening the structure's severe vertical character.

About the time that Johnston inscribed this print "to a fellow artist" in June 1939, the Le Pretre Mansion was the subject of a series of detailed architectural drawings—twenty-six sheets in all—made between 1938 and 1940 by Cecil R. Coleman, Alvyk Boyd Cruise, H. Kenison, Emory N. Maddux, Louis Sarrazin Jr., Uriel J. Theriot, and Chester H. Wicker under the auspices of the Historic American Buildings Survey (HABS). The series includes elevations, floor plans, and section drawings of architectural features like cornices, window moldings, doorframes, ornamental plaster, and decorative ironwork.

The "fellow artist" in Johnston's inscription is unknown. After Johnston's move to the Vieux Carré in 1940, she became part of the artistic circle of the neighborhood.

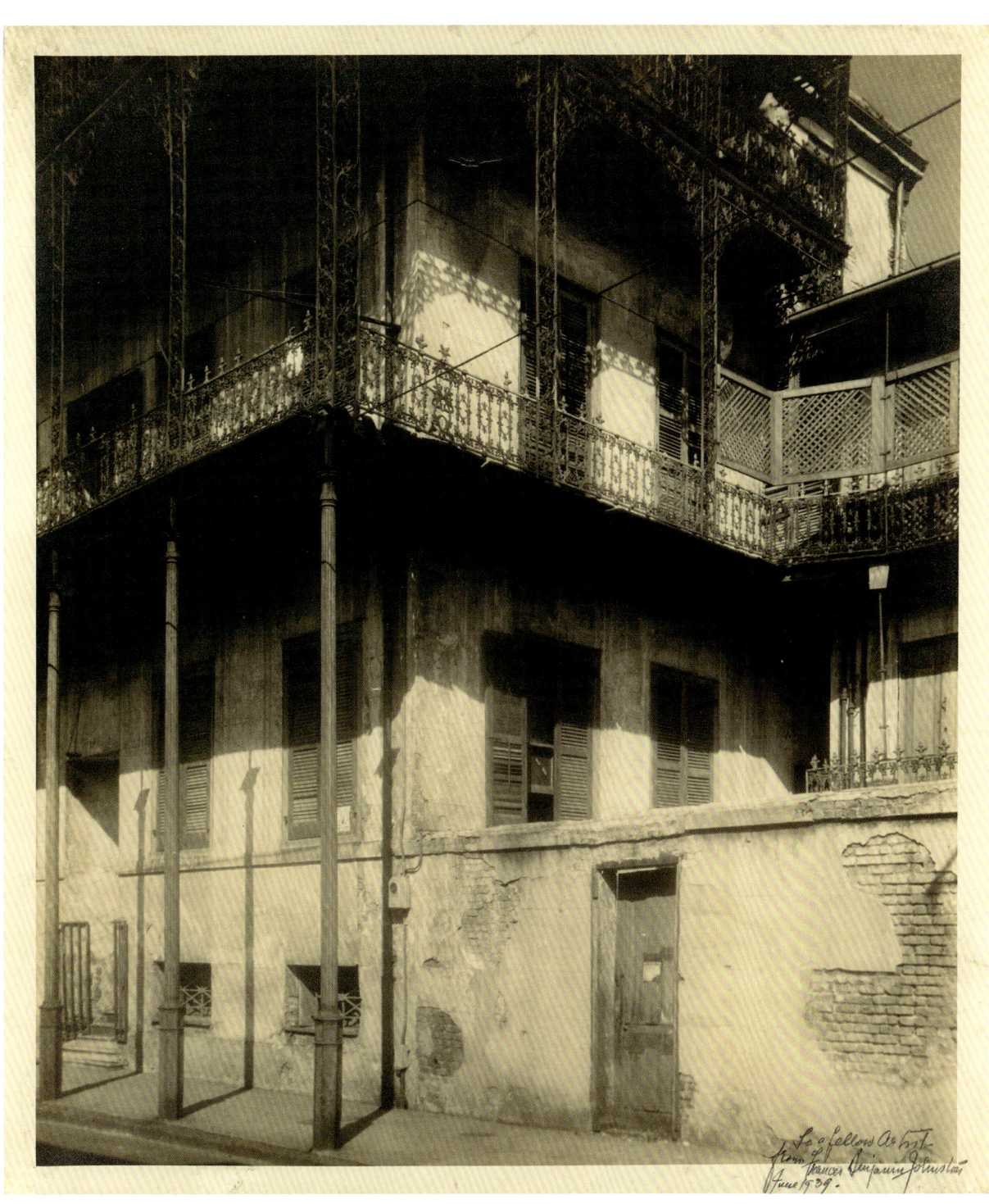

Le Pretre Mansion, between 1938 and June 1939

by Frances Benjamin Johnston
gelatin silver print, 18 × 15 in.
1978.227

Eugene A. Delcroix (1891–1967)

Eugene A. Delcroix's soft-focus paeans to New Orleans's French Quarter were just one facet—a very visible one—of a career that used photography to promote economic activity in the region. Visitors purchased Delcroix's gauzy landscapes and views of historic architecture through varied retail outlets. They tucked the photographs into suitcases before returning home from the Crescent City, dispersing Delcroix's take on New Orleans throughout the country. In 1938 and several times in the 1940s, Joseph S. W. Harmonson of New Orleans published a distillation of Delcroix's vision under the title *Patios, Stairways and Iron Lace Balconies of Old New Orleans*.

But a second side of Delcroix's work was promoting the growth and economy of New Orleans's upriver neighbor, Jefferson Parish. For some thirty years, beginning in the mid-1930s, Delcroix's photographs of the parish's natural beauty, new businesses and industry, prominent civic figures, and grand ambitions for growth saw publication in the *Jefferson Parish Yearly Review*, a chamber of commerce–type yearbook that presented past triumphs and future projections of prosperity for Jefferson Parish, whose precincts extend on both sides of the Mississippi River above and opposite New Orleans, and south to Grand Isle on the Gulf of Mexico. The island was a favorite subject and setting for Delcroix, who had spent time there as a boy because of his mother's teaching job. His legacy is as both an artist and a documentarian.

Delcroix began his photography career in the studios of established practitioners in New Orleans, whose bread-and-butter trade was studio portraiture: Anthony H. Hitchler and C. Bennette Moore (p. 106). Delcroix remained a steadfast user of glass plates long after film had become the preferred medium for professional photographers. His photographs often eradicated any temporal references, making his work hard to date. His pictures that were reproduced in a publication can at least provide a "no later than" time of execution. A limited geographic range of his subjects and his revisiting these same places over the course of his career also make precise dating difficult.

The photographs here present examples of the two sides of Delcroix's work. The view of St. Louis Cathedral through the architectural framing of a casement window with a fanlight head typifies the Tonalist reduction that he employed to obliterate detail, emphasize compositional elements, and efface temporal clues. The photograph of a trapper's compound in lower Jefferson Parish is from his series on the families who practiced that seasonal occupation and made the harvesting of fur-bearing mammals—muskrat, nutria, and mink—a significant economic engine for the region.

Fan window, no later than 1938
by Eugene A. Delcroix
gelatin dry plate negative, 7 × 5 in.
gift of Joel Jergins and Mrs. Eugene Delcroix, courtesy of the New Orleans Museum of Art, 1984.189.3171, © Eugene A. Delcroix Estate

Trapper with muskrat, no later than 1939
by Eugene A. Delcroix
gelatin dry plate negative, 7 × 5 in.
gift of Joel Jergins and Mrs. Eugene Delcroix, courtesy of the New Orleans Museum of Art, 1984.189.850, © Eugene A. Delcroix Estate

Trapper's cabin, no later than 1939
by Eugene A. Delcroix
gelatin dry plate negative, 5 × 7 in.
gift of Joel Jergins and Mrs. Eugene Delcroix, courtesy of the New Orleans Museum of Art, 1984.189.1569, © Eugene A. Delcroix Estate

Contemporary gelatin silver prints made by THNOC staff are reproduced.

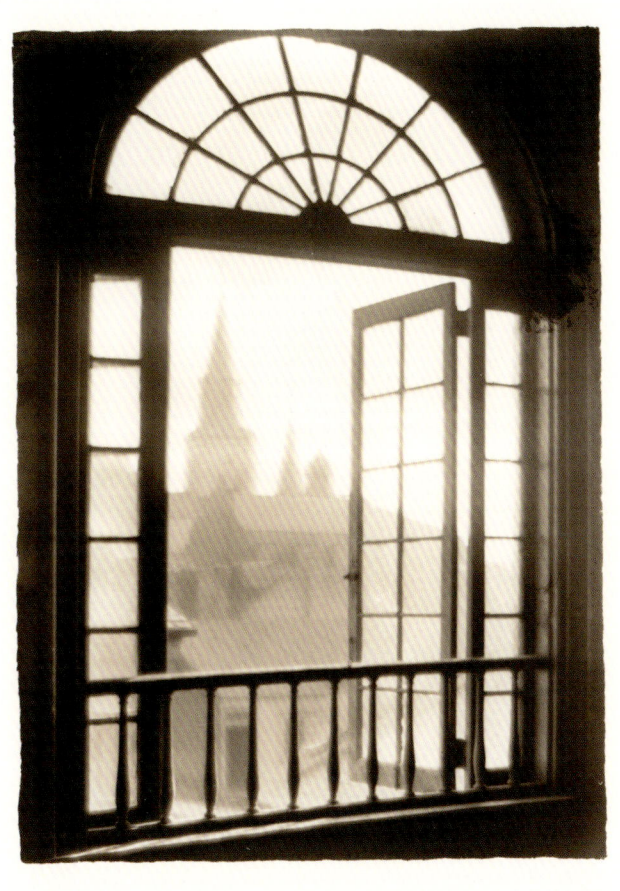

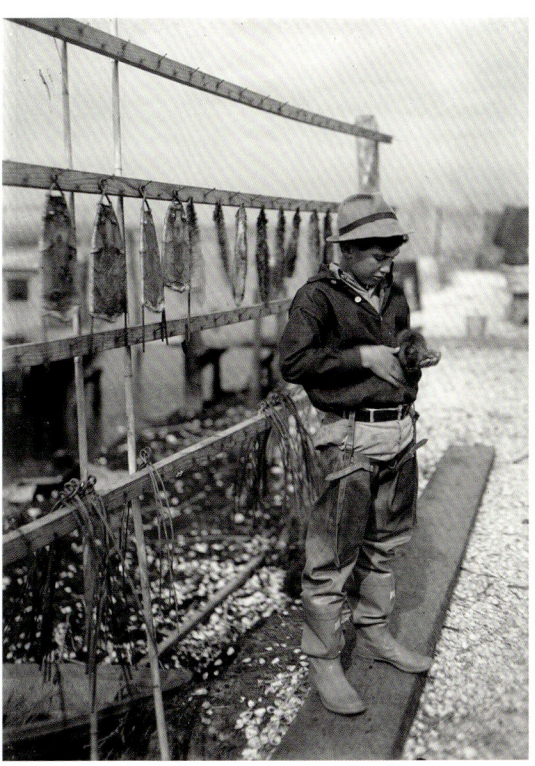

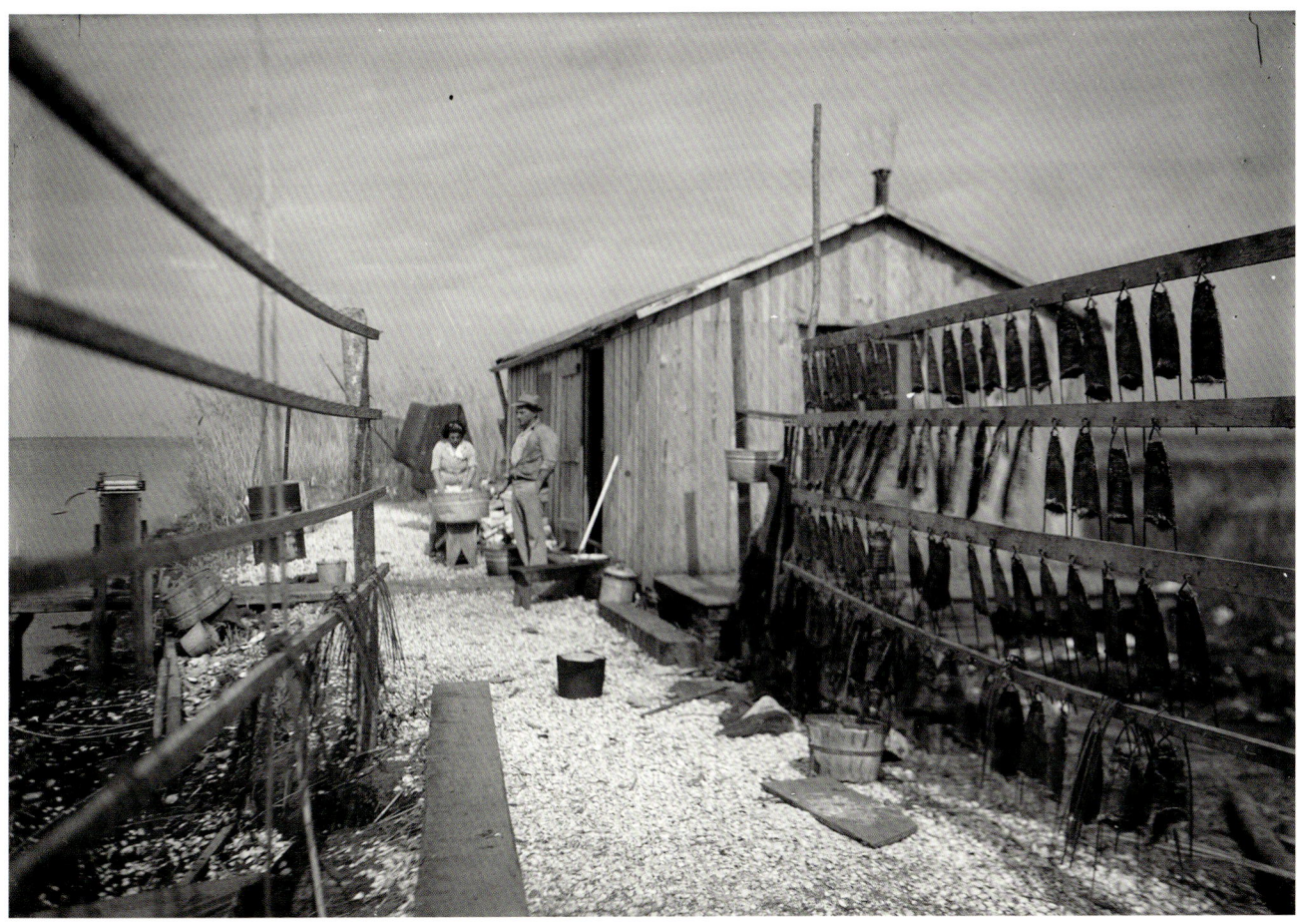

Joseph Woodson "Pops" Whitesell (1876–1958)

Joseph Woodson "Pops" Whitesell came to New Orleans in 1918 from his native Indiana and made the city his home for the next forty years. Whitesell lived in the French Quarter, a locus of bohemian life, residing in and working out of a narrow dependency (or slave quarters) behind an eighteenth-century townhouse on St. Peter Street. Passing through his studio were clientele that ranged from society men and women, young brides, and Mardi Gras royalty, to the photographers, painters, sculptors, writers, and other artists who populated his circle of friends and acquaintances. Many of these creative people were also his French Quarter neighbors. Whitesell's early installation in the firmament of French Quarter characters garnered him inclusion in the 1926 tongue-in-cheek publication *Sherwood Anderson and Other Famous Creoles* by William Spratling and William Faulkner.

This portrait of a neighbor, Isaac Monroe Cline, is a study in contrasts. Not only is the pure line of Cline's profile (from his pants cuffs to the top of his head) an element of visual stability in the chaos on and around his desk, but the chaos itself offers a suggestion of dissonance between the discipline of science (Cline is described as "scientist" in Whitesell's title) and the clutter of the scene, as well as the idea that scientific breakthroughs may well come from seemingly disorganized thoughts.

Cline was a meteorologist, and in an early episode of his professional life he downplayed the warnings that a strong hurricane approaching Galveston, Texas, in September of 1900 was cause for alarm. The storm struck the unprotected and unprepared city directly on September 8, with a loss of many thousands of lives, including Cline's wife and the child she was carrying. When the National Weather Service (NWS) moved its operations from Galveston to New Orleans in 1901, Cline followed.

The lessons Cline learned in 1900 shaped his post-Galveston career; he became an excellent forecaster and an advocate for preparation in the face of extreme weather events. Before retiring from the NWS in 1935, he authored two books; two more followed, about weather events and forecasting. Over the next two decades, he pursued an interest in painting and opened an antiques store, the Art House, on St. Peter Street. Cline died in 1955, three years before his friend Whitesell.

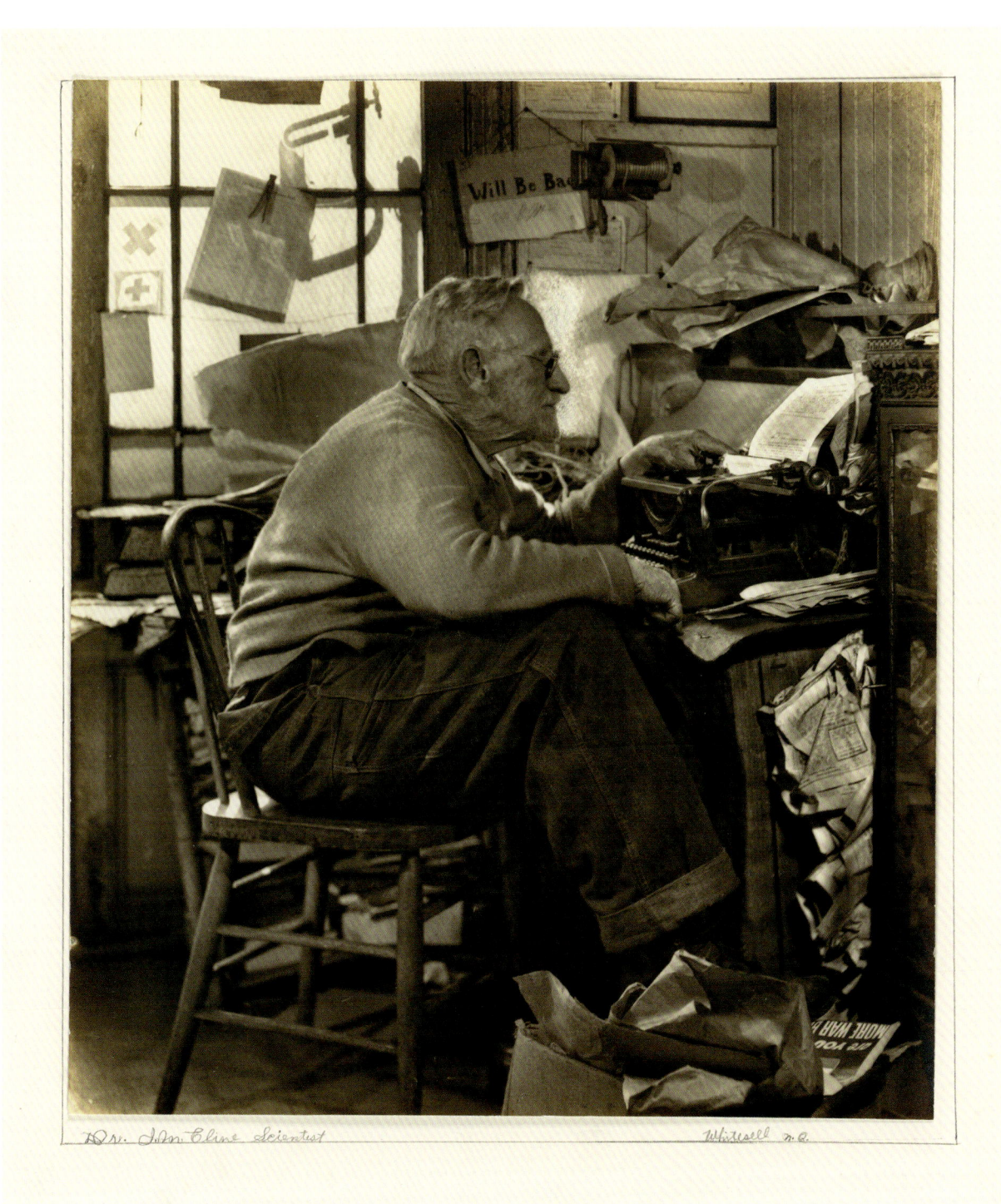

Dr. I. M. Cline, Scientist, between 1945 and 1950
by Joseph Woodson "Pops" Whitesell
gelatin silver print, mounted, 19¹⁵⁄₁₆ × 15⅞ in.
The L. Kemper and Leila Moore Williams Founders Collection,
1957.104.1

Florestine Perrault Collins (1895–1988)

Houses around the world contain boxes and drawers full of photographs, photo albums with carefully mounted pictures, frames displaying photos on desks and walls, and all manner of devices that store image files. All of these containers hold pictures of children. Though ubiquitous, they are often paradoxically private, significant mainly to those who know the subjects. This elegantly composed studio portrait of a young Theodore St. Leger is such a photograph—among many billions preserved in numerous places, both public and private. What parent wouldn't be proud of a child whose picture recorded a singular life event, but also transmitted a seriousness beyond his years? Florestine Perrault Collins's practice thrived on memorializing subjects like young Theodore, dressed for a school play as part of a graduation ceremony.

In 1909 Florestine Perrault began working in a photography studio to help with family expenses. This experience allowed her to learn the technical and business of the trade and led to establishing her own studio, which she initially operated in her home. At the time Perrault took up photography, the field was—like many aspects of life in the United States—segregated racially, and the overwhelming domain of male practitioners. As a Black woman, she fit neither the gender nor race of most of the nation's photography studio owners. Indeed, Perrault (who would later use her husbands' surnames, Bertrand and Collins) was among just 101 women listed as photographers in the 1920 US census.

In a biography of Collins, Arthé A. Anthony avers that societal attitudes toward women working outside of the home, as well as her first husband Eilert Bertrand's wishes for a traditional domestic life, may have hindered her early practice as a photographer. Anthony suggests these mores were involved in limiting Collins mainly to photographing "the domestic world of black Creoles and other African Americans who lived in New Orleans's downtown wards." But by 1923, she was able to establish a dedicated studio for her work on North Claiborne Avenue in one of the city's Black business districts. She later moved to South Rampart Street (another Black commercial neighborhood) and during the 1930s took out numerous advertisements in the *Times-Picayune* and *New Orleans States* for studio assistants and salespeople for her portrait packages. Other ads in 1939 announce the reopening of a newly enlarged business. During World War II, the Collins Studio (as it was known) advertised for receptionists and retouching specialists. In August 1949 the notices in newspapers are of a different character, offering the equipment of the Collins Studio for sale with the note "owner retiring."

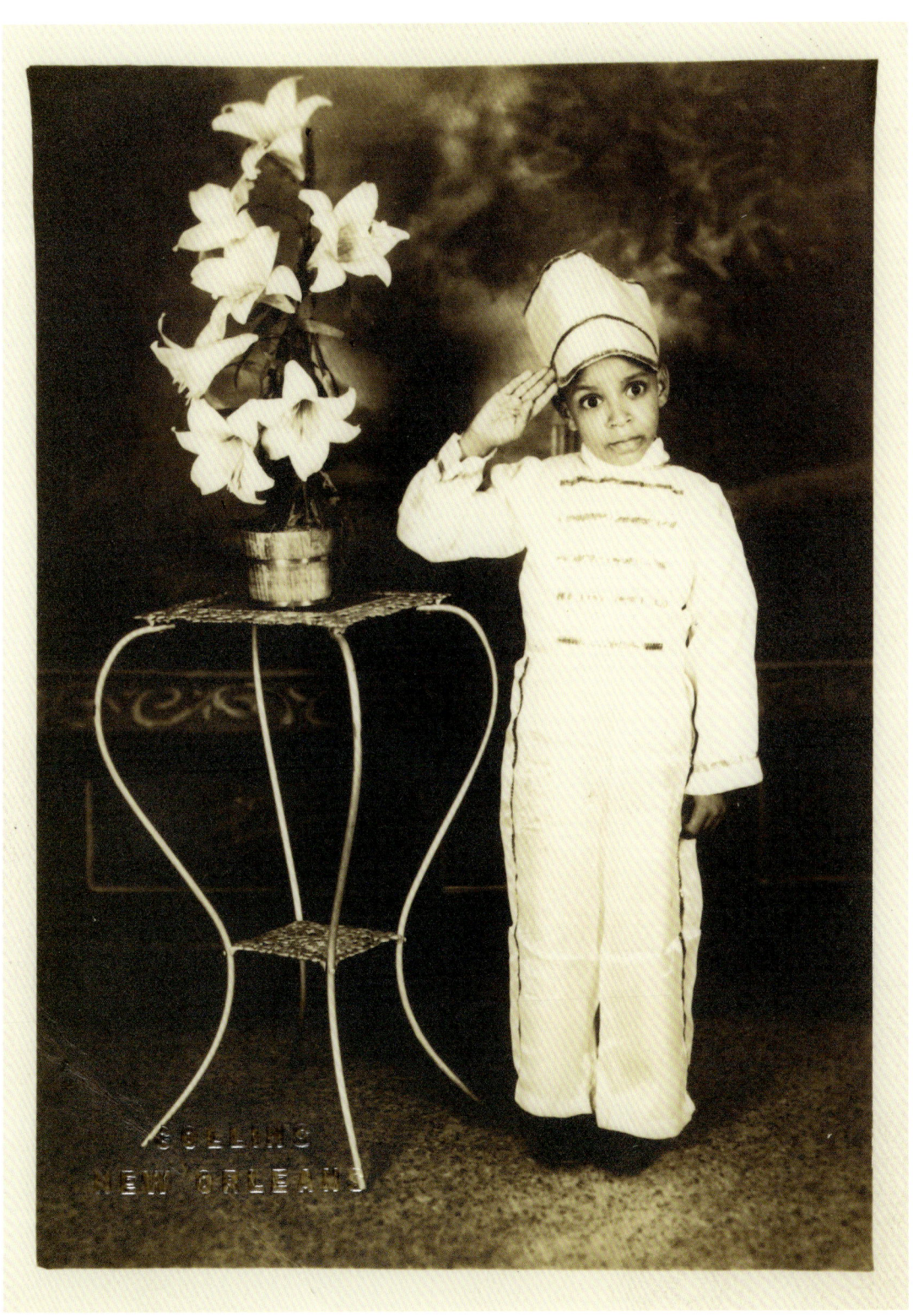

Little Theodore in Soldier Suit in Graduation Play, June 9, 1940, Age 5½ Years

by Florestine Perrault Collins
gelatin silver print, 5⅜ × 3⅜ in.
2001.79.5

Stuart M. Lynn (1906–1997)

Kentuckian Stuart Moore Lynn arrived in New Orleans in the late 1930s and for more than thirty years pursued a photographic career that ranged from architectural subjects and city landmarks to the antiques trade and cemeteries. In 1949 Lynn published a book of pictures—*New Orleans*—that presented the city of his day. This publication contained elements of modern New Orleans and its port, like the streetscape shown here, as well as many references to the city's nineteenth-century architecture and cemeteries.

With Lynn's camera planted at the edge of the Vieux Carré, this photograph shows a glimpse of New Orleans's business district and may be viewed symbolically as looking from the old city toward the new, with its vibrant commercial activity, big hotels, and skyscraper office buildings. The relative tranquility of the scene masks the looming entry of the United States into World War II, when the city would become a hub of activity for fighting that war.

Lynn's technical photographic methods varied little from mainstream commercial practices, and some photographic artists of the era also embraced this approach. Lynn's prints were based on large-format black-and-white negatives, processed and printed to offer a full spectrum of tones from inky black to pure white, and presented on papers that produced a glossy, brilliant surface. This glossy character was achieved through the technique of ferrotyping—squeegeeing a wet print face down on a shiny metal plate (or heated metal drum). After drying in this manner, the print popped free from the metal surface, having achieved a very smooth and reflective surface. Such high-gloss prints presented the maximum amount of detail contained in the negative and were the choice for photographs meant to be reproduced in books, magazines, and newspapers.

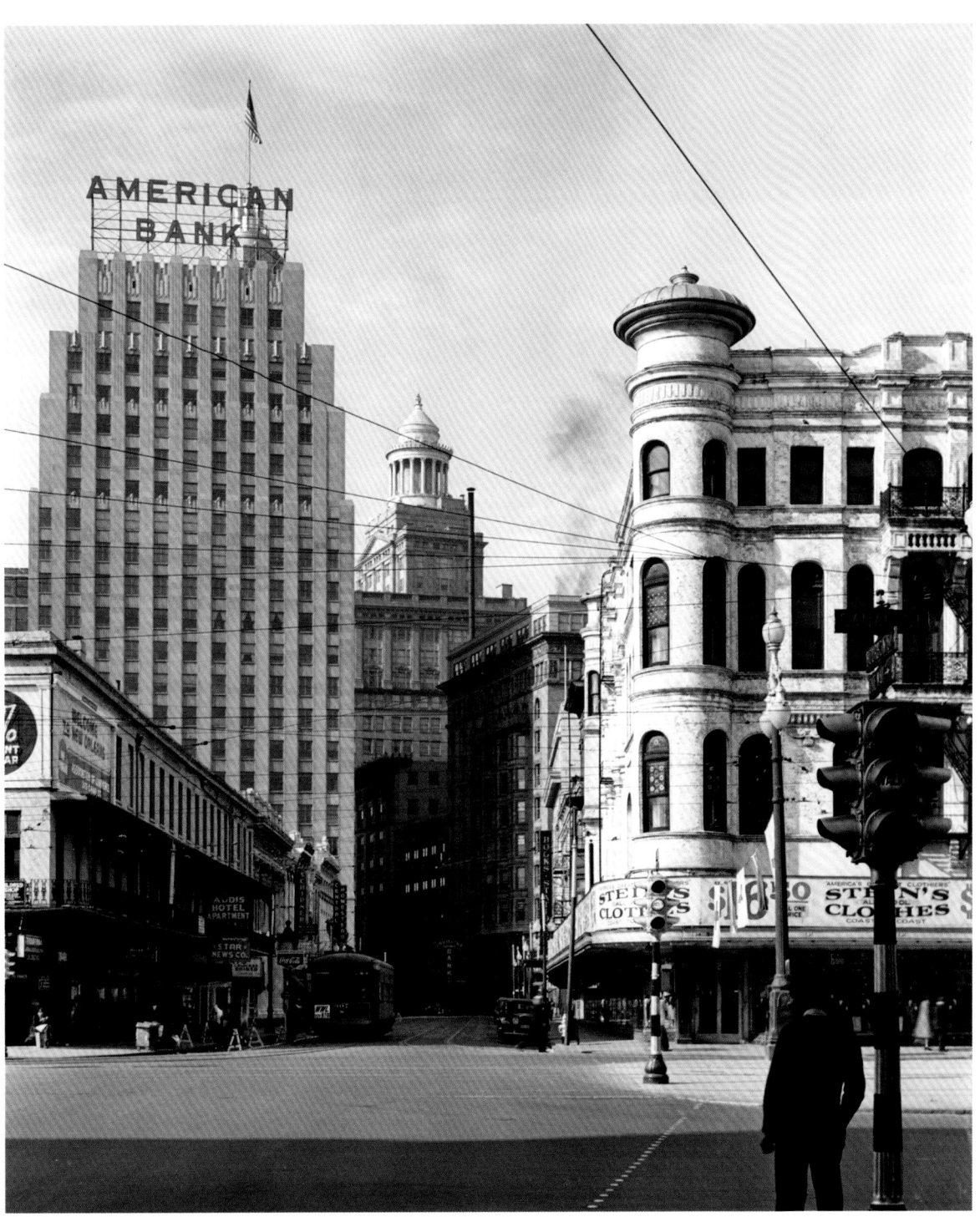

View of Canal and Carondelet Streets, 1941
by Stuart M. Lynn
gelatin silver print, 10 × 8⅛ in.
gift of Stuart M. Lynn, 1978.102.1

Clarence John Laughlin (1905–1985)

Clarence John Laughlin began photographing creatively about 1932, with the desire to use the pictures as a means of illustrating his poetry and fiction. Before the US entry into World War II, Laughlin had worked as a photographer for the Army Corps of Engineers, had a one-man exhibition at the Isaac Delgado Museum of Art in New Orleans and another at the Julien Levy Gallery in New York, secured a book contract with Houghton Mifflin Company that resulted in the publishing of *New Orleans and Its Living Past*, and had a tryout as a *Vogue* fashion photographer. A conscientious objector during the war, Laughlin was assigned to a photography unit of the Office of Strategic Services in Washington, DC. After the war, Laughlin's bread and butter as a commercial photographer was making pictures of contemporary architecture of the postwar era. Meanwhile, he pursued his own project focused on Louisiana's crumbling plantation architecture, first published by Scribner's in 1948 under the title *Ghosts along the Mississippi*. From the outset, Laughlin arranged his photographs in thematic categories of his own creation. By the end of his active career in the mid-1960s, this classification included twenty-two distinct groups.

Even a prosaic form like architectural photography could spur Laughlin's thinking in unexpected directions. Two examples shown here were made at Belle Grove plantation, an abandoned complex on Bayou Lafourche near White Castle, Louisiana. One is a "straight" photograph of the conditions presented to Laughlin and his camera: a hulk of a building— one of the largest plantation manor houses of the nineteenth century—deteriorating almost before his eyes, yet still an architectural presence receding behind a scrim of Spanish moss. The photograph is one of several hundred plantation buildings and sites that Laughlin began photographing in the mid-1930s, and the series provides the foundational basis for the one hundred pictures included in *Ghosts*.

Without moving his camera position very much, Laughlin recasts this scene in the second picture, incorporating many of the same elements. In this view the architecture becomes a stage set for the draped figures, a symbolic personification of the past. Such apparitions are found principally in another of Laughlin's series, *Poems of the Inner World*, which began as a reaction to the start of World War II in Europe in the fall of 1939—though as in this example, the mysterious figures sometimes appear in other series.

Well armed with an imagination and facility with words that served his particular approach to photography, Laughlin explored buildings and cemeteries of an earlier era with what he saw as their metaphorical underpinnings providing a portal to the subconscious mind. To accompany his more elliptical photographs, Laughlin wrote captions that encouraged viewers to see what the picture represented in symbolic terms. His comment on *Farewell to the Past, Number Three* is "The feeling of tragic farewell is intensified by an increase in the number of hands." This type of work was self-directed and self-funded, as were portraits like *"Mother" Brown*. The projects he pursued mixed the corporeal, photographable world with elements of fantasy, providing a runway for his imagination. Laughlin's captions helped the viewer's own thoughts gain speed until they took off in a flight of fancy, or insight.

Laughlin rarely received commissions for portraits, but he sought out or stumbled across subjects he thought would render compelling, even symbolic, photographs. In his hierarchy of classification, these portraits were usually placed in one of two categories: *Visual Poems* or *Images of the Lost*. The portrait here is from the latter category. For Laughlin, the term "lost" was very broad but had implications of the subject being lost in the world, not fitting in, or being out of sync with time. It carried a physical meaning as well as a psychological one.

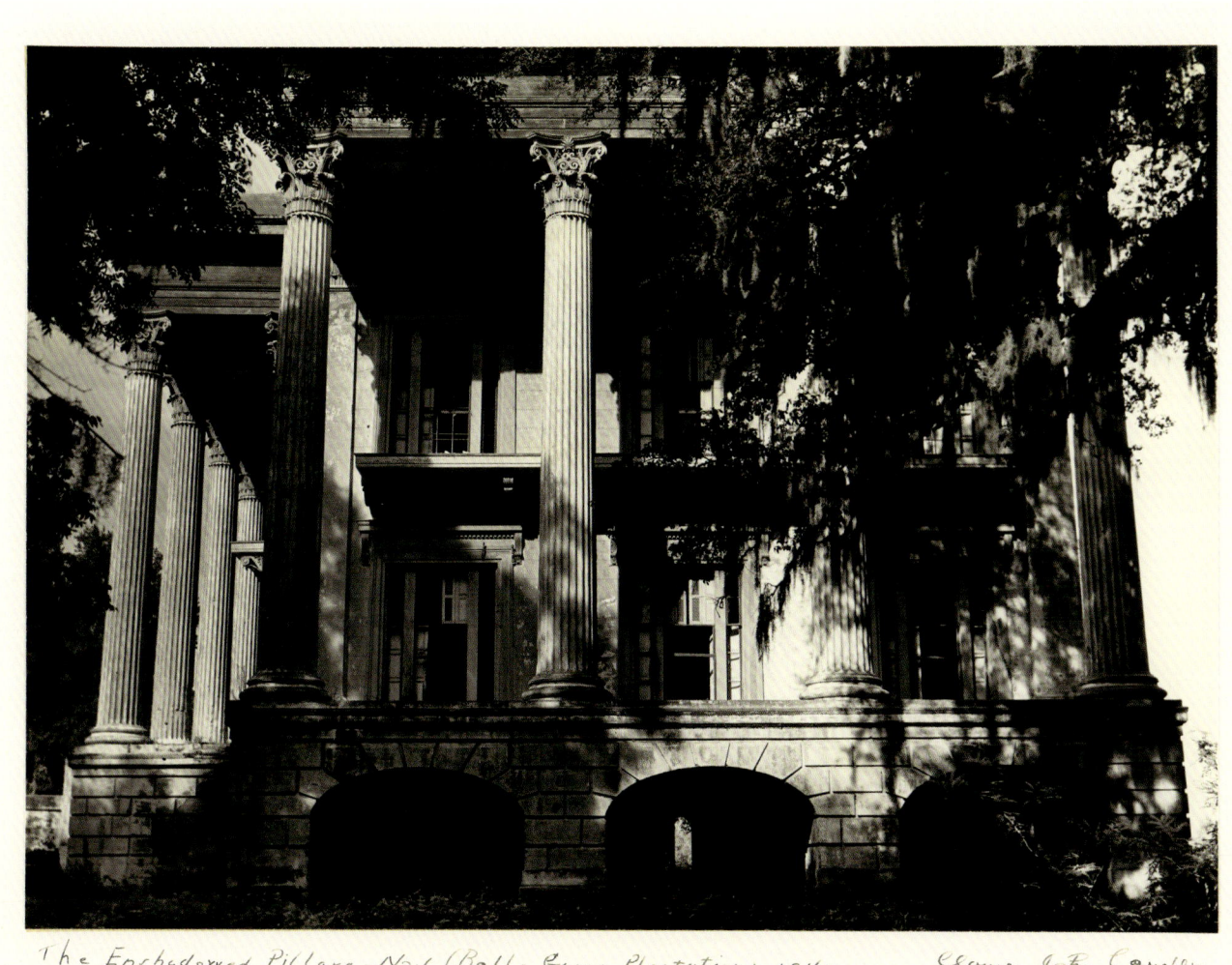

The Enshadowed Pillars—No. 1 (Belle Grove Plantation),
1940

by Clarence John Laughlin
gelatin silver print, mounted, 14 × 17 in.
gift of WDSU-TV, 1985.131.3

The dignified subject of the portrait at right is identified by Laughlin as "Mother" Brown, the leader of a religious congregation that worshiped in St. Daniel's Spiritual Temple, the building against which she stands. Located at 1117 Loyola Avenue, it was heavily damaged by fire in 1953, a condition Laughlin also recorded in a different photograph. The site is now subsumed by the roads and elevated highways flanking the New Orleans Union Passenger Terminal, which opened in 1954.

This particular print is presented in Laughlin's preferred exhibition style: a lacquered print dry-mounted to a stiff board, signed and titled at the lower margin. Like other Laughlin photographs, its back displays his coded information about the negative and print processing.

The photograph is from a portfolio of images that Laughlin sold to Kemper and Leila Williams, the founders of The Historic New Orleans Collection, and is one of the few documentable acquisitions of photographs made by the couple in establishing the content of The Historic New Orleans Collection. Unlike other artists' practice of selling portfolios that consisted of the same set of photographs, Laughlin allowed his clients to select twelve prints from his work. He then prepared the photographs and presented them to the buyer in a cloth-covered case with a letterpress sheet that recapped highlights of Laughlin's career to that point.

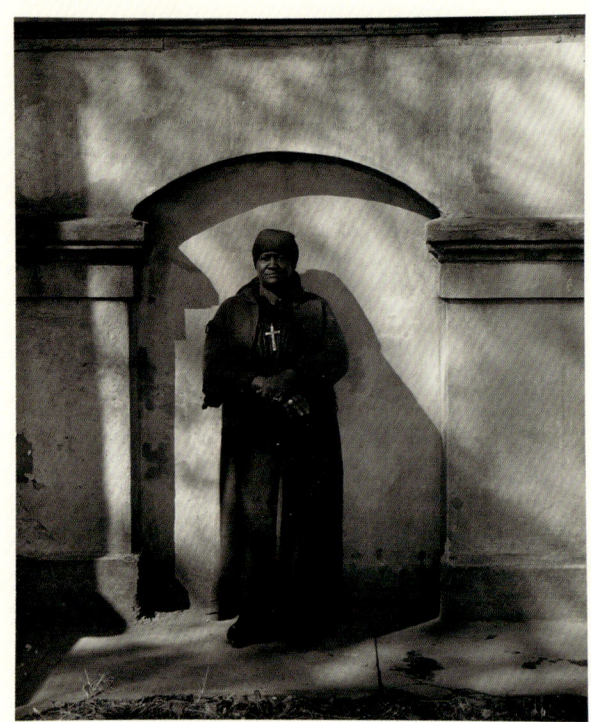

"Mother" Brown, 1945
by Clarence John Laughlin
gelatin silver print, mounted, 17 × 14 in.
The L. Kemper and Leila Moore Williams Founders Collection,
1950.61.295.5

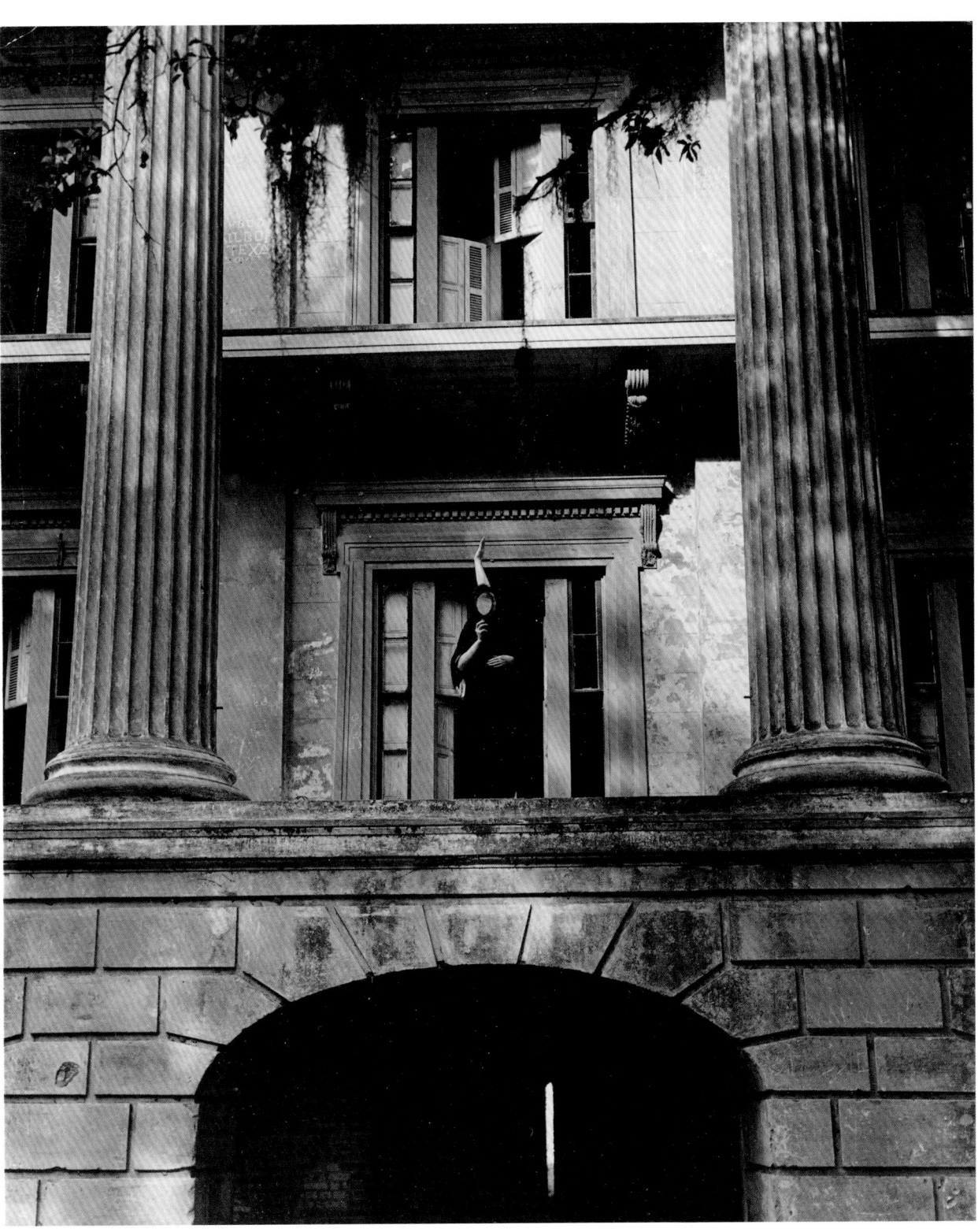

Farewell to the Past, Number Three, 1940
by Clarence John Laughlin
gelatin silver print, 7⅞ × 9¾ in.
*The Clarence John Laughlin Archive at The Historic New Orleans
Collection, 1983.47.4.654*
A 1946 gelatin silver print is reproduced.

Todd Webb (1905–2000)

Todd Webb was a photographer for the Standard Oil Project, a globe-spanning post–World War II documentary photo effort meant to show the positive effects of the Standard Oil Company in the communities where it operated. With its sweeping scope and arsenal of photographic talent, the undertaking is sometimes regarded in the same light as the various federal photographic projects of the Great Depression. Indeed, Standard Oil tapped Roy Stryker, the person principally responsible for administering the earlier work, to head its program. Louisiana was one of the hundreds of places documented, and Todd Webb was one of dozens of photographers who participated.

Webb made this photograph in June 1947 in the southwestern Louisiana town of Abbeville, near the Gulf Coast, a region of intense oil exploration and drilling, both on land and offshore. Webb spent a number of weeks in Abbeville that summer while working as a still photographer for *Louisiana Story*, a film by Robert Flaherty that also centered on the oil industry (p. 142).

Among Webb's photographs in Louisiana, this picture seems more overtly socially attuned to its time and place than his images of oil derricks and refineries, the coastal landscape of the oil industry, and outlets for the sale of Standard Oil's products. The scene shows a sharply defined racial separation common during postwar America. The sunlight brilliantly illuminates the principal Roll of Honor—a list of deceased war veterans—that identified white soldiers. Literally in the shadow of this signboard is the smaller, less tidy Roll of Honor for African American soldiers who lost their lives in the same conflicts. Webb's journal of his days in Louisiana (running intermittently from April 1947 through January 1948) contains numerous references to the segregation and racial discrimination that he witnessed.

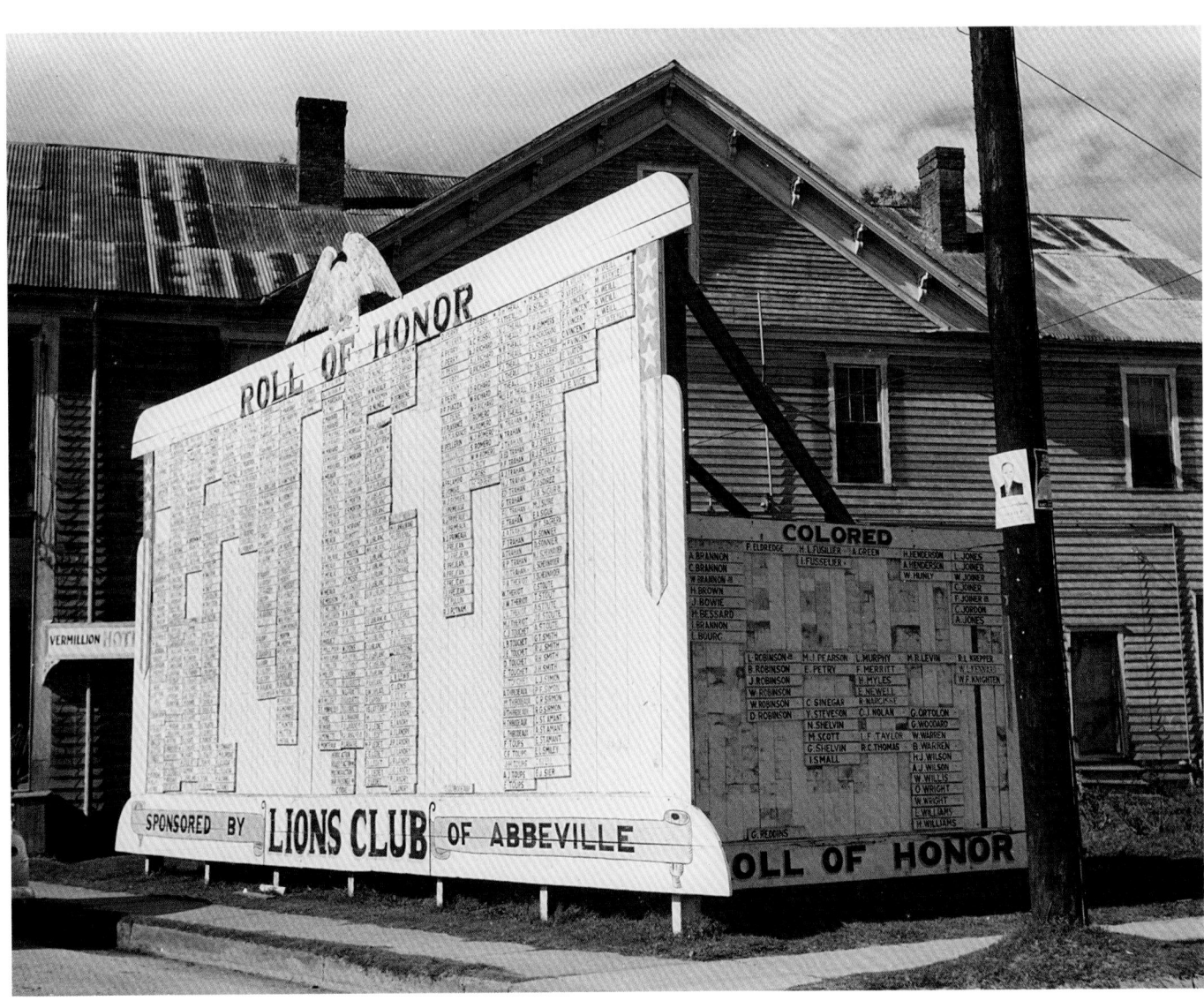

Roll of Honor, Abbeville, Louisiana, 1947

by Todd Webb
gelatin silver print, 7⅛ × 8⅞ in.
1978.90.6, © Todd Webb Archive

Guy Bernard (1905–1982)

In November 1948, when Guy Bernard made this picture, it described a small—even minor—part of the city's skyline, but nonetheless the purposes of the buildings and their finely maintained condition suggest an affirmation of permanence. Over seven decades later, barely a trace of this view survives. Other than the curved roadbed of St. Charles Avenue containing streetcar tracks corralling a circular park, and the elongated onion-domed steeple of St. John the Baptist Catholic Church in the middle-right distance, this viewscape has been obliterated: the double towers of Temple Sinai and the full-service filling station are gone.

When Barthélémy Lafon laid out the street in 1807, the park at the center of the roundabout was called Tivoli Circle. In 1884 it was renamed for Confederate general Robert E. Lee, and a column surmounted by a monumental standing figure of Lee was installed, where it remained for over a century and a quarter. The Lee statue was removed in 2017; in 2022 the city council restored the name Tivoli Circle to the street, and the small park at its center was named Harmony Circle.

Bernard earned an undergraduate degree at New Orleans's Loyola University and a graduate degree from the Eastman School of Music in Rochester, New York. He was a musician and music teacher at Loyola by profession, and a photographer by avocation. Bernard's obituary doesn't mention his activities in that realm, however, despite some of his pictures being published in books devoted to Louisiana historical subjects. It is unknown what compelled him to make this view, but not knowing why it was made doesn't diminish the clear information it displays or its relevance to the collection of a history museum.

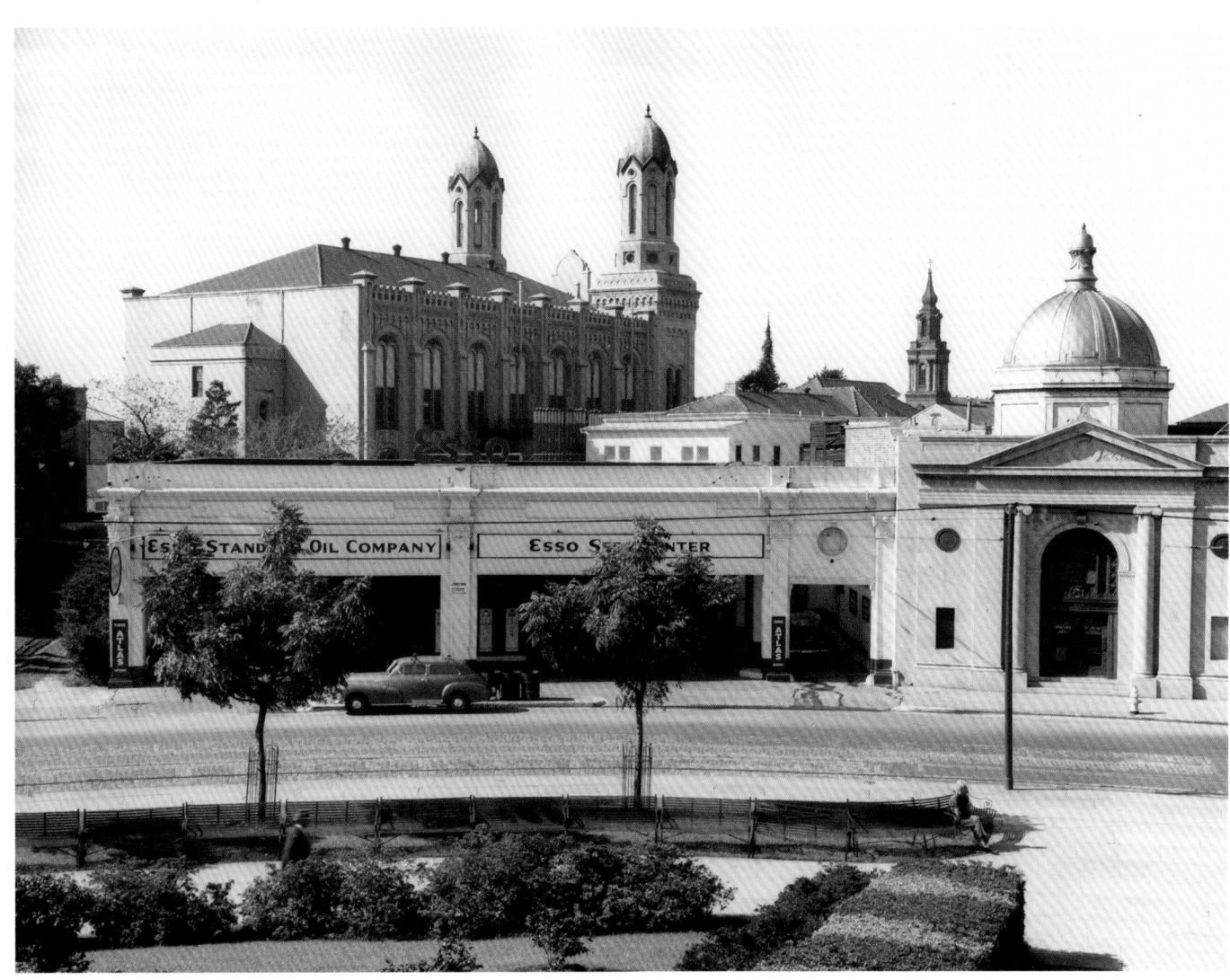

Old Temple Sinai and St. John's Church, 1948
by Guy Bernard
gelatin silver print, 8 × 10⅛ in.
Guy F. Bernard Photographic Archive at the Historic New Orleans
Collection, 2000.46.2.1721

Elemore Madison Morgan Sr. (1903–1966)

On February 20, 1949, Robert Flaherty's award-winning film *Lousiana Story* made its Louisiana premiere at Frank's Theatre in Abbeville. The town's connection to the event was hardly casual. The film's young star, Joseph Boudreaux, was from the area, and other locals, as well as the region itself, were among the prime elements of the film, commissioned by the Standard Oil Company. The film was scripted and shot to show the way that the company's drilling operations could coexist with a community that was largely dependent on natural rhythms of the seasons. Flaherty, his wife, Frances (who cowrote the script), and members of the crew lived in Abbeville during the filming.

Elemore Morgan's photograph of the assembled crowd, many of them dressed in their Sunday best, suggests the importance of the event. This photograph and dozens of others were reproduced in *All This Is Louisiana*, a paean to the state by popular novelist Frances Parkinson Keyes, published in 1950.

After occupations as a draftsman and tire store owner, Morgan operated his photography business from Baton Rouge. For nearly a quarter of a century, he made pictures of clarity, restraint, and documentary richness. Harnett T. Kane's *Bayous of Louisiana* (1943) contains some of Morgan's earliest work. Beginning in 1951 and for many years following, he was the principal photographer for the Louisiana Forestry Association's trade publication, *Forests and People*, and he traveled the state, photographing industry activities. Other publications that display his talent are *The Sixties Ended It: A Book of Architectural Photographs* (1959) and *The Face of Louisiana* (1969), published posthumously.

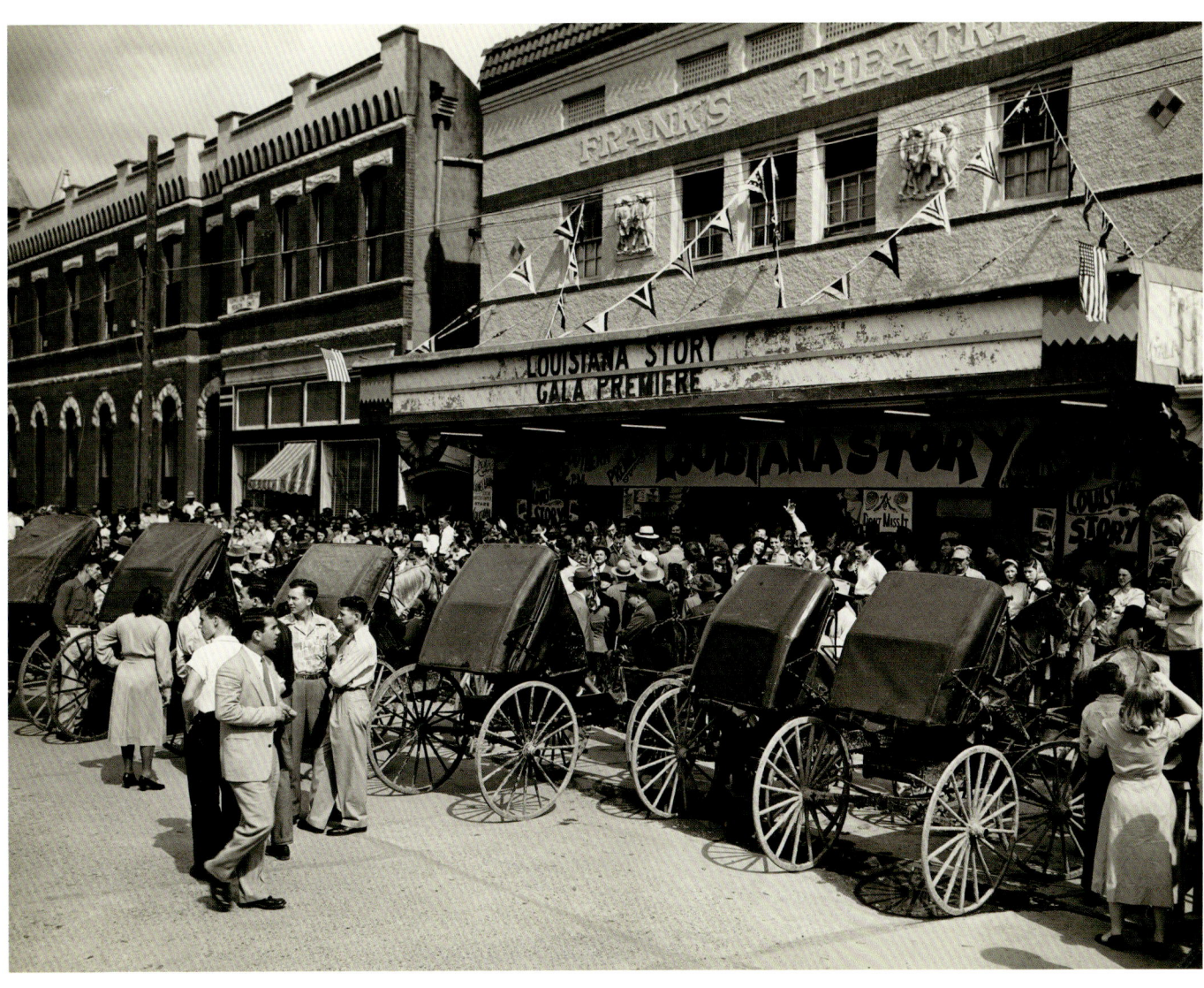

Buggies parked in front of Frank's Theatre, Abbeville, showing *Louisiana Story*, 1949

by Elemore Madison Morgan Sr.
gelatin silver print, 8 × 10 in.
gift of Leonard V. Huber, 1976.139.125, © Elemore Morgan Sr. Estate

Joseph Anthony Lucia Sr. (1914–2002)

Reporter, photographer, editor, publisher: this quartet of roles fit the career (sometimes simultaneously) of Joseph Anthony Lucia Sr. of Lutcher, Louisiana, which began with a part-time job at the *River Parishes Journal* during high school in the early 1930s and continued until 1977. While enrolled at Tulane University, he worked on the *Hullabaloo*, the school's newspaper. Though this marked the start of a longtime career as a journalist and news photographer, he ultimately started a photographic practice in his hometown while maintaining his newspaper job. Lucia served an array of clients seeking advertising pictures; the recording of lifetime milestones like weddings, birthdays, pageants, and important anniversaries; and tracking the region's economic growth through the opening of new schools and businesses. In an era of segregation and Jim Crow legislation, Lucia was the rare white practitioner to serve African American as well as white clients.

Lucia began his full-time journalism career in 1937, the same year he graduated from Tulane University, joining the *Times-Picayune* and reporting on and making photographs for the court and crime beat. Another early platform for his photography was an illustrated quarterly magazine he started, the *St. Jamesian* (the town of Lutcher is in St. James Parish), whose brief publication from 1945 to 1946 spanned six issues. Its publishing calendar made the stories oriented more toward features than hard news. Its recap of social activities in the preceding quarter, along with the advertising in its pages, conveys a flavor of the River Parishes in the immediate postwar years. Though the River Parishes are not far from New Orleans or Baton Rouge, their character is decidedly more rural and small town, as clearly shown in Lucia's photographs.

Lucia's pictures illustrated here reflect the activities of the people he lived among. Even when working at the *Times-Picayune*, he commuted the nearly fifty miles between Lutcher and New Orleans every day. The connection to his birthplace reinforced the communal and familial ties implicit in many of his photographs. Lucia presents the particulars of a place—both the sharp edges and the smooth contours of life—that differ from more populous places but reveal a common desire to mark the moments of importance in any life. Such pictures permit an examination not only of change over time, but of the persistence of traditions.

In 1949 Lucia and two partners purchased a weekly paper, *L'Observateur*, based in St. John the Baptist Parish, just downriver from St. James Parish. In 1959, now the paper's sole owner, Lucia moved its offices from Reserve to LaPlace but continued with his work at the *Picayune*. Five years after his 1977 retirement, Lucia received the Louisiana Press Association's President's Award for his lifetime contributions to the field.

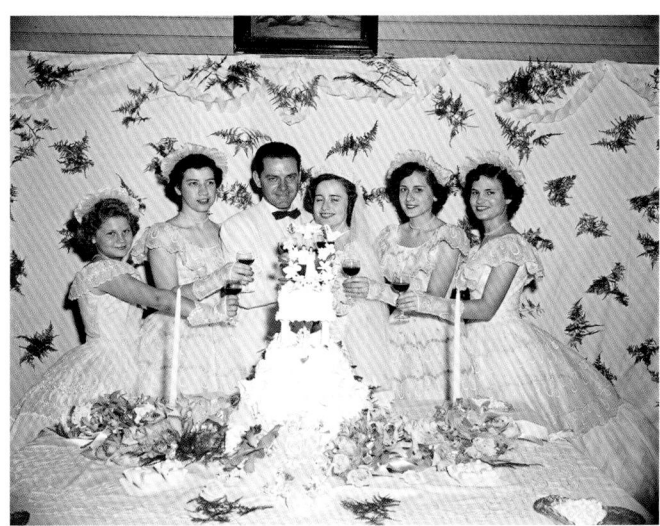

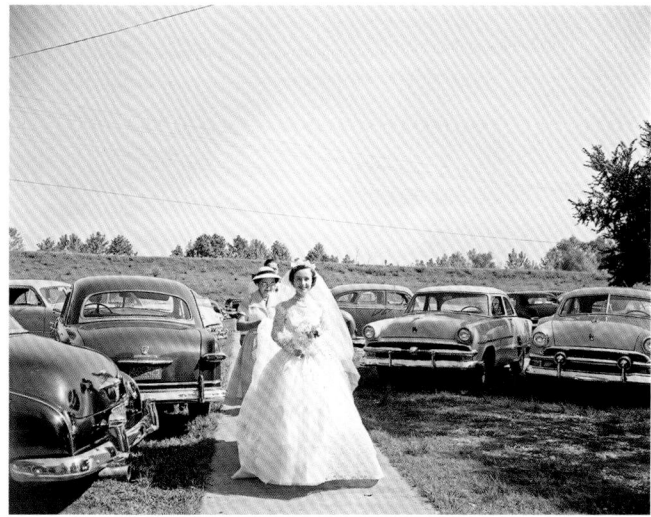

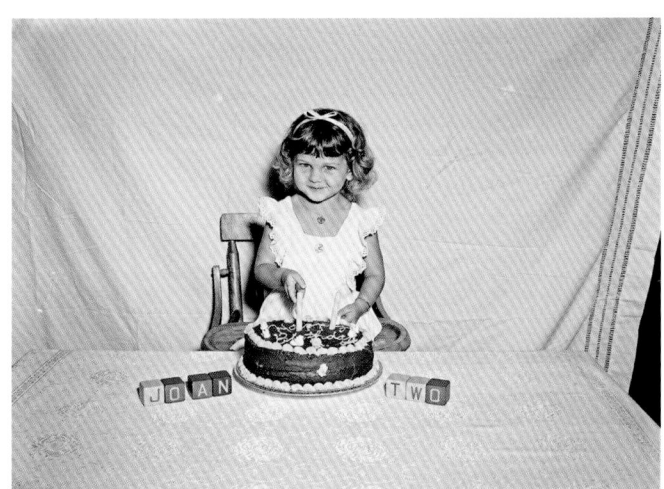

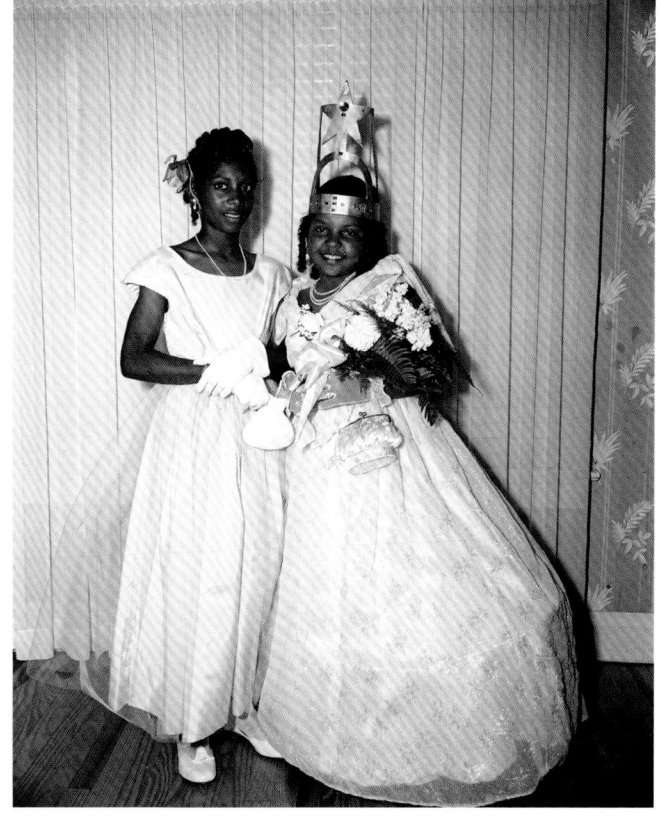

***Borne Wedding*, circa 1954**
by Joseph Anthony Lucia Sr.
gelatin silver negative, 4 × 5 in.
2021.0031.1.1

***Borne Wedding*, circa 1954**
by Joseph Anthony Lucia Sr.
gelatin silver negative, 4 × 5 in.
2021.0031.1.2

***Joan's Birthday*, 1950s**
by Joseph Anthony Lucia Sr.
gelatin silver negative, 4 × 5 in.
2021.0031.1.3

***Julia Parker*, 1950s**
by Joseph Anthony Lucia Sr.
gelatin silver negative, 4 × 5 in.
2021.0031.1.4

Ralston Crawford (1906–1978)

Visual artists often known for works in a single medium sometimes excel in more than one. Ralston Crawford was such an artist, achieving high levels of critical recognition as a painter, draftsman, printmaker, and photographer. The Historic New Orleans Collection is fortunate to hold examples in each of those categories, and photographs (over thirty in all) are the most numerous. Though it could be argued that Crawford was drawn to the tout ensemble of the city, which he first encountered in the late 1920s and to which he frequently returned after the late 1940s, the subjects of cemeteries and jazz musicians stand out among his photographs. During the 1949–50 academic year Crawford taught at Louisiana State University in Baton Rouge, an experience that offered him him regular access to New Orleans. When Crawford was buried, it was in New Orleans's St. Louis No. 3 Cemetery, accompanied by music from jazz musicians he had identified for the occasion, along with a post-burial celebration that he arranged in advance.

The bold composition and contrasting elements of Crawford's photographs such as this one translated well to his lithographs of New Orleans cemeteries. Indeed, parallels among certain of his photographic subjects (ships and docks as well as cemeteries, for example) may be found in his paintings, prints, and drawings. An exception to this "sharing" across media are Crawford's photographs of jazz musicians and the world of funeral and celebratory parades that they often inhabited. These subjects exist only as photographs within his artistic realm.

One role the artist plays through his or her work is presenting to an audience a new, unexpected, or different side of something that they think they already know. The mediation of the artist transforms the subject for the viewer, providing new appreciation, understanding, and insight. In New Orleans, a Catholic city from its outset, generations of New Orleanians have made regular visits to the graveyards, especially on All Saints' Day. But how many of them saw what Crawford presents in this picture: a taut composition of geometric shapes, a study in tonal contrast, and a jumble of shadows that defy simple description?

Cemetery vault with iron fence, 1950s
by Ralston Crawford
gelatin silver print, 10 × 7⅛ in.
1983.33.6 , © 2023 Estate of Ralston Crawford / Licensed by VAGA at Artists Rights Society (ARS), NY

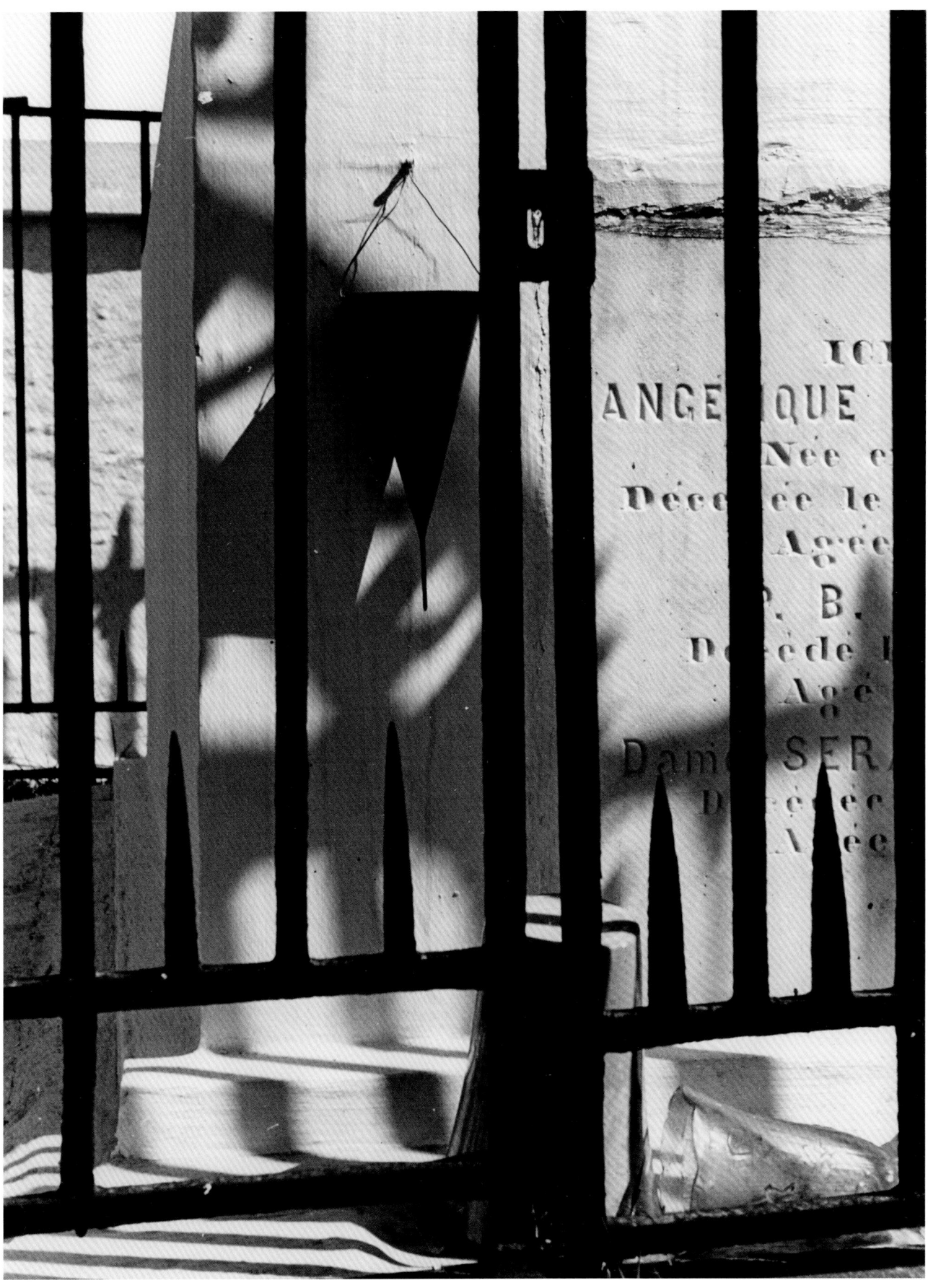

Homer Emory Turner (1898–1981)

One use of photography since its earliest days has been as an aide-mémoire by artists working in other media. Beginning in 1843, David Octavius Hill and Robert Adamson made nearly 500 photographic portraits to assist Hill in creating a massive painting of 470 clergymen establishing the Free Church of Scotland, completed in 1866. Likewise, in 1872 in New Orleans, Victor Pierson and Paul Poincy used portrait photography by Theodore Lilienthal to ensure accurate likenesses in a large painting of the participants in the annual parade of New Orleans firemen. Ralston Crawford made photographs that bear striking resemblances to certain of his prints and paintings. Which brings us to Homer Emory Turner, an American painter of the mid-twentieth century.

A small number of Turner's New Orleans paintings are in the holdings of THNOC. Accompanying them are nearly two hundred color slides that he made of the region in the early 1950s. The photographs here are two views of Canal Street made at night, illuminated by streetlights and electrical signs. The painting Turner executed resembling the photographs shows how he chose to transform what the camera recorded. He compressed the painting's perspective and selectively excluded or included some additional elements. Turner also narrowed the angle of view, choosing a more tunnel-like effect in the painting than the one rendered in the camera's images. While the photographs show no evidence of precipitation, Turner's use of a rain-slicked street provides mirrored reflections of the colored lights, energizing the lower portion of the composition in a way that is absent in the photographs. Though the photos' description of the streetscape gives a sense of a bustling downtown street at night, the painting fairly crackles with that energy.

Turner graduated from Centenary College in Shreveport, Louisiana, in 1918. After a thirty-seven-year career with the federal government, Turner retired in 1959. Upon his death in 1981, the college noted that Turner had been working as a professional artist. The date of materials here suggests he was an active painter for a long period of time.

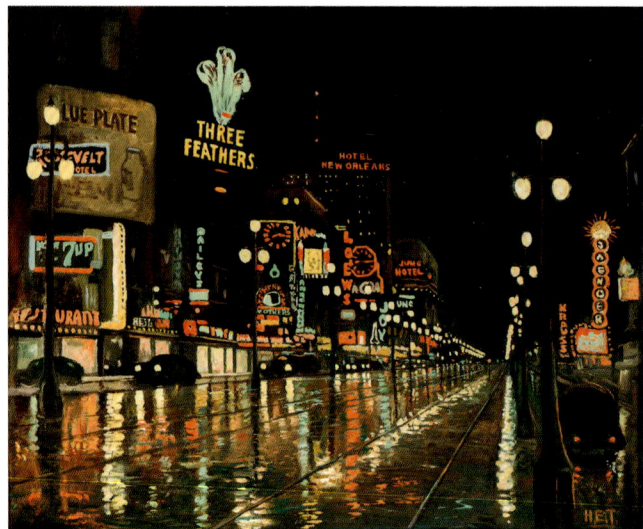

Canal Street at night, circa 1952; by Homer Emory Turner; oil on canvas, 23¹⁄₁₆ × 27 in. (framed dimensions); *gift of Beverly Turner Lynds, 2002.66.1, © Homer Emory Turner*

Two views of Canal Street at night, circa 1952
by Homer Emory Turner
color transparency, 35 mm
gift of Beverly Turner Lynds, 2002.84.105, .108, © Homer Emory Turner

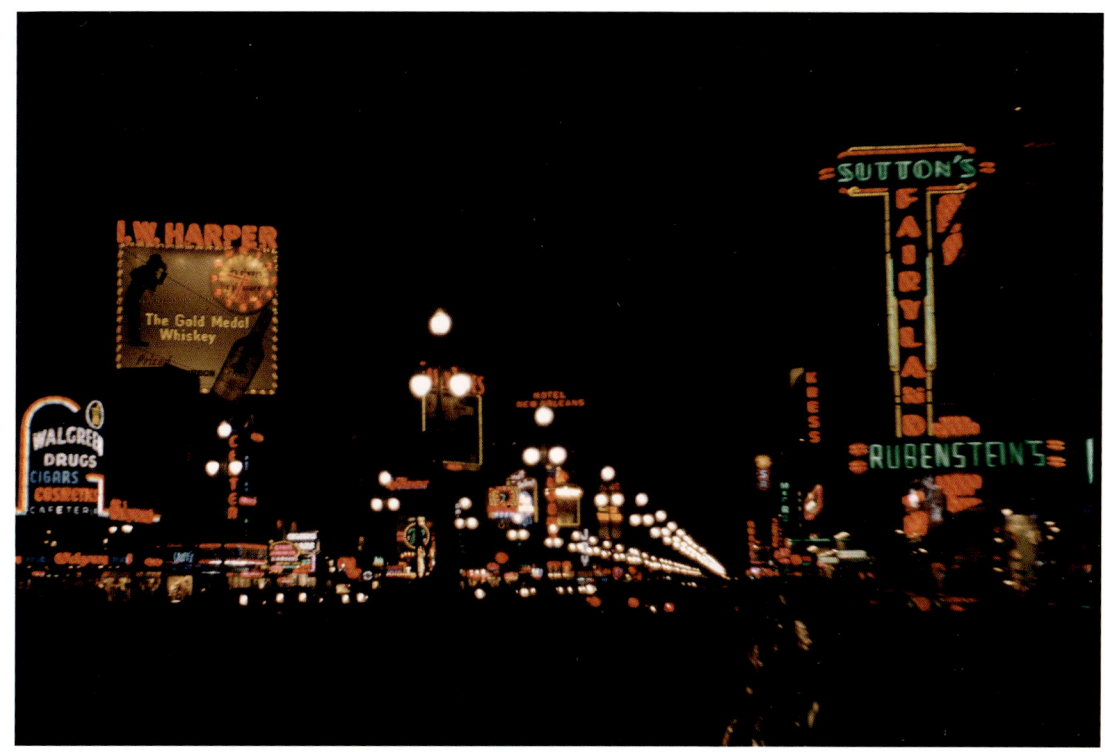

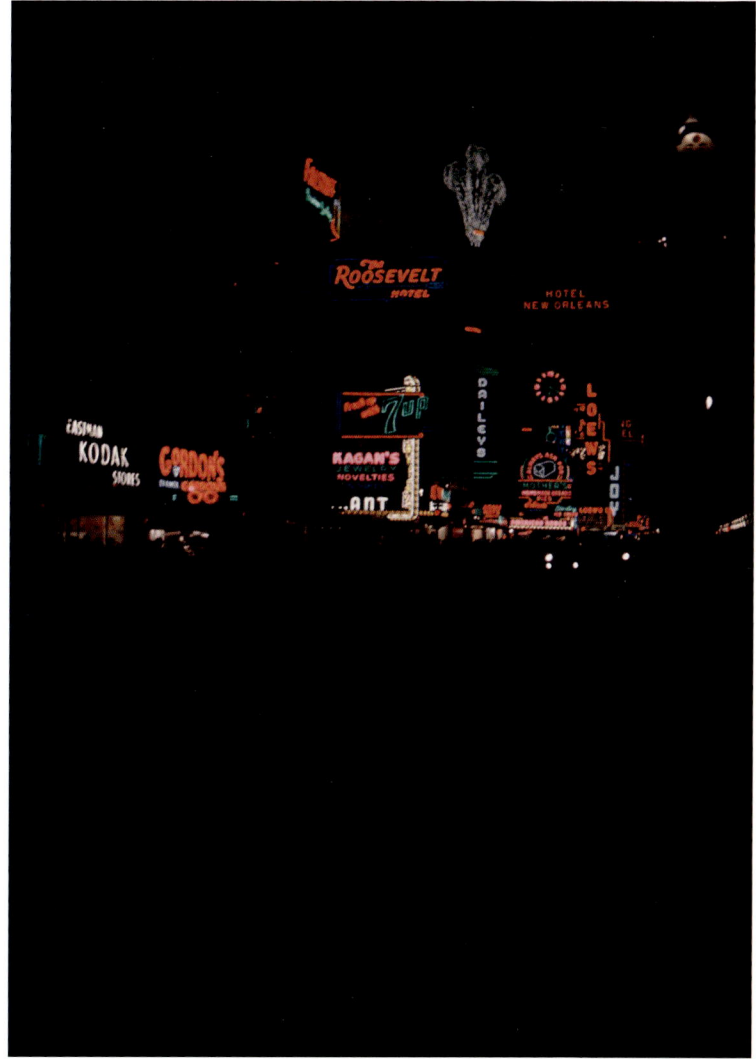

Beatrijs Kuyck-Hechtermans (b. 1931)

Museums and archives, including The Historic New Orleans Collection, are full of letters from all eras of the history they collect. Sometimes a letter is useful or interesting because of the content, sometimes because of who wrote it, or to whom it was addressed. The postage applied to the envelope can also add historical value. The person who completed the delivery is rarely considered. The present photograph gives one letter carrier a face, if not an identification.

To Beatrijs Hechtermans, a young woman from the Netherlands, New Orleans must have appeared quite different from her homeland. The daughter of a Dutch diplomat, Consul General Edmond Louis Hechtermans, she had attended photography classes at the Institute of Design in Chicago just prior to moving to Louisiana. Photographs of that city are in the collection of the Chicago History Museum.

With the loan of a friend's jeep, Hechtermans explored New Orleans on a very intimate scale, photographing much of what she encountered: people, street activities, the river and its batture community, the surrounding countryside, and children, developing the film and making prints in darkroom facilities she had set up.

Regardless of race or class, adult subjects are equally dignified and seem to sense the importance of having their photograph taken. But pictures of children—usually in candid poses, though some as formal portraits—were a favorite subject for her camera as well. The New Orleans public school system, still segregated at that time, illustrated its brochures and annual reports with Hechtermans's photographs, in images that show both sides of the system. Her deft touch with the camera comes through in her photographic technique and communication with the subjects of her portraits, such as this one. She recalls making the photograph on the day he delivered a letter from her husband-to-be.

During her sojourn in New Orleans, Hechtermans met Norcom Jackson Jr. of New Orleans, and the two maintained a friendship by correspondence over time and distance. It was to Jackson that she entrusted the photographs produced in New Orleans, and through his intercession and the generosity of Kuyck-Hechtermans, this archive became part of The Historic New Orleans Collection's holdings.

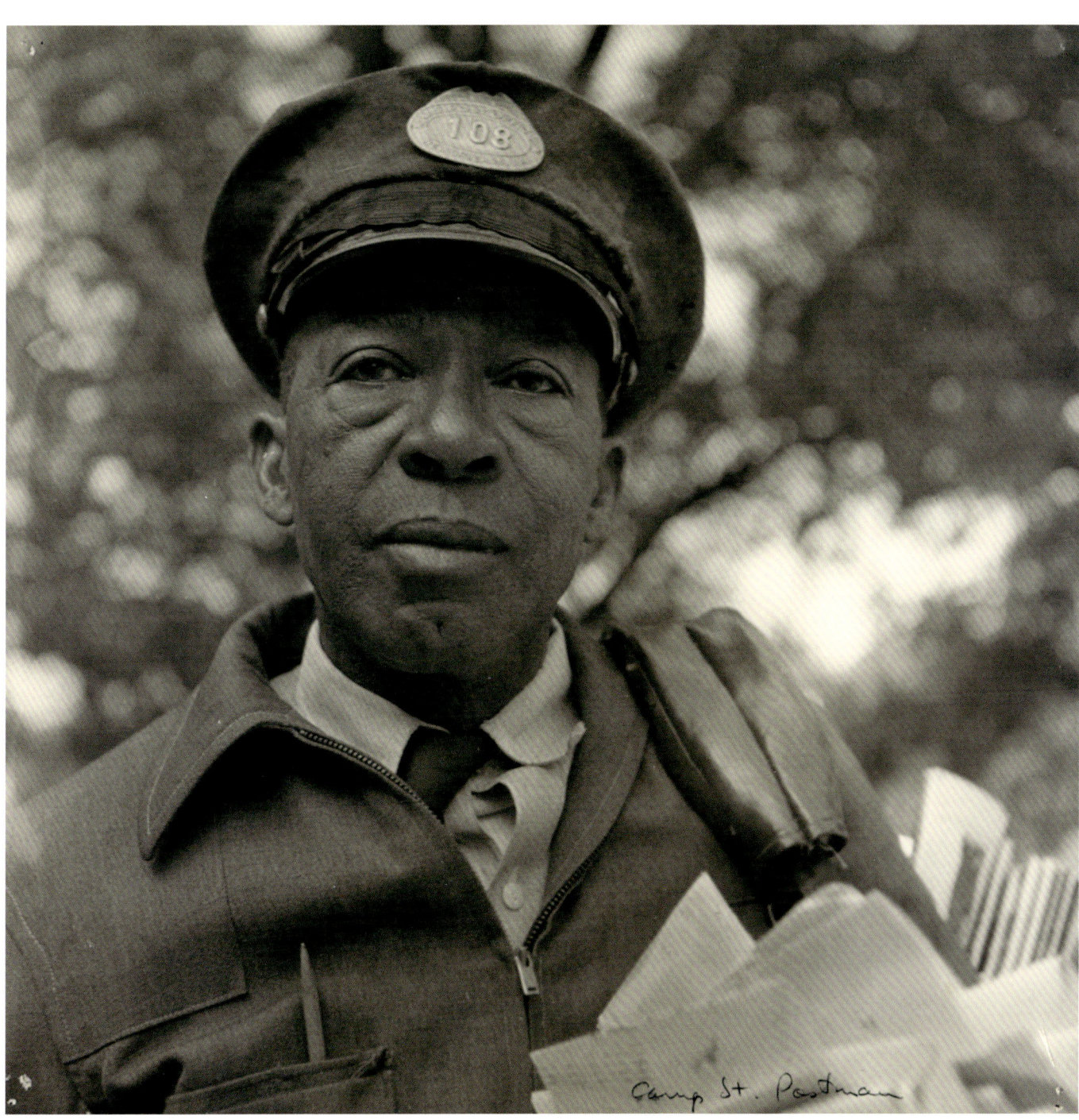

Camp St. Postman

***Camp Street Postman*, 1953**
by Beatrijs Kuyck-Hechtermans
gelatin silver print, 7¼ × 7½ in.
gift of Beatrijs Kuyck-Hechtermans, 2013.0213.2.5

Milton Melton (1916–2011)
Jack Robinson (1928–1997)

Since 1963 the Bourbon Street Awards in the French Quarter have been one of the focal points of New Orleans Mardi Gras. Gay men model their elaborate costumes for the public and a panel of judges. The awards began well after these photographs were made, but even without the incentive of a formal competition, some maskers went all out in designing and fabricating their costumes for a day when expectations were high. These photographs from the 1950s offer two takes on costuming.

Milton Melton's masker walking in the 700 block of Royal Street, near the corner of St. Peter Street, is replete with silver face makeup and a crown surmounted by feathery, palm-like fronds. The backdrop of the laundry business and the front of a 1955 Plymouth add a note of the everyday as counterpoint to the fantasy of both Mardi Gras in general and the masker in particular. Melton was a French Quarter resident for decades and a dedicated amateur photographer.

A similar casual feeling comes from Jack Robinson's photograph made on Mardi Gras day 1954 in the 300 block of Bourbon Street, but there is the dynamic energy of an ensemble instead of a solitary masker. The group of revelers includes the classic theatrical characters of Harlequin and Pierrot in the center, with others less readily defined. Robinson lived in New Orleans and worked as a graphic artist during the early 1950s. His Mardi Gras photographs are a sort of time capsule, a subject he did not return to after moving to New York in early 1955, where he ultimately became a successful fashion photographer.

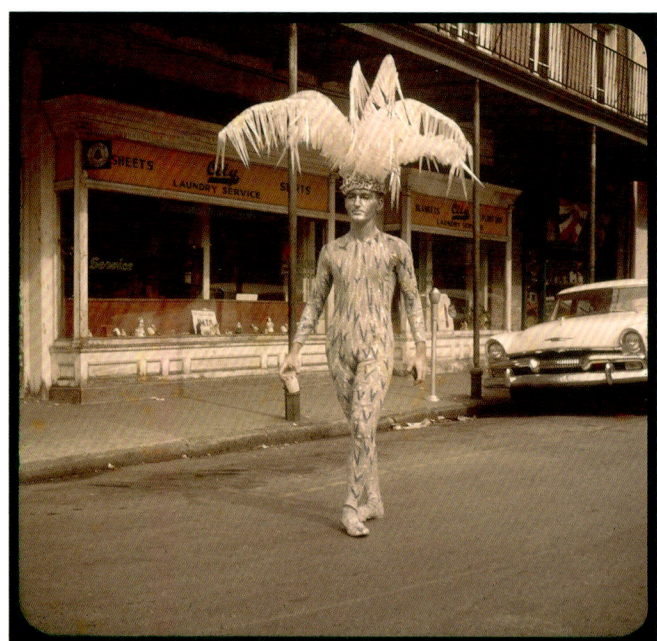

Mardi Gras costume, after 1955
by Milton Melton
color transparency, 2 ¼ × 2 ¼ in.
gift of Stephen Scalia, 2012.0172.8

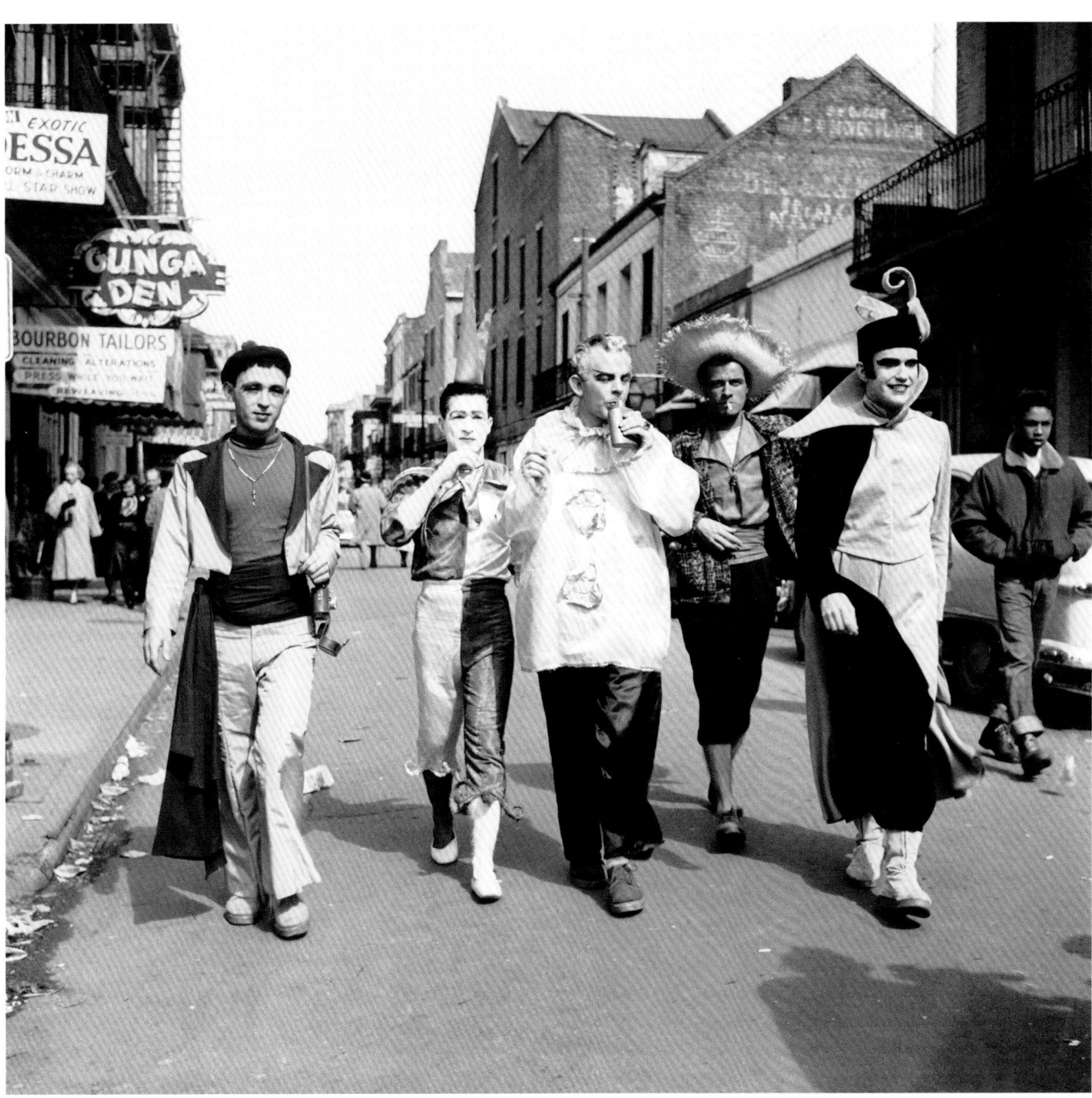

Bourbon Street, 1954
by Jack Robinson
inkjet print, 9¾ × 10 in.
gift of Howard Philips Smith, 2020.0095.1.6, © Jack Robinson, The
Jack Robinson Archive, LLC; www.robinsonarchive.com

The inkjet print was made in 2017 from a 1954 negative.

John Bernard (1916–1993)

The widespread phenomenon of photographing a New Orleans jazz funeral accelerated in the decades after World War II to where it is today, with photographers scattered throughout the throng. Initially, those not associated with the deceased were drawn into the crowd not only because the music carried for blocks but also because white photographers were fascinated by the cultural event so foreign to them. These processions offered a moment to flout segregation, allowing white onlookers a view (if they knew where to look) of African American traditions that were otherwise invisible to them.

In the 1950s, white photographers making such pictures did so for professional reasons as well as personal ones. Ralston Crawford, Florence Mars, and Lee Friedlander visited New Orleans frequently for decades, and significant portions of their work address the street performance of music and other aspects of life as lived by traditional jazzmen. In the early years of these photographers' interest in the subject, Jim Crow laws were still in effect, and associating too closely with the Black musicians they admired constituted a crime.

Businessman Jules Cahn (p. 178) of New Orleans had no professional motive for filming and photographing musicians in such settings. Later photographers Michael P. Smith, Matt Anderson, Christopher Porché West, and Harold Baquet, among others, offered their own takes on the performances at funerals and during social aid and pleasure club parades, as the cast of players and musical styles changed.

John Bernard, a New Yorker who moved to New Orleans in the early 1950s, falls generationally with Cahn, Crawford, and Friedlander. Like Cahn, Bernard (an architect) also photographed funeral and other parades because of personal interest rather than as a profession. The examples here show both a capacity for the individual portrait (trumpeter Thomas Jefferson) during a parade rest as well as the ritualized marching and playing during the parade. That picture shows snare drummer Freddie Kohlman and bass drummer Christopher "Happy" Goldston. Andrew Morgan plays the clarinet.

For over a decade beginning in 1952, Bernard followed the music all over New Orleans and the surrounding area. His dedication, insight, and technical command of the medium embody the best and original meaning of *amateur*.

Andrew Morgan, Freddie Kohlman, and Happy Goldston, 1953
by John Bernard
gelatin silver negative, 2¼ × 2¼ in
The John Bernard Photographic Archive at The Historic New Orleans Collection, 1999.41.1.1.79

Thomas Jefferson, 1955
by John Bernard
gelatin silver negative, 2¼ × 2¼ in.
The John Bernard Photographic Archive at The Historic New Orleans Collection, 1999.41.1.2.82

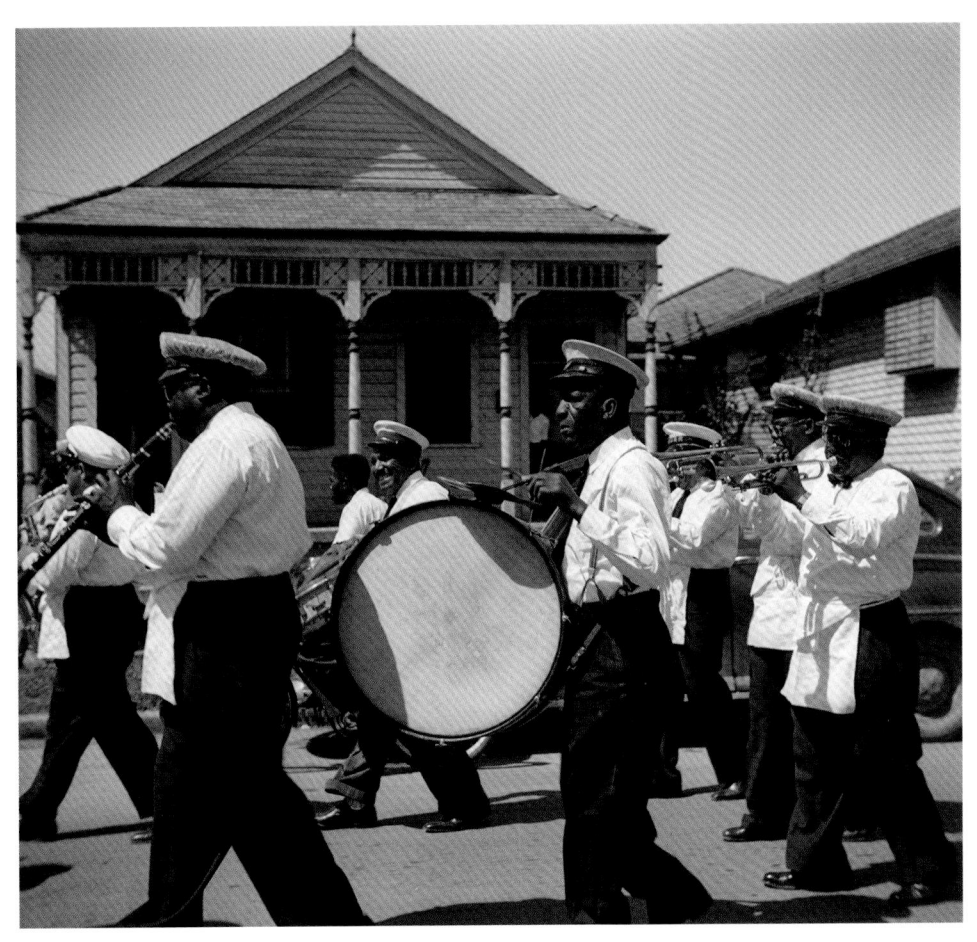

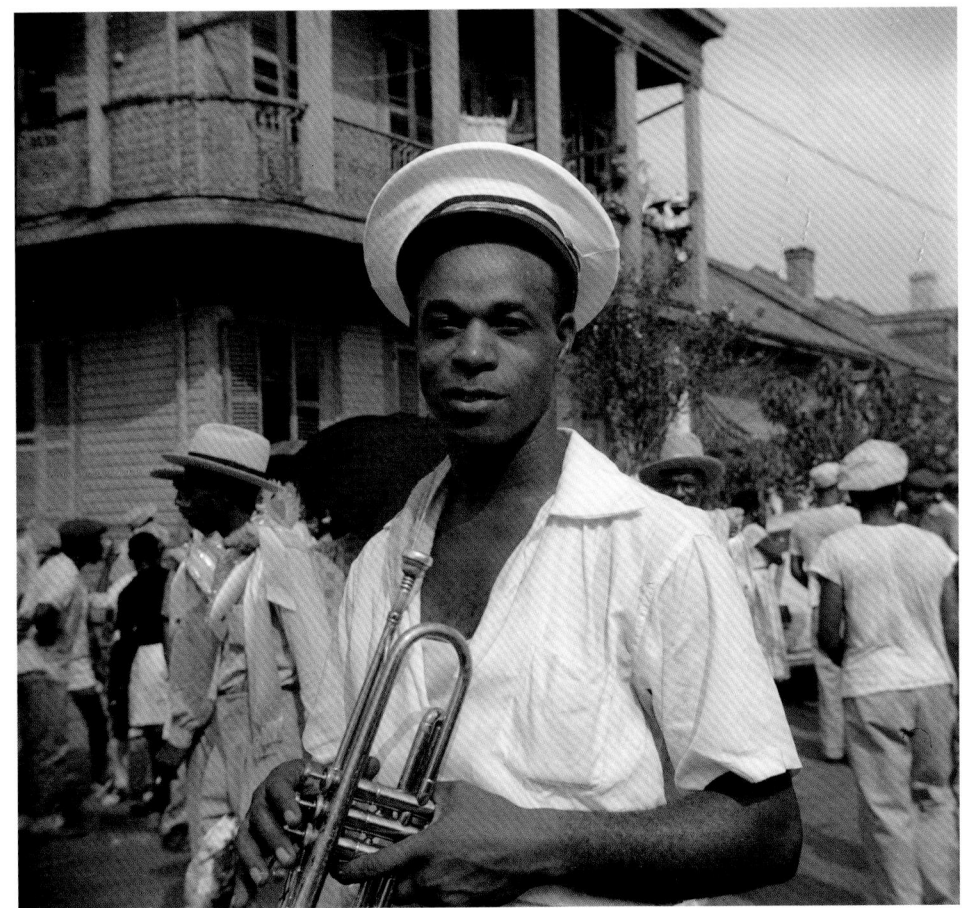

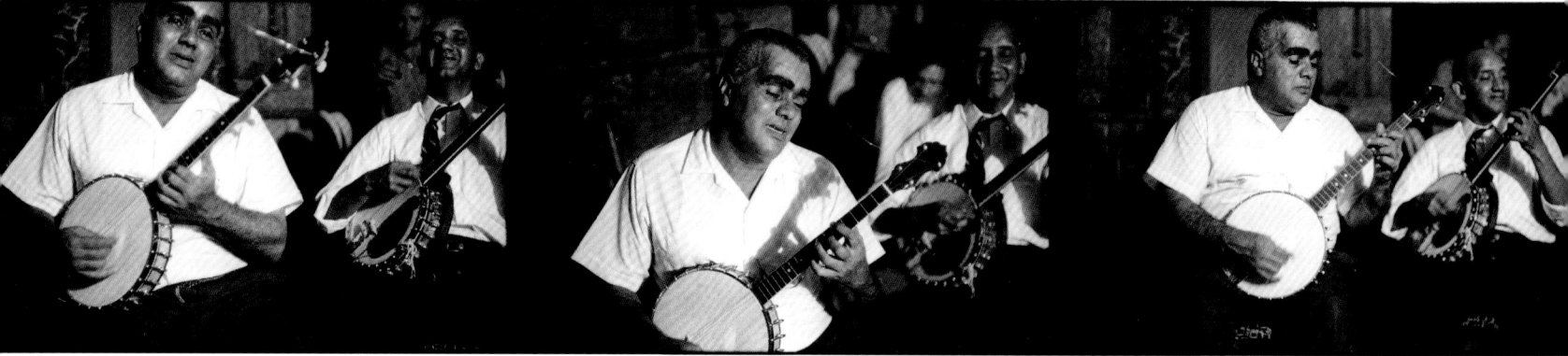

Lyle Bongé (1929–2009)

Contact prints are made by placing negatives directly on the photographic paper without enlargement. Contact prints made from roll film negatives are useful in determining a photographer's approach to the subject, assuming that some adjacent frames are variations on the subject. This strip of six frames of 35 mm film by photographer Lyle Bongé illustrates that point. From left to right, the first three capture banjoists George Guesnon (l.) and Emmanuel "Manny" Sayles (r.), before trombonist Jim Robinson becomes the subject. Bongé then skips to clarinetist Paul D. "Polo" Barnes, before jumping back to Robinson in a wider view that shows the trombone to better advantage, along with the musician's powerful arm and air-filled cheeks.

When Bongé, who lived on the Mississippi Gulf Coast in Biloxi, made these photographs in 1960, he had been a regular presence in the Vieux Carré, especially at Mardi Gras, since 1955. In *The Sleep of Reason: Lyle Bongé's Ultimate Ash-Hauling Mardi Gras Photographs*, James Leo Herlihy describes Bongé's frenetic, amphetamine-fueled approach to photographing revelers on and near Bourbon Street. According to Herlihy, Bongé would work in close quarters and anticipate, recognize,

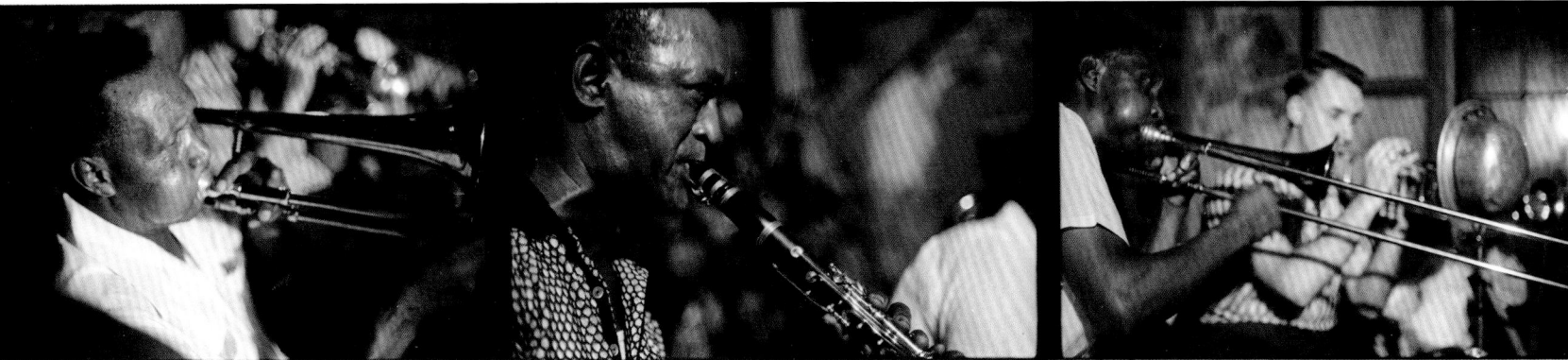

and execute pictures he wanted to make—a streetwise talent
that would come in handy when photographing musicians
performing as well.

The location of the action is the Associated Artists Gallery,
in the 700 block of St. Peter Street in the French Quarter,
which opened in 1954. In addition to displaying art for sale,
founder Larry Borenstein invited jazz musicians to play in the
gallery. Over time, the musical performances eclipsed the
popularity of the artworks on display. The year after Bongé
made these photographs, the gallery became the full-time
music venue Preservation Hall.

Jazz at Larry Borenstein's Associated Artists Gallery, 1960
by Lyle Bongé
gelatin silver negatives, 35 mm
1997.94.51 i-vi

Abbye A. Gorin (1927–2017)

From a steady trickle of immigrants in the 1840s to a torrent following the Civil War, Italians (many from Sicily) came to represent one of the most numerous ethnicities among the city's population. The downriver section of the French Quarter was home to so many Sicilian families in the late nineteenth century, the neighborhood became known as "Little Palermo." This area abutted the fruit and vegetable market, where Italian merchants and purveyors were very visible. Grocery stores, bakeries, and other shops serving the desires of the populace emerged from this setting. Among those operating such a business was Angelo Brocato, born in Cefalù, Sicily, who started an ice cream parlor.

Italian immigrants—especially Sicilians—and the generations that followed them have played a central role in New Orleans's food production, from importing and farming to retail sales and restaurants. The Brocato family and their business hold a prominent place in the continuum of New Orleans culinary history.

Angelo Brocato's Italian Ice Cream Parlor, established in 1905, offered baked goods of their own production, candies and other sweets, coffee service, and perhaps most famously, ice cream and fruit ices made on site. This group portrait with two generations showing mother and sons (Angelo died in 1946), was made in their French Quarter shop at 615–617 Ursulines Street, where mosaic tiles in the sidewalk still mark the "ladies' entrance." Brocato's operated there from 1921 until 1981, when it moved to its present location in the Mid-City neighborhood.

Abbye Gorin photographed for well over half of her life, both in service to the company she and her husband founded, and to explore subjects that fascinated her. Multiple interests, including historic preservation, cultures outside of her own, modern architecture, history, and design informed her photography in varying ways. Her archive is at The Historic New Orleans Collection.

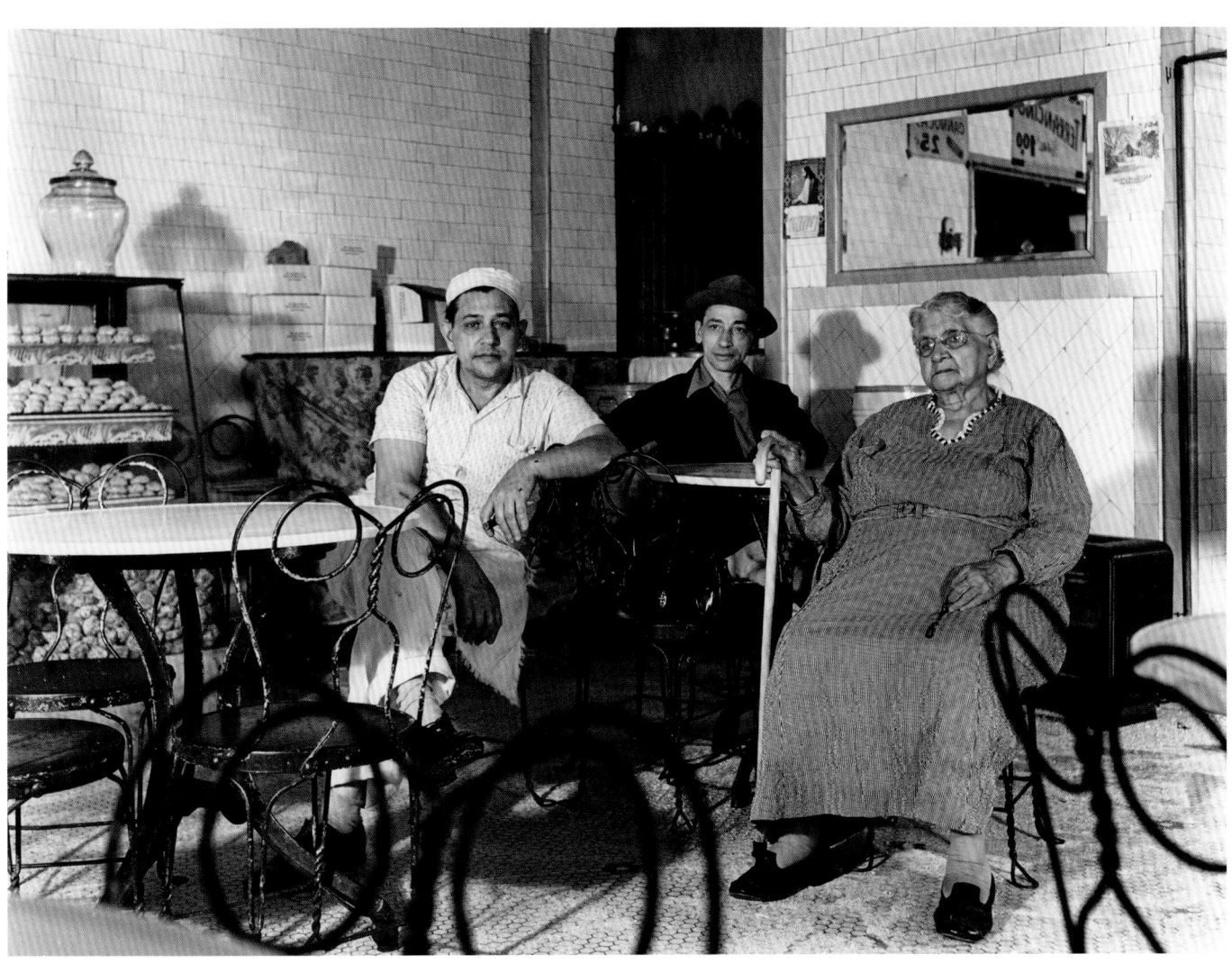

Mama Brocato and Boys, circa 1960
by Abbye A. Gorin
gelatin silver print, 8 × 10 in.
gift of Abbye A. Gorin, 2004.0140.1.1

The gelatin silver print was made in 1984 from a circa 1960 negative.

Maurice Martinez (1934–2022)

Photographers and a photography-consuming public often seem to consider the historical record as comprising only dramatic, singular, or newsworthy events, and however important those might be in aiding the understanding of history, they are not the only means of understanding. The simple and honest acts of everyday routine that are the throughline of living—keeping house, engaging in conversation, or preparing a meal—are worthy subjects but also ubiquitous to the point where photographing them seems unnecessary. This picture counters the fallacy of that thinking.

The maker of this photograph, Maurice Martinez, recalled the details of it vividly: the person is his grandmother, Marie Bousquet Bernard, sweeping the sidewalk in front of her large home, at 1767 North Roman Street in New Orleans's Seventh Ward. He described the activity as a commonplace social event in the neighborhood, during a time when neighbors watched out for neighbors and thought nothing of disciplining other people's children if conditions warranted it. The Roman Grocery, a corner store, anchors the background of the sidewalk vista. One can imagine the critical role that this business played in the neighborhood, serving families and individuals, the young and the old. Sweeping a surface clean is a renewal of sorts, and Martinez opined that an element of religion and forgiveness could be read into this simple act.

Dr. Martinez, a New Orleans native and educator, poet, writer, musician, photographer, and filmmaker, used his cameras as a way of understanding his varied interests in music, history, New Orleans Creoles and their traditions, and the transmission of culture from generation to generation.

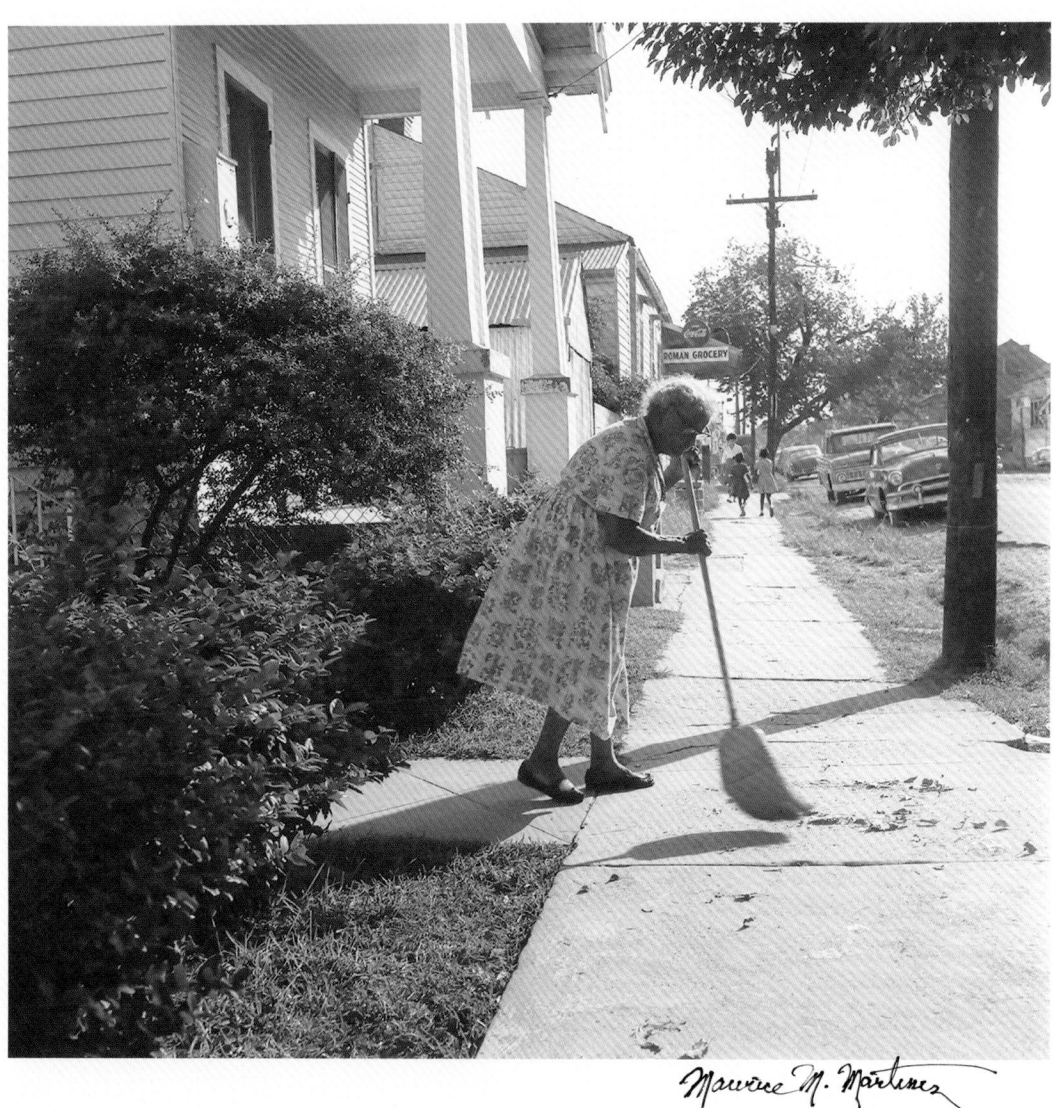

7th Ward, N. Roman Street, after 1961
by Maurice Martinez
inkjet print, 14 × 11 in.
*acquisition made possible by the G. Henry Pierson Jr. Photography
Fund, 2020.0099.1*

The archival inkjet print was made in 2019.

Norman Thomas (life dates unknown)

The rubber stamp on the back of Norman Thomas's photographs identifies him as "Writer-Photojournalist (ASMP), Latin America and Deep South," with an address of 544 St. Peter Street in the Upper Pontalba building, overlooking Jackson Square. The parenthetical notation ASMP identified him as a member of the American Society of Magazine Photographers. Though The Historic New Orleans Collection holds thirty-five photographs of New Orleans scenes made by Thomas, the University of California at Santa Barbara's summary of Thomas's archive in their collection barely mentions New Orleans. Latin America seemed to be his main beat.

The picture here embodies the notion of Bourbon Street as a place apart from other areas of the French Quarter and from New Orleans life in general. The risqué entertainment offered in the legally licensed clubs proved popular with locals as well as visitors but also prompted periodic morality crusades. The group of three well-dressed couples in Thomas's photograph shows a range of reactions from bemusement to active interest.

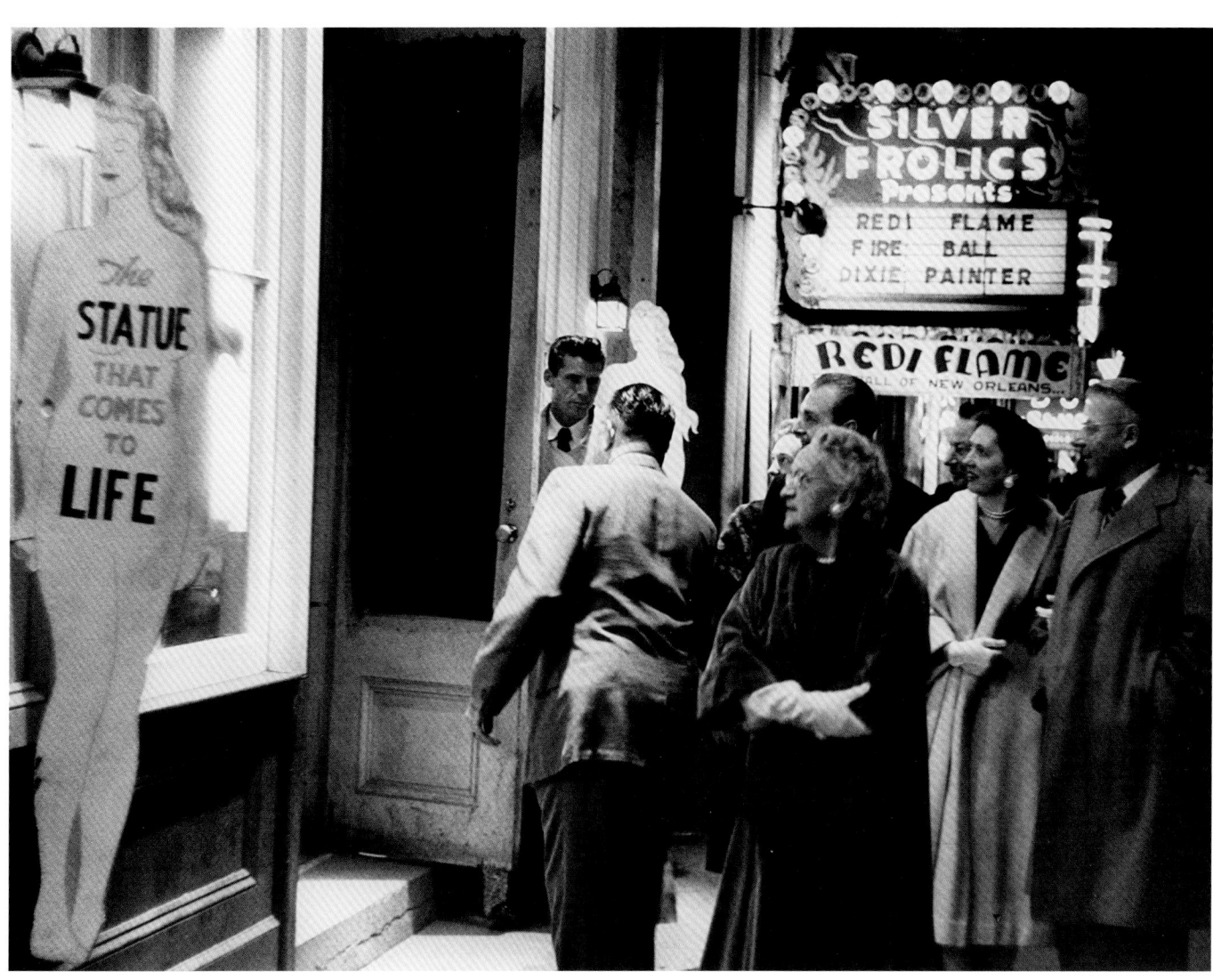

Bourbon Street, between 1961 and 1963

by Norman Thomas
gelatin silver print, 7½ × 9⅜ in.
1998.107.20

Leonard Freed (1929–2006)

Knowing who made this photograph (Leonard Freed) and the general character of what it shows (people in prison), divining its particular subject may not be too difficult: an incarceration system that obviously treated white and Black prisoners quite differently. The disparities between the races—not limited to incarceration—were the subject of Freed's 1969 publication *Black in White America*, an extended photo essay using pictures made between 1963 and 1965.

The back of this photograph is heavily marked with the telltale signs of its history as an object: rubber stamps, assorted manuscript notations, technical photography data, and conflicting print dates—both 1964 and 1965 are given—among them. Another of these markers is a label from the Magnum photo agency (a collective that Leonard Freed joined in 1972), pasted to the mounting board bearing the typewritten inscription "White female means for white women only in the New Orleans prison."

Given the date of the photograph and the appearance of the scene depicted, the photograph was likely made in what was at the time called the Orleans Parish Prison, which opened in 1930. As newer elements were added to the complex, it became referred to as the Old Parish Prison. Examination of the picture's details—concrete walls and ceilings, metal reinforcements riveted to key joints in the walls, double steel doors with observation windows, and the vertical bars that define the farthest distance shown in the picture—all underscore the nature of the facility. The area shown appears to be a treatment room rather than a prison cell. At the time this photograph was made, providing uniforms for women inmates in Orleans Parish was a rather new practice. In a letter from Criminal Sheriff Louis A. Heyd Sr. dated August 20, 1957, reproduced in the pamphlet *Parish Prison Progress, 1954–1958*, Heyd noted that two thousand uniforms had been recently acquired.

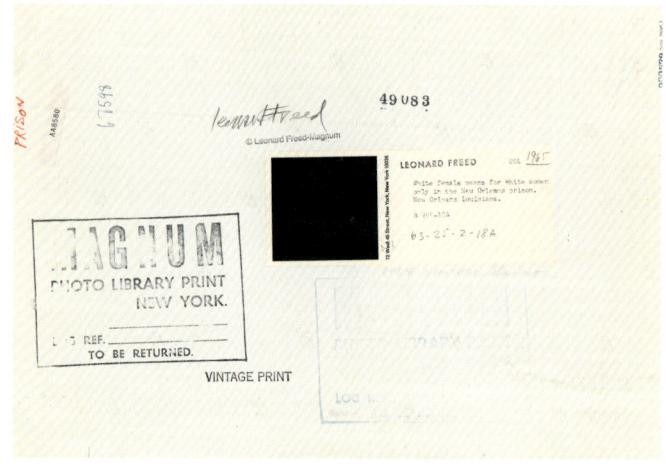

The expressions of the subjects photographed range from stoic and reserved to wary and campy. In isolation, the character of the photograph loses some of its edge. In the context of Freed's book, the differences between the jailed experience of Blacks and whites becomes clear.

Segregated ward in Orleans Parish Prison, 1963
by Leonard Freed
gelatin silver print, 13⅝ × 9¾ in.
2021.0145.1, © Leonard Freed / Magnum Photos

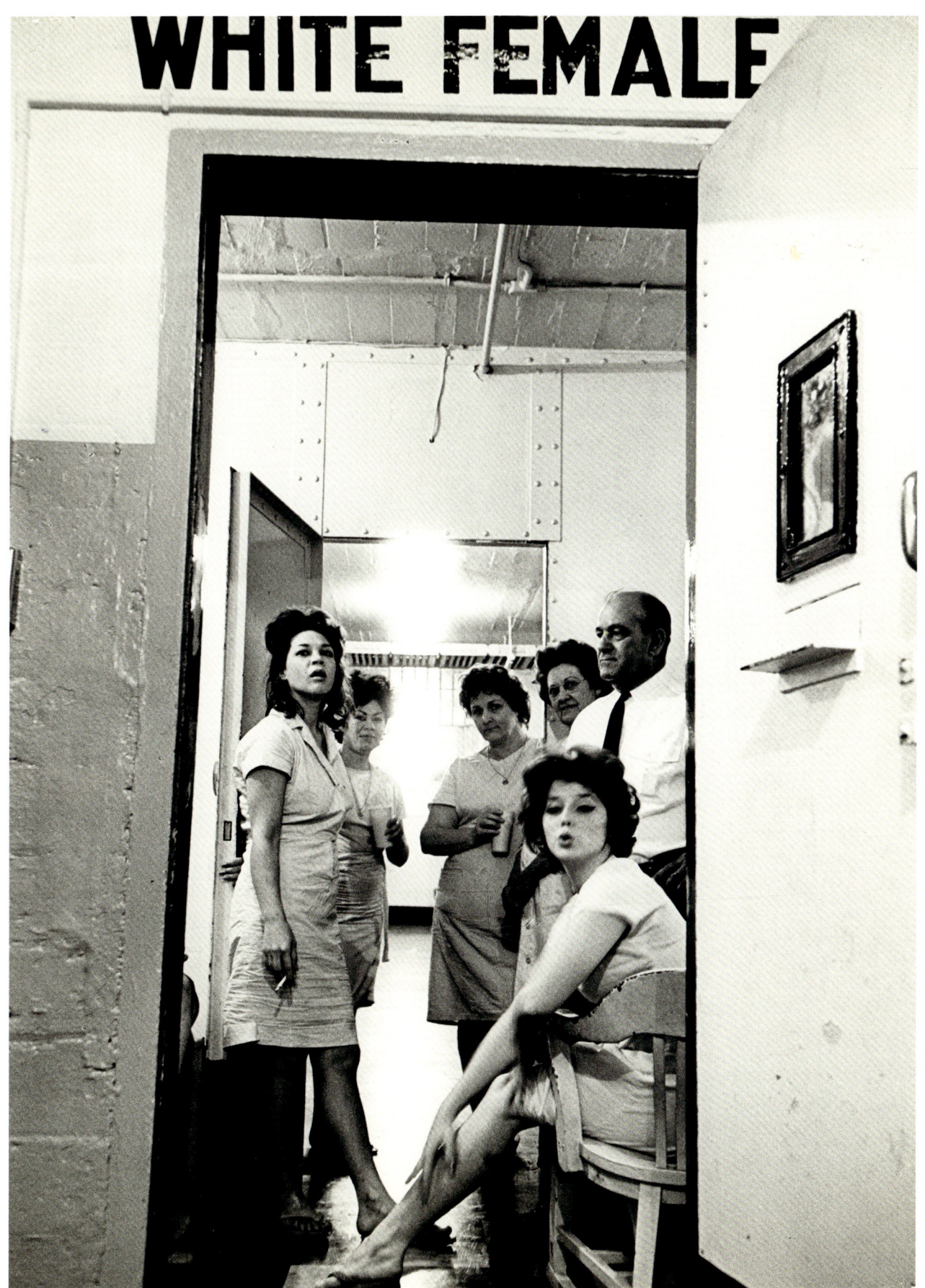

Sam R. Sutton (1912–1985)

The ubiquity of satellite imagery today may make aerial photography seem less exotic than it was when these pictures were made. However, the view provided by an automated satellite is not visually innovative, at least in a deliberate way. Meanwhile, the use of remotely controlled drones has opened up a new world of aerial photography, one that offers even a closer bird's-eye view than that provided by a piloted aircraft. Together, these options present a spectrum of possibilities for aerial photography for both documentary and aesthetic purposes.

Unlike the aerial photograph by Betsy Swanson (p. 171), which represents an anomaly in her work, the career of Sam Sutton—early on with Chester "Chet" Dyer and in later solo practice—produced nothing but aerial photographs. The Sutton/Dyer archive at THNOC represents some three decades of New Orleans and the surrounding region as seen from the air, from the mid-1950s until 1983, and reveals how the city's density and infrastructure changed dramatically in the years following WWII. With Sutton's single-engine, high-wing monoplane; a 4 × 5-inch camera; and his knack for selecting cooperative weather conditions, angle of view, and time of day, the photographs collectively produced an aerial portrait of the city.

Aerial photographs offer a unique perspective on terrestrial subjects. Sutton's notes don't always log the altitude from which the photographs were made, but those that do indicate a height of four to twelve thousand feet. The quasi-omniscient view of an airplane-mounted camera presents aspects of life on the ground in ways that an earthbound observer cannot see: the web of highways and railroads, the building densities of neighborhoods, even the arpent lines of early eighteenth-century land grants, preserved in the layout of modern streets.

The pictures here represent some of the areas where change occurred most dramatically during the second half of the 1950s and throughout the 1960s: the corridor for the approach to the High Rise Bridge over the Industrial Canal, the Mississippi River Gulf Outlet, the NASA Michoud Assembly Facility, New Orleans East, and the area near the shore of Lake Pontchartrain developed for the University of New Orleans's campus.

The early years of Sutton's practice were a harbinger for the direction his career would take. Throughout the 1960s and 1970s, his photographs tracked Interstate 10 as it snaked through the metro area, the construction of the Rivergate Convention Center at the foot of Canal Street, the expansion of suburbs and exurbs onto vacant lands in every direction from New Orleans, and the construction of the Louisiana Superdome.

Aerial view of New Orleans East, 1966
by Sam R. Sutton
gelatin silver print, 8 × 10 in.
gift of Sam R. Sutton, 1984.166.2.438

Aerial view of Mississippi River Gulf Outlet, from NASA facility to Chandeleur Sound, 1969
by Sam R. Sutton
gelatin silver print, 8 × 10 in.
gift of Sam R. Sutton, 1984.166.2.748

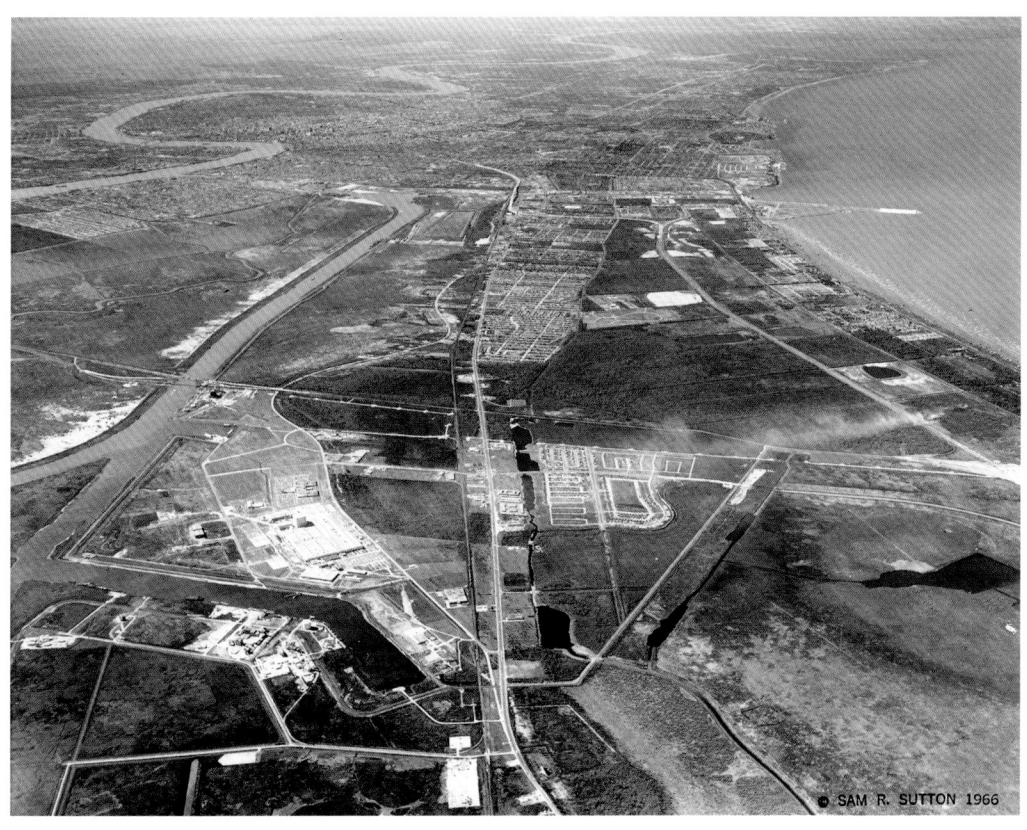

© SAM R. SUTTON 1966

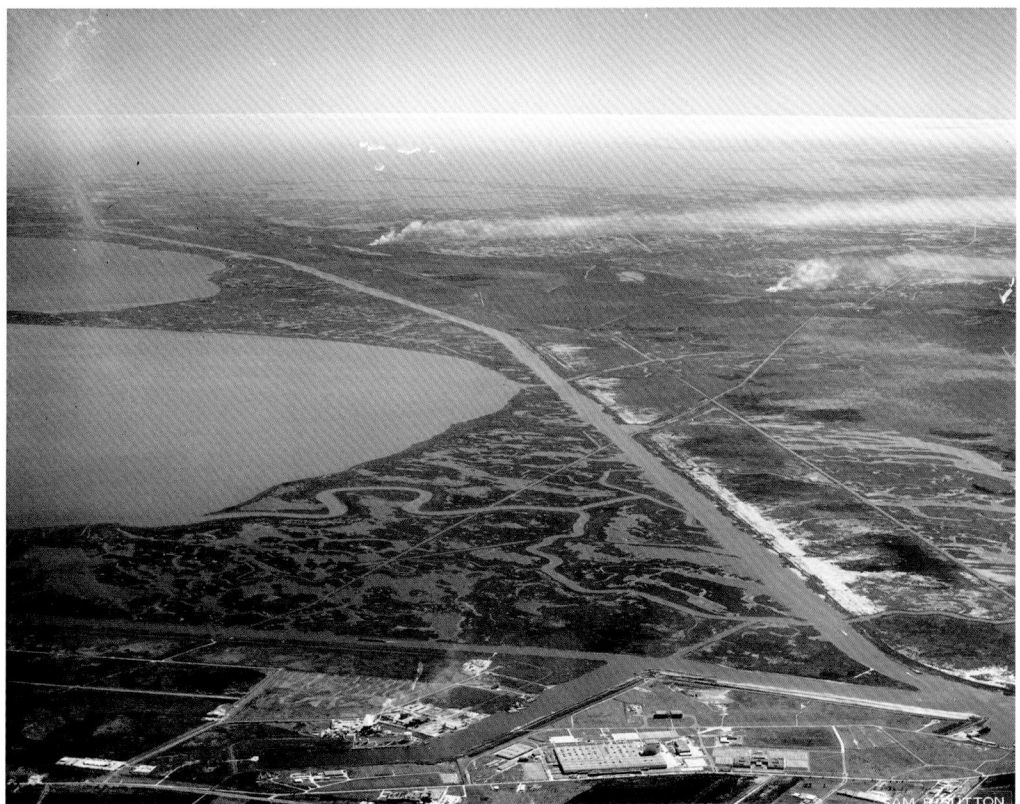

SAM R. SUTTON

Roy Octave Trahan (1913–2000)

The New Orleans Saints of the National Football League played their inaugural season in 1967. Tulane Stadium (also known as Sugar Bowl Stadium) was the site for home games. Despite the fate of a poor record that often befalls expansion teams, the Saints drew a large following of dedicated fans. Pregame and halftime entertainment was part of the draw.

On November 12, 1967, the Saints hosted the Dallas Cowboys. The Cowboys prevailed, 27–10. The entertainment package that day included demonstrations of a jet pack by stuntman Jim Pitts, seen here flying through the goalposts of the stadium's north endzone. Roy Octave Trahan's photographs from this event also show the jet-powered Pitts talking with another popular flying figure of that era: a costumed actress portraying Mary Poppins.

The mosaic of fans against which Pitts is presented, and the visual compression and flattening of the pictorial space by Trahan's use of a telephoto lens, causes the main subject to blend into the background, creating a "Where's Waldo" effect. It requires a double take to separate Pitts from the hundreds of fans who appear in this view. Also noticeable in this selection of fans is the fact that the seating is desegregated, a condition that had been achieved only a few years before the picture was made.

Trahan enjoyed a New Orleans–based photography career that lasted over five decades. His practice ranged from educator to studio portraitist and editorial photographer for numerous nonprofit agencies in New Orleans. Trahan also specialized in object photography for the city's antiques and auction trades.

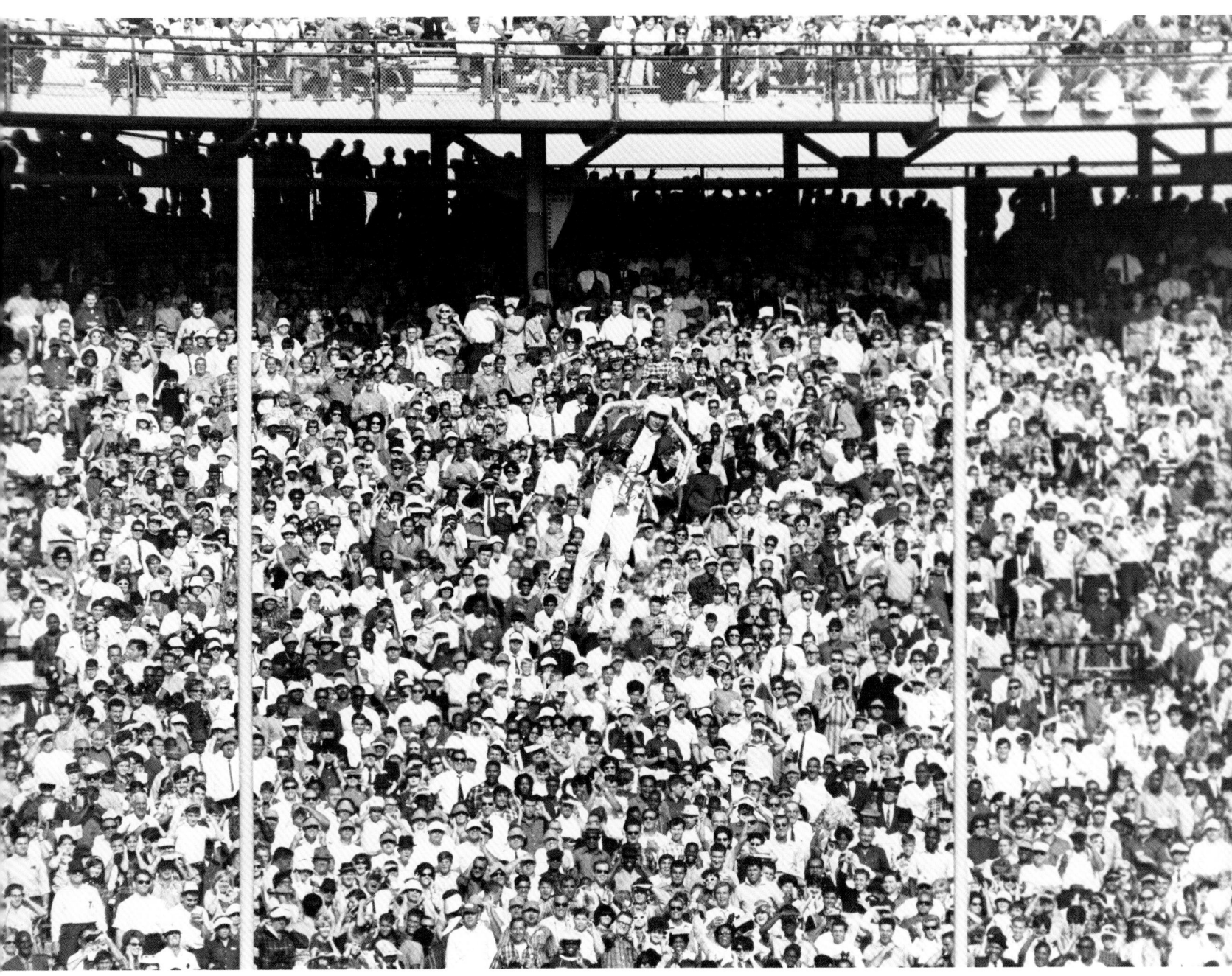

Jet pack at Saints-Cowboys game, 1967
by Roy Octave Trahan
gelatin silver print, 7 ½ × 10 in.
gift of Roy Trahan, 1990.16.1.1247

Betsy Swanson (b. 1938)

Betsy Swanson made tens of thousands of film negatives of historic architecture, mostly in the metropolitan New Orleans area, and by far the majority of them were made with her feet planted firmly on the ground. But to better examine the context of some buildings and historic sites, she would take to the air to provide a broader view. Such is the case with this photograph of Seven Oaks plantation made in 1968.

The site lies a few miles up the Mississippi and on the opposite bank from New Orleans. According to a marker on the road adjacent to the property, the house was occupied until 1957. The building, which sat neglected in the middle of an oil storage tank facility, was demolished in 1977.

Swanson graduated from Newcomb College in New Orleans and received a master of fine arts degree from Tulane University. Her photographs are often concerned with documenting historic architecture both as individual structures and as part of their surrounding contexts. Some of her work involved photographing sites and conditions for the preliminary phase of establishing state and national parks in South Louisiana. She also made thousands of photographs used in the first six volumes of the New Orleans Architecture series, begun in 1971, which examines historic neighborhoods of New Orleans. Though the photographs in those books are not a census of buildings in historic neighborhoods, they are extensive inventories of nineteenth- and twentieth-century New Orleans building stock, made at a time when development and real estate speculation placed individual structures or entire blocks in jeopardy. Her 1975 book, *Historic Jefferson Parish: From Shore to Shore*, devoted to architecture and historic sites in Jefferson Parish, complements Eugene A. Delcroix's earlier work done in the parish.

Seven Oaks Plantation House, Westwego, La., **1968**
by Betsy Swanson
gelatin silver print, 13¾ × 9¼ in.
gift of John Geiser III, 2008.0145.7, © Betsy Swanson

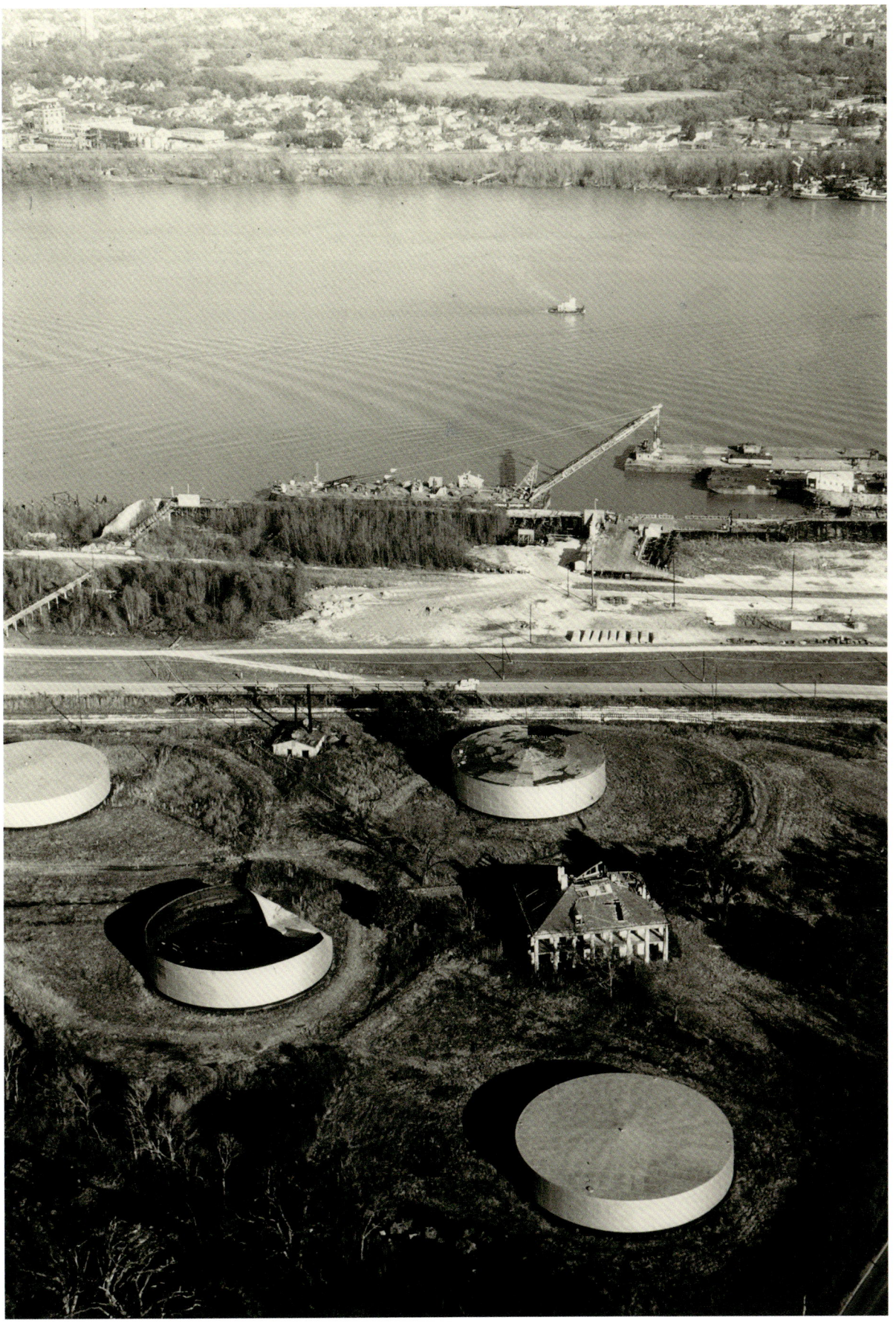

George D. Berkett (1910–2002)

Choices are part of making a photograph, and George D. Berkett chose to match the distortion of a fish-eye lens with the counterculture interior of a head shop on Decatur Street in New Orleans's French Quarter. This picture reminds us that all camera images are based on circular projections of a lens onto the plane of the film. They appear square or rectangular only because a frame inside the camera isolates a part of the image that the photographer sees in composing and limits the film's exposure to that rectangle or square. With this lens, the image is free to extend to the very perimeter of the projected circle.

Berkett's picture concentrates political, musical, and social symbols of US anti-establishment youth culture within the circle of imagery. The camera position seems to be on a countertop or table, allowing the view to embrace nearly an entire hemisphere of ceiling and walls, all of which serve as display surfaces for artwork. The vertiginous perspective and other distortions of the optics suggest an analogy of drug-induced reverie. At least one poster visible references the hallucinogen LSD.

Other posters promote folk singer Tom Paxton, David Blue, and the Butterfield Blues Band, and mainly feature albums that were released in 1965 and 1966. Contemporary political figures (Mao Zedong, Fidel Castro, and Ho Chi Minh) and historic ones (Karl Marx and Joseph Stalin) are displayed incongruously on the ceiling alongside Lon Chaney Jr.'s Wolf Man character and Bela Lugosi's Dracula.

Lower Decatur Street was a locus of counterculture activity during the tumultuous 1960s and early 1970s. In addition to Davis's shop, there was an experimental jazz workshop and a free medical clinic. The *Vieux Carré Courier*, a weekly paper focused on historic preservation and other forms of activism, had its offices nearby.

Berkett, an orthopedic surgeon, was a longtime amateur photographer. One portfolio of his photographs consists solely of those made with the fish-eye lens. He counted many New Orleans visual artists among his friends, and another group of his photographs consists of their portraits.

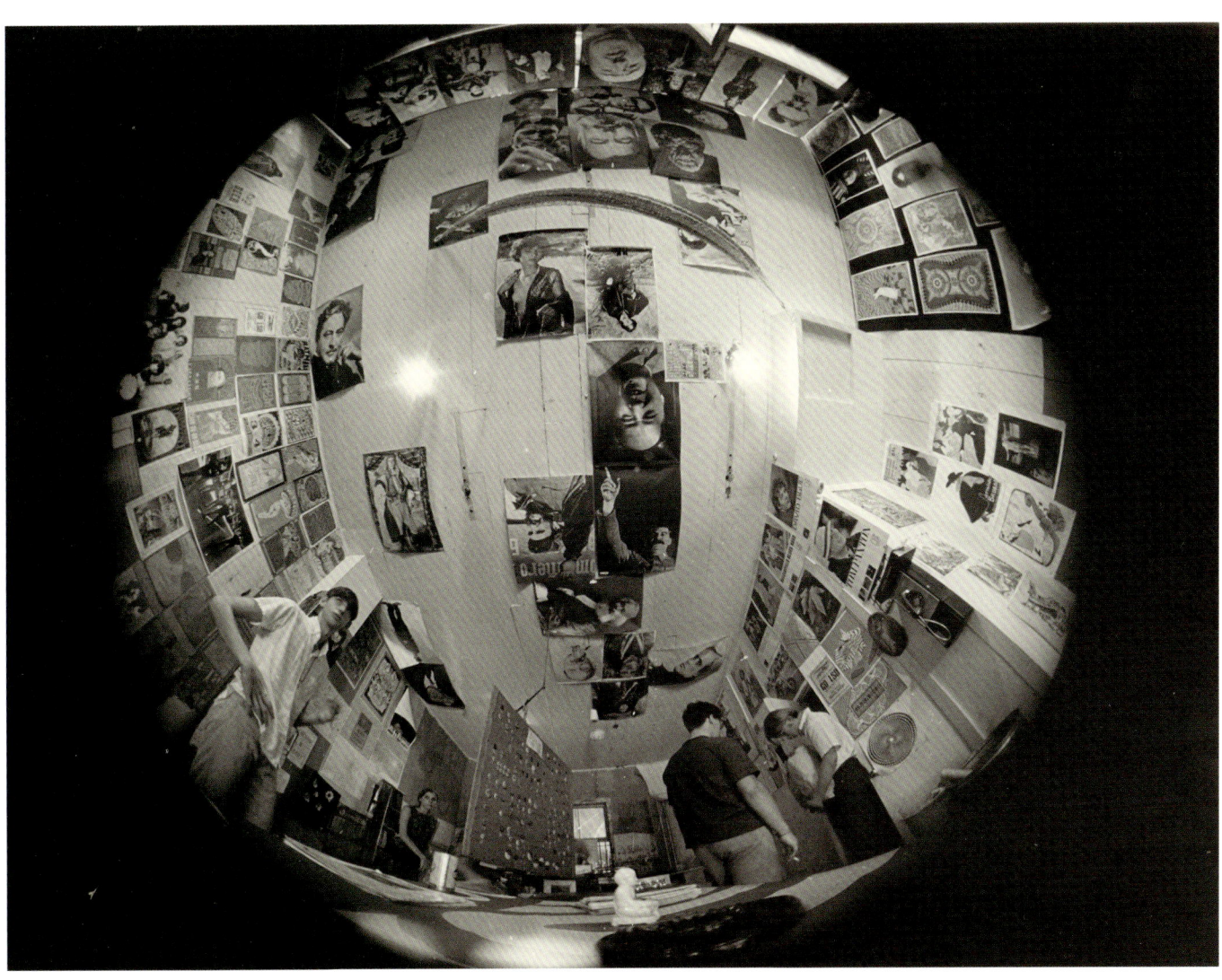

**Arthur Quentin "Quint" Davis Jr.'s head shop on Decatur
Street, late 1960s**

by George D. Berkett
gelatin silver print, 11 × 13⅞ in.
gift of George D. B. Berkett, 1987.199

Matt Anderson (b. 1948)

Due to this picture's clarity, nearly all the people among the dozens in the frame who gathered for this protest against the Vietnam War could be identified. But individual identity was not the intent of this photograph. Its message is conveyed in their numbers, showing support for a common cause—rethinking the United States' participation in the war. There is no apparent end to the people, giving the picture a compressed visual effect, as well as a psychological one that suggests the crowd extends far beyond what is captured within the frame.

On October 15, 1969, the national Moratorium to End the War in Vietnam took place, with an estimated two million participants across the country. Though this photograph was made in New Orleans, the scene was replicated throughout the United States on college campuses, in auditoriums, and in city streets and town squares. A month later, another moratorium was held in Washington, DC, with an estimated turnout of half a million, distilling the voices from scattered communities into a single one that addressed the nation's political leaders and elected representatives. Among a large portion of the country's youth, the Vietnam War was not popular, but protesting it was.

Matt Anderson, a student at Tulane University, was the head photographer of the school's newspaper, the *Hullabaloo*, and covered the New Orleans moratorium for the paper. Anderson's photograph was made at the culmination of a march that began on Freret Street at the point where the Tulane and Loyola university campuses meet. By the time the group reached New Orleans City Hall and the adjacent Duncan Plaza, where the marchers settled in to hear speeches, the assembly had grown much larger and was not limited to student participants.

Following his years at Tulane, Anderson continued a career as a freelance photojournalist, with his pictures often appearing in newsmagazines and newspapers. The *New York Times* frequently tapped him for regional assignments between 1979 and 2004. In New Orleans, Anderson regularly photographed events for performing arts magazines and journals, including the productions of two ballet companies and the New Orleans Symphony.

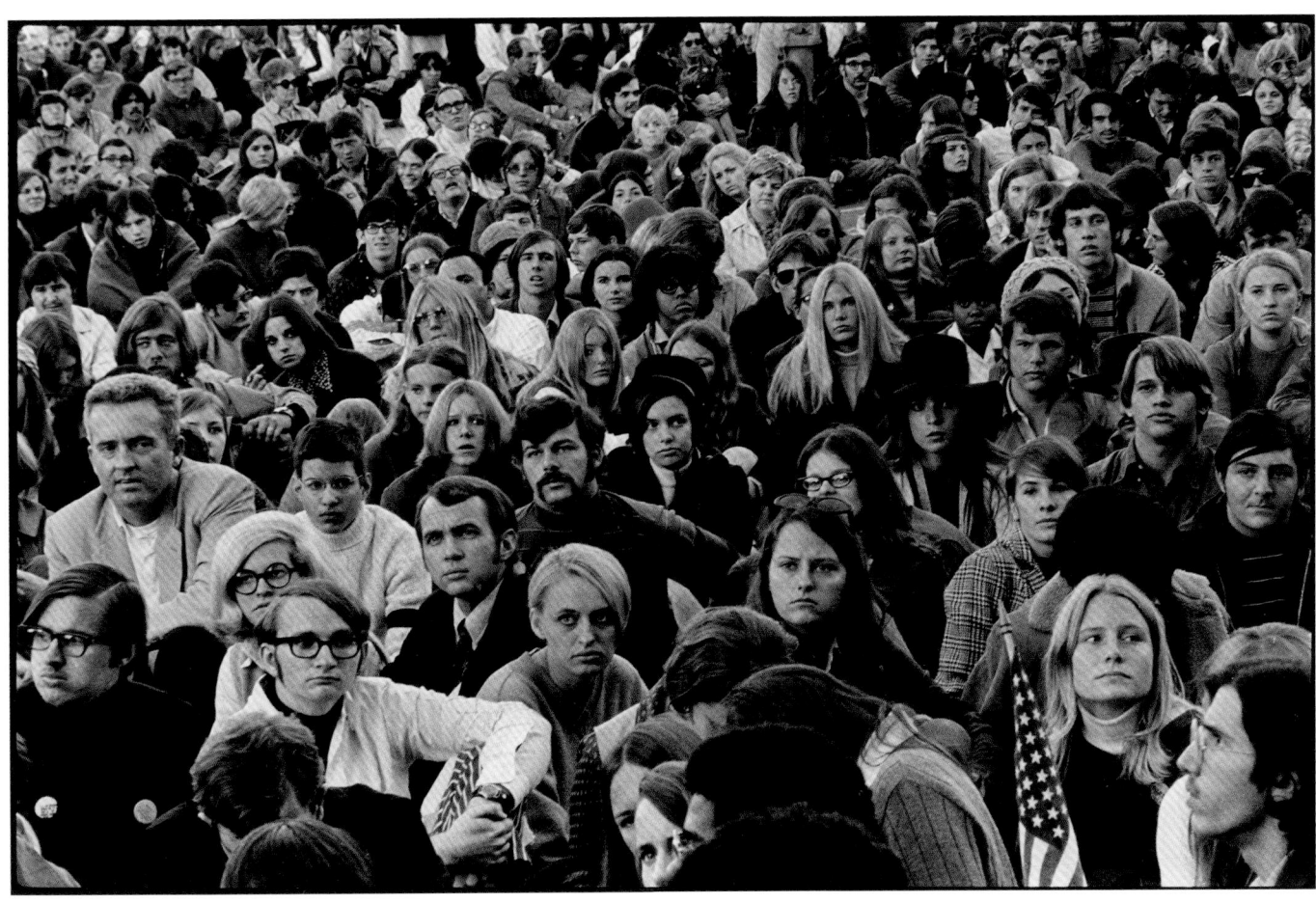

Moratorium to End the War in Vietnam, New Orleans, 1969

by Matt Anderson
gelatin silver print, 10½ × 14 in.
gift of Matt Anderson, 2002.12.5, © Matt Anderson

Donald Muir Bradburn (1924–2012)

The history of any place is usually considered in terms of founding and settlement, native populations, the in- and out-migrations that shape a place's culture, military conflicts, and great events; individuals with fame or infamy also influence a locale's development. Lost among these several histories are natural history and art history, which can add a deeper understanding, and therefore deserve representation within the holdings of any museum that presents a wide view. The photographs of Donald Muir Bradburn bring together threads of these specialized histories and, in doing so, offer a context for appreciating the others.

Since the mid-twentieth century, a very public discussion has carried on about the science and economics of Louisiana's vanishing coastal areas (both marshes and the actual shoreline of the Gulf of Mexico), how they are vanishing, and how this condition can be addressed. The conversations often center on balancing the impact of the oil and gas industry with the needs of traditional, generational work patterns in the area as well as with the natural setting that provides beauty, wide-ranging recreational opportunities, critical wildlife habitat, and a buffer from strong hurricanes that protects inland communities.

The longtime chief of pathology at Touro Infirmary, Bradburn photographed the natural enviroment of Louisiana and the surrounding waters that he visited often. With a particular emphasis on the region's ornithology, both resident and migratory, he embraced the overall fabric of the natural world. His profession as a pathologist may have made him more aware of the fragility of the world's environment and the forces—both natural and human—that could cause imbalance and destruction. Working with his botanist wife, Anne Strickland Bradburn, he studied, recorded, and inventoried flora and fauna of some Gulf Coast barrier islands. Their work was critical to Horn Island—pictured here—and nearby Petit Bois Island receiving the protection of inclusion in the National Wilderness system in 1978 and later, as part of the Gulf Islands National Seashore.

The Donald M. Bradburn Archive at THNOC holds many thousands of 35 mm color slides and prints made from black-and-white negatives of Horn Island and its neighbors. Among the earliest is one from 1950. This print, made from a later negative, shows one of Dr. Bradburn's favorite locations on the island's north side.

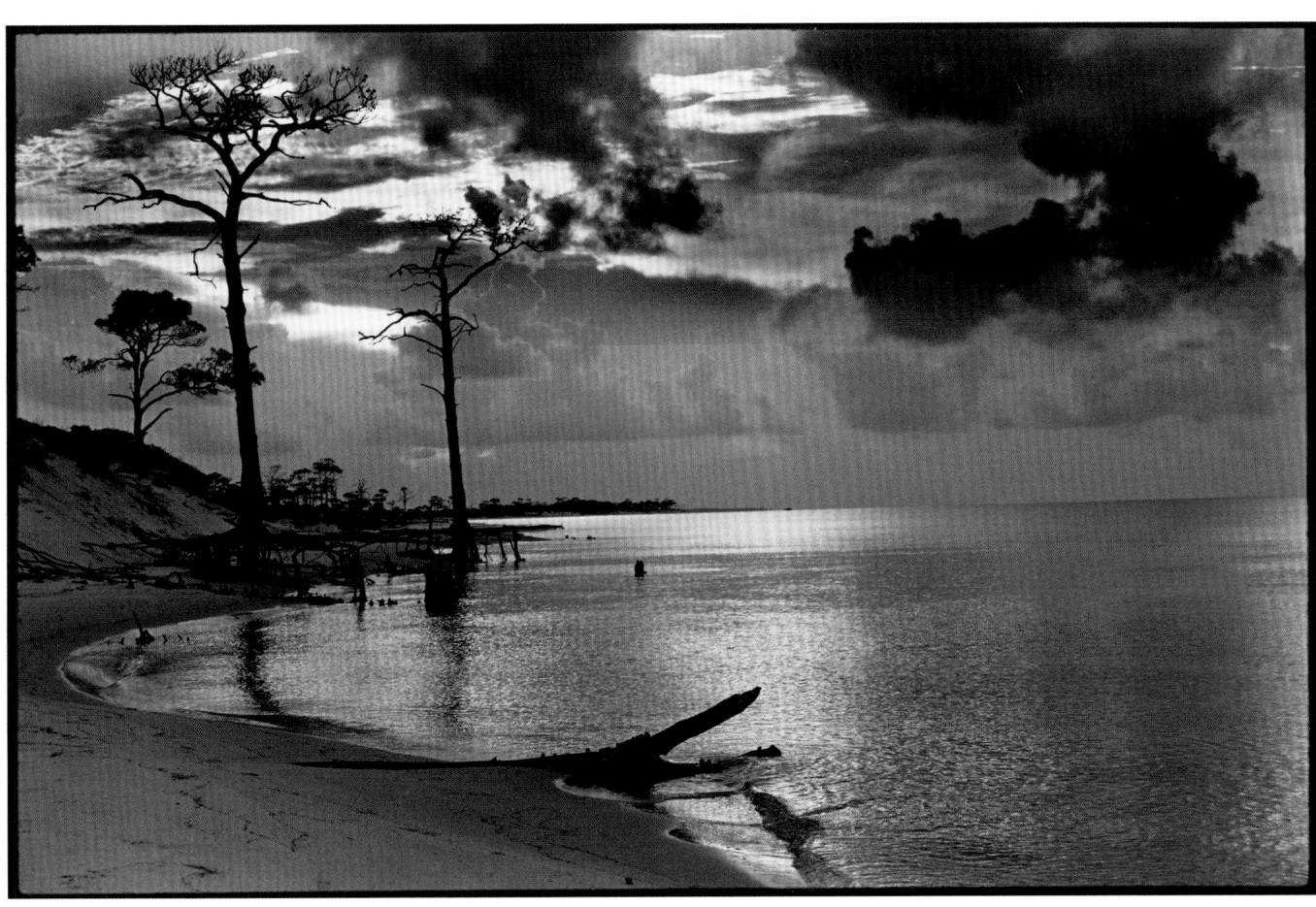

Sunset, North Shore, 1970s?
by Donald Muir Bradburn
gelatin silver print, 11 × 14 in.
gift of Anne S. Bradburn, 2015.0035.1.2.1

Jules Cahn (1916–1995)

To characterize this image as portraiture is a little misleading, though there is no doubt that Jules Cahn's photograph is accurate in presenting the likenesses of known subjects. Cahn had photographed or filmed each of these people separately numerous times, and his relationships with them extended beyond acquaintance into friendship. Perhaps this familiarity permitted Cahn—a businessman as well as avocational photographer and moviemaker—to capture Sister Gertrude Morgan and Noel Rockmore side by side but disengaged from each other in this moment. Cahn's archive—consisting of thousands of items including negatives, still photographs, 16 mm film footage, and videotapes—is held by THNOC.

The picture was taken on the grounds of the first music and cultural event now known as the New Orleans Jazz and Heritage Festival. In the early years of the festival—far more modest in size than today's version—it was held in Congo Square, adjacent to the French Quarter.

Morgan's immersion in her book is as intense as any rendered in a seventeenth-century Netherlandish genre scene. She was a legendary preacher of the Gospel, both spoken and sung. A self-taught artist, her works exuded visionary images of New Testament messages. Rockmore was a trained painter whose New Orleans output was defined by expressive portraits of jazz musicians, friends, and acquaintances in his French Quarter. His intense gaze, almost challenging the photographer, is both penetrating and benign.

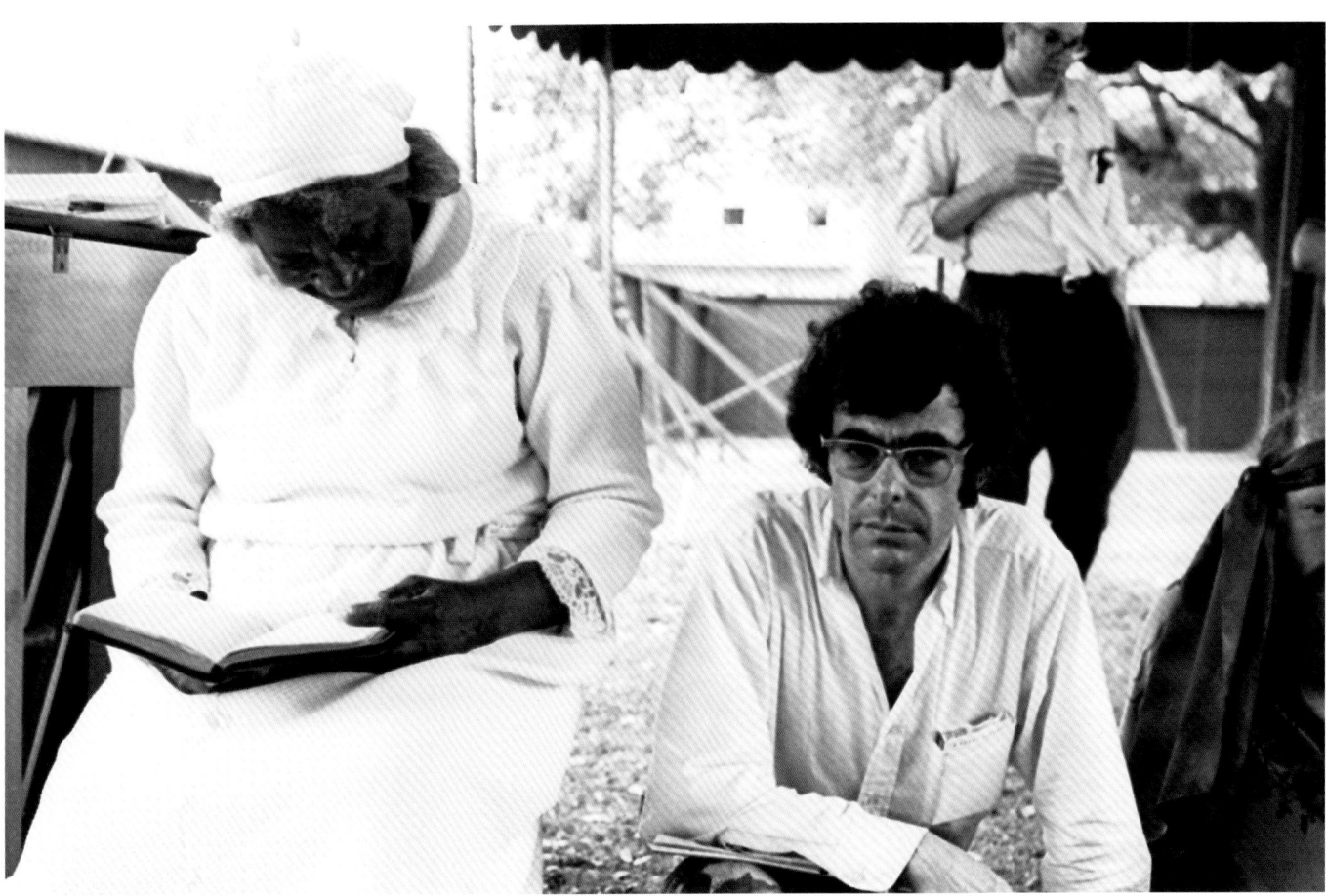

**Sister Gertrude Morgan and Noel Rockmore, New Orleans
Jazz and Heritage Festival, 1970**
by Jules Cahn
inkjet print, 8½ × 11 in.
Jules Cahn Collection at THNOC, 2000.78.8.41

The inkjet print was made in 2014 by Melissa Carrier from a
1970 negative.

Girard Mouton,III (b. 1952)

Without the protective coloration of a momentous event, larger-than-life personality, or other such trappings we associate with "history," it can be difficult to see the importance of a simple and joyous picture of a youngster, such as this one made by Girard Mouton,III. Children's history, in all its multifaceted character, is a part of any history—world, national, or local. This unidentified subject is lost in a moment of childhood, which from the expression on his face, consists equally of bliss and determination. The vehicle that transports him to this state is of simple construction, a form that by the 1970s, when this photograph was made, had become so traditional as to not require a plan.

But one could argue that the event resonates on a symbolic level as well. The setting for this photograph is an activity sponsored by the New Orleans Recreation Department (NORD). For a number of years, the city agency held an annual Skatemobile Derby, where young participants built and raced scooters of their own creation. The program was started in the 1950s by Morris F. X. Jeff Sr., who oversaw the NORD activities for African Americans. The codified discrimination of the era did not permit racially integrated programs, and the Skatemobile Derby was Jeff's solution to the exclusion of Black children from the Soap Box Derby program. In the next decade, following the Civil Rights Act of 1964, Jeff would see many barriers to discrimination fall as he became the program director for all of NORD, creating activities that served all of the city's children.

Mouton made this picture with his first camera. Though he continued to photograph many aspects of life in New Orleans, especially as experienced by the city's African Americans, his research and publishing on New Orleans's African American photographic history is of equal and lasting importance. Mouton is widely known as an official photographer of the New Orleans Jazz and Heritage Festival and over more than thirty years has made many thousands of pictures of the performers on stage as well as the exuberant fans.

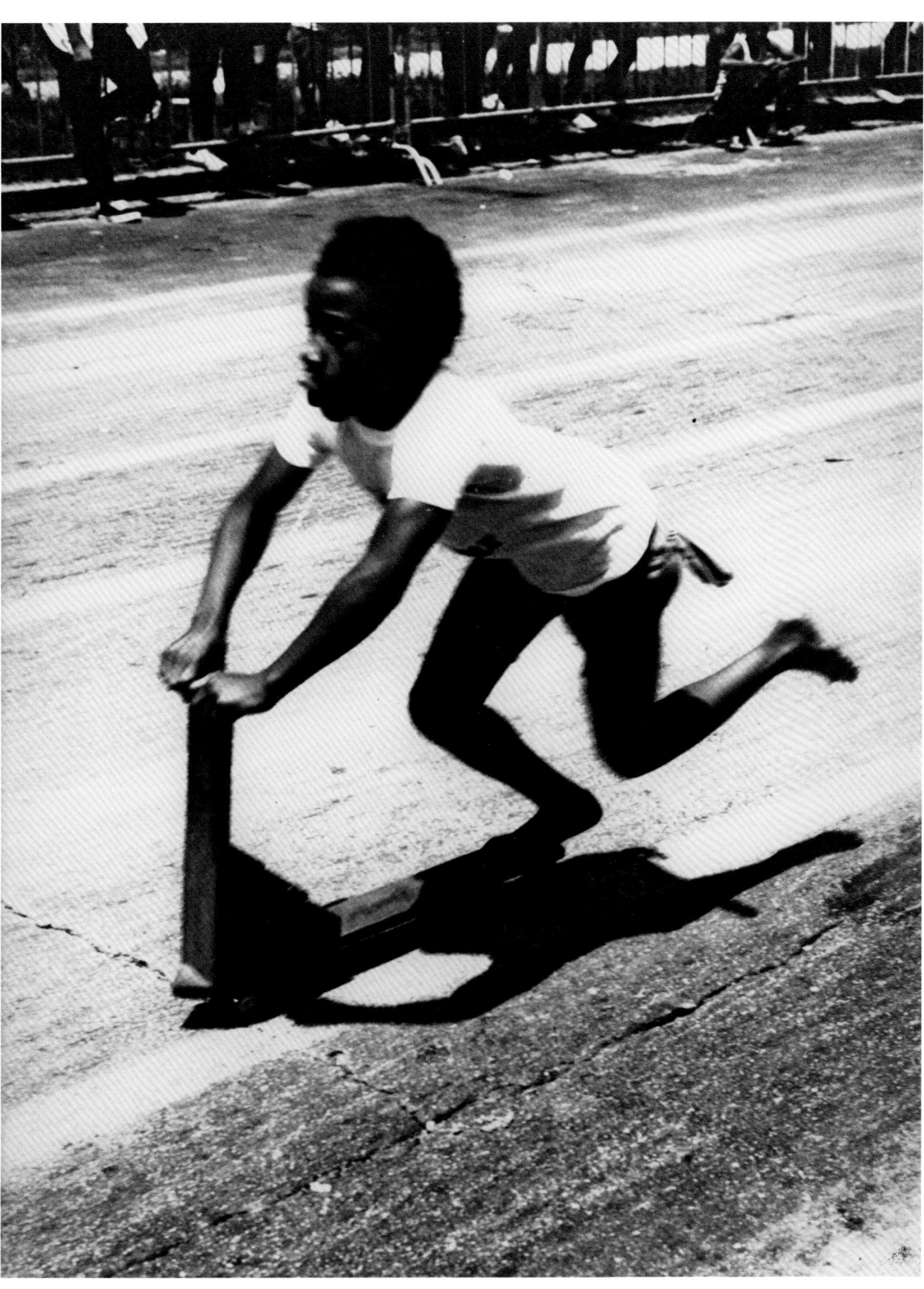

***NORD Skatemobile Derby,* 1972**
by Girard Mouton, III
inkjet print, 11 × 8½ in.
gift of Girard Mouton, III, 2021.0024.3, © Girard Mouton, III

The inkjet print was made in 2015 from a 1972 negative.

National Aeronautics and Space Administration (NASA) (established 1958)

This photograph contains elements of history both in the portrayal of its subject and in its status as an object. The principal subject is the Bonnet Carré Spillway during an opening in April 1973, when the Mississippi River was dangerously high. Following historic flooding of the river in 1927, the spillway system was designed to divert some of the floodwater into areas (in this instance, Lake Pontchartrain) that would be less damaged by flooding, thereby reducing the pressure on the levees that protect cities and towns downstream.

This photograph shows a section of the Mississippi River that flows northwest to southeast between Baton Rouge and New Orleans; the lake is in the upper right corner. The odd coloring is due to the use of visual data from both visible spectral bands and a near-infrared spectral band. In this combination, green foliage reproduces as red, and bodies of water as dark blue or black. The white glint of sunlight off of the water at the bottom left of the photograph is an exception. Infrared signatures of roads, buildings, and factories often show as silvery-white or gray. Selectively using portions of the nonvisible spectrum permits seeing conditions—such as water movement and plant growth—that are not always easily discerned using only the visible spectrum. Compared with Richard Sexton's traditional black-and-white photograph of the spillway at ground level, it is clear how viewpoint and technical factors affect perception (p. 274).

When this photograph was made in the spring of 1973, it documented only the fourth time that the spillway had been opened in its forty-year life to that point. All 350 bays were opened, and the sheet of water extending from the control structure on the Mississippi River to Lake Pontchartrain attests to the diversion capacity of 250,000 cubic feet of water per second at that level of operation. Before the end of the twentieth century, the spillway was opened an additional four times.

Between 2018 and 2020 the process was repeated each year, though not at full capacity.

The boundaries of land parcels (often wedge-shaped) evident in the picture harken to original colonial concessions. Such grants had narrow frontage on the river—the principal route of commerce and communication in eighteenth-century Louisiana—permitting each owner a spot on this important artery. What the concessions lacked in frontage, they made up for in depth, often extending miles away from the river.

The images resulting from the Mercury and Gemini manned space flights spurred the US government to collect photographic data about the Earth. Scientists could use those pictures to aid in understanding physical characteristics of the planet, unachievable from terrestrial viewpoints. A dedicated program for orbiting satellite imagery production initiated in the mid-1960s reached fruition in 1972, when a satellite dubbed Landsat 1 began collecting data. The picture here is from that first Landsat operation. NASA launched Landsat 9 in 2021 to capture images vital to understanding and managing worldwide challenges such as deforestation, climate change, and natural and human-made disasters.

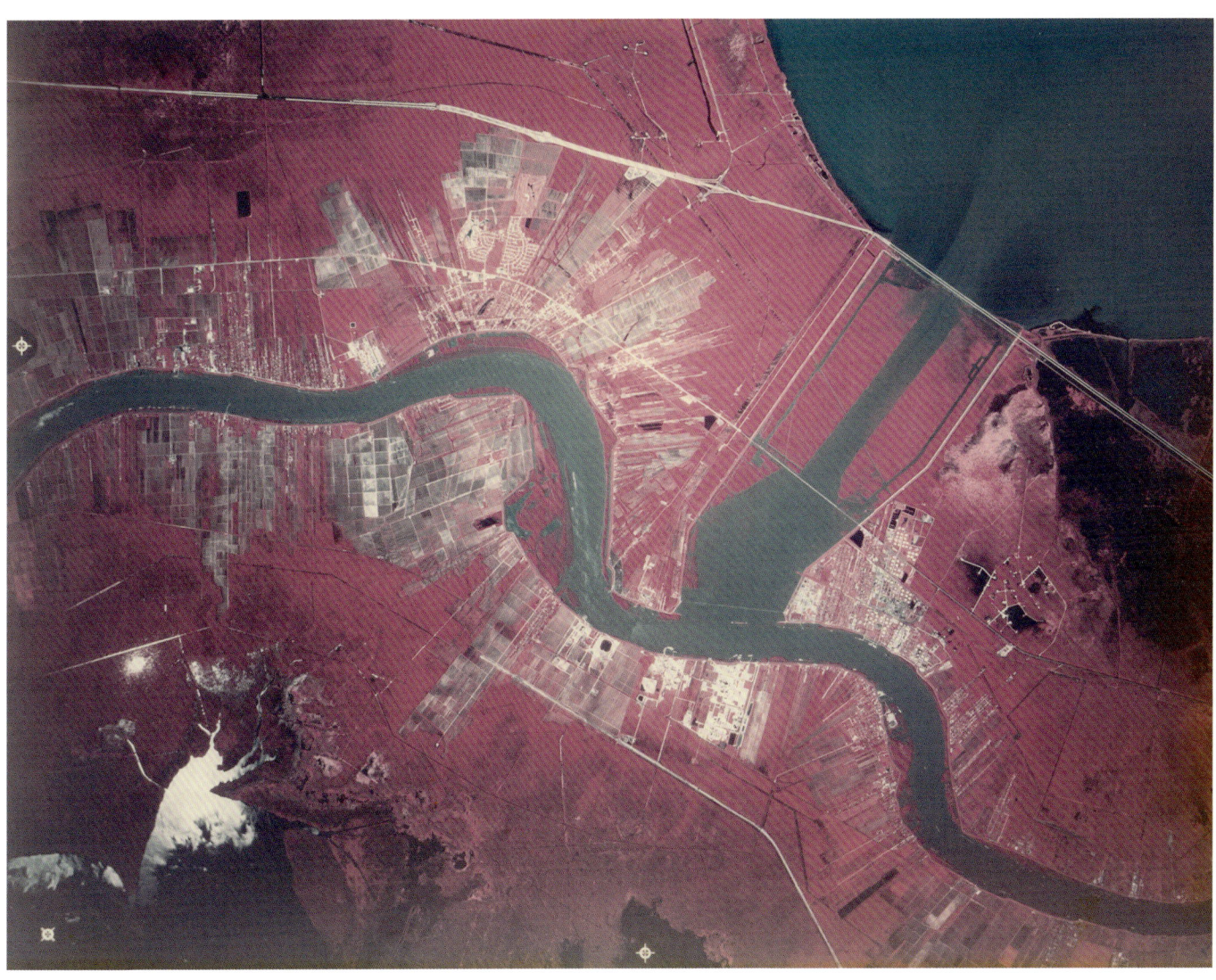

Bonnet Carré Spillway flowing into Lake Pontchartrain, 1973
by NASA
chromogenic print, 11 × 13⅞ in.
gift of Dode Platou, 1976.6.1

Charles F. Weber (1905–1980)

By the time Charles F. Weber, principal in the eponymous advertising and commercial photography firm in New Orleans, made a portrait of Clay Shaw, he would have known of the fateful connection it had with a portrait he had made nearly a decade before of Jim Garrison. In the years between the making of the photographs, national and local events brought the two figures together in an unexpected way.

Shaw was a successful businessman, civic leader, and champion of historic preservation; Garrison was the district attorney of New Orleans, elected in 1962. He served for a decade in that office, during the time of President John F. Kennedy's assassination and the subsequent investigation headed by US Chief Justice Earl Warren. Garrison was openly skeptical of the Warren Commission's conclusion that Lee Harvey Oswald—a one-time resident of New Orleans—acted alone in shooting the president in 1963. The district attorney launched his own investigation into the crime, focused heavily on the theory of a conspiracy hatched in New Orleans with Shaw as a principal figure. Shaw stood trial in 1967, and in the end—about a year later—a jury took less than an hour to acquit him of all charges.

Weber's photographs of each man present them in different phases of their careers and lives. Shaw's was his official portrait as president of the New Orleans French Market Corporation, a position he held from 1971 to 1972. His engagement with the camera shows someone confident, though perhaps still a little wary from the disruption in his life. The full-frame version showing Garrison was likely made to test a lighting setup. Finished pictures from this session at Weber's are of a bust-length view, not cropped from this photograph. The light stands, diffusers, background, and electrical cables snaking across the floor give a sense of the control that studio portraits offer both the subject and the photographer.

Though the Garrison probe was fruitless in its quest to overturn the Warren Commission findings by convicting Shaw, the effort inextricably linked these two public figures. Clay Shaw died in 1974, just a few years after Weber photographed him. Garrison died in 1992.

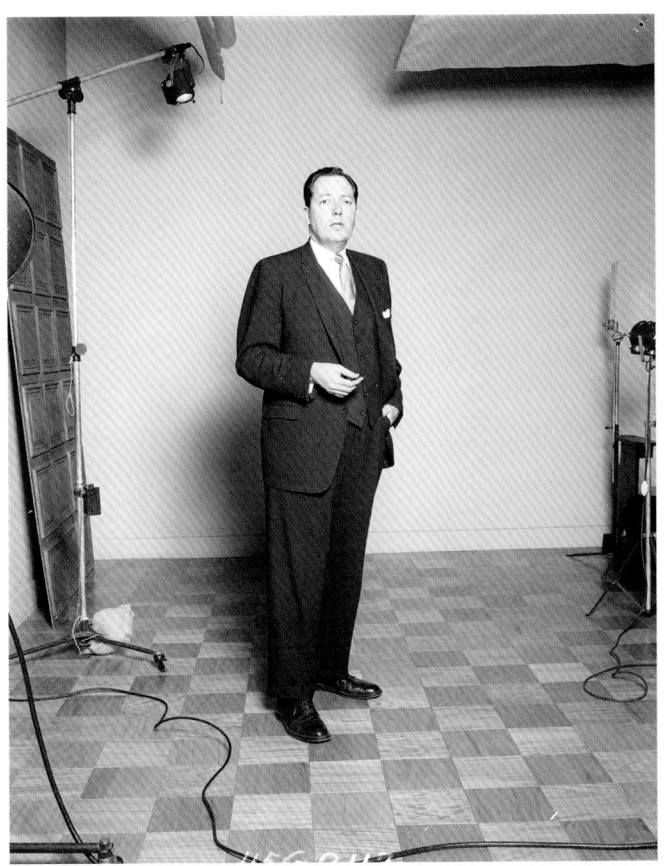

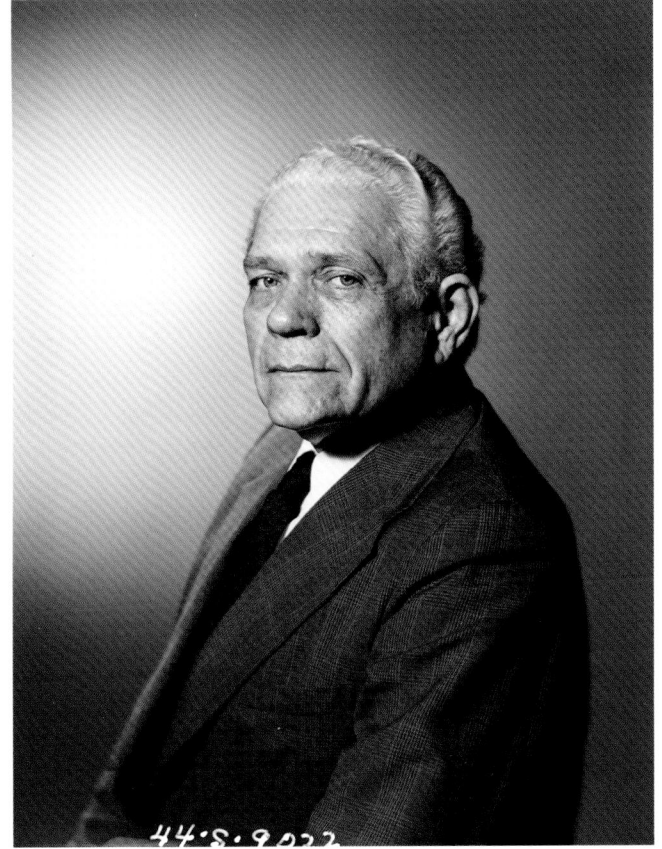

Jim Garrison, 1962
by Charles F. Weber
gelatin silver negative, 5 × 4 in.
2012.0208.2.414

Clay Shaw, 1971?
by Charles F. Weber
gelatin silver negative, 5 × 4 in.
2012.0208.2.110

John Uhl (b. 1933)

John Uhl was born in the Algiers section of New Orleans, which lies opposite the French Quarter across the Mississippi River. A construction industry executive and a dedicated amateur photographer, he would visit his old neighborhood to photograph places that had changed as well as areas that remained as he remembered them. Uhl's Proustian excursions took him from the Algiers ferry landing and the levee to houses and businesses. It is safe to say that any picture seen by a random viewer will provoke a reaction that is different from that of the person who made it. Uhl made photographs for his own reasons, but that is not to say they hold no interest for other viewers.

Such photographs in a history museum's collection preserve details that might otherwise be overlooked or forgotten. Frank's Food Store provided the neighborhood not only groceries but short orders like po-boy sandwiches and "chicken in a box," both noted on the signage. A few customers wait by the takeout window, where snowballs or to-go orders were dispensed.

When this photograph was made, scores of corner stores like Frank's were scattered throughout New Orleans and the surrounding communities. Though such places still exist, most have gone out of business over the past half-century. In addition to its varied offerings, Frank's had the typical features of a neighborhood store: the clipped corner entryway, the metal awnings over the door and take-out window, and signs and menus affixed to the exterior walls or set on the sidewalk. The glass and metal door may have replaced the typical screen doors of such establishments, likely coming about with the introduction of air-conditioning. The bicycle parked in front with its banana seat, angel-wing handlebars, and purposely mismatched tires (knobby in back, standard in front) are indicators not only of a time, but possibly of the clientele: corner groceries were places for children to buy comic books and candies, baseball cards and soft drinks, or perhaps to pick up a missing ingredient for a family member in the midst of dinner preparation.

Were this picture in an art museum, one might examine it from a standpoint of genre (street photography), compositional balance (how the awnings, fire hydrant, and bicycle create four corners for focusing the text-rich signage), and its place in Uhl's body of work. But in a history museum the image provides a wealth of information for the historian, sociologist, or preservationist to mine.

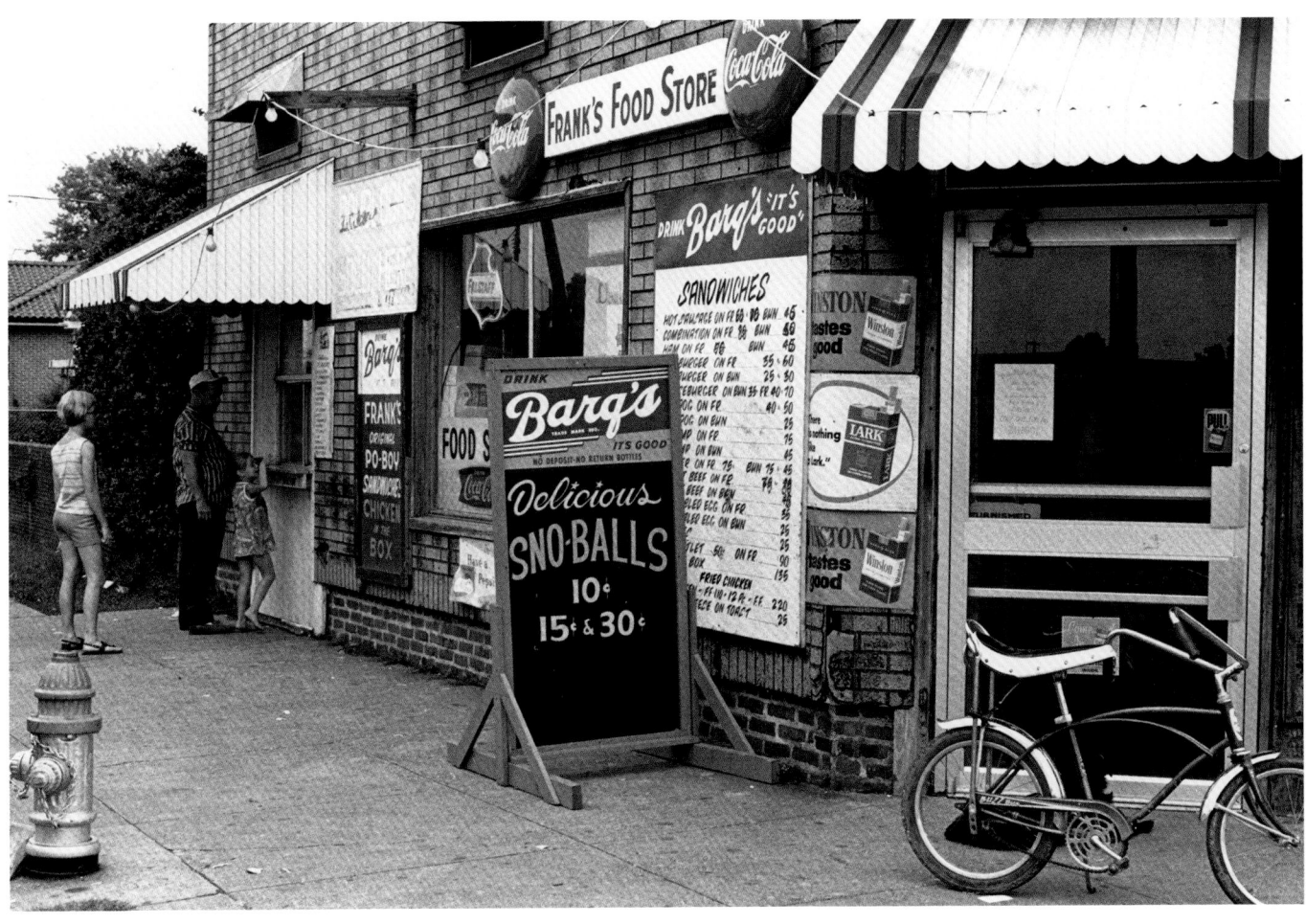

Frank's Food Store, circa 1970

by John Uhl
gelatin silver print, 5 × 7 in.
gift of John Uhl, 1984.190.56

Charles H. Traub (b. 1945) and Douglas Baz (b. 1943)

What do photographs mean in their own time? How does "their time" affect how we view them? Photographs are almost always and inextricably tied to their phantasmal counterpart—memory. Looking at a picture, recent or ancient, is like rubbing Aladdin's magic lamp and seeing the apparition that emanates from it. The photograph, like the genie, bends to our command—one of memory or personal experience.

In 1973 and 1974, Douglas Baz and Charles H. Traub spent several months living in Louisiana's Cajun area, the south-central and southwest portion of the state. Drawn to the area because it was so unlike the America they had known in the Northeast and Midwest, they wanted to photograph its lifeways and landscape. To be sure, Louisiana Cajuns of the 1970s were more modern than their immigrant ancestors who settled the region beginning in the late eighteenth century, but many still engaged in seasonal occupations of trapping, fishing, moss gathering, and hog butchering. These sources of income and sustenance were being replaced by employment in the oil industry and other businesses, however. The more than three thousand photographs Baz and Traub made in their sojourn caught the region in a time of transition.

Other photographs from Baz and Traub's Louisiana residency, published by THNOC in 2020 as *Cajun Document*—their name for this collective and collaborative project—may better capture distinctive Cajun foodways and folkways, and better express the artists' sense of wonder at encountering a culture that struck them as exotic.

But this picture of Port Fourchon represents the past meeting the present at a particular moment during the development of *Louisiana Lens*: August 29, 2021, when Hurricane Ida made landfall at Port Fourchon. This whopper of a storm, whose strength has been equaled only twice in Louisiana's history, came ashore with winds of 155 miles per hour, wreaking tremendous destruction. Port Fourchon appears here in embryonic form, before extensive development by offshore industries serving oil and gas production. In a century, will this photograph be viewed as the foundation of a bustling industrial complex or a ruin that lies beneath the sea, a casualty of an eroding coast? The photograph will not have changed during this time, but what it shows certainly will have.

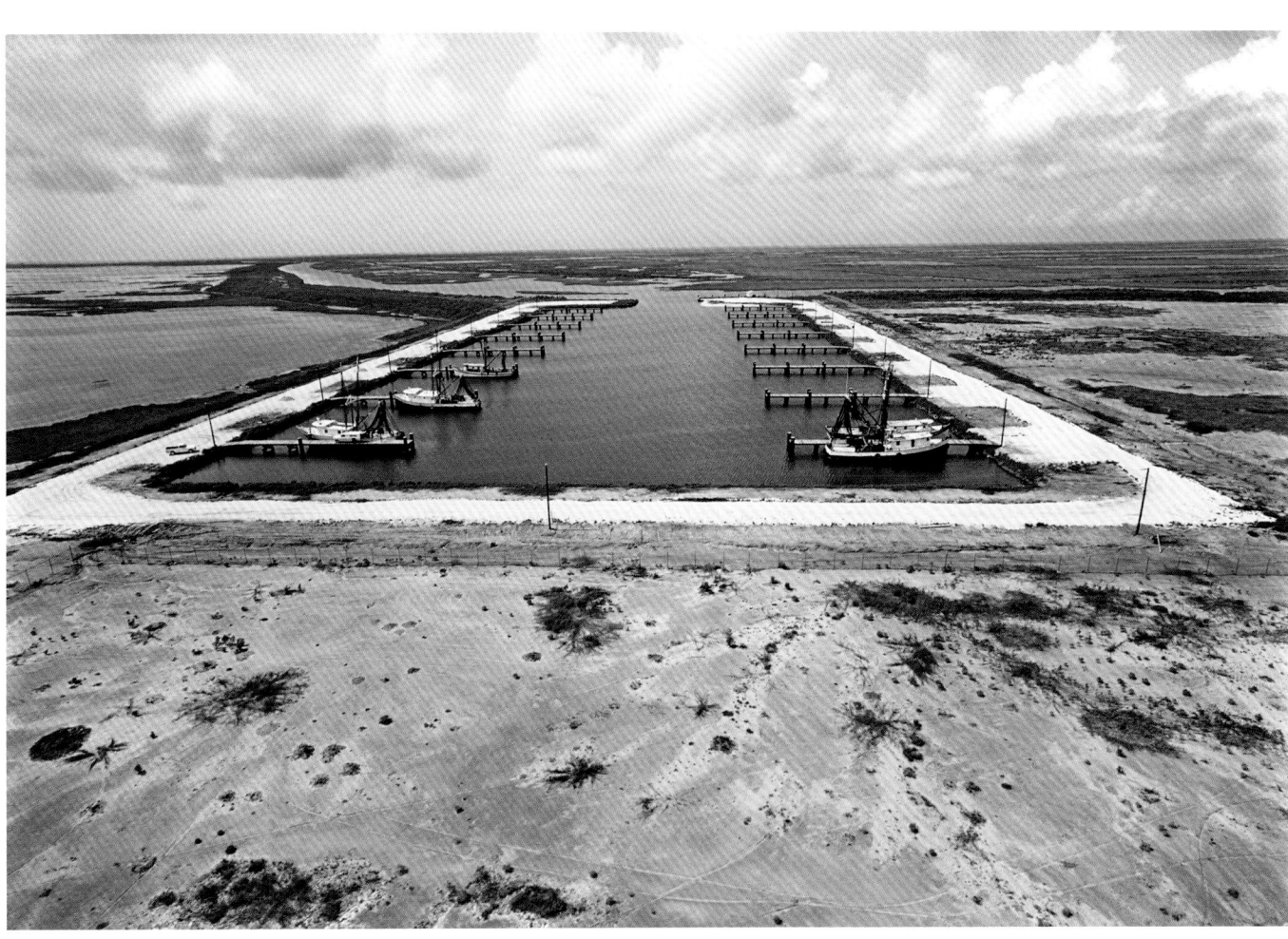

Port Fourchon Marina, Golden Meadow, 1973–74
by Charles H. Traub and Douglas Baz
inkjet print, 21 × 29 in.
2019.0362.100, © Douglas Baz and Charles H. Traub

Debbie Fleming Caffery (b. 1948)

Debbie Fleming Caffery grew up in southwest Louisiana, in the heart of the state's sugarcane fields and processing plants. Around 1973 she began photographing the milieu of sugar production—its mills, fields, laborers, and the inhabitants of the region, often her family and friends. Her photographs from this period present a visual terroir that makes them unmistakably of the locale and unmistakably hers.

Caffery's pictures of sugar growing and processing places are descriptive to a degree, but hardly documentary. This photograph's overall character seems more emblematic than particular. While many of her photographs of people are titled with the subjects' names or nicknames, this man is identified only by his role in the community. The live oaks framing the simple wooden structure are endemic to south Louisiana, as is the Spanish moss that hangs from them. The building surmounted by a bell appears to be a place of worship. Bells not only call congregants to services but have also signaled the start of another day of labor in the field or sugar factory.

With the long and narrow boards of the facade emphasizing the vertical elements of the structure, the man appears incongruously dwarfed by a structure that most likely contains only one room. The photograph does not have the visual obscurity of deep shadow and elimination of details found in some of Caffery's later photographs, but the ambiguity between the grace and patience of the present moment with the historical past presents its own paradox.

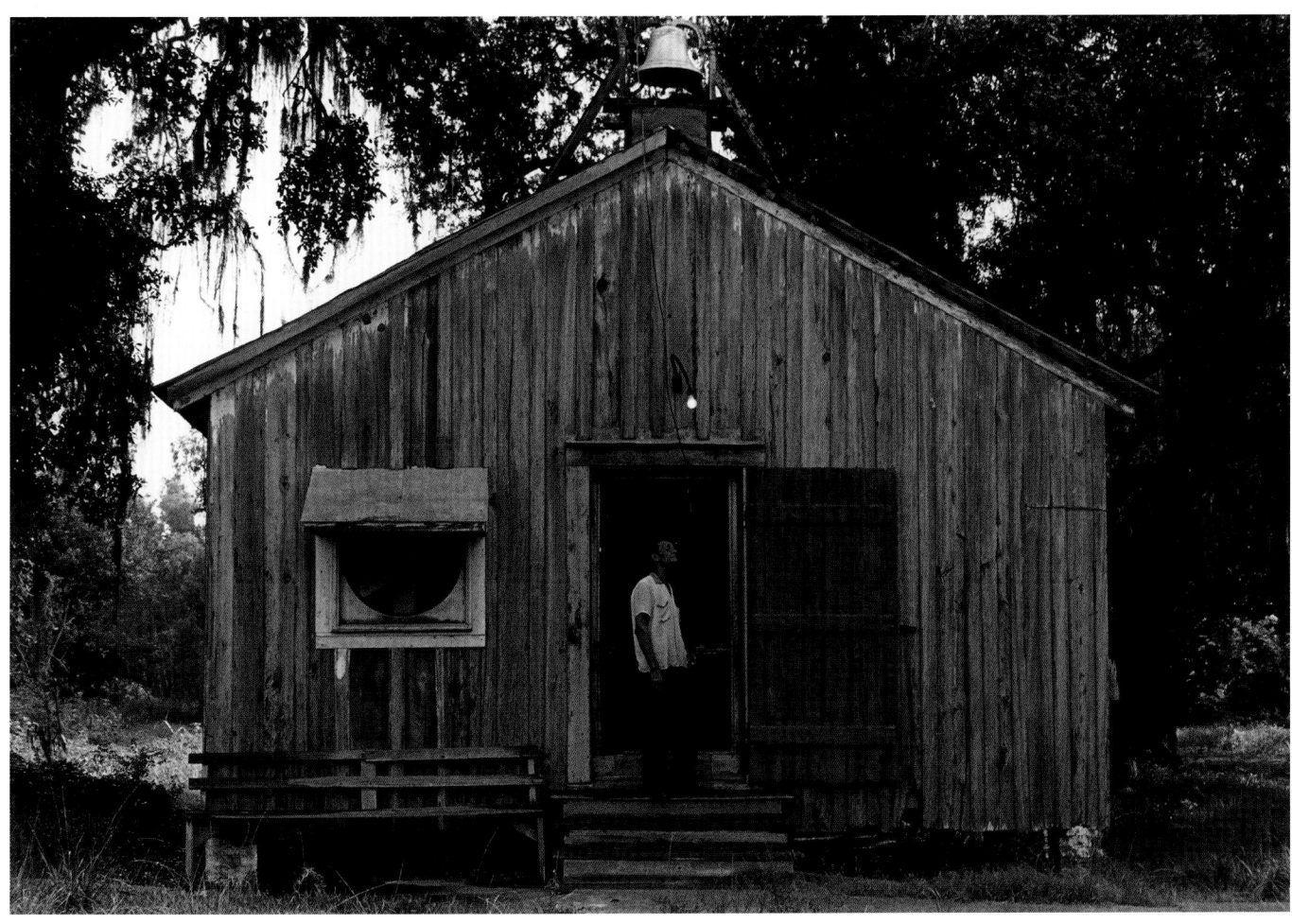

Deacon, 1974
by Debbie Fleming Caffery
gelatin silver print, 16 × 20 in.
gift of an anonymous donor, 2014.0198.1.4, © Debbie Fleming Caffery

Johnny Donnels (1924–2009)

Johnny Donnels was a painter and draftsman who worked as a police sketch artist creating renderings of suspects from eyewitness accounts before he discovered his affinity for photographic expression in the 1960s, when he traded one of his paintings for a camera. For the next four decades, Donnels photographed the French Quarter, the location of both his studio and gallery. The Quarter's architecture—nearly unchanging in form but visually different in varying light and weather—and the dignity of traditional funeral parades were subjects he never seemed to tire of exploring. His subjects were also often people he knew—artists, writers, and musicians—and the titles he gave some photographs, such as this one picturing residents of the building where his studio was housed, underscored his sense of humor and playfulness.

Like Sister Gertrude Morgan (p. 174), Louise "Gypsy Lou" Webb, seen here at left, was the subject of multiple Noel Rockmore portraits. She and Rockmore, on the right, appear as the dominant figures in *Homage to the French Quarter*, the artist's monumental 1975 painting depicting dozens of Vieux Carré inhabitants.

Webb and Rockmore had also collaborated on a publishing project a decade before this photograph was made. Gypsy Lou and her husband, Jon Webb, operated the Loujon Press out of their French Quarter apartment, and they commissioned Rockmore to create artworks for an edition of Charles Bukowski's collection of poems, *Crucifix in a Deathhand* (1965). Loujon had previously published another volume of poems by Bukowski, *It Catches My Heart in Its Hands* (1963).

The Webbs moved to Tucson, Arizona, in 1965, and while there published two works by Henry Miller, as well as continuing to publish their cultural and literary journal, *The Outsider*. Their books and the journal received high critical praise for content and production, but Loujon ceased operation with the death of Jon Webb in 1971. Noel Rockmore died in 1995. Gypsy Lou returned to New Orleans and remained in the area until her death in 2020 at age 104.

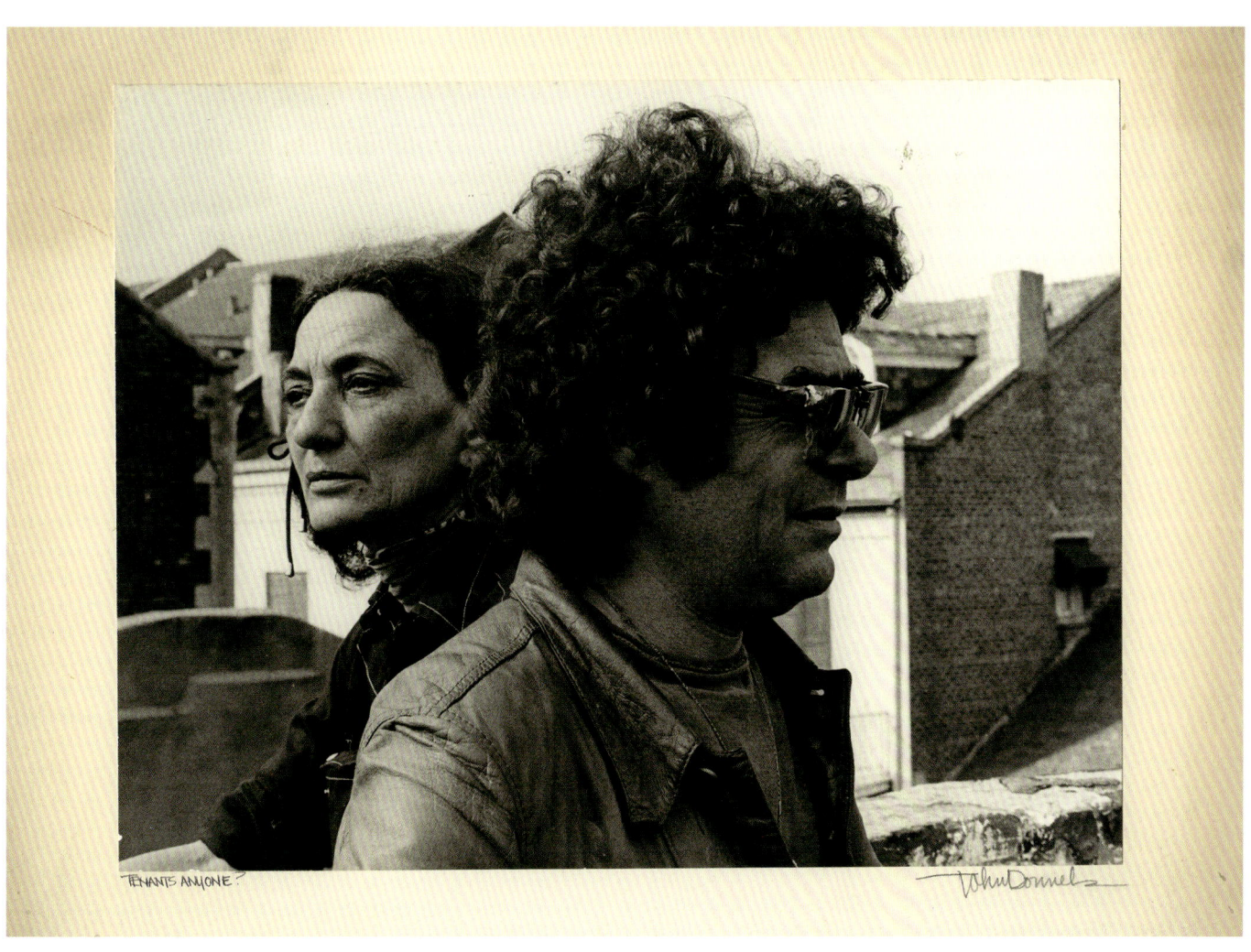

Tenants Anyone?, 1975
by Johnny Donnels
gelatin silver print, mounted, 15 × 20 in.
gift of Joan T. Donnels, 2010.0068.1.2

Michael P. Smith (1937–2008)

Michael P. Smith's first published work in book form, *Spirit World: Pattern in the Expressive Folk Culture of Afro-American New Orleans* (1984), was an extended look at Black spiritualist churches in New Orleans and a tour de force of both photography and respectful cultural investigation. Presented here is one photograph among hundreds, showing a ceremony at the Holy Family Spiritual Church of Christ in the city's Lower Ninth Ward. Smith's camera was present through the decades at Mardi Gras Indian practices and street appearances, jazz funerals, and the parades of social aid and pleasure clubs. In short, he covered the city's cultural calendar while maintaining a commercial practice that focused on editorial assignments for a range of clients, including the photo agency Black Star.

In the Spirit: The Photography of Michael P. Smith from The Historic New Orleans Collection contains many of his most widely known works: photographs from his perennial appearances at the New Orleans Jazz and Heritage Festival as well as other New Orleans music venues. The example seen here shows Blue Lu and Danny Barker (left and center, respectively) with pianist Tuts Washington at Tipitina's, the club Smith helped to launch. His determination to get close to the performers, along with his unerring instinct for composition and timing, combined to convey the vibrancy of New Orleans music within the limitations of still photography.

Smith's photograph of the corner of South Claiborne and Washington Avenues epitomizes his observation that some neighborhoods in New Orleans are "cultural wetlands." Deconstructing this photograph's visual and implied elements offers insight into Smith's focused take on African American culture in New Orleans during the time he photographed, from the late 1960s until the early years of the twenty-first century.

The overwhelming majority of Smith's photography was done with handheld instruments that used roll film in 35 mm and (rarely) 6 × 6 cm formats, but for this picture Smith employed a 4 × 5-inch, tripod-mounted view camera using sheets of film. The photograph depicts human activity from a distance, set against architecture and a torrent of advertising on a busy corner. In the catalog of a history museum, one could define the "subject" as one chooses—advertising, street life, or commerce, to name a few.

Despite the predeterminations that go into using a view camera (e.g., tripod position, framing of the scene, and lens and shutter settings that must be accomplished in advance), the element of spontaneity in this picture reflects the nimbleness of Smith's handheld camera work. This may be best understood by the figure at the far right, walking out of the frame, his foot barely blurred by a shutter speed too long to capture it cleanly in mid-step. With the exceptions of the man with the staff and the person at the far left who seems to look directly at Smith, the groups of people on the sidewalk, perhaps waiting for a bus, are engaged with each other.

In keeping with his metaphor of cultural wetlands, Smith shows two types of businesses that fostered both tradition and conversation: a record store and a barbershop. Other such places where neighborhood residents met included bars, sweetshops, corner groceries, and churches. Over time, Smith captured all those community incubators and more.

In this richly layered photograph, the posters promoting gospel concerts, political candidates, dances, and musical reviews happening around town in large and small venues add to the notion of community. One of these places is the ILA (International Longshoremen's Association) Union Hall, which stood opposite the corner shown in the photograph. The union hall—now demolished—was a place where many African American cultural activities took place. With his camera set squarely between the two corners, Smith places himself in the middle of the cultural wetlands he deemed so important.

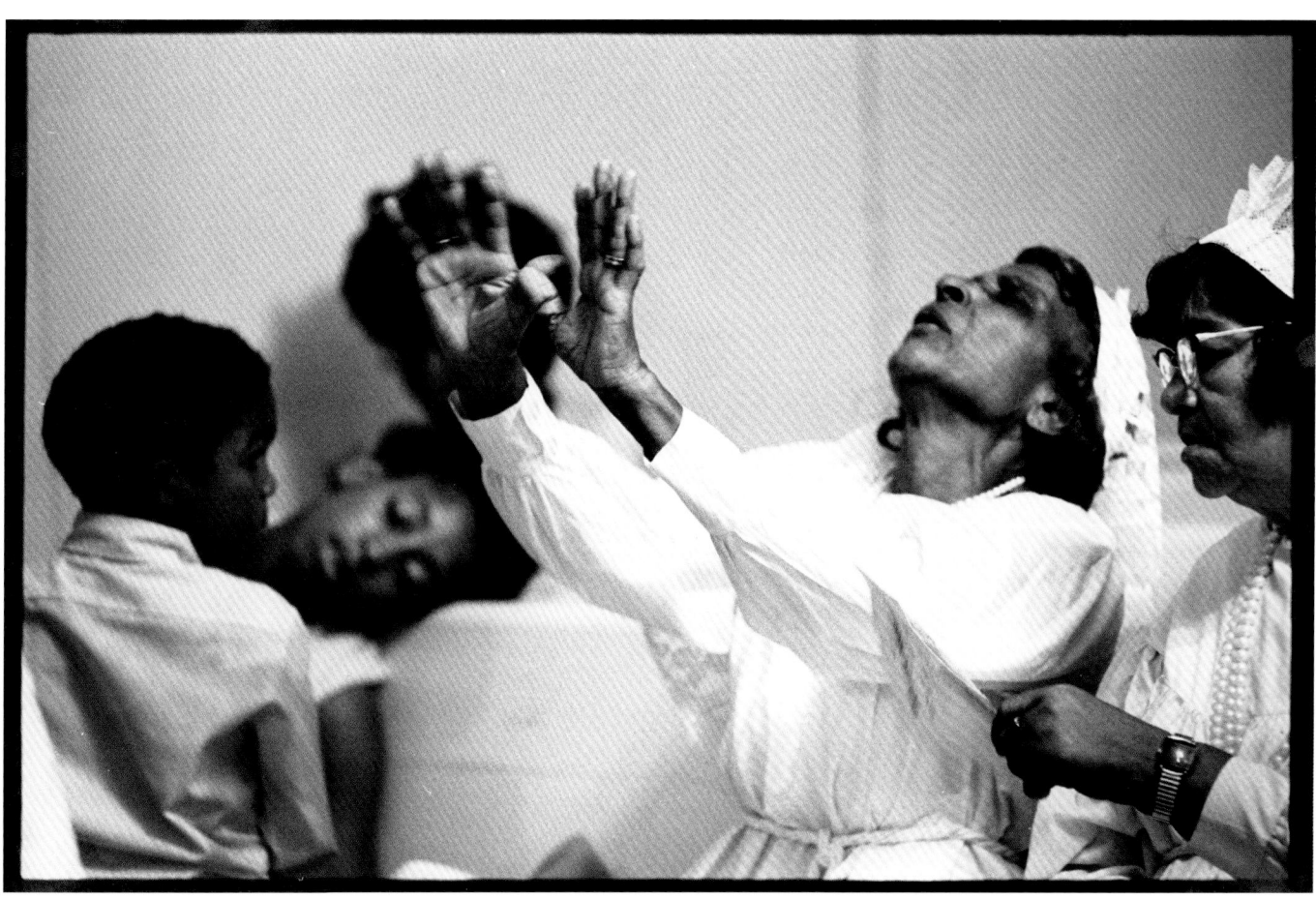

***Holy Family Spiritual Church*, 1973**

by Michael P. Smith
gelatin silver negative, 35 mm
2007.0103.1.302.1, © The Historic New Orleans Collection

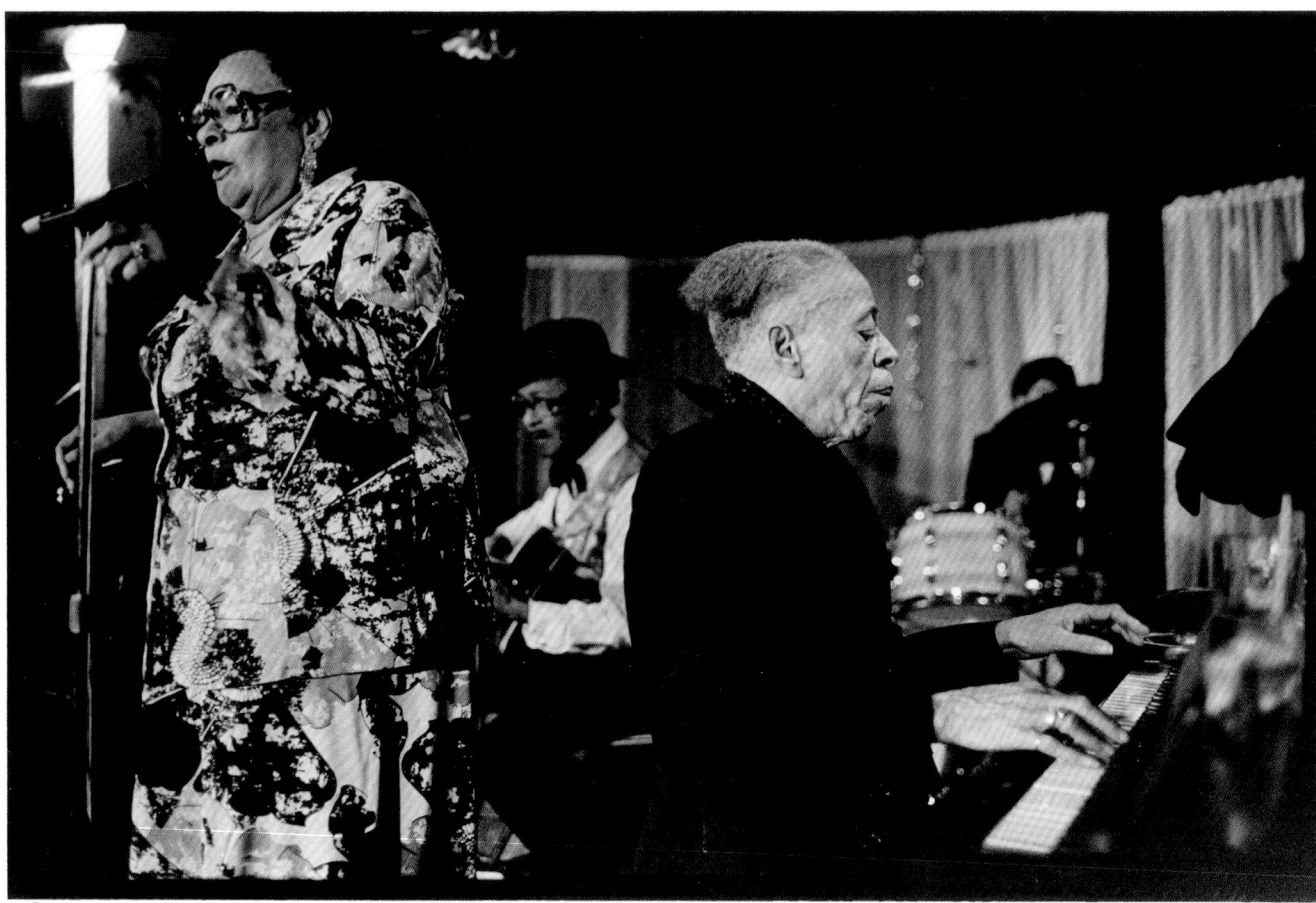

Lu & Danny Barker with Tuts Washington at Tips handwritten caption · 1575/31 · Michael P. Smith, 1978

Lu & Danny Barker with Tuts Washington at Tips, 1978
by Michael P. Smith
gelatin silver print, mounted, 14 × 17 in.
gift of Master Digital Corporation, 2011.0307.16, © The Historic New Orleans Collection

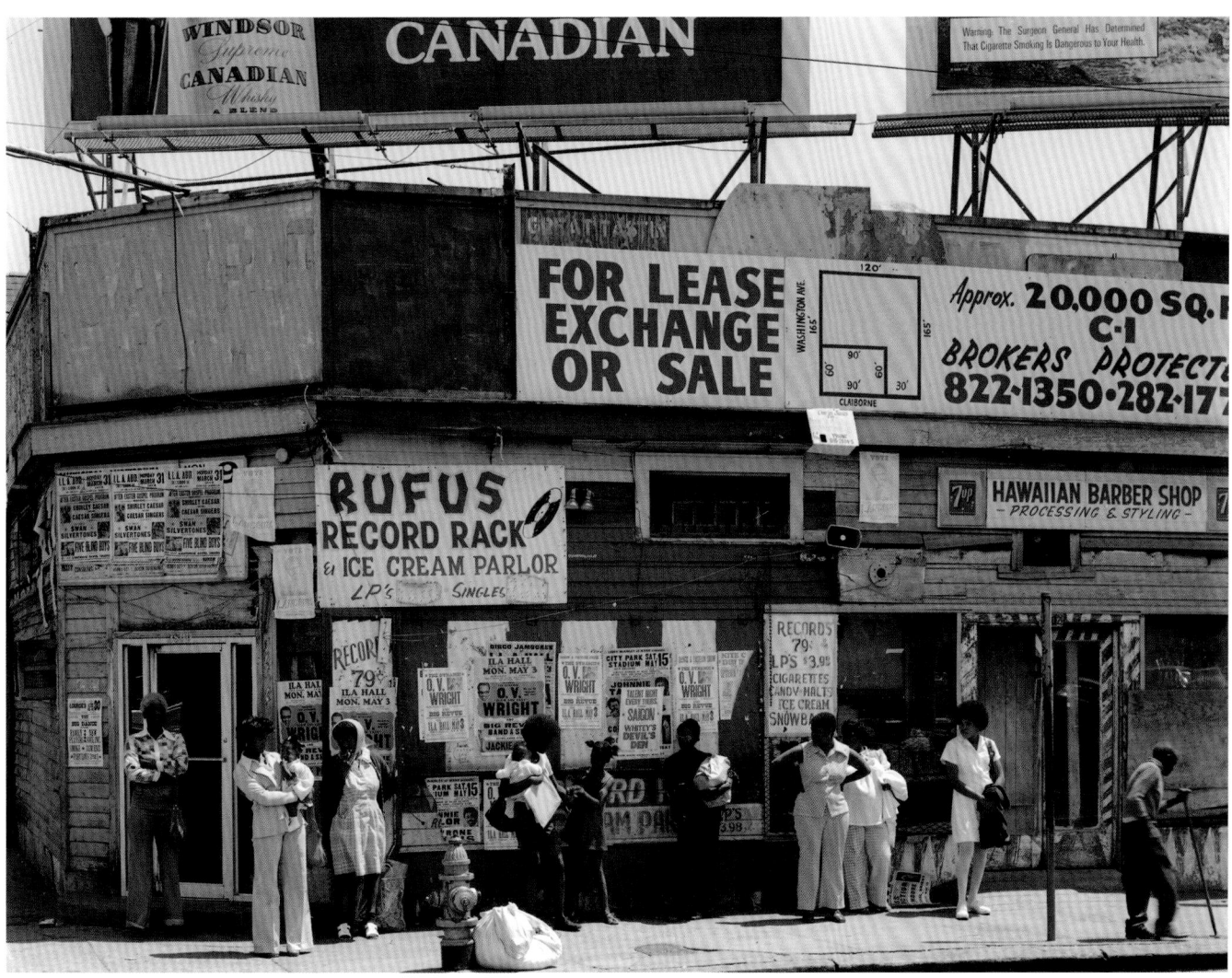

Claiborne and Washington, 1976

by Michael P. Smith
gelatin silver negative, 4 × 5 in.
2007.0103.1.1.8, © The Historic New Orleans Collection

Josephine Sacabo (b. 1944)

Josephine Sacabo's photograph is one of a portfolio of the city's markets and street vendors commissioned from her by The Historic New Orleans Collection for a 1976 exhibition on the subject. At the time, her work was strongly grounded in the tradition of black-and-white, documentary-style photography identified with a group of New Orleans photographers whose work was inspired by the city, its people, and its traditions. In time, Sacabo's photography became mostly concerned with the human figure, often catalyzed by literary and poetic texts, and rendered in deep, shadowy tones that she presented in both photographs and photogravure prints.

Comparing her photograph with one by Stuart Klipper (p. 245) of the same site made a quarter century later, the primary changes to this seafood market appear to be only minor and cosmetic. But the signs tell another story. In Sacabo's picture, the market still sells turtle meat, which is not in evidence in Klipper's picture. Indeed, the later picture shows an expansion of the market's offerings beyond seafood, including prepared foods such as jambalaya as well as chicken and ribs. At present, though the market building remains, it now houses an upscale food court rather than a traditional market.

Turtle soup is a dish that can trigger strong emotions. It is rightly seen as an exotic delicacy in most of the United States, yet for much of the twentieth century, turtle soup was a regular offering on New Orleans menus. But the basis of the dish—turtles—became increasingly threatened through excessive harvest of one species after another. Turtle farms took up some of this trade but could not raise their product fast enough to meet demand. In the last quarter of the twentieth century, the commercial catch of wild turtles was mostly banned in the United States, though recreational catch is still permitted in some places.

The apex predator alligator snapping turtle (often known as "cowan" in Louisiana) is now the primary species used for turtle soup, though in late 2021 the US Fish and Wildlife Service proposed listing it as a threatened species under the Endangered Species Act.

Lama's St. Roch Market, 1976
by Josephine Sacabo
gelatin silver print, 14 × 11 in.
1976.128.25

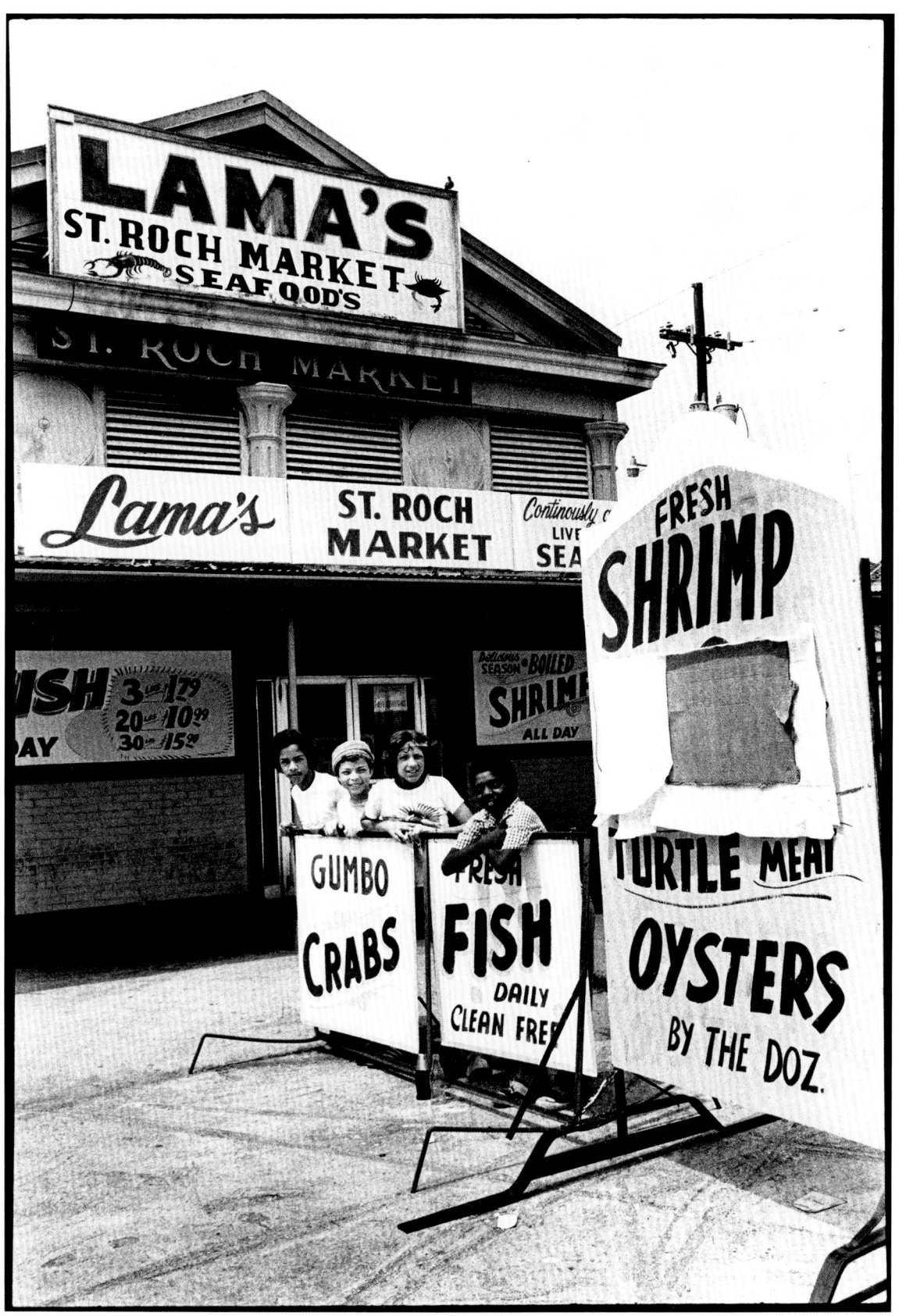

Christopher R. Harris (b. 1945)

In 1977, as his play *Vieux Carré* was being prepared for production in New York, Tennessee Williams came to New Orleans (where he maintained a residence) with Christopher R. Harris and David Chandler, a writer for *People* magazine. One of the places Williams brought them in a walkabout of the French Quarter was 722 Toulouse Street, where he had lived in a garret apartment when he first arrived in the late 1930s. Nearly all the action of the autobiographical play is set in this building. Williams seems almost wistful as he faces the light coming through the dormer. The walls, no longer covered with plaster, have perhaps given up their memories in the nearly four decades between his first visit and the one memorialized in this photograph.

One might imagine the playwright thinking of *Vieux Carré's* opening lines spoken by the main character known only as The Writer: "Once this house was alive, it was occupied once. In my recollection, it still is, but by shadowy occupants like ghosts. Now they enter the lighter areas of my memory." Harris's photograph puts the older Williams in conversation with his younger self.

Also in the party was Richard Alfieri, playing the lead in the New York production, who also absorbed the atmosphere of Williams's room and asked if he could take a scrap of broken plaster as a talisman.

The building was in the process of being restored to its early nineteenth-century appearance, for use by The Historic New Orleans Collection. It was being changed from the updated structure of the late nineteenth century (with its additional half-story added to the upper level) that Williams had experienced during his tenancy. The building had been acquired by Kemper and Leila Williams, founders of The Historic New Orleans Collection (and no relation to the playwright), shortly after the latter moved out. During the Williamses' ownership, the building had a garage on the first floor and living quarters for housekeeping staff on the upper levels.

Williams and the other visitors spent some time walking through rooms whose future occupants would be archivists and curators rather than the mismatched set of tenants that Williams encountered in early 1939, and whom he placed in the setting of his play.

Harris is a photojournalist whose work appeared in gallery exhibitions and was published in national and international periodicals during the last quarter of the twentieth century and well into the twenty-first. He has enjoyed a long career in photographic education at the university level that covered the transition from film photography to digital imaging. Harris's published articles often concentrate on legal issues in the age of digital photography.

Tennessee Williams at 722 Toulouse Street, 1977
by Christopher R. Harris
gelatin silver print, 14 × 10⅞ in.
1994.143.2, © Christopher R. Harris

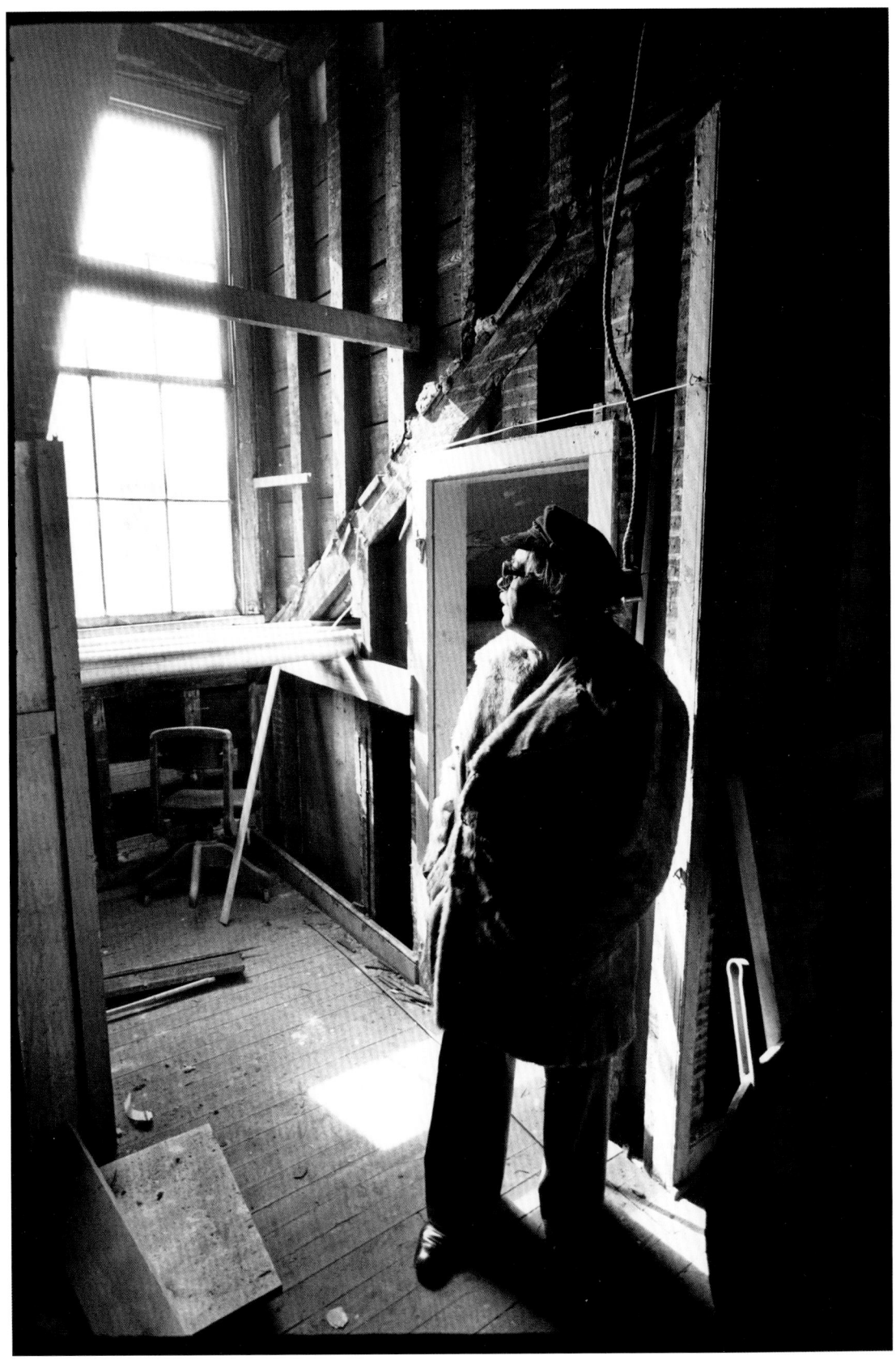

Jim Zietz (b. 1956)

In addition to being the nexus of the perique tobacco industry in Louisiana, St. James Parish is a center of sugar fields and sugar production, both historically and at present. The building in Jim Zietz's photograph is the Hymel House on the east bank of the Mississippi River. Hymel, a surname initially associated with the lands bordering the Mississippi River between New Orleans and Baton Rouge, likely derives from the Germanic Himel, and the region where this building is found has been called "the German Coast" for centuries. German-speaking immigrants came to Louisiana in the early eighteenth century to establish farms to feed the colonial population, and today numerous descendants from dozens of families still live in the area.

Jim Zietz's career in photography was anchored by his role as head photographer for Louisiana State University's flagship campus in Baton Rouge, and in that capacity he thoroughly chronicled activities on campus, the visits of speakers and dignitaries, and other events that are the ebb and flow of life at an institution with a student population of nearly thirty-five thousand.

Zietz's work and interests extended beyond the boundaries of the campus. His photographs of Cajun Mardi Gras in rural Louisiana demonstrate how widely that holiday celebration differs from what happens in New Orleans. His portraits of Louisiana musicians, especially those in Baton Rouge, capture performers at rest and in concert. Zietz worked with decorative arts historians for decades to photograph significant examples of Louisiana's material culture, and with architectural historians to document hundreds of historic buildings.

His photograph of the Hymel plantation house shows the building in a state of decay, and perhaps on the brink of collapsing. Several years after Zietz made his photograph, the structure was the subject of ten measured drawings for the Historic American Buildings Survey (HABS) in 1983 (p. 114). By the late 1990s, the Hymel House was no longer standing.

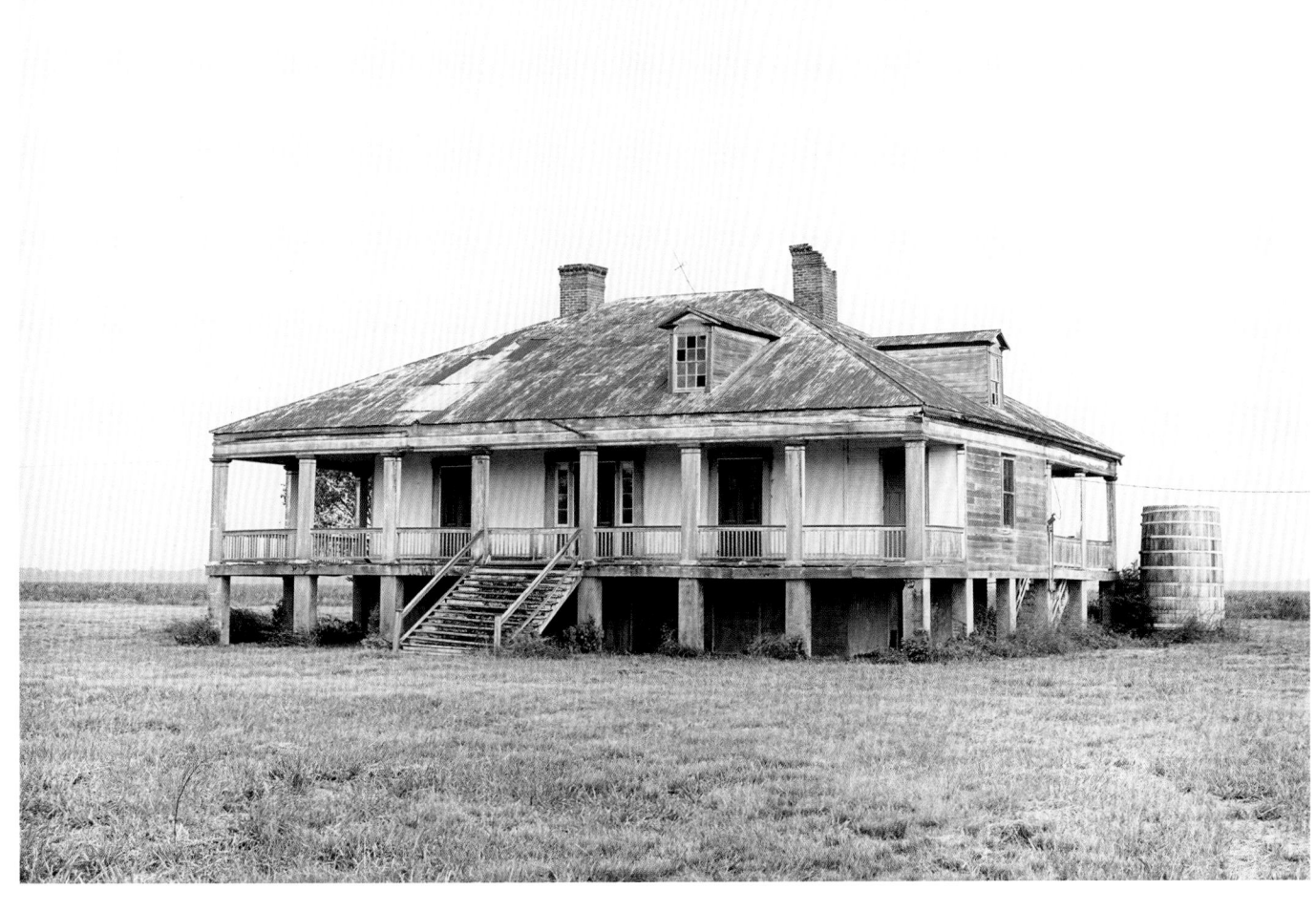

Hymel House, 1977
by Jim Zietz
inkjet print, 13 × 19 in.
2020.0202.1, © Jim Zietz

The inkjet print was made in 2019 from a 1977 film negative.

William Karam Jr. (b. 1948)

For much of the developed history of New Orleans, the banks of the Mississippi River were exclusively dedicated to industrial uses such as wharves, cargo handling, and railroads rather than recreational purposes. The river, walled off figuratively and sometimes literally from the populace, was not designed for residents' leisure activities. Through the decades, one could appreciate the magnificence of North America's central waterway from the deck of one of several ferryboats that crossed at New Orleans. When the first bridges spanning the river were built (1935 in adjacent Jefferson Parish and 1958 in New Orleans), motorists could glimpse the river from an elevated viewpoint, but however interesting a view they afforded, these crossings were not a pastime in and of themselves.

In the last quarter of the twentieth century, many cities around the country began reconsidering their relationship with waters that bordered their precincts and converted these areas into parks for pure enjoyment. New Orleans got its first real taste of this trend in the mid-1970s, as former industrial areas of the French Quarter began to be redeveloped for the public.

Between 1969 and 1972 NASA's Apollo space missions to the moon resulted in six human landings, and the astronauts' explorations of the surface were called moonwalks. And though NASA's Michoud Assembly Facility had built the booster rockets for these missions, it was not only New Orleans's connection to the Apollo program that gave this riverfront park its moniker. From 1970 to 1978, Moon Landrieu was mayor of New Orleans. Because of his administration's role in this riverfront project, which opened to the public in 1975, the promenade was given the name Moonwalk.

Since its launch, the Moonwalk has undergone two upgrades—most recently in 2018 for the tricentennial of New Orleans's founding—and with expansion and additional landscaping and hardscaping, it looks much different from the simple wooden boardwalk flanked with benches that appears in William Karam Jr.'s photograph. The city's current master plan calls for a nearly unbroken linear riverfront park several miles long, to connect residents to the geographic feature that prompted the city's settlement over three centuries ago.

Karam's photograph of a foggy atmosphere with strong backlighting eliminates many details and emphasizes the graphic character of this scene. A native of Louisiana, Karam received a fine arts degree from Northwestern State University in Natchitoches. His main discipline in the fine arts program was painting, but his years as a resident of New Orleans saw him make many photographs around his French Quarter neighborhood.

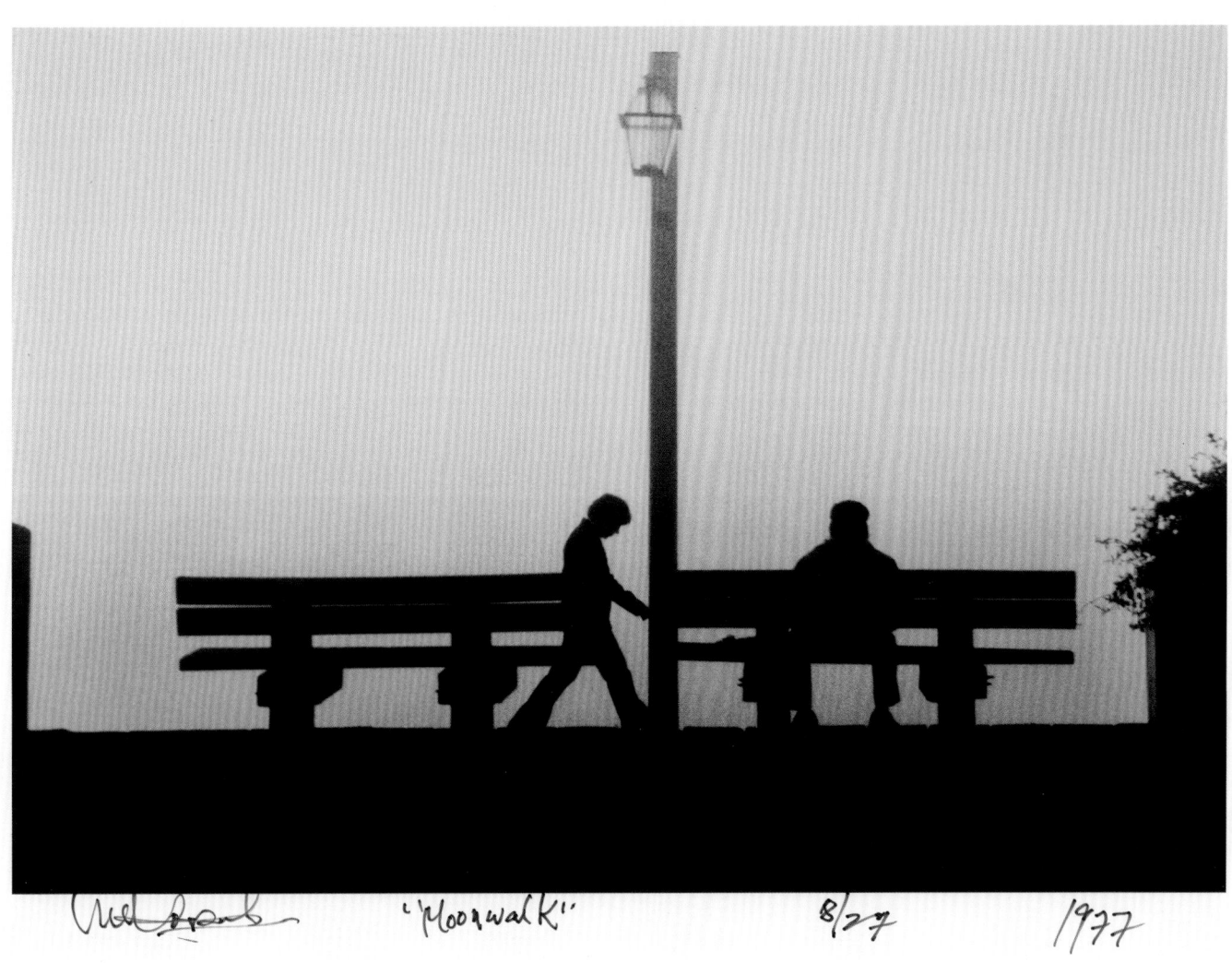

"Moonwalk" 8/27 1977

Moonwalk, 1977
by William Karam Jr.
inkjet print, 8½ × 11 in.
gift of William Karam Jr., 2017.0159.1, © William Karam Jr.

The inkjet print was made in 2012 from a 1977 negative.

Owen F. Murphy Jr. (b. 1948)

Owen F. Murphy Jr. is loosely associated with a group of New Orleans–based photographers whose careers began in the late 1960s and continued for decades. The general character of their work was based on a 35 mm reportage style exploring the daily rhythms of New Orleans's environment—its neighborhoods, foodways, music, streetscapes, residents, and festivals. In addition to Murphy, others associated with this era include Harold Baquet, D. Eric Bookhardt, Keith Calhoun, Luis Castrillo, Sandra Russell Clark, Barry Kaiser, Joshua Mann Pailet, Chandra McCormick, Jack Pickett, David Richmond, Josephine Sacabo, and Michael P. Smith. Kaiser and Richmond were instrumental in founding the first gallery in New Orleans dedicated to photography, the Photo Exchange, a place where, as Murphy recalled, "independent artists forg[ed] their own identities and individual destinies via collective efforts."

The elevated portion of Interstate 10 in this photograph, built upon the neutral ground (or median) of North Claiborne Avenue, was a little more than a decade old when Murphy made this picture. It was later included in *Créoles of New Orleans* (1987), with photographs by Murphy and text by Lyla Hay Owen, published through funding from the Arts Council of New Orleans. The expressway in Murphy's photograph looms over the ground-level street activity, dwarfing the human figures. It casts both a literal and figurative shadow on the Tremé and adjacent neighborhoods that had been home to many Creole families since the suburb was first laid out in 1810. Black-owned businesses had flourished along North Claiborne, and stately rows of mature live oaks lined its parklike neutral ground. When urban planners routed I-10 through the heart of Tremé, the oaks were cut down and the grass was paved over, depriving the neighborhood of a greenway as well as dividing it physically. Many homes and businesses were expropriated and demolished to make way for the elevated highway's

on- and off-ramps. With six lanes of traffic causing a constant background roar, the expressway decimated the neighborhood's economy, along with its physical character and ambiance. What the photograph can't show is what intangible aspects of Tremé were lost.

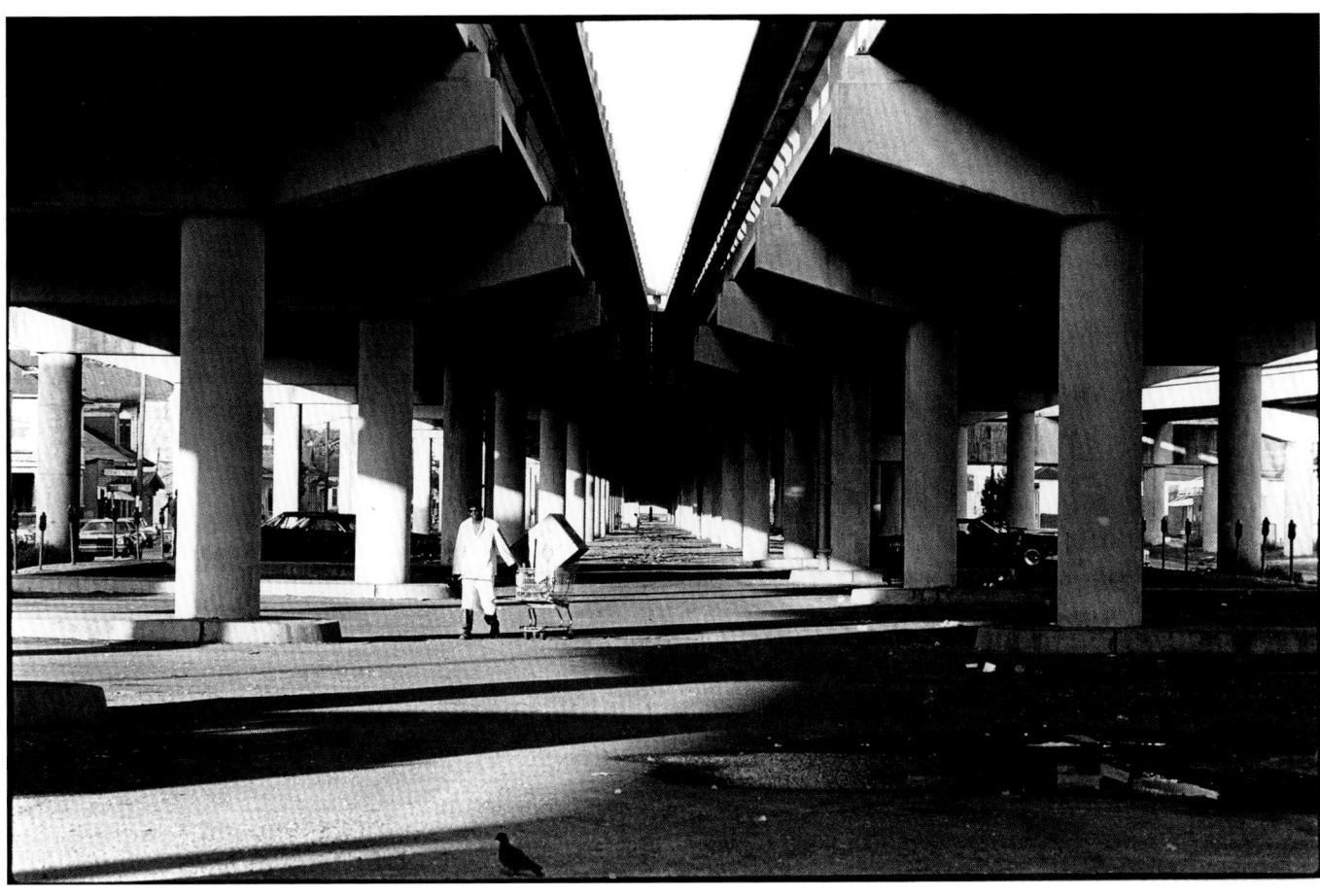

Where There Was Once an Avenue of Oaks, 1978
by Owen F. Murphy Jr.
gelatin silver print, 14 × 18 in.
gift of Arts Council of New Orleans, 1996.93.57, © Owen F. Murphy Jr.

Stephanie B. Dinkins (1913–1997)

In Stephanie B. Dinkins's archive at The Historic New Orleans Collection, one negative sleeve containing two strips of film is inscribed "Parlange and Hawaii," giving an inkling of the breadth of her photographic work. Parlange, a plantation home in New Roads, Louisiana, and the Hawaiian Islands are thousands of miles apart, but it is the differences among places and cultures worldwide that drove Dinkins's creative impulses. With the exception of Antarctica, she photographed on every continent of the world.

Dinkins was born in the Cajun town of Charenton and attended Tulane University's Newcomb College, graduating with a degree in French and an interest in English literature. Following her graduation she moved to New York and worked as an editor before joining the newly formed United Nations, helping to produce the agency's radio projects. After leaving the UN she continued this work as a freelance correspondent for the organization and for commercial radio networks, proposing and writing her own stories. An assignment to Saudi Arabia for which she also made photographs marked her turn to photography.

After a globetrotting career, Dinkins returned to Louisiana in the 1960s and remained anchored to the state for the remainder of her life. She photographed extensively in the Cane River area near Natchitoches and around False River near New Roads. The town where Dinkins was born was barely one hundred miles from where the photograph of this young girl was made. As befits a person grounded in journalism, Dinkins's photographs are often done in series. Other pictures of the same subject indicate that the setting for this picture was a church.

Dinkins first used color film in 1957 but continued to employ black-and-white film extensively. When interviewed by Diane M. Moore for her book *Their Adventurous Will: Profiles of Memorable Louisiana Women*, Dinkins observed,

"I have discovered, like so many others before me, that Louisiana is not only beautiful, it is picturesque, mysterious, and even exotic."

Young girl near New Roads, 1980
by Stephanie B. Dinkins
gelatin silver print, 10 × 8 in.
gift of an anonymous donor, 2016.0339.2.1

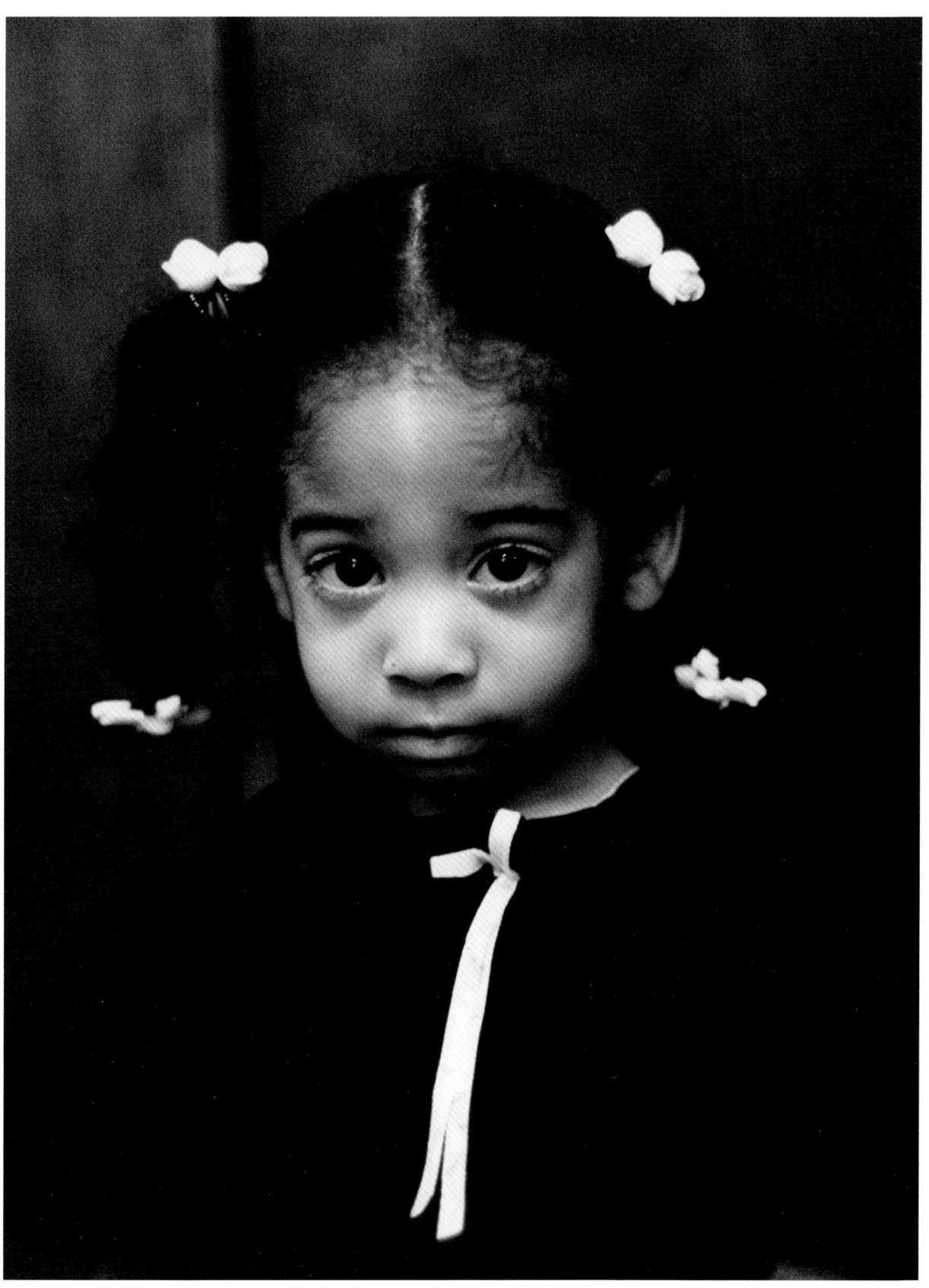

Warren Gravois (b. 1937)

The small scraps of paper on the ground visible in the photographs of these tombs might be mistaken for litter or wind-deposited detritus. But closer examination of the alphanumeric codes suggests something more systematic. The numbered squares, when matched with an index, identify individual tombs in a large-scale documentation project that was a joint effort of the nonprofit group Save Our Cemeteries, the University of New Orleans, and The Historic New Orleans Collection.

The debut issue of THNOC's *Quarterly* (January 1983) described the documentation process:

> The project, which began in August of 1981, set out to document thoroughly the aged tombs and wall vaults contained within several historic New Orleans cemeteries. All information inscribed on the tombs and vaults was carefully transcribed, and the material and condition of the tombs were recorded. This information has been typed on cards and indexed for ease of use. In addition, an 8 × 10 black-and-white photograph of each tomb has been filed with the written information, so that design motifs will be readily apparent.
>
> The four cemeteries included in the National Register of Historic Places, St. Louis No. 1, St. Louis No. 2, Lafayette No. 1, and Odd Fellow's Rest, were surveyed initially. Because of the value and success of the project, the survey was extended to include the nineteenth-century sections of Cypress Grove and Greenwood cemeteries. . . . Approximately 5,300 tombs and 7,000 wall vaults have been documented. Photographer Warren Gravois, of Gulf South Photography, has shot over 8,000 photographs.

Over time the project was extended to include a total of nine cemeteries. In addition to those mentioned in the

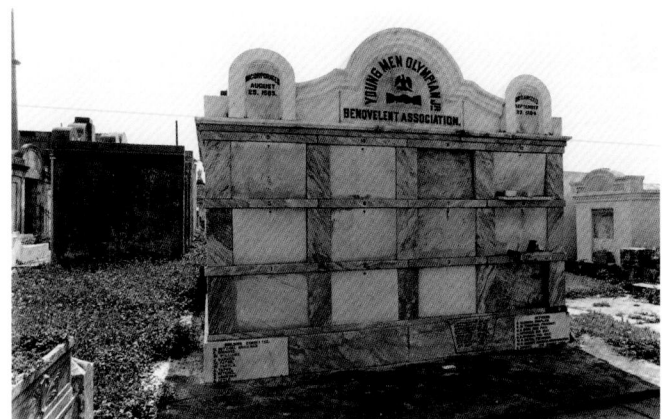

quotation above, Lafayette No. 2, St. Joseph No. 1, and St. Joseph No. 2 are included. The total number of items increased to 11,525.

The two photographs here hint at some of the many ways that such an inventory can be used besides documenting the tombs' condition at the time the photographs were made. The gravesite surrounded by a Gothic-style cast-iron fence suggests not only the design influences of historical revival architectural styles (heavily represented in the city's cemeteries) but also speaks to a strong nineteenth-century business of iron foundries and importers in New Orleans. The society tomb of the Young Men Olympian Jr. Benevolent Association attests to the prevalence of such vaults in many New Orleans cemeteries and is especially significant, as this group is the oldest of such organizations founded by African Americans for African Americans still extant.

Lafayette Cemetery No. 2, between 1981 and 1983
by Warren Gravois
gelatin silver print, 8 × 10 in.
Survey of Historic New Orleans Cemeteries, Williams Research Center, The Historic New Orleans Collection, MSS 360.4.297

Lafayette Cemetery No. 1, between 1981 and 1983
by Warren Gravois
gelatin silver print, 10 × 8 in.
Survey of Historic New Orleans Cemeteries, Williams Research Center, The Historic New Orleans Collection, MSS 360.3.649

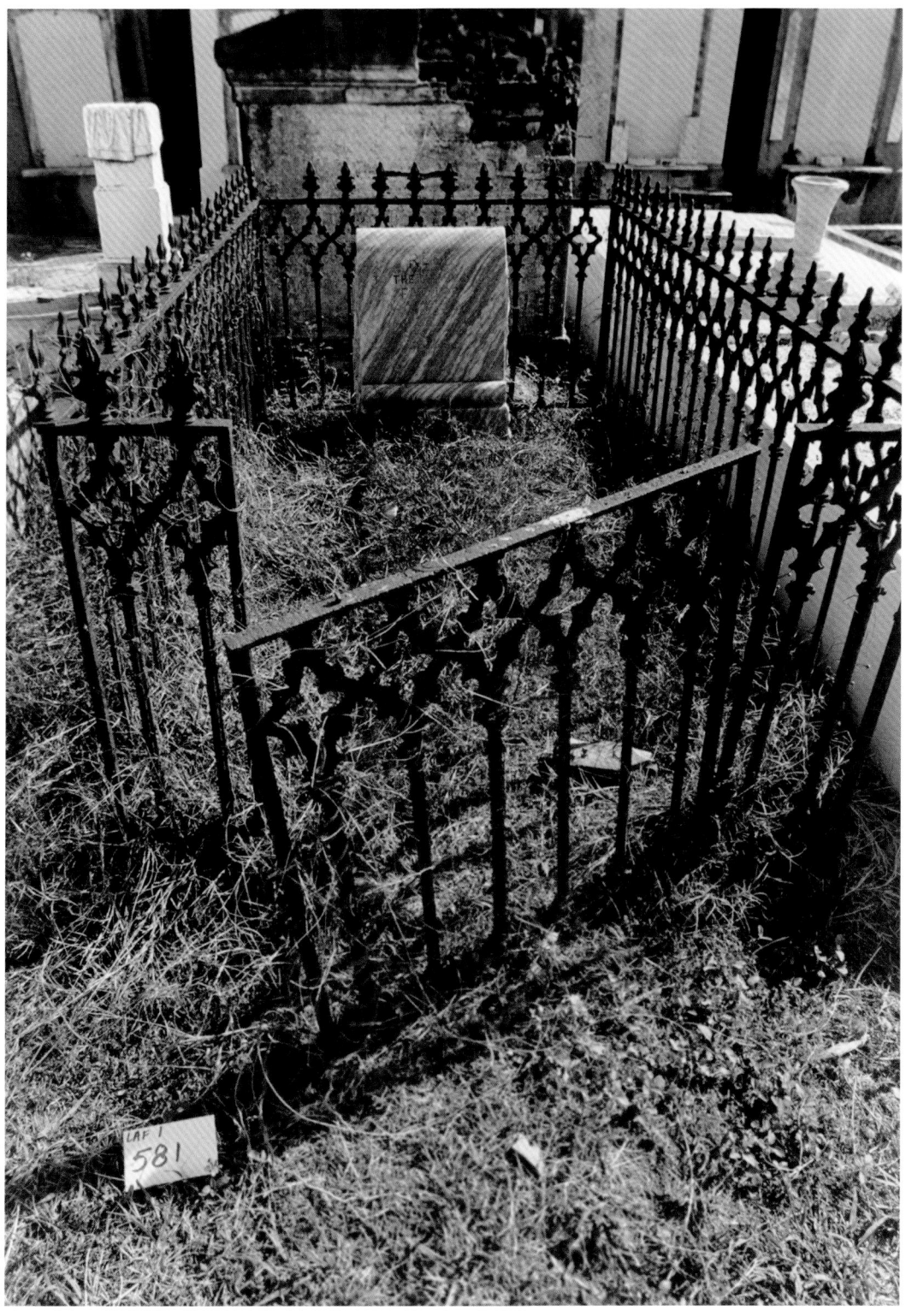

A. J. Meek (b. 1941)

The confrontation with an 8 × 10 view camera usually gives a portrait subject pause. Typically, the camera and its required tripod together stand at least as tall as the human being photographed, and the photographer, invisible under the focusing cloth, gives instructions or encouragement. The session is hardly conducive to spontaneity. Framing the portrait, focusing the scene on the camera's ground glass screen, and adjusting the lens aperture and shutter speed all take place in a manner that would have been familiar to George F. Mugnier and his contemporaries. The entire setup may command respect for the process, but the time it takes might also help to relax the subject. Mr. Wilbert Pryer's stance conveys that respect as well as his own sense of confidence in this social transaction, the contours of his figure serving as a counterpoint to the rigid lines presented by the building and paving.

A. J. Meek is a photographer and photographic educator who has worked in Louisiana since the early 1980s. The majority of his photographs were made with large format cameras that use individual sheets of film rather than cameras that make successive pictures on the same roll of film. If his technical approach has been narrow, his subjects have been wide ranging. Extended series of pictures include industrial subjects, landscapes, the pepper production of Avery Island, and places of worship.

This portrait is from a series that Meek undertook in the 1980s in rural Louisiana communities along the Mississippi River and throughout the state. The photograph is an example of a contact print, a process sometimes used to produce pictures from an entire roll of film on one sheet of photographic paper, to assess the merits of each individual frame (see examples on p. 158–59 and 243). In this case, however, each frame occupies the entire sheet.

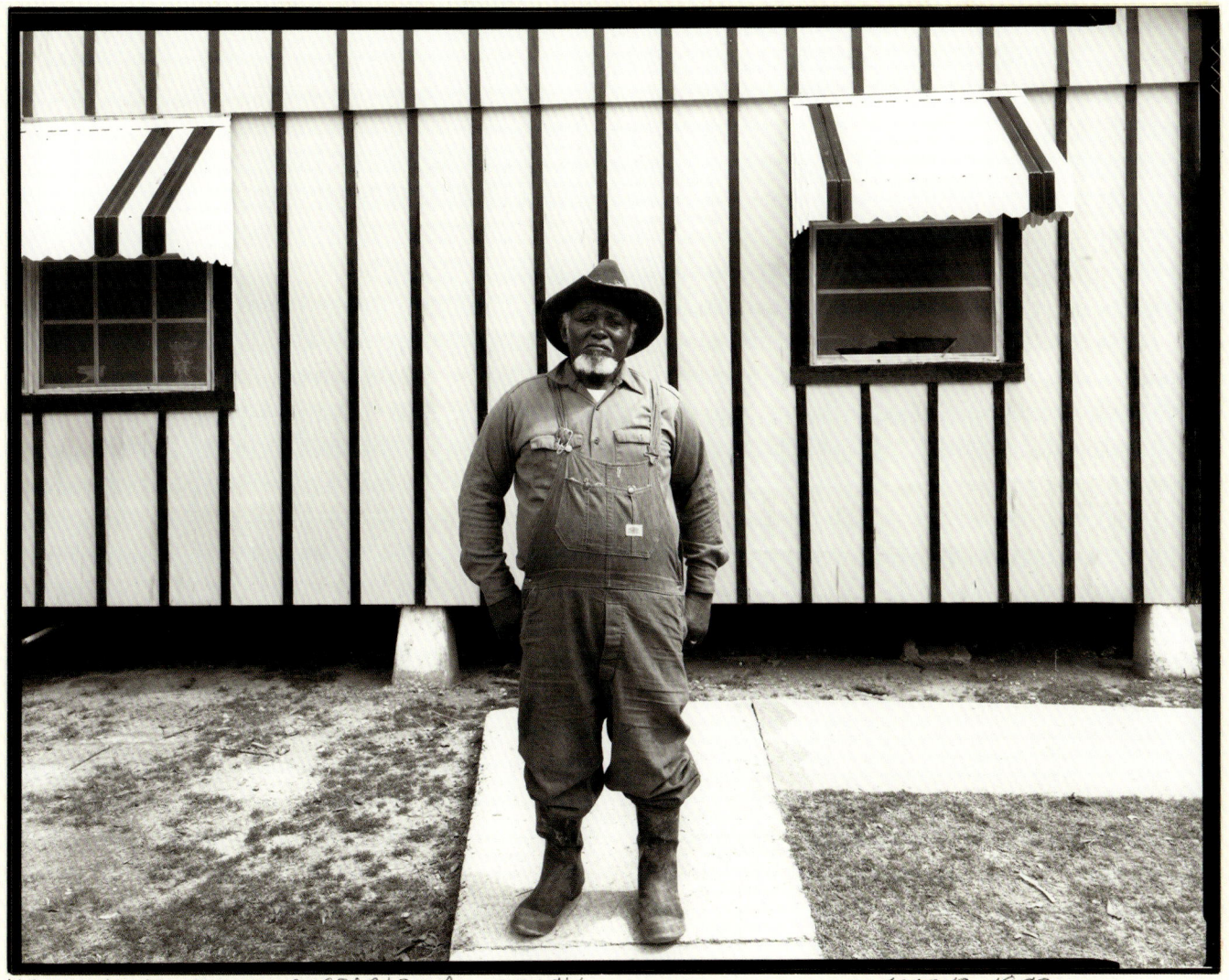

MR WILBERT PRYER, ROSEDALE, LA. NEG #1   MAR 12, 1982

Mr. Wilbert Pryer, Rosedale, LA. Neg #1, 1982
by A. J. Meek
gelatin silver contact print, 8 × 9⅞ in.
gift of A. J. Meek, 2013.0022.9.266

Christopher Porché West (1958–2023)

Born in Los Angeles, Christopher Porché West came to New Orleans, the city of some of his Louisiana ancestors, to conduct research for his senior thesis at the University of California, Santa Cruz. He was especially interested in the historic community of free people of color and their contemporary descendants, traditions, and networks.

Prior to the abolition of slavery, free people of color in New Orleans inhabited a stratum of legal identity that placed them under whites and above the enslaved in terms of rights. Members of this vibrant community achieved financial success in fields as varied as real estate, journalism, music, and skilled trades such as carpentry, ironwork, plastering, and masonry.

In 1995, after several extended trips to New Orleans, Porché West made the city his permanent home, continuing full-time photographic exploration of the subject that first drew him to the city. As his work progressed, he enlarged the context of the traditions he photographed in New Orleans to include parallel ones in Cuba and Haiti.

The photograph here shows a modest barbershop in the Tremé section of New Orleans. Such small businesses have functioned as compact community centers for the neighborhoods they serve, where people meet and talk while conducting the nominal commerce of the enterprise. This symbolic role is further emphasized by the sign that is generic rather than specific: BARBER SHOP. Not "So-and-so's" Barbershop. Despite the "closed" sign on the door, the man on the stoop seems on the lookout for potential trade or conversation, renewing on each day a tradition of engagement and inquiry that has existed for generations.

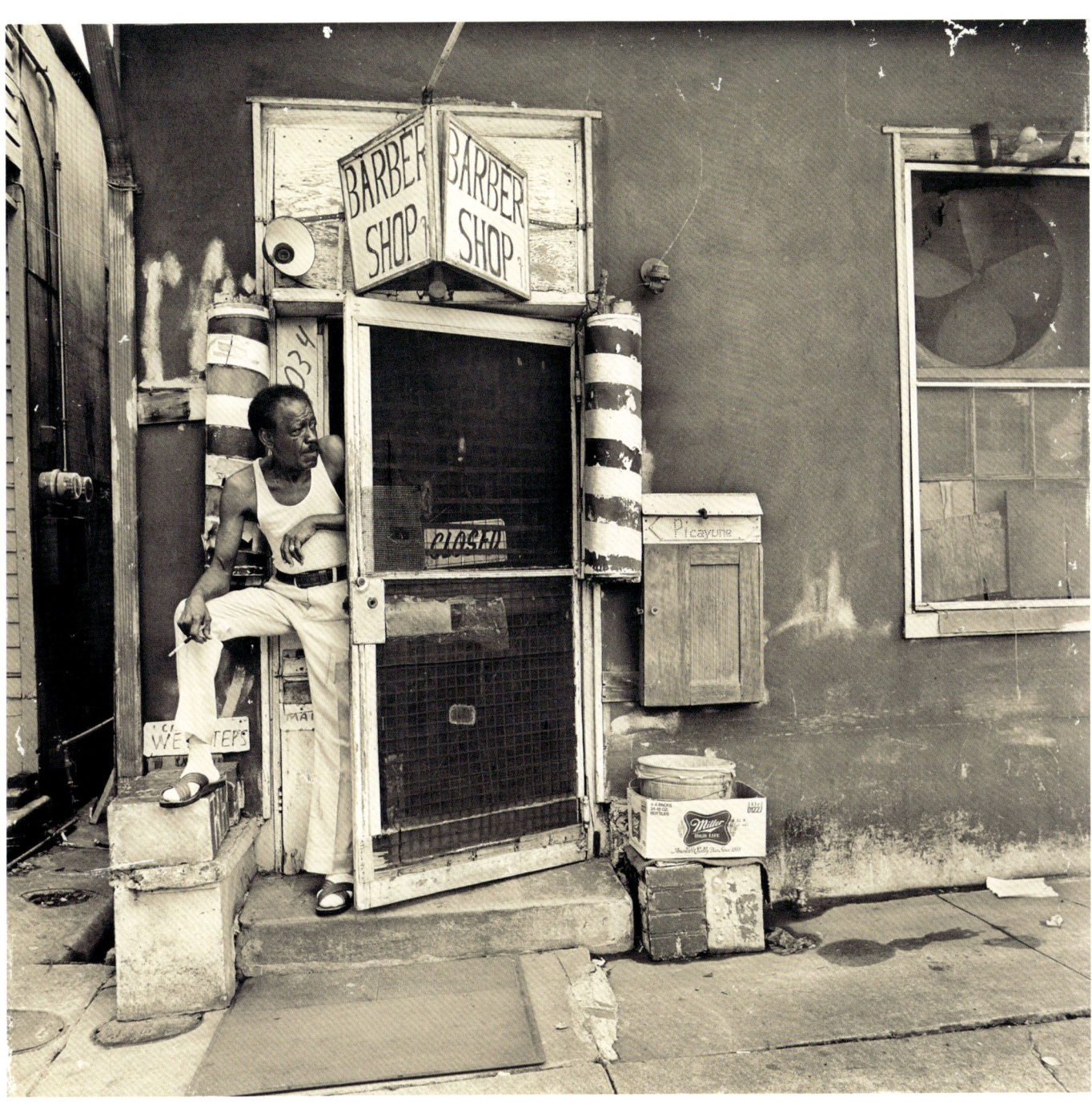

Tremé Barber Shop, 1982
by Christopher Porché West
inkjet print, 15¾ × 15¾ in.
acquisition made possible by Tim Mink, 2017.0035.1, © Christopher
Porché West

The inkjet print was made in 2017 from a 1982 negative.

Allen Hess (b. 1950)

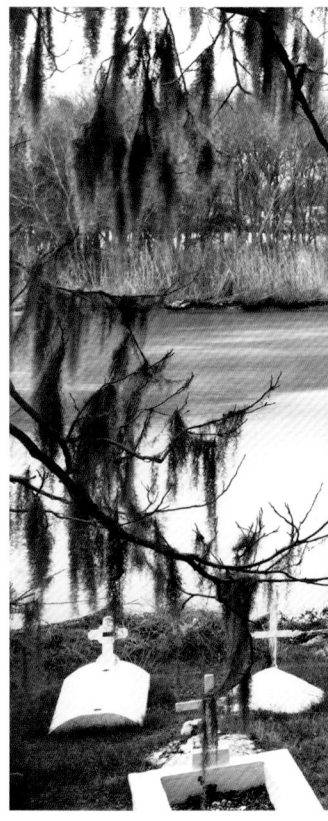

Allen Hess's tranquil scene of a waterside cemetery is practically an encyclopedia of Louisiana symbols. His choice of camera, an 8 × 20-inch banquet camera, emphasizes the flatness of the coastal landscape. His vantage point, a shell mound overlooking Bayou Barataria, was built up by generations of Native Americans who lived in the area prior to the arrival of European settlers in the early eighteenth century. The oak trees and Spanish moss symbolize both endemic nature and "the Old South." The cemetery testifies to the long history of Catholic burial in the region, while the bayou itself adds a layer of geographical meaning as the early means of travel and communication for inhabitants, whether Indigenous or transplanted. The barges, barely visible against the far bank in the background, allude to the industries that now operate in part of this area.

It is unlikely that the photographer had all (or any) of this in mind when this photograph was made. The choices that Hess made as an artist were limited but critical: camera position and natural conditions that affected how the scene was illuminated. Like any photograph, this one takes a transient moment and forever fixes it, permitting a leisurely analysis and interpretation for future observers. In looking at this image, we make it a part of our personal history, though we were not there at its creation.

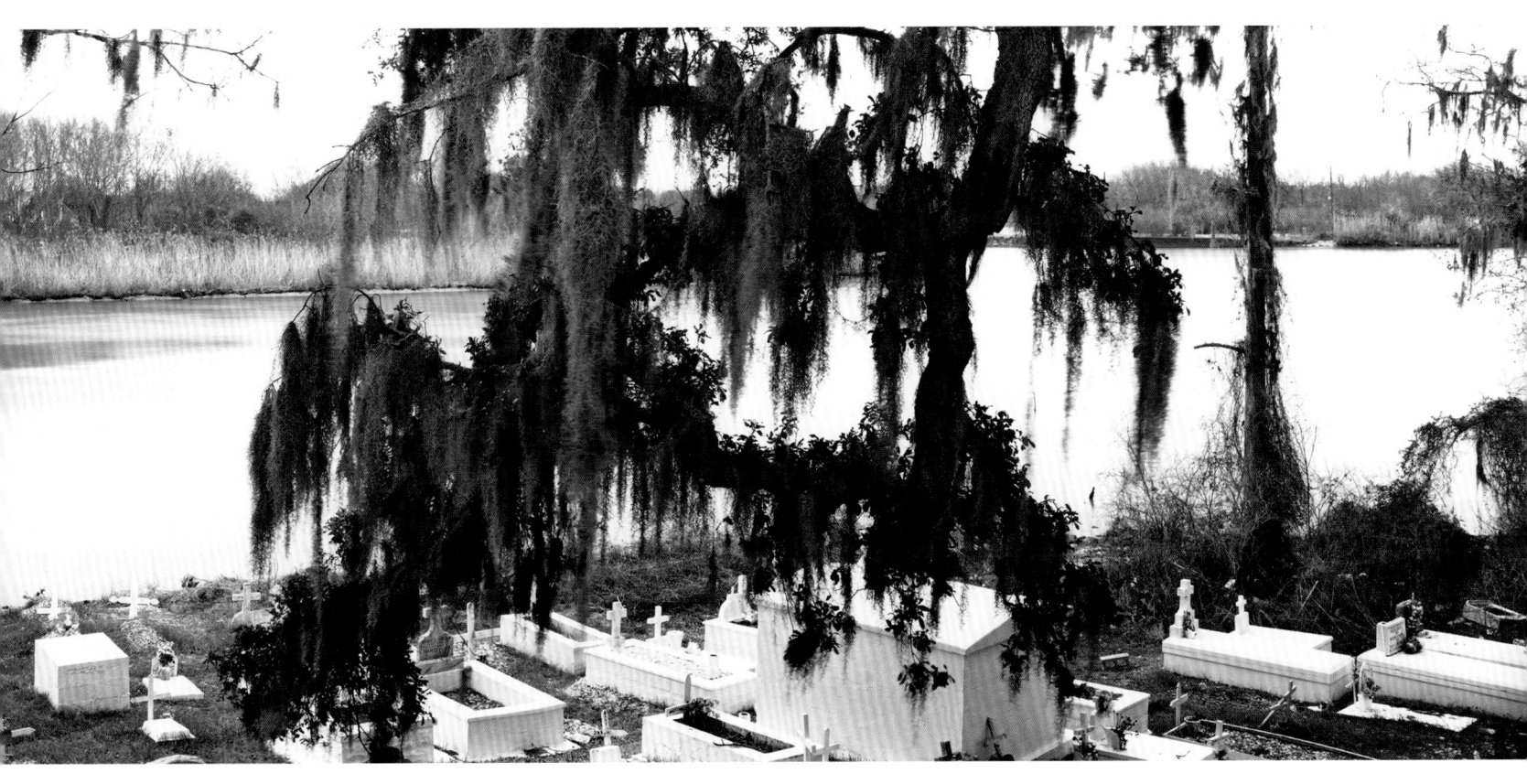

***Fleming Cemetery, Bayou Barataria,* 1982**
by Allen Hess
gelatin silver print, 16¾ × 39⅝ in.
1991.51.1, © Allen Hess

The gelatin silver print was made in 1989 from a 1982 negative.

Alan Karchmer (b. 1954)

A century after presenting the World's Industrial and Cotton Centennial Exposition in 1884, New Orleans again launched a world's fair to attract international attention and spur regional economic development. Unlike its predecessor, held on the pastoral grounds of a park, the Louisiana World Exposition centered its campus in the city's gritty riverfront warehouse district, which had been largely abandoned by the storage, transfer, and light industry sectors that were its mainstay from the mid-nineteenth to mid-twentieth centuries. Though the economic fortunes of the neighborhood had waned, the building stock was very much intact and included some very fine examples of commercial architecture of its heyday. Because not all of this architecture was likely to survive the development of the fairgrounds and its exposition areas, a study and photographic inventory of the several dozen square blocks was commissioned under the auspices of the Preservation Resource Center of New Orleans.

The principal photography sought to document the block faces of each street, providing context of the buildings on each side. Because of the photographic techniques used, detailed information about individual structures can be determined. Photographer Alan Karchmer, who holds a degree in architecture, followed the guidelines of the New Deal–era Historic American Buildings Survey (HABS). Beginning in 1982, he systematically photographed the district using a view camera with 4 × 5-inch black-and-white film. The view camera permitted a rectified view of each exposure that maintained parallelism of the structures' vertical and horizontal elements. Following HABS stipulations, each negative contains a scale (an eight-foot pole divided into foot-long black and white segments) to permit calculated measurements. To capture the varied character of the area, Karchmer also produced hundreds of 35 mm color slides that show casual street scenes and significant building details.

The view shown here is the even-numbered side of the 400 block of Julia Street and consists of three images that together present the illusion of a single block. This effect today is accomplished digitally, but in the early 1980s, three scaled prints were spliced together to achieve the same effect. The four-story brick structure with granite pillars and lintels on the first floor, along with its cast-iron window lintels on the upper floors, appears largely as it might have when first completed circa 1850 (the central ground floor opening appears to have been modified with a roll-up door). The street's brick pavement reads clearly, with partially visible railroad tracks attesting to the use of spur lines and rail sidings that sometimes directly accessed these structures.

Karchmer undertook this project fairly early in a career that currently spans over forty years of practice on several continents. Publications devoted to architecture of the late twentieth and early twenty-first centuries regularly include his work.

Like the 1884 exposition, the 1984 world's fair ended in the red. But the event sparked interest in reinventing the former commercial zone, which now thrives with apartments, restaurants, and entertainment venues for both visitors and residents.

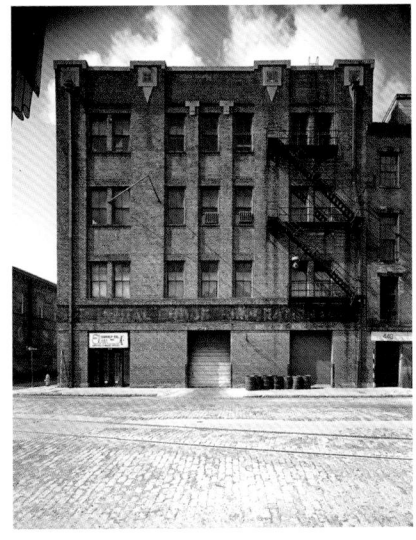
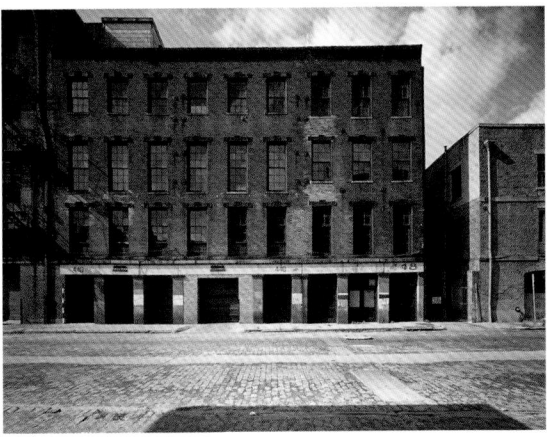
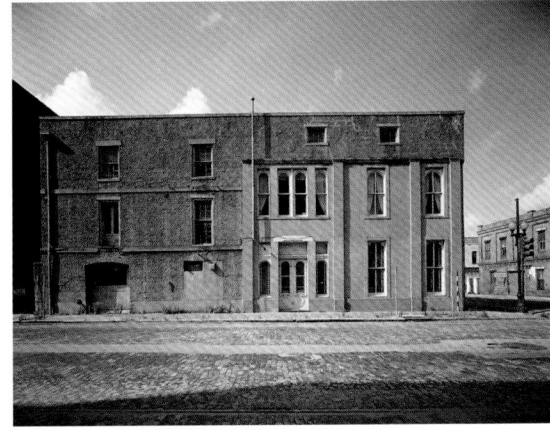

Images from the Warehouse Documentation Project, 1982

by Alan Karchmer
gelatin silver negatives, 4 × 5 in.
1990.6.347, .346, .345, © Alan Karchmer

Howard Philips Smith (b. 1956)

The Piazza d'Italia, a plaza in downtown New Orleans completed in 1978, is often cited as an early example of postmodern architecture, though an unusual one, since it is not a building but a public cityscape. The piazza is the design of architect and educator Charles Moore, working with New Orleans–based August Perez and Associates. Several years later, Moore would be critical in designing another piece of public (though temporary) architecture: the Wonder Wall of the Louisiana World Exposition in 1984.

The Piazza d'Italia's fortunes have ebbed and flowed. The project was conceived to recognize the Italian presence in New Orleans history and encourage greater appreciation for Italian contributions to local society and culture. The grand scheme of the plaza, with renovated buildings adjoining and surrounding it—so as to give a sense of discovery when encountered—was never implemented. At the time of its construction, the Piazza d'Italia would have been in close proximity to the riverfront's Spanish Plaza and the now-relocated equestrian statue of Joan of Arc, two other projects referencing ethnic and cultural contributions to New Orleans history.

Maintenance of the neon lighting and water features—including a fountain shaped like a map of Italy and water jets that emulated classical architectural elements—proved difficult, and the site fell into disrepair as the anticipated surrounding elements failed to materialize. The condition prompted one wag to comment that the piazza was the country's first postmodern ruin. A city effort to renovate the piazza for the three hundredth anniversary of New Orleans in 2018 returned many of its components to operational status, but the original concept with the context of surrounding buildings is no longer possible, due to a drastically altered streetscape.

Howard Philips Smith's photograph of the piazza is one in a series he made when the setting was new and its whimsical elements mostly operating as planned. Though ablaze with its neon lighting, Smith's rendering of the subject in black, white, and gray tones seems the antithesis of Moore's colorful, vibrant, and playful design. The series of photographs that Smith made is somewhat ironic in its treatment of a postmodern setting with a very modernist approach to photography. But it can be argued that the inventiveness of the Moore and Perez design can lead to different perceptions and reactions by those who encounter it, as Smith's photograph shows. Smith included the piazza work in his larger series *A History of Empty Places*.

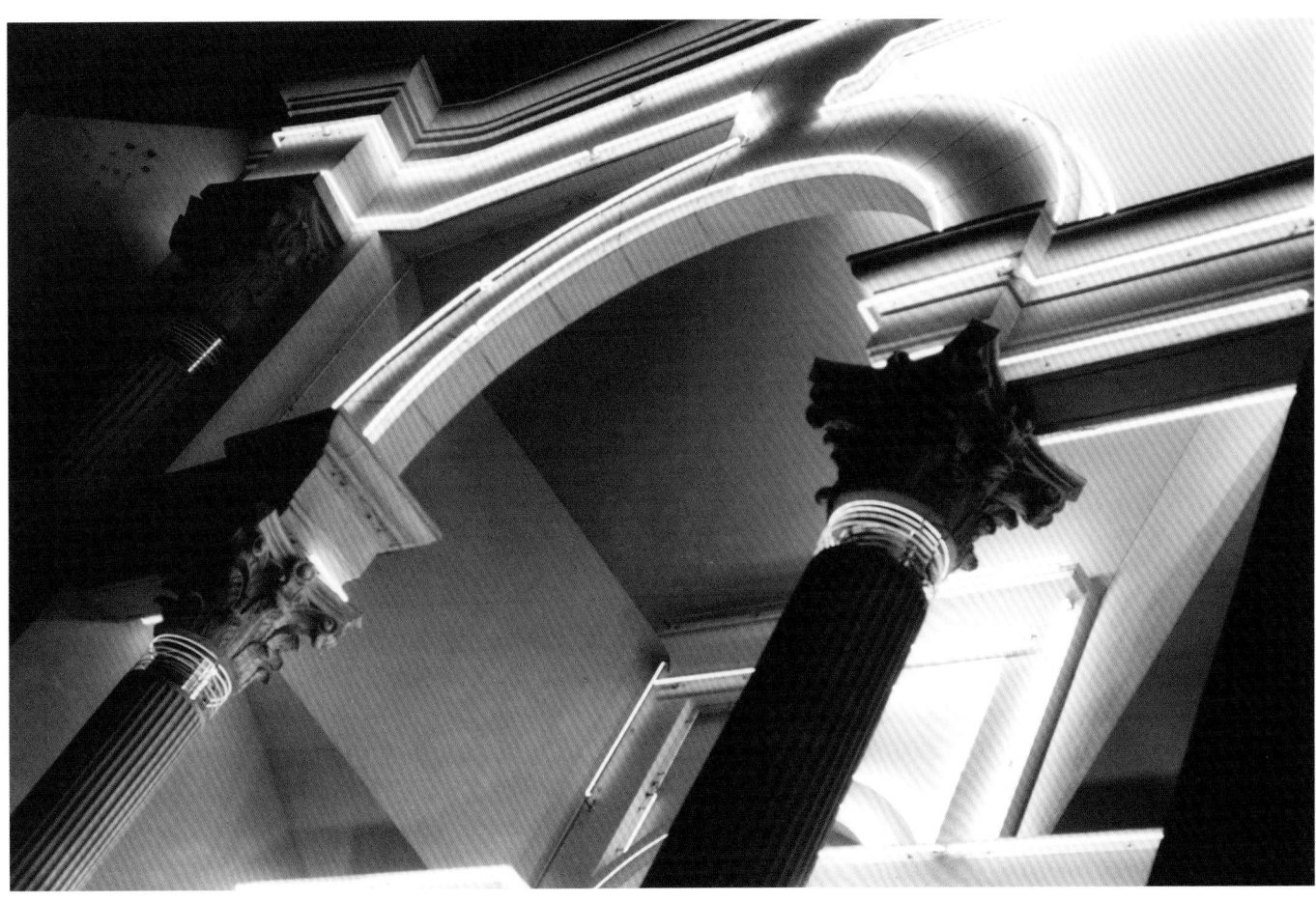

Piazza d'Italia, 1983
by Howard Philips Smith
gelatin silver print, 11 × 14 in.
gift of Howard Philips Smith, 2021.0005.4.10, © Howard Philips Smith

David Leeson (1957–2022)
Kurt Mutchler (b. 1958)
G. Andrew Boyd (b. 1955)

The 1984 Louisiana World Exposition (LWE), staged along the Mississippi River waterfront, boasted an appropriate theme: *The World of Rivers—Fresh Water as a Source of Life.* The fair offered many attractions to locals and visitors—exhibitions of art, science, industry, culture, musical performances, food and drink, and a setting that permitted viewing the river up close. Indeed, opening access to the Mississippi for public enjoyment might be one of the LWE's most enduring legacies. But despite its many attributes, the fair was not a financial success, a point seized upon in the press coverage.

The City of New Orleans had its own pavilion and collaborated with The Historic New Orleans Collection to produce a historical exhibition on water and its management in the city and to solicit some contemporary artistic reactions to the subject. The organizing principle of the exhibition centered on rain, nearly every drop of which must be pumped and channeled out through canals, lest flooding occur. The principal works of the exhibition, created specifically for the event, were a cartoon mural by Will B. "Bunny" Matthews describing the operations of the Sewerage and Water Board, small sculptures by contemporary artists based in New Orleans referencing water and rainfall, and a series of commissioned photographs on the theme of rain.

Photojournalists David Leeson, Kurt Mutchler, and G. Andrew Boyd produced a total of fifty-three photographs for the *Rain* exhibition. Other photographers were invited to submit additional entries, swelling the photographic portion of the installation by dozens more items. The assembled collection offers a moment-in-time reflection on the many ways that rain permeates the ebb and flow of New Orleans life. In fact, Mutchler's and Boyd's photographs were made on the same date.

Leeson's dramatic photograph of a lightning bolt over Lake Pontchartrain was taken from the causeway that spans twenty-four miles across the lake. The nighttime setting emphasizes the lightning flash, which seems nearly solid when compared to the squiggly lines of moving automobile lights and vibrating reflections emanating from puddles on the shoulder of the roadbed. The photograph captures the dichotomy of weather as as a vector for both nourishment and destruction, and implies the role of the lake as a reservoir to manage excess precipitation. When rainfall exceeds the capacities of the mechanisms to carry it away, results can vary from the grim struggle for survival captured in Mutchler's boatman, or the whimsy of Boyd's photograph showing a telephone conversation in chest-high water, and an umbrella that collects rain instead of shedding it.

Leeson was on the staff of New Orleans's *Times-Picayune* (as were Mutchler and Boyd) when he made the pictures for the *Rain* exhibition. He later joined the *Dallas Morning News* and was awarded a 2004 Pulitzer Prize in photography for his frontline coverage of the Iraq War. Boyd remained with the *Times-Picayune* as both a photographer and administrator of the photojournalist staff. Mutchler continued his photographic career as a deputy director of photography at *National Geographic* magazine.

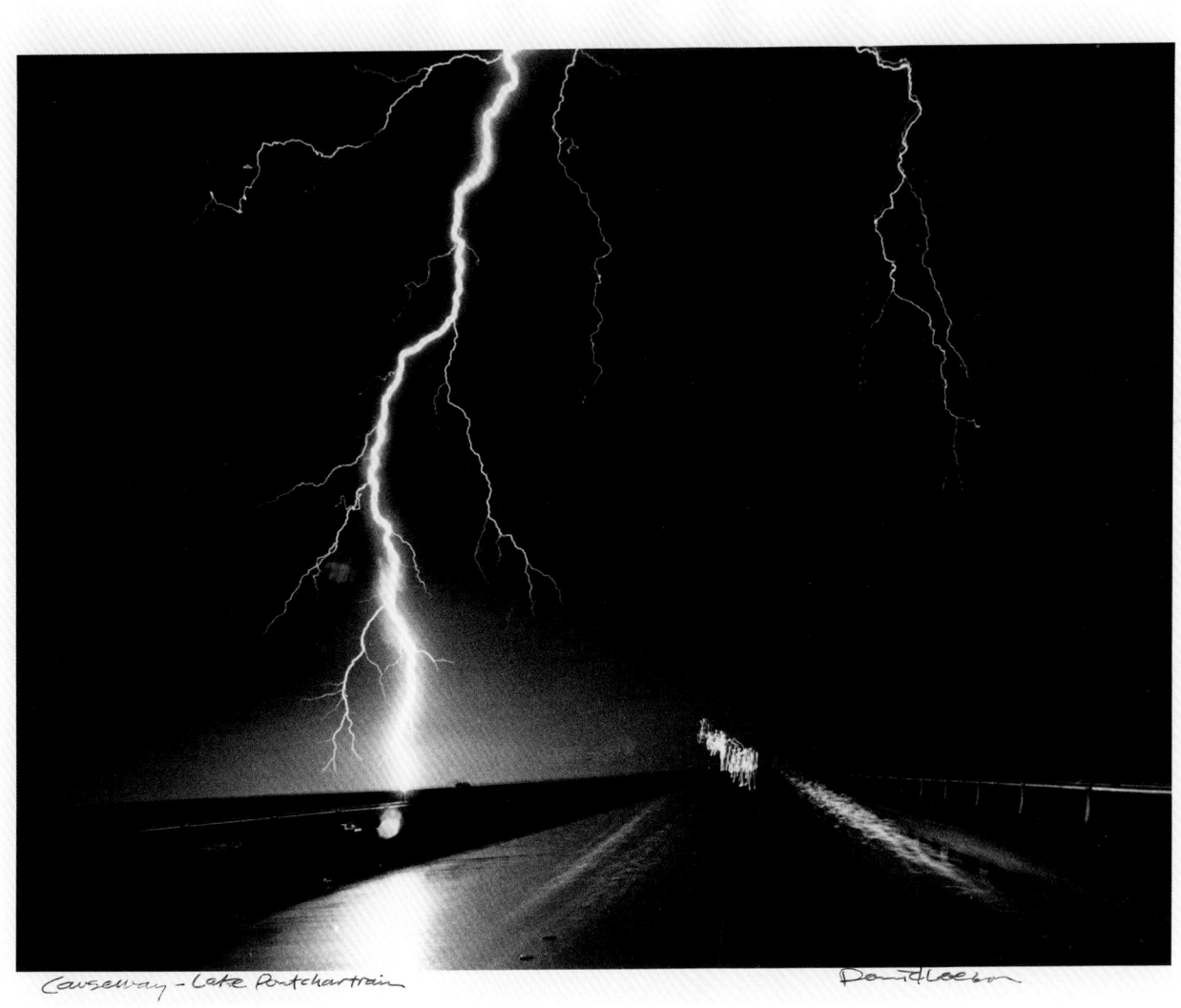

Causeway—Lake Pontchartrain

David Leeson

Causeway—Lake Pontchartrain, 1983 or 1984

by David Leeson
gelatin silver print, 14 × 10⅞ in.
1985.148.7, © David Leeson / The Times-Picayune

223

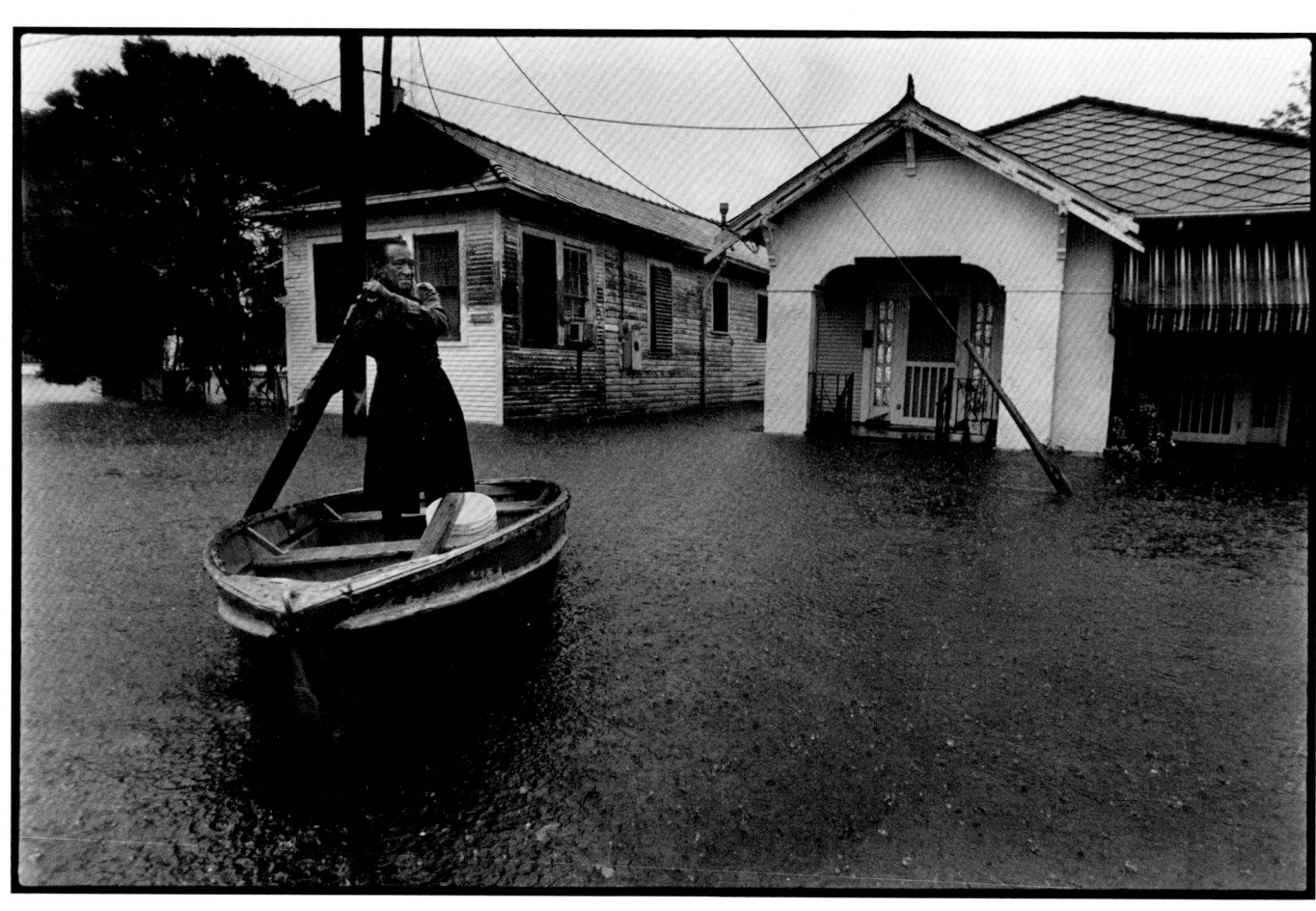

Flooded street, 1983
by Kurt Mutchler
gelatin silver print, 11 × 14 in.
1985.147.2, © Kurt Mutchler / The Times-Picayune

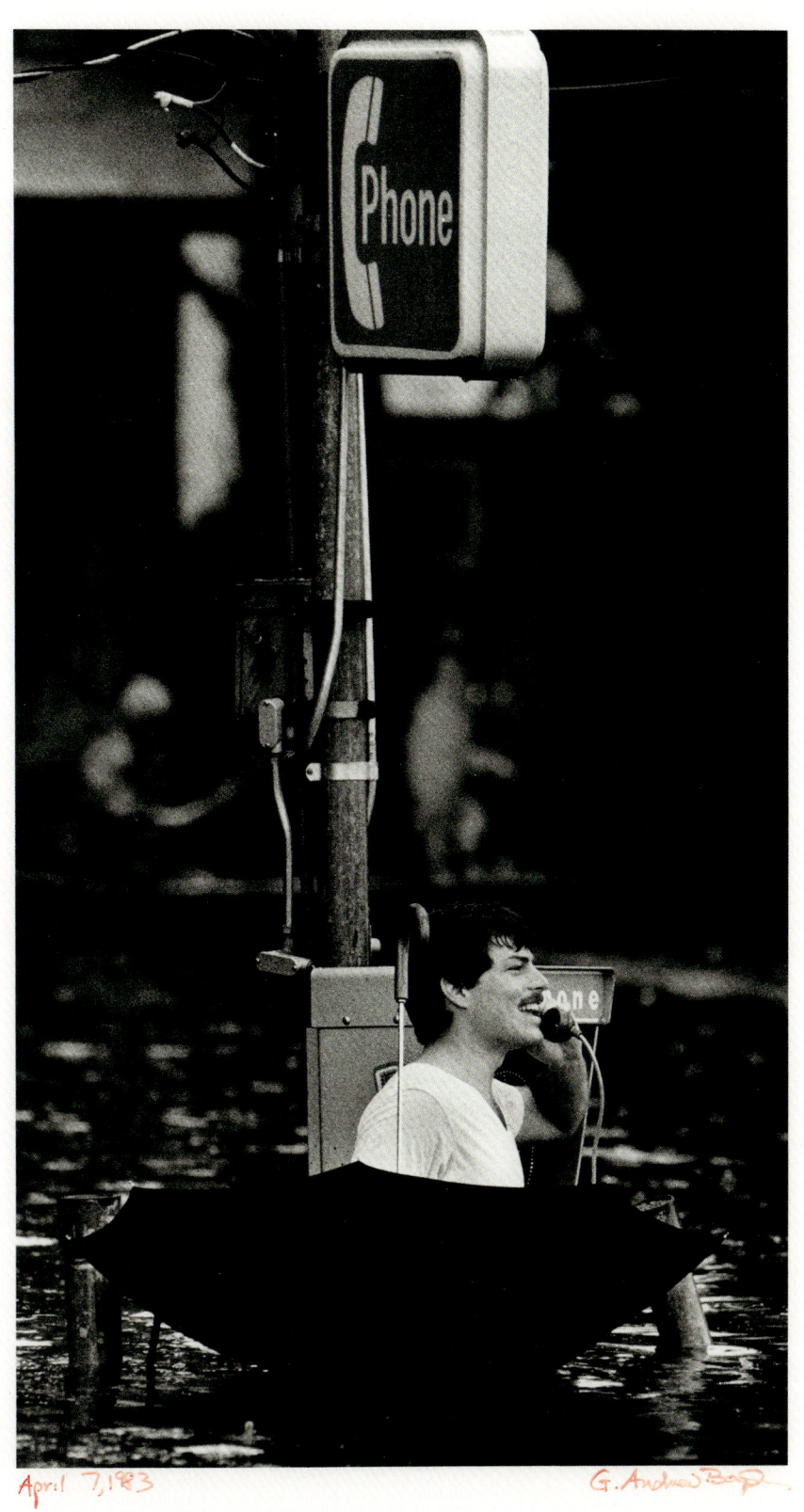

April 7, 1983
by G. Andrew Boyd
gelatin silver print, 10¾ × 14 in.
1985.152.11, © G. Andrew Boyd / The Times-Picayune

Franck-Bertacci Photographers (active 1980s–1994)

Before the mid-1930s, the only way to cross the Mississippi River between New Orleans and Vicksburg was by ferry. In December 1935 the Huey P. Long Bridge opened, carrying rail traffic as well as automobiles, trucks, and buses. The bridge began and ended in Jefferson Parish, immediately upstream from New Orleans. Another span crossing at Baton Rouge opened in the summer of 1940. In the River Parishes that lie between these cities, the lack of any bridge limited enterprises such as cargo terminals, refineries and chemical processing plants, agricultural businesses, and power generating facilities.

In the late 1950s and early 1960s, bridges at New Orleans (Greater New Orleans Bridge, later renamed Crescent City Connection, 1958, 1988) and Donaldsonville (Sunshine Bridge, 1964) were added, but numerous ferries still remained to serve pedestrians as well as vehicles. Until 1980, the easiest way to cross the river at points from New Orleans to Baton Rouge—134 river miles away from each other—might have been one of the automobile ferries that served major towns along the banks of the river. In 1976, a terrible accident between the ferryboat *George Prince* and the cargo tanker *Frosta* that killed more than seventy people at the Destrehan-Luling crossing contributed to a decline in ferry usage, but not in the need to cross the river.

In the 1980s, a bridge-building boom of sorts occurred, seeing three spans constructed: one running parallel to the Greater New Orleans Bridge and two in the River Parishes— the Hale Boggs Memorial Bridge connecting Destrehan and Luling, providing a critical component of Interstate 310, and another one upriver linking Gramercy and Wallace.

This view, made by Franck-Bertacci Photographers, shows the construction of one of the Gramercy bridge's tower foundations. A coffer dam of steel sheet piling to exclude the river's flow has been built around the site from which the tower will rise. Tons of metal reinforcment and hundreds of cubic yards of concrete will fill the void and stand above the river's surface before the dam is removed. Once the towers are in place, the superstructure and roadway of the bridge follow. This bridge, known as the Veterans Memorial Bridge, opened to traffic in 1995.

Franck-Bertacci Photographers, based in New Orleans, was often called upon by government entities and businesses to document the progress of construction projects. Schools, shopping centers, car dealerships, bank buildings, and other tangible signs of capital investment and progress passed before the firm's lens. It is tempting to suggest that through their operations, which covered nearly the entire twentieth century, Charles L. Franck Photographers and the successor firm, Franck-Bertacci, provided a comprehensive view of New Orleans—but that would be misleading. Like any commercial photographic enterprise, they were commissioned by others and took the pictures they were directed and paid to take. There was no comprehensive plan to systematically document New Orleans and the region. Furthermore, the firms specialized in industrial photography, recording brick-and-mortar infrastructure subjects, rather than people, events, news, or pictures designed to promote social awareness or record cultural traditions. Nonetheless, the nature of the work and the time period it covers make the Franck and Franck-Bertacci archives a rich source for understanding the economy and infrastructural growth of the region.

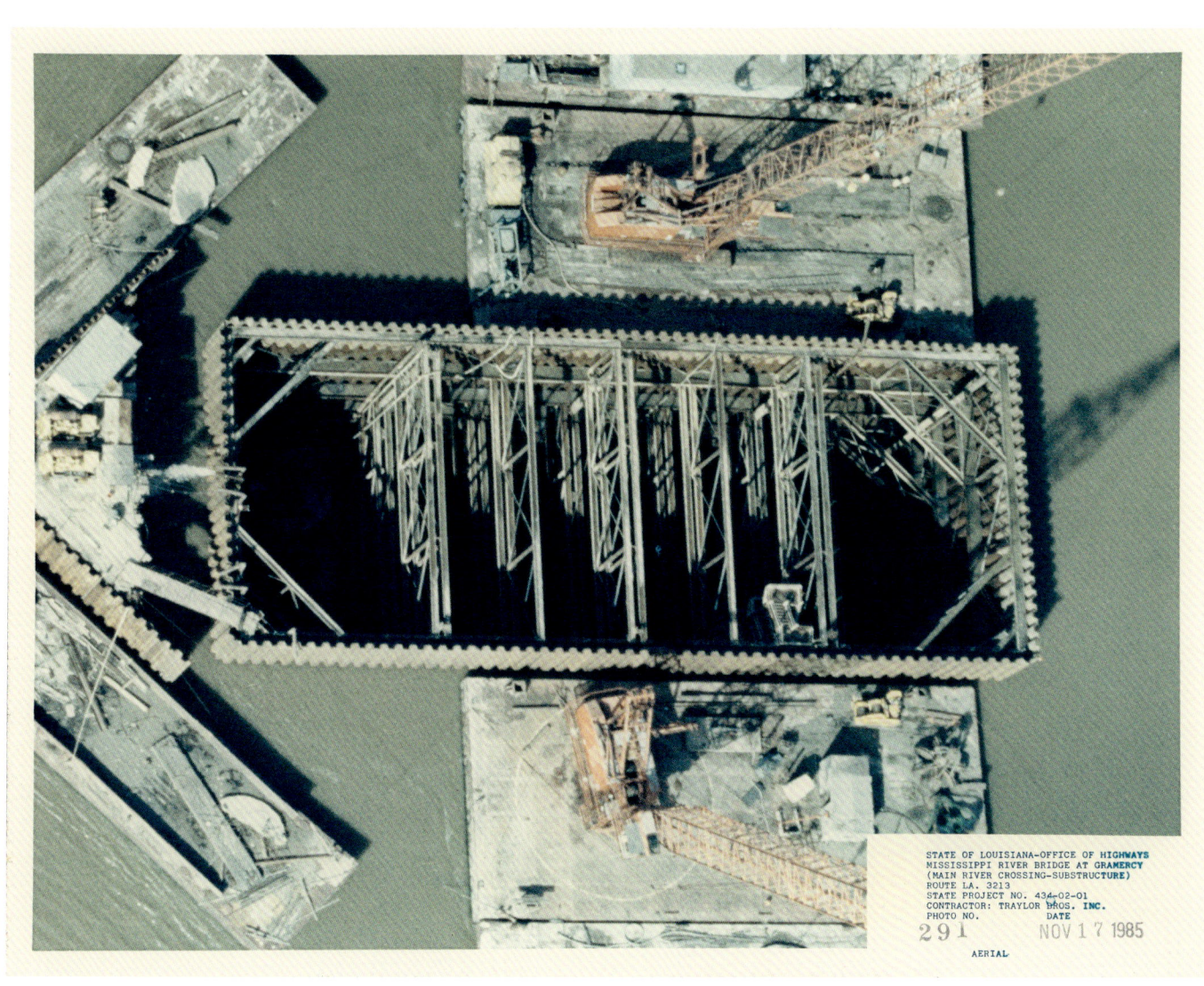

STATE OF LOUISIANA-OFFICE OF HIGHWAYS
MISSISSIPPI RIVER BRIDGE AT GRAMERCY
(MAIN RIVER CROSSING-SUBSTRUCTURE)
ROUTE LA. 3213
STATE PROJECT NO. 434-02-01
CONTRACTOR: TRAYLOR BROS. INC.
PHOTO NO.   DATE
291   NOV 17 1985
        AERIAL

Aerial view of the construction of the Mississippi River bridge at Gramercy, 1985
by Franck-Bertacci Photographers
chromogenic print, 8 × 10 in.
The Franck-Bertacci Collection at THNOC, 1994.94.3.913

Michael A. Smith (1942–2018)

In anticipation of the 1984 Louisiana World Exposition, the French Quarter underwent a major infrastructural upgrade. Streets and sidewalks were rebuilt, street lighting improved, and gas, electric, and water services all received updates to welcome the increased visitorship that the city anticipated.

The Historic New Orleans Collection commissioned Michael A. Smith to photograph New Orleans as the prospect and implementation of the exposition transformed the city. From 1984 to 1986, Smith, who was based in rural Pennsylvania, visited New Orleans several times for extended periods and produced a portfolio of 405 photographs. The pictures were made with three different view cameras that produced negatives with dimensions of 8 × 10 inches, 8 × 20 inches, and 18 × 22 inches.

The disruption that the city's improvements entailed was consequential and wearying to residents, businesses, and visitors. A celebration was planned to acknowledge the end of the construction and to encourage the local population to rediscover the Vieux Carré. A festival of modest aspirations in 1984, the French Quarter Festival has grown into an attraction that rivals Mardi Gras and the New Orleans Jazz and Heritage Festival in popularity and attendance. The dozens of food booths and hundreds of acts on multiple stages showcasing nearly two thousand of the area's musicians offer attendees two of the city's most visible cultural elements, set against a third: the architecture of the Vieux Carré.

The second annual French Quarter Festival in Jackson Square is the subject of Smith's photograph. Captured within the frame is an encapsulation of the early city of New Orleans: the Place d'Armes, or parade ground, renamed Jackson Square in the mid-nineteenth century; St. Louis Cathedral, which has been the site of a Catholic church since the city's founding; the buildings of church and state flanking the cathedral (the Presbytère on the right and the Cabildo on the left); and the implication of the Mississippi River, which flows past the scene behind the photographer's position.

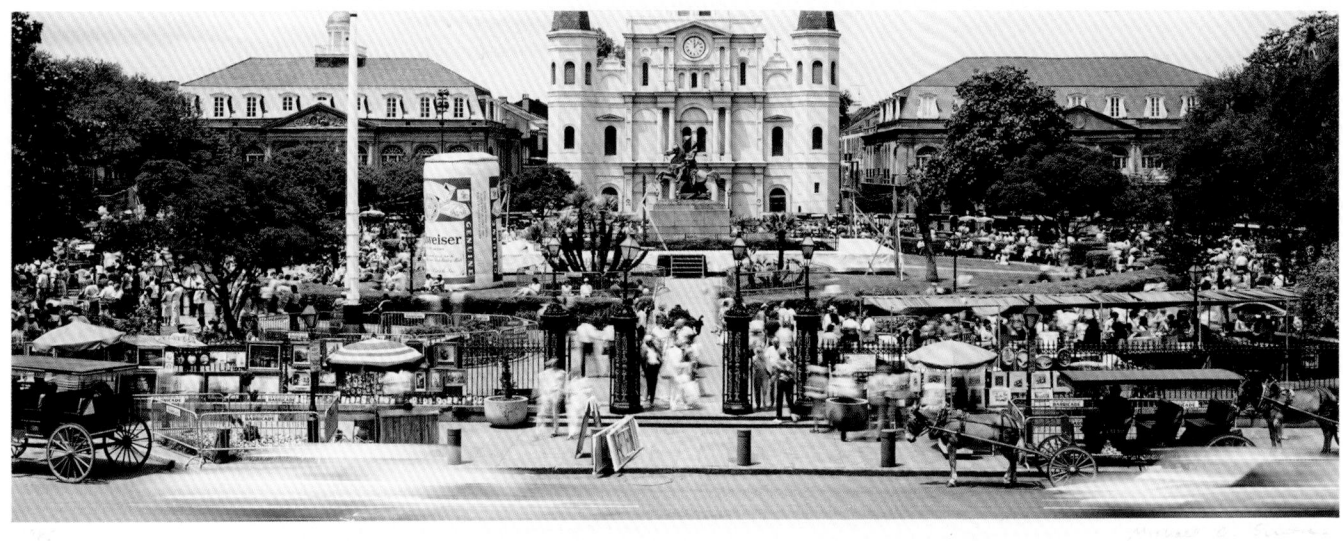

French Quarter Festival from Washington Artillery Park, 1985

by Michael A. Smith
gelatin silver contact print, mounted, 7¾ × 19½ in.
1986.125.257, © Michael A. Smith

Tina Freeman (b. 1951)

Tina Freeman's wide-ranging career in photography has spanned many countries of the world, but this portrait was made within an hour's drive of her New Orleans studio. From portraiture to interiors, and architecture to landscapes, the direct and clean presentation of what lies before her lens has appeared in books, magazines, and exhibitions for more than forty years.

Louisiana's coastal areas have been occupied for centuries, first by Native Americans and later by people from nearly every other continent. Until the early twentieth century, the natural bounty of this region permitted a life based around seasonal occupations including hunting, fishing, shrimping, oystering, trapping, and other pursuits. The waterfowl populations of coastal Louisiana offered sport and subsistence hunting of ducks and geese (and, until the passing of the Lacey Act in 1900, hunting for the commercial market), and concurrent with this activity grew a tradition of making decoys.

Jett Brunet is a second-generation carver—his father Andrew "Tan" Brunet and brother Jude Brunet are also noted practitioners of the art. Jett comes from a region along Bayou Lafourche rich with that tradition and with many talented artisans; for more than a century the slivers of buildable land along the bayou's banks have been home to carvers who made decoys for hunting, at first, and later as decorative works for collectors. Jett Brunet's carvings began as realistically painted interpretation of waterfowl, but in more recent years, he has chosen to leave areas of the sculptures without decoration to emphasize form and material over detail.

Tina Freeman's portrait of Brunet was made the year after he won his first Ward World Championship Wildfowl Carving Competition at the age of twenty-one. He is presented with assurance, surrounded by the simple tools and setting of his studio.

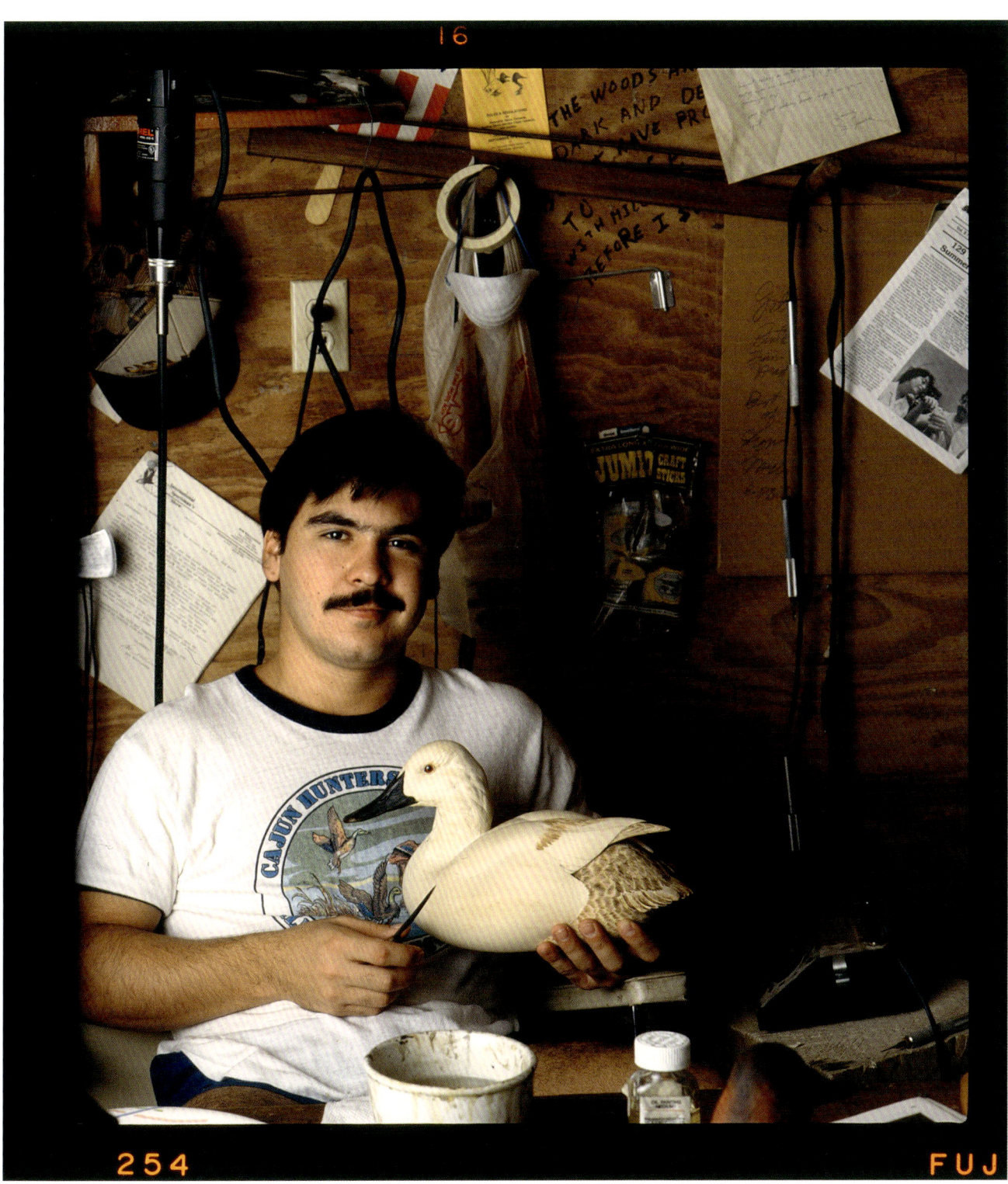

Jett Brunet, Duck Decoy Craftsman: Portrait with Decoy,
1986
by Tina Freeman
color transparency, 2¼ × 2¾ in.
gift of Tina Freeman, 2020.0151, © Tina Freeman

Mitchel Osborne (b. 1943)

The popular perception of Mardi Gras in New Orleans is a wide-open public event featuring costumes, music, and parades along the defined routes to which Carnival organizations, or krewes, adhere. But most groups also have far more private events—usually referred to as balls—open only to members and their invited guests. Some organizations, like Zulu, allow tickets to be purchased to these events. Activities at the balls can include the presentation of the krewe's king, queen, and court, as well as musical performances, tableau presentations, dancing, and socializing. Formal wear for men and women in attendance is typically required, though less-formal events by new organizations are redefining what a Mardi Gras ball can be.

The Zulu Social Aid and Pleasure Club's ball is known to be a good time, and Mitchel Osborne's photograph made at the 1988 ball conveys some of its excitement, supplied in part by Dejan's Olympia Brass Band. By the time this photograph was made, Harold Dejan's band had been operating for thirty years. His leadership and adherence to the early twentieth-century jazz tradition that he experienced as a young musician was an important element in keeping the roots of jazz a vibrant part of New Orleans music.

The photograph appears to be made using both a slow shutter speed (blurring parts of the photograph) and flash (which renders some sharpness in the action). The combination of techniques is effective in capturing the energy of the event while still preserving detail.

Osborne's photography covered a lot of ground. He contributed documentary-style photographs in black and white to a book on the plight of Louisiana's sugarcane workers during the 1970s. He covered the 1984 Louisiana World Exposition and the 1987 visit of Pope John Paul II to New Orleans. The wide spectrum of Mardi Gras activities he has photographed includes the costume balls of the gay Krewe of Armeinius, the marching group Society of St. Anne, and the bawdy and irreverent Krewe du Vieux, along with more traditional organizations like Zulu and the Krewe of Hermes. Many of his Mardi Gras photographs were made while informally roaming the streets on Fat Tuesday, photographing individuals enjoying the festivities. His photographs illustrate four books about Mardi Gras published over more than three decades, beginning with *New Orleans, the Passing Parade* (1980).

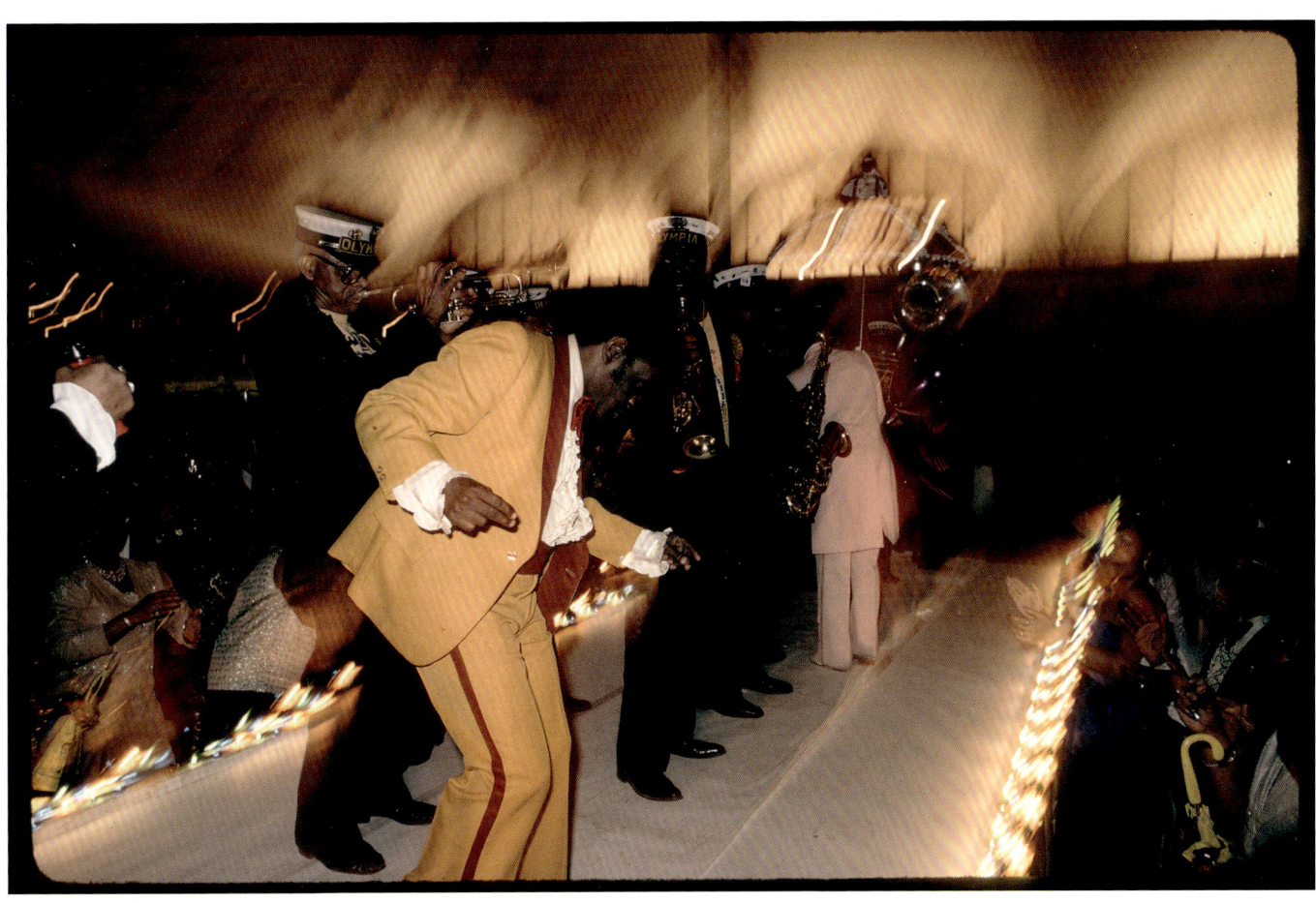

Zulu Social Aid and Pleasure Club ball, 1988

by Mitchel Osborne
color transparency, 35 mm
gift of Mitchel Osborne, 2007.0001.308, © Mitchel Osborne

Rick Olivier (b. 1957)

Rick Olivier grew up in White Castle, Louisiana, and began photographing professionally at the age of sixteen. Olivier now lives in New Orleans, and though he is best known for his location portraits, particularly of musicians, this picture speaks to his early career and a time when small trades, rather than national retailers with international supply chains, still furnished everyday goods to a local clientele.

This photograph was made inside of Cancienne Broom and Mop Factory in Thibodaux, just down Bayou Lafourche from where Olivier grew up. At one moment in history, Thibodaux supported five broom-making operations, though Cancienne's is the only one still going. The enterprise started in 1933, its output keeping the floors of many south Louisiana homes and businesses clean and tidy. By the time Olivier made his photograph, the business had been for nearly two decades under the proprietorship of founder Cleveland Cancienne's son-in-law, Bruce Robertson, who also introduced mops to the company's line. The third generation—Robertson's daughter and son-in-law—later joined the business.

Olivier's book *Zydeco!*, with coauthor Ben Sandmel, was selected as Humanities Book of the Year in 2000 by the Louisiana Endowment for the Humanities. His interest in music is not limited to photographing the people who make it: Olivier and Rob Savoy are the cofounders of the band Creole String Beans, for which the photographer has served as vocalist and guitarist since 2003.

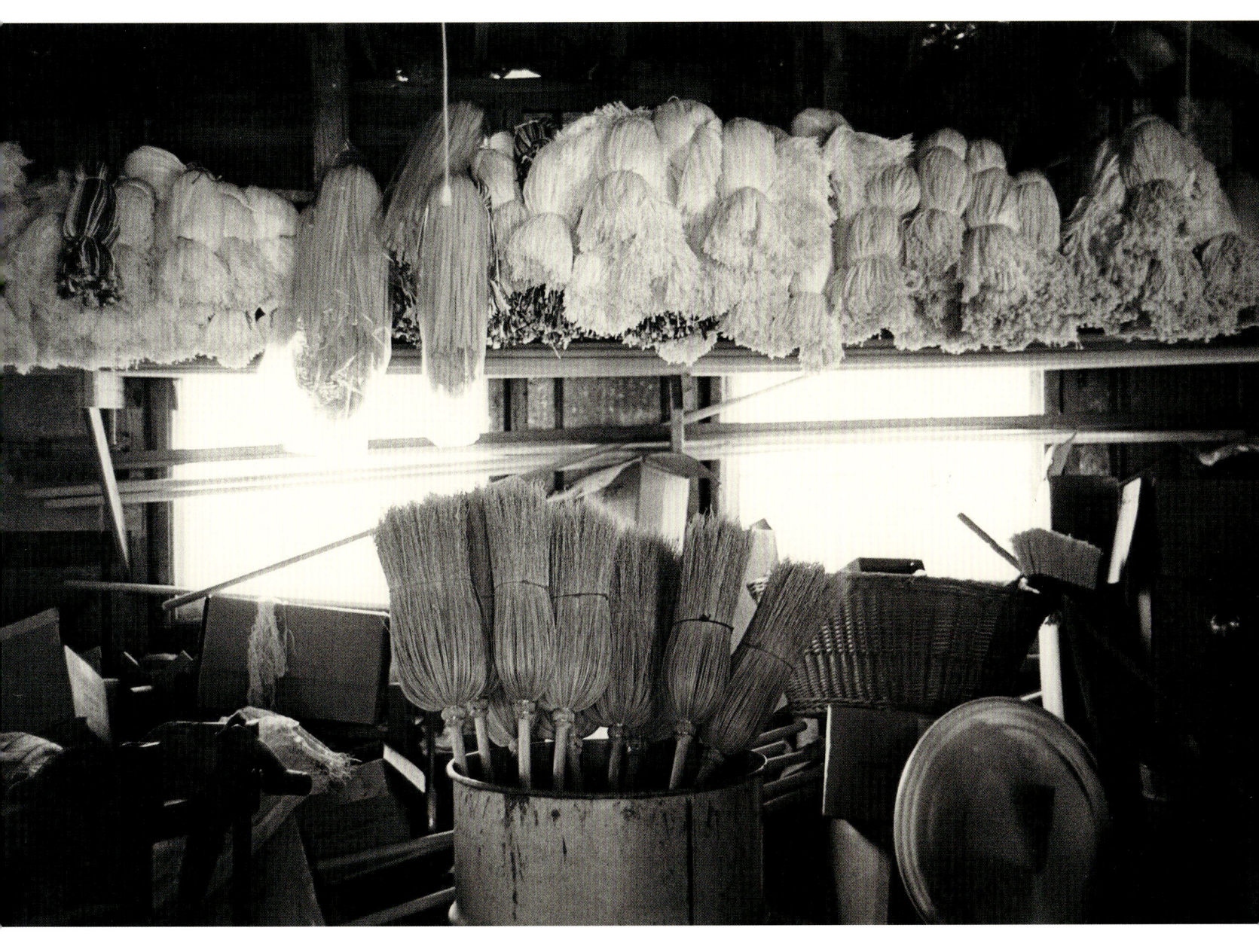

Cancienne Broom and Mop Factory, Thibodaux, LA, 1989
by Rick Olivier
gelatin silver print, 11 × 14 in.
1989.73.5, © Rick Olivier

Randell Brent Vidrine (b. 1950)

Randell Brent Vidrine's photographs are a form of self-exploration overlaid with identifiable documentary circumstance. His use of the camera was purely for what it could record about himself and the slice of the world he confronted at a particular moment. Vidrine used chromogenic black-and-white film, which could be processed and proofed in snapshot form in the (then) ubiquitous color film chemistry available at drugstores and photo processing labs. After evaluation, he would seek the darkroom expertise of photographer Vincent Palumbo (1927–2003) to achieve a final vision in a black-and-white print for which the film was designed.

Vidrine lives in New Orleans but is from Ville Platte, in Louisiana's Acadian parishes. He sometimes returned as an adult to make photographs in his boyhood surroundings; this portrait, made in the town of Washington, Louisiana, is one of those. The photograph has elements of foreboding: a partially hidden face; a hammer whose purpose is yet to be known; a vista at the end of a shadowy passage, glimpsed through a half-opened door.

Like another Louisiana photographer, Clarence John Laughlin, Vidrine used photographs as a starting point for examining the world, using a camera to cross-examine what he saw with his eyes. He amplified the visual result through prose and poetic narrative to characterize the personal journey that each photograph represented for him. Vidrine's commentary on the masked man with the hammer can set the viewer's mind at ease. His caption reads:

> The man in the doorway is James Fontenot, who practices law in Abbeville, Louisiana. The setting is what James calls the Eagle Hotel, although the structure is uninhabited and has gone by at least two other names since its construction in 1852. James purchased the building a short time before the making of this photograph and has made its restoration one of his many serious avocations. I had set up my tripod for this exact image without a human subject, when the proverbial light bulb gave me a different idea. Instantly I climbed a steep ladder to the attic, where I knew James was mixing lime (thus his use of the mask) and doing carpentry. I interrupted him to describe the picture I had in mind and begged him to come down. The polite exasperation with which he acquiesced was vintage James Fontenot. To me, the image he posed for represents an incognito Christ biding His time before the Second Coming, through His mercy and goodness doing what He can to repair man's decadent moral structure near the close of the 20th Century. As for my reluctant model James, after sitting for the pictures he ecstatically returned to "literal" carpentry.

Fontenot's plans for the historic structure were not fully realized, and a change in ownership saw the completed renovation of the structure and its rebirth as a hotel in 2016.

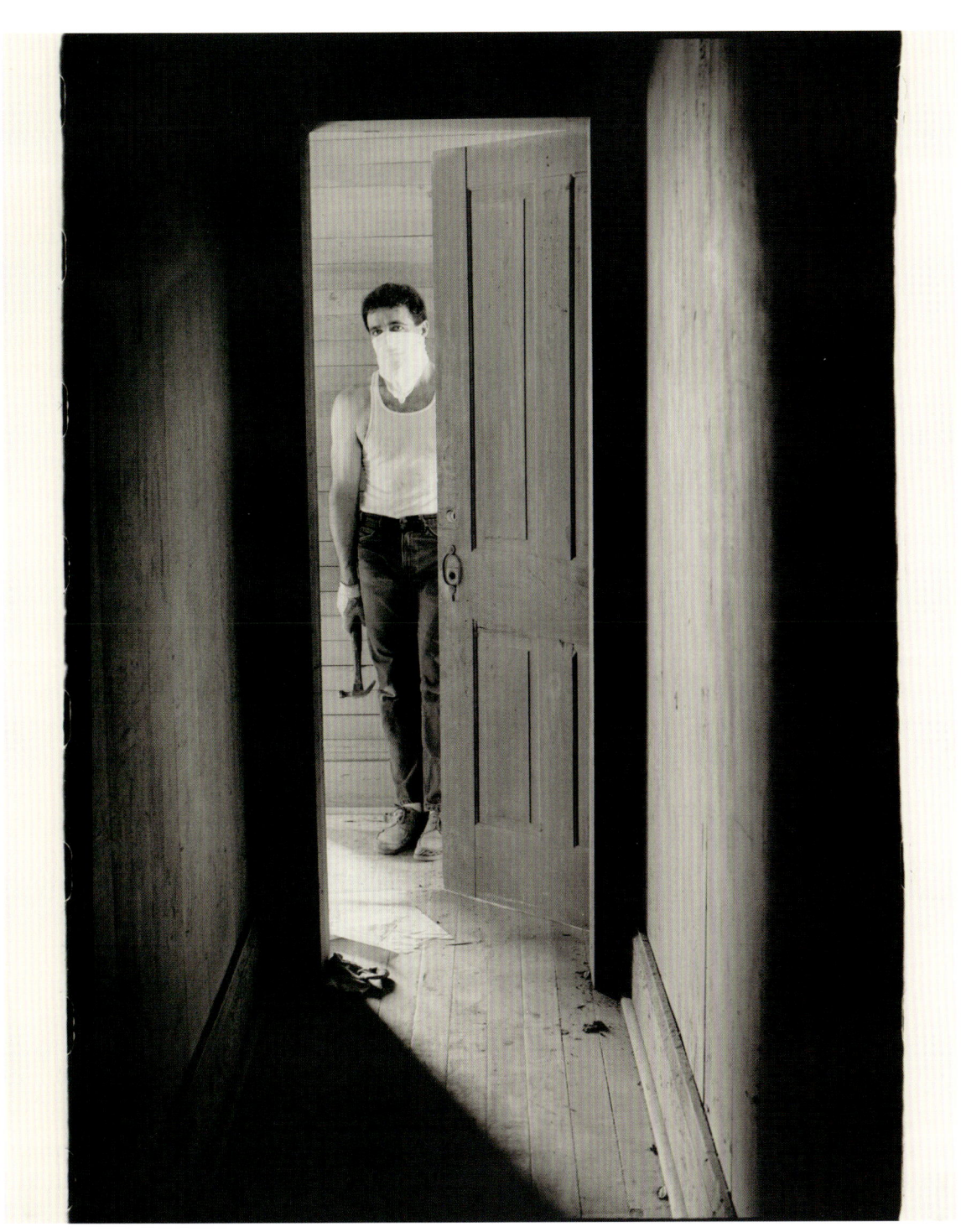

Man with a Hammer, 1990
by Randell Brent Vidrine, printed by Vincent Palumbo
gelatin silver print, 20 × 16 in.
gift of Randell Brent Vidrine, 1997.29.2

Harold Baquet (1958–2015)

Harold Baquet's career as a photographer began in the late 1970s. He was drawn to both everyday and newsworthy events, and his work was an important visual component of a local and national Black press. An obituary tribute revealed that Baquet considered himself a "one-man photo news agency for the African American community in New Orleans." Baquet's photographs were published locally in the *Data News Weekly*, the *New Orleans Tribune*, and *Figaro*; his work also appeared in such national publications as *Rolling Stone*, *Ebony*, *Jet*, and *Essence* magazines.

Besides his freelance contributions, Baquet served as official photographer for New Orleans mayors Ernest N. "Dutch" Morial (1978–86) and his successor, Sidney Barthelemy (1986–94). Baquet's coverage of political figures and events from this era is rich and deep. His photographs illustrate the connections New Orleans had to national movements involving concerns spurred by the civil rights movements of the 1960s, with Baquet usually focusing on individuals and groups that advocated for these causes. The example reproduced here shows a meeting in New Orleans between Mayor Morial (second from right) and the Reverend Jesse Jackson (third from left, his face partially obscured), about Jackson's Rainbow Coalition—an organization that grew out of Jackson's run to be the Democratic presidential nominee in the 1984 election.

In 1989, Baquet became the head photographer for Loyola University New Orleans, a position he held for the rest of his life. In a published interview for the *New Orleans Review*, conducted in 2007 by Laura Camille Tuley, Baquet connects his photography work to the trades of masonry, plumbing, and carpentry practiced by his forebears: "I wanted a working nuts-and-bolts understanding of my craft, and I did it through thousands and thousands of exposures, just like that craftsman does it through thousands and thousands of hand-set tiles or hand-set bricks or precise cuts or nails driven into lumber."

Harold Baquet's archive, including tens of thousands of negatives and prints, was given to The Historic New Orleans Collection by his widow, Cheron Brylski, in 2016. It represents decades of work by a gifted photographer who first became entranced with the technical aspects of photography as a teenager. In Brylski and Baquet's 2009 book, *In the Blink of an Eye: Photographic Memories of a New Orleans No More*, he acknowledges that his fascination with photographs as objects came much earlier in his life, realizing "that they represented something precious in time and space."

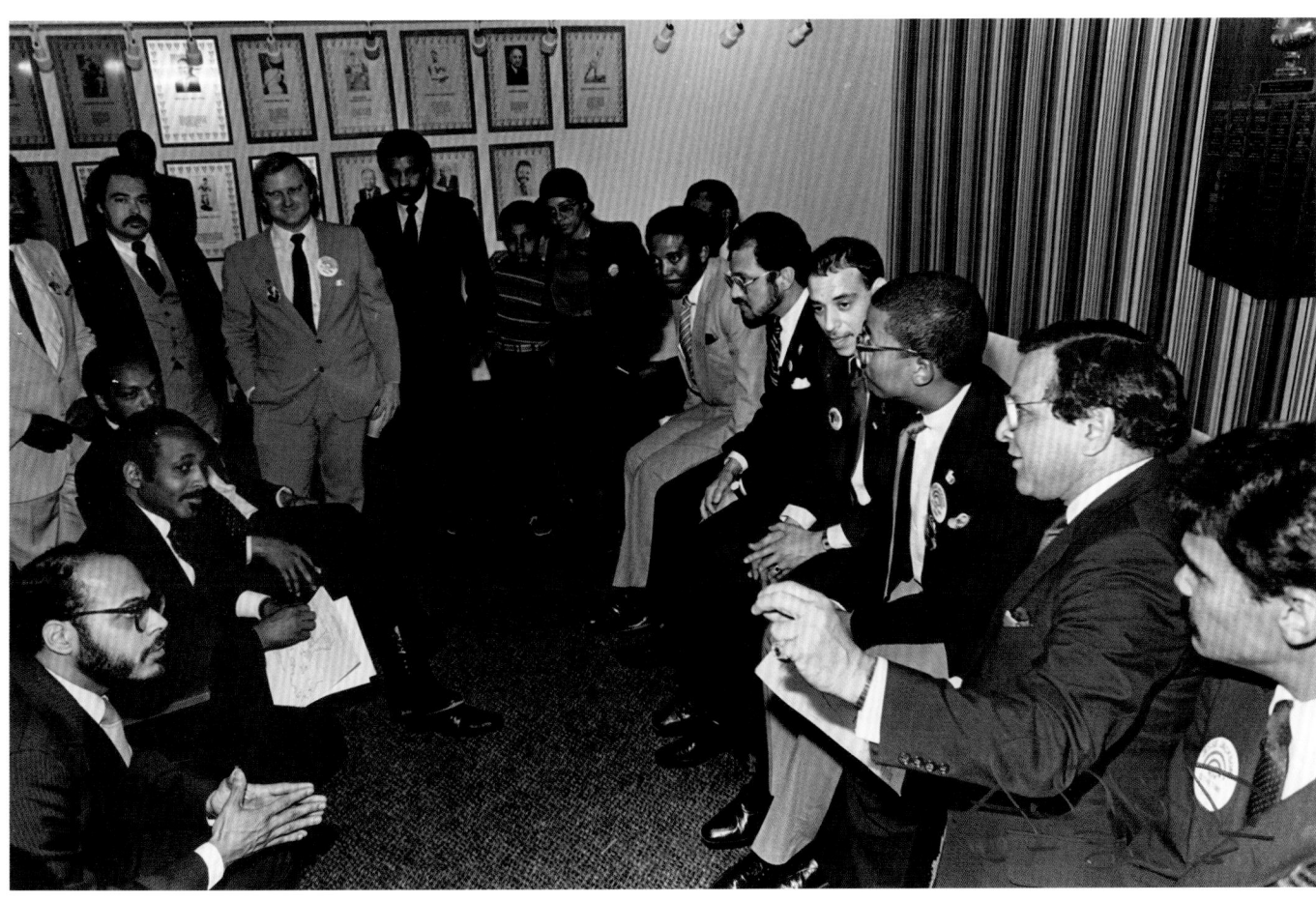

Rainbow Coalition, circa 1985

by Harold Baquet
gelatin silver print, 16 × 20 in.
gift of Harold F. Baquet and Cheron Brylski, 2016.0172.4.65

Stan Strembicki (b. 1952)

For nearly a century and three quarters, Mardi Gras in New Orleans has been marked with parades that occupy the streets in the days leading up to Fat Tuesday, as well as those parades that happen on the day itself. Stan Strembicki's photograph was made at Hermes—a night parade named for the Greek god associated with several areas of life, from trade and luck to thievery and language—as it was getting ready to roll. It is both a document of that moment and a masterfully created photographic print.

The flambeaux carriers, crouched in a line along the curb with their kerosene-fired torches lit, await their cue to begin their night's work, which will occupy the next several hours. The devices (and those who carried them) were fixtures in night parades during the pre-electricity days of Mardi Gras, when their flickering illumination served a practical as well as a decorative purpose. The advent of electric street lighting, and in more recent decades, floats with their own sources of generator-powered illumination, largely negated the need for flambeaux to furnish light. Nonetheless, their appearance in certain parades is both traditional and anticipated.

When the parade leaves the assembly area and the floats pass by them, the men will file into the procession and walk between the floats to provide some illumination, as well as to inject an element of spectacle for the onlookers along the route. New Orleans Police Department officers attend every parade for public safety and offer assistance for any emergencies.

The dynamic range of this photograph—that is, the spectrum of white, grays, and black between the lightest and darkest parts of the print—incorporates the entire possibility offered by the gelatin silver process. The delicately rendered smoke from the torches, the intense glint on the officer's highly polished shoe, and the inky blackness of the distant sky are all points of engagement for the viewer.

Strembicki's career as a photographic artist and university-level educator spans decades. Mardi Gras is a recurring subject in his work.

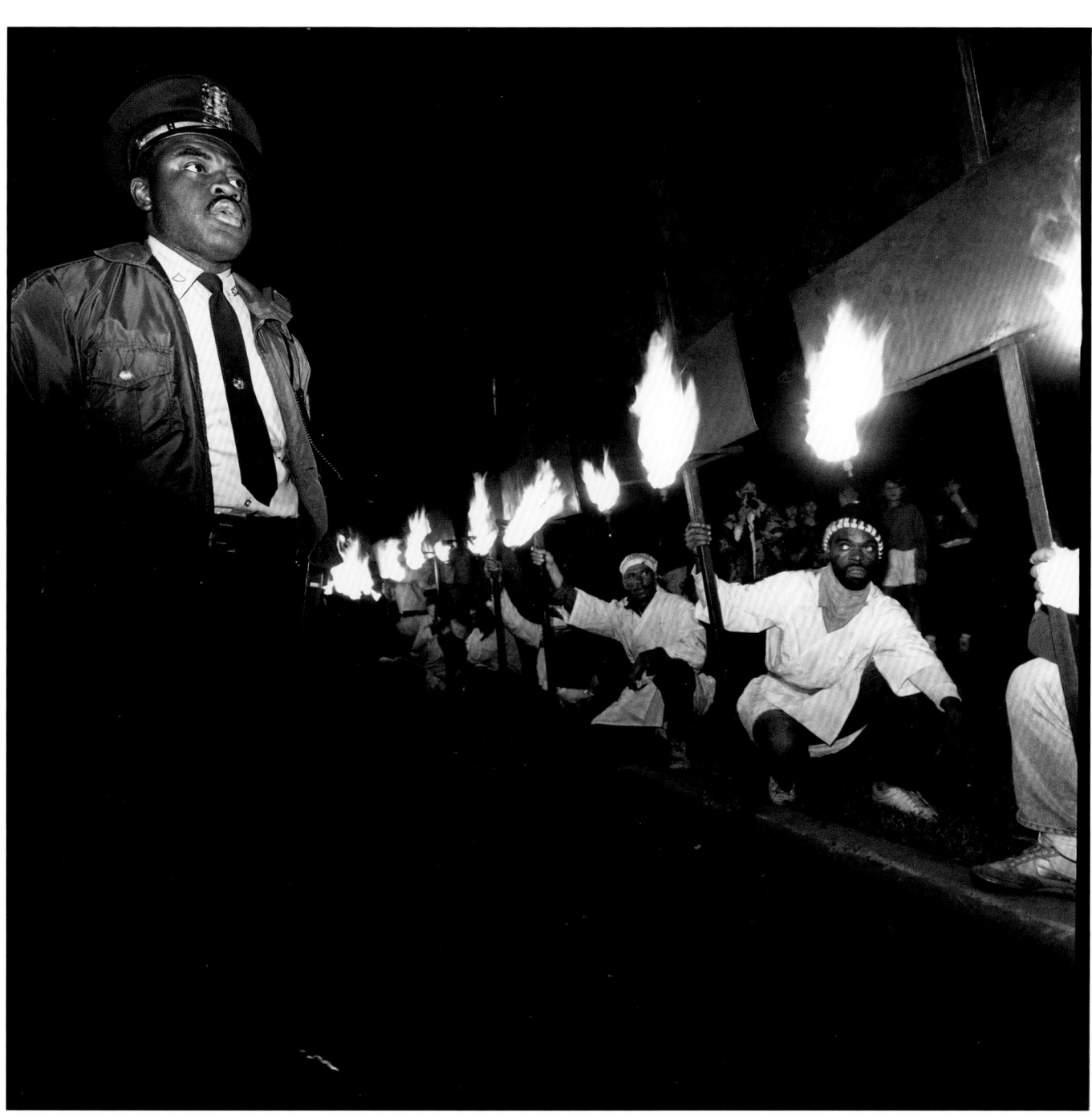

***Flambeaux, Hermes Parade,* 1991**
by Stan Strembicki
gelatin silver print, 20 × 16 in.
gift of Stan Strembicki, 2004.0049, © Stan Strembicki

The gelatin silver print was made in 2003 from a 1991 negative.

Rusty Costanza (b. 1964)

From magician conventions and whopper soft-shelled crabs to politicians, sporting events, fires, and hurricanes, a daily newspaper chronicles both the quirky and the quotidian. The *Times-Picayune* has been a constant in New Orleans journalism since the early twentieth century, its name persisting to this day despite recent media mergers and acquisitions. A portion of the newspaper's negative archive, covering the years 1983 through 2000 and containing millions of individual frames of film, is now housed at The Historic New Orleans Collection. The archive comprises black-and-white and color negatives and represents the seventeen years of the paper's operations before all its reporting photography became digital. The negatives are housed in sleeves containing coded information about assignment, page placement, and other aspects of the newspaper's prepress operations.

G. Andrew Boyd, the *Times-Picayune*'s chief photographer at the time, recalls that the shift to color film in the late 1980s required that the staff be retrained to visualize their work in color. The *Picayune* first deployed color reportage for breaking news on May 11, 1988, when a disastrous fire destroyed the cupola and third floor of the Cabildo on Jackson Square. In 2001, the switch to digital photography took place, and one of the benefits was that the new technology (not requiring darkroom processing) could push the press deadline back by hours.

Combining two Louisiana passions—politics and football—this photograph captures a brief encounter between two controversial candidates in a runoff for Louisiana's governorship: David Duke, a former grand wizard of the Ku Klux Klan, and former three-time governor Edwin Edwards. Rusty Costanza, a staff photographer for the *Times-Picayune* hired the year before, made the pictures. Costanza would enjoy a twenty-two-year career at the newspaper and was part of a Pulitzer Prize–winning team in 2006 for coverage of Hurricane Katrina.

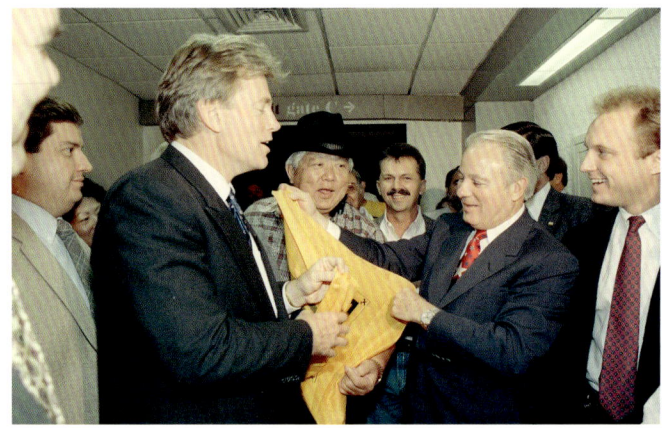

The photograph was taken inside the Louisiana Superdome, where the two candidates saw the New Orleans Saints prevail over the Tampa Bay Buccaneers, 20–7. Only hours before, Edwards and Duke had learned that the primary election held the day before placed them in a runoff for the state's highest elected office.

The runoff election presented Louisiana voters with a dilemma: a vote for Duke would empower someone whose racist and bigoted opinions had defined his public life; a vote for Edwards would return to office a former governor who had dodged federal charges for bribery associated with awarding hospital licenses. Public sentiment seemed to coalesce around a bumper sticker widely circulated at the time of the runoff: "Vote for the Crook: It's Important." Edwards won the election with over 60 percent of the vote and served his fourth term as governor. He would soon find himself under federal indictment for crimes associated with casino licensing in Louisiana during that last term. He was found guilty.

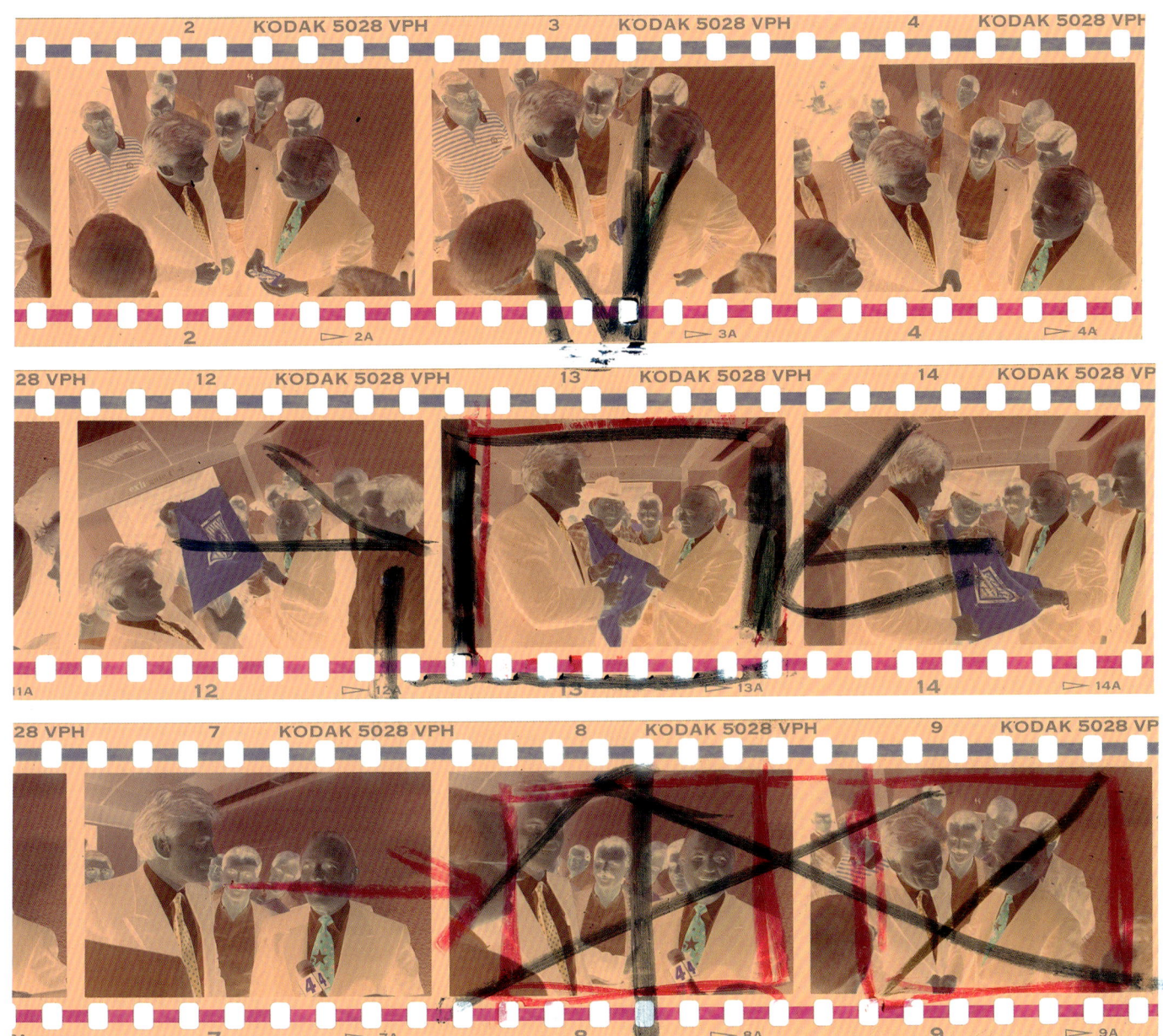

David Duke and Edwin Edwards meet in the Superdome, 1991

by Rusty Costanza

chromogenic negative, 35 mm

donated by NOLA Media Group, 2015.0437.4.1, original materials

© Rusty Costanza/The Times-Picayune

Stuart Klipper (b. 1941)

New Orleans has long been a city of public markets. From the late colonial period until the rise of private markets and grocery chains between the world wars, city-owned public markets anchored neighborhoods, provided controlled and sanitary locations for the sale of foodstuffs, and supplied revenue to the municipal treasury. The expansion and annexations of suburbs throughout the nineteenth century drove additions to the network of public markets. The system reached its peak during the first decades of the twentieth century at thirty-four structures, and though nearly all are now gone, a handful remain under private ownership. One of these, the St. Roch Market near the border of the Marigny and Bywater neighborhoods, is seen here. The subject of the photograph is not so much the market structure as the numerous signs advertising the wares, hours of operation, and available services.

Stuart Klipper, a regular visitor to Louisiana, made this picture over a decade before Hurricane Katrina struck New Orleans in 2005, and many neighborhood residents were displaced due to the floods that came after. This photograph, in the panoramic format for which the Minnesota-based Klipper is known, is part of the series *A City as Once Seen*, published under that title as a limited-edition artist's book in 2009. In the years following Katrina, the St. Roch Market was renovated and operates as a food court.

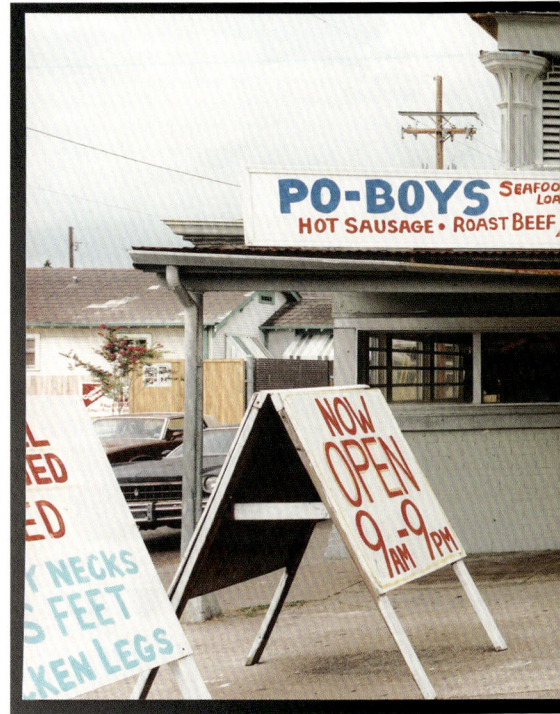

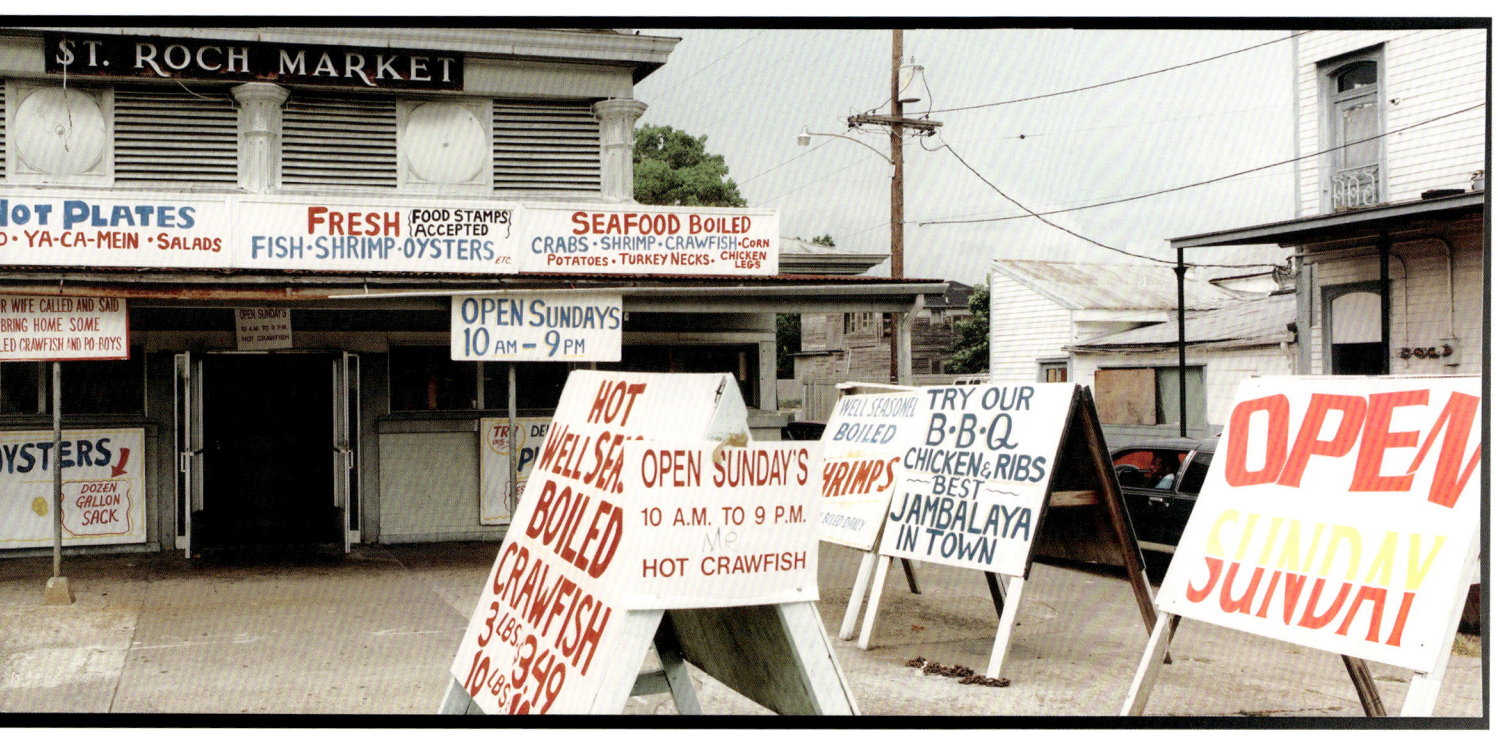

***St. Roch Market, St. Claude Ave., Upper 9th Ward,
New Orleans, 1992***
by Stuart Klipper
inkjet print, 9¾ × 29¹¹⁄₁₆ in.
gift of Stuart Klipper, 2016.0250.2, © Stuart Klipper

The inkjet print was made in 2008 from a 1992 negative.

Sandra Russell Clark (b. 1949)

After a point in photography's history when gelatin dry plates, flexible film, and the handheld camera had become mainstream, photographic technologies became more varied, building on proven techniques while extending the limits of chemistry and optics that opened new possibilities of pictorial expression. This effect was in no small way due to the efforts of photographers themselves, many of whom were, and are, artists, tinkerers, casual or professional scientists, and curious individuals who defy easy categorization.

One such tool appropriated by artists is infrared film, the original uses of which were scientific and military. The emulsion of this product responds to the longer-waved near-infrared end of the spectrum (rather than far-infrared, which is mostly thermal energy). The process was pioneered in 1910 by US physicist Robert W. Wood, and the widespread use of the product became possible in the 1930s. Film that rendered infrared wavelengths in color was introduced in the early 1940s, adding different capabilities to what had been only a black-and-white option. By 2007, just shy of a century from its proof of concept and in the rising face of digital photography, infrared film emulsion was commercially discontinued.

Black-and-white infrared photographs have a different appearance from those made on panchromatic film (a black-and-white film sensitive to all colors of the visible spectrum), depending on the subject chosen and technical factors of exposing, processing, and printing. In landscape photographs, green foliage reproduces as white, while blue skies are nearly black. Because the focal point of infrared rays may be slightly different from the focal point of visible light, a blurriness to the contours of the subject may exist if the lens is uncorrected for this difference or the photographer has not compensated for this effect. Some photographers choose their subjects to exploit these otherworldly or dreamlike characteristics of infrared photography.

Sandra Russell Clark has made the use of infrared photography a signature element of her work. Another aspect of Clark's output is her dedication to bodies of work on a single theme. Her 1980s Louisiana Dreamscape series, incorporating infrared film, chemical toning, and hand-applied coloring, is a group of pictures grounded in Louisiana coastal landscapes. Their execution exemplifies a trend that chose to stress (if not broadcast) artistic choices and counter the impression that photographs were noncreative objects, derived only from the mechanics and optics of camera and lens, and the chemistry of the process.

The photograph reproduced here is from Clark's mid-1990s series *Elysium* (also published as a book with that title), an interpretive assessment of aspects of some New Orleans cemeteries. The specific subject is a corner of the chapel on the grounds of St. Roch Cemetery. The chapel dates from 1876, when it was completed by Father Peter Leonard Thevis in fulfillment of a promise he made when his congregation was spared during one of New Orleans's regular epidemics of yellow fever. A cemetery was soon built around the chapel. In a variation of traditional ex-voto paintings, grateful supplicants who have prayed to St. Roch for relief from a spectrum of maladies often return to place an emblem related to the cure of their affliction—heart, limbs, ears, eyes—through the intercession of the saint. Others leave a simple plaque with the word *Thanks* or *Merci* on it.

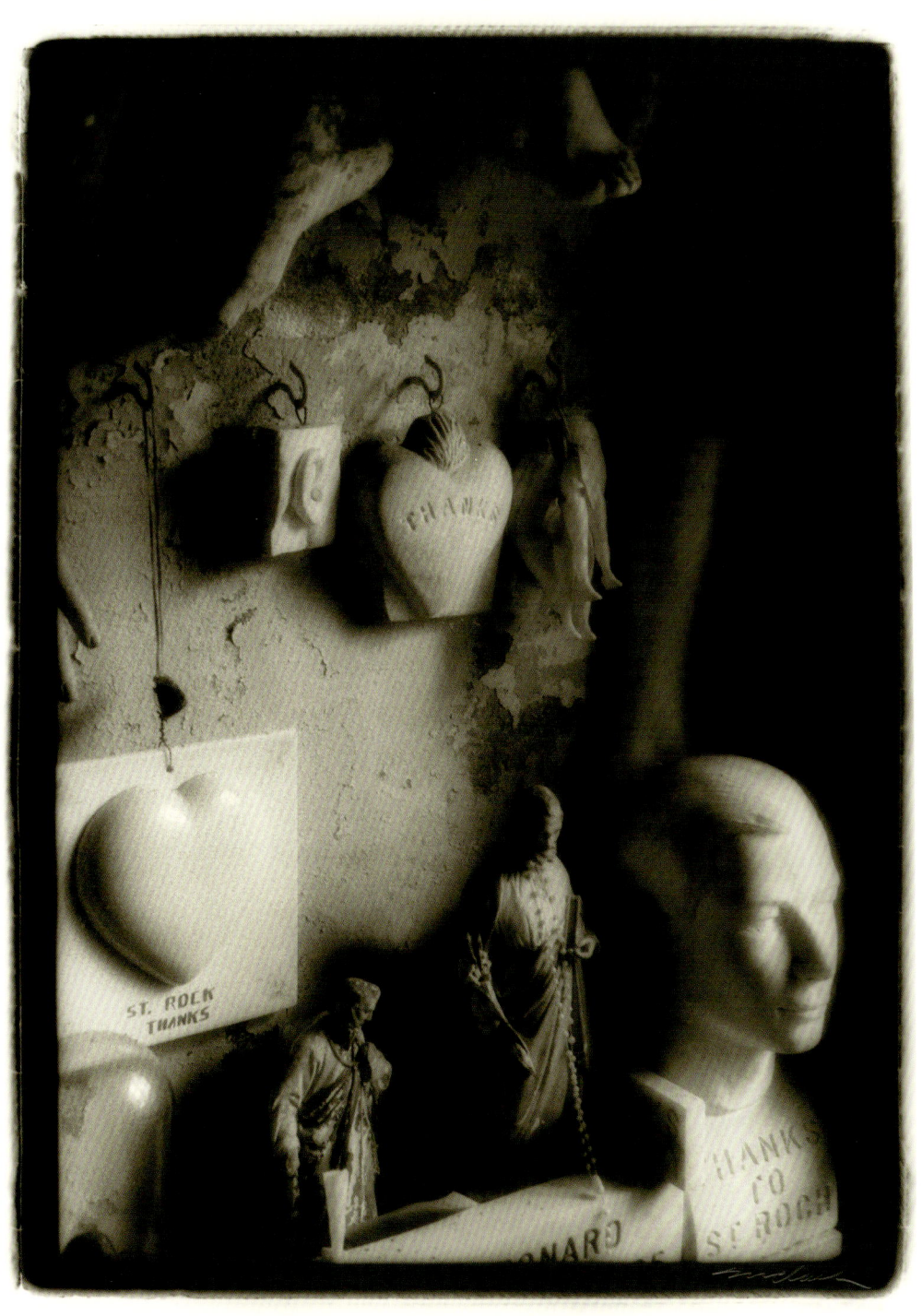

St. Roch I – Head and Heart, 1997
by Sandra Russell Clark
gelatin silver print, 15¾ × 19¾ in.
2013.0108.10, © Sandra Russell Clark

Jonathan Traviesa (b. 1976)

New Orleans singer, songwriter, and musician Ernie K-Doe was born Ernest Kador Jr. in 1933 and died in 2001. He was not just a musician, songwriter, performer, and entrepreneur but also a showman. K-Doe's persona was built on his own supreme confidence and the indispensable support of his wife, Antoinette. She was a significant partner in his renaissance in the 1980s and the launch of the Mother-in-Law Lounge, a barroom, music club, and community gathering spot, long after his 1961 number one hit single "Mother-in-Law" had left the charts. She also fashioned some of the colorful outfits that K-Doe wore in his performances, including the Uncle Sam costume seen here. He wore it to a July 4, 1999, concert in Washington, DC, at the Washington Monument.

The opening of K-Doe's club was a leap of faith to reaffirm his position in New Orleans's musical firmament, but it was also an act of defiance in the face of the withering presence of the elevated expressway on Claiborne Avenue, which it bordered (p. 206). The location would have defeated the efforts of other business owners, but the lounge, managed by the K-Does and subsequently by family member Betty Ann Fox McGee, proved durable. Now under the ownership of New Orleans musician Kermit Ruffins, the club still operates as a mecca for New Orleans music and its fans.

Jonathan Traviesa's photography often involves portraiture, with the subject placed in a setting of familiar objects or surroundings. About this photograph, Traviesa recalls that the K-Doe portrait was his first commissioned assignment, and though elements of the session were prearranged, and there were specific expectations about how the subject should be presented, within that framework there was ample opportunity to improvise.

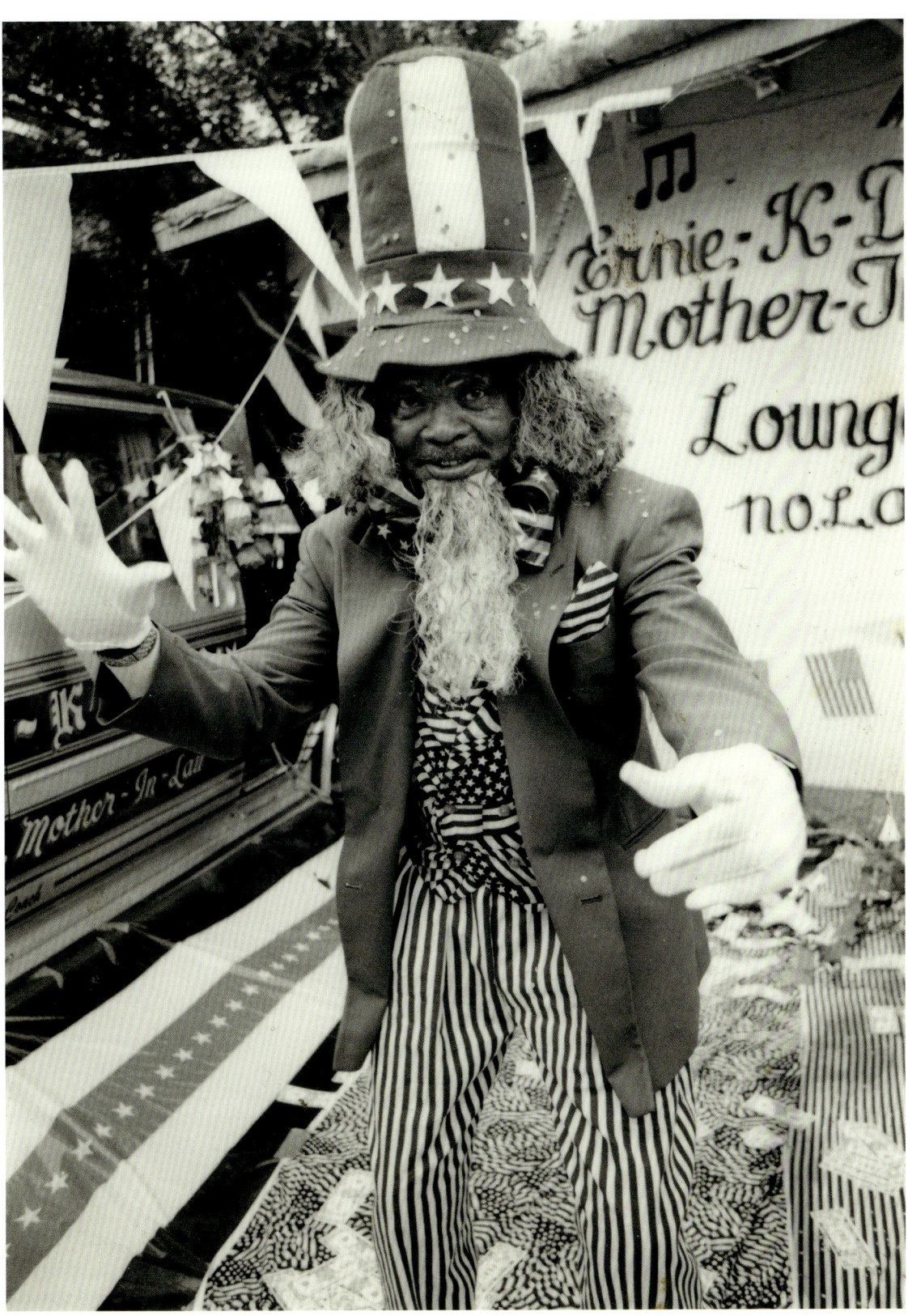

Ernie K-Doe Dressed as Uncle Sam, 1999

by Jonathan Traviesa
gelatin silver print, 9⅞ × 7⅞ in.
gift of Betty Ann Fox McGee, 2009.0232.5, © Jonathan Traviesa

A DIGITAL EXPLOSION

2000–PRESENT

Chris E. Mickal (b. 1955)

Wind was among the destructive forces of Hurricane Katrina, which struck New Orleans early in the morning on August 29, 2005; floodwaters followed when the levees failed. The impact of the flooding—damaged buildings steeped in standing water—lingered long after the storm had dissipated. With power down throughout much of the area, the city's public water system was essentially unavailable, making the threat of fire another primary concern. Because some buildings in flooded areas could not be reached, they burned, paradoxically, to the waterline.

Fighting fires with traditional fire equipment was impossible, so helicopters—customarily used in battling forest fires—were deployed. Carrying large buckets and dipping them into the Mississippi River, the helicopters released water on burning structures. Chris E. Mickal, a chief of the New Orleans Fire Department, captured both the destruction and the often heroic efforts of those fighting the fires.

Mickal donated several hundred pictures that bear witness to the efforts made by his department and by some out-of-state units that came to assist in the aftermath of the disaster. He also contributed two audio interviews that serve as a narrative background to activities shown in some photographs. He frequently frames the scene in a clear but stunning way. This photograph of a conflagration on Napoleon Avenue establishes the difficult situation facing first responders: a raging fire in a neighborhood beset by flooding and downed trees. Without streetlighting—due to the power outage—sundown presented a further problem for firefighters. Another picture from the series Mickal made of this event features a boat with workers rescuing survivors or looking for victims.

No single picture, film, essay, painting, book, or interview could summarize the society-altering force of Hurricane Katrina. For this reason, THNOC began Through Hell and High Water: Katrina's First Responders Oral History Project, offering users an opportunity to listen to interviews, look at pictures and videos, examine official reports and studies, and absorb the words of those who experienced this historical catastrophe first hand. Through this collection, an understanding of the event, in both its broad and specific contours, can begin to take shape. The project supplements other holdings that offer additional perspectives on the storm's effects, including paintings, drawings, and other photographs.

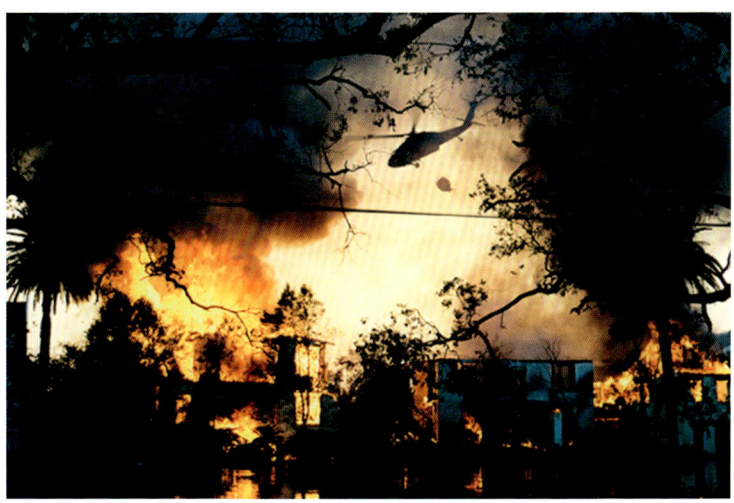

Napoleon Avenue fire, 2005

by Chris E. Mickal
digital image
gift of Chris E. Mickal, MSS 571.7.40.701, © *Chris E. Mickal, NOFD*
Photo Unit

Robert Polidori (b. 1951)

When New Orleans became accessible to outsiders covering the effects of Hurricane Katrina, Robert Polidori was among the first in line to visit the place that had been his home during part of his teenage years, when his father was working at the NASA Michoud Assembly Facility, in New Orleans East, on the booster rockets that first brought astronauts to the moon. The many hundreds of photographs he made over the course of the next several months collectively give a sense of how this storm and flood affected individual lives. Polidori entered many buildings that had been evacuated by their owners, finding within them the indiscriminate destruction left by rising, flowing, and standing water; oppressive heat and humidity; mold growth; and other forces.

One thing lost in seeing a photographic image (printed in a book or displayed on a screen), rather than a photographic object, is the sense of materiality that the latter version possesses. Polidori's prints from the Hurricane Katrina series are huge. This example is approximately 51 × 67 inches in dimension and mounted to a stiff panel of aluminum and polymer. The size not only permits a detailed look at the flakes of peeling paint, crumbs of plaster, water-damaged fabrics, and deposited dirt in the room but also provides an immersion in the setting. At close range, the size of the picture essentially surrounds the viewer, allowing them to symbolically stand in the room. The photograph becomes an elegy to a place and the people that inhabited it. Such an effect offers an inkling of the residents' experiences, as well as the anguish faced by others whose circumstances differed in details but not in overall effect.

The muted palette of this photograph is both literally descriptive of this location and emblematic of the brownish-gray pall of deposited sediment the receding floodwaters left in so many parts of the city. That patina of destruction covered surfaces—interior and exterior—throughout New Orleans and the neighboring communities.

The photograph was made in the city's Lower Ninth Ward. When the downriver floodwall of the Inner Harbor Navigation Canal (also known as the Industrial Canal) failed, waters augmented by tidal surge and unfavorable winds rushed through the neighborhood, inundating it and large portions of adjacent St. Bernard Parish. The silent grandeur of the scene is appropriate to what it depicts but also masks the chaos that produced it. Polidori shows us only the aftermath, his picture allowing us to imagine the lives that may have been lived in this room. In that sense, like all pictures, it is a nuanced, layered, and personal history between subject and viewer.

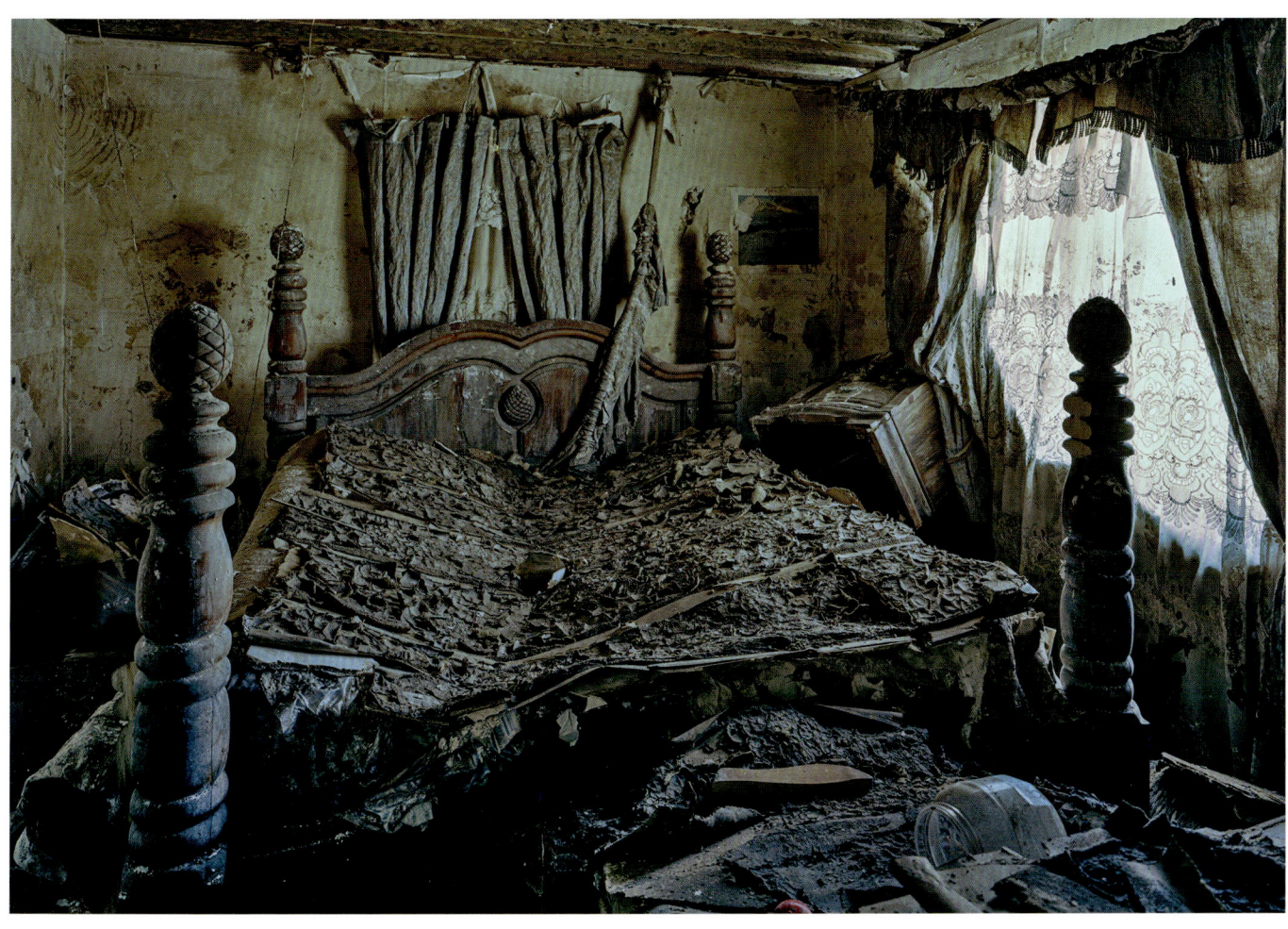

6328 North Miro Street, New Orleans, La., 2005
by Robert Polidori
digital chromogenic print, mounted, 51¾ × 67¾ in. (framed
dimensions)
2008.0090.2, © Robert Polidori

Stephen Wilkes (b. 1957)

The subjects of Stephen Wilkes's photographs of post-Katrina New Orleans are often portraits of survivors like Carroll Herbert standing in front of his tire shop on St. Claude Avenue. The form—a type of occupational portrait that shows a person with attributes of their profession—is nearly as old as photography itself. From the nineteenth century, countless daguerreotypes, cartes de visite, and other portrait formats show nameless and identified people gazing at the viewer, often brandishing an object that telegraphs what they do in life: a blacksmith with a hammer and anvil, a musician with an instrument, an astronomer with a telescope. Wilkes's portrait of Carroll Herbert follows that tradition by showing both what his subject does and the pride that person exhibits in that occupation, even when confronted with destructive forces of nature.

Another type of photograph that Wilkes made in post-Katrina Louisiana and Mississippi is testament to the devastating power of wind and water. These pictures convey a silence bereft of a palpable human presence. In the photograph showing a portion of a double shotgun house's facade, Wilkes has captured the glyphic markings used by rescue teams to indicate whether a building had been checked and to assign it a status. Teams from throughout the United States were dispatched to New Orleans in the wake of the storm and flood, and they employed a marking system developed a few years earlier by the Federal Emergency Management Agency (FEMA).

The X-shaped markings, usually applied with spray paint, provide shorthand information: the top portion shows the date the structure was visited; the right quadrant indicates hazards or sometimes that no entry ("NE") to the structure occurred; the bottom quadrant records whether living people or bodies were found inside; and the left quadrant identifies the unit that conducted the search. The two Xes in Wilkes's photograph reveal that this house was initially searched by the Drug Enforcement Agency (DEA) on September 10, 2005, and then searched again on September 21 by a unit identified as FL2, which may represent Urban Search and Rescue South Florida Task Force 2. The zeroes at the bottom of both Xes indicate that no people—alive or dead—were found in the house.

In depicting places of abandonment, Wilkes's pictures of post-Katrina New Orleans complement other projects undertaken by the Connecticut-based photographer. In the case of his series of the Ellis Island Immigration Station (1998–2003) and Bethlehem Steel (1998), the abandonment he shows reflects a change in use of those places, and an effect on disrupted lives that is different in character from what happened in Hurricane Katrina. But knowing this doesn't reduce the poignancy of the portraits or the "still life" pictures.

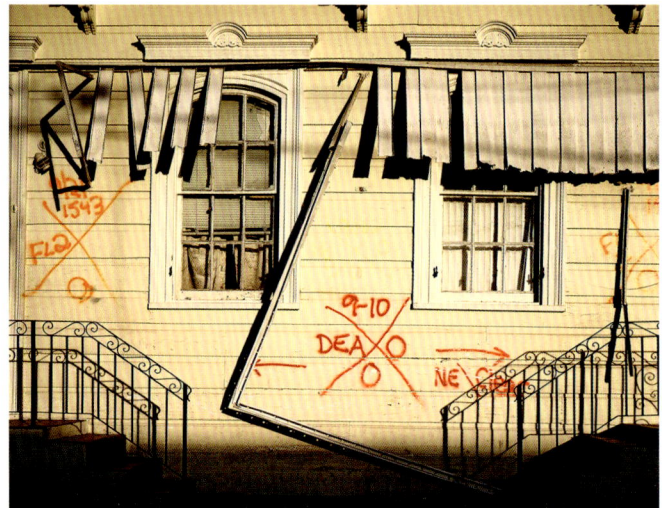

Search and Rescue Markings, Holy Cross, **2006**
by Stephen Wilkes
inkjet print, face mounted, 30 × 38 in.
gift of Stephen and Bette Wilkes, 2011.0195.10, © *Stephen Wilkes,*
www.stephenwilkes.com

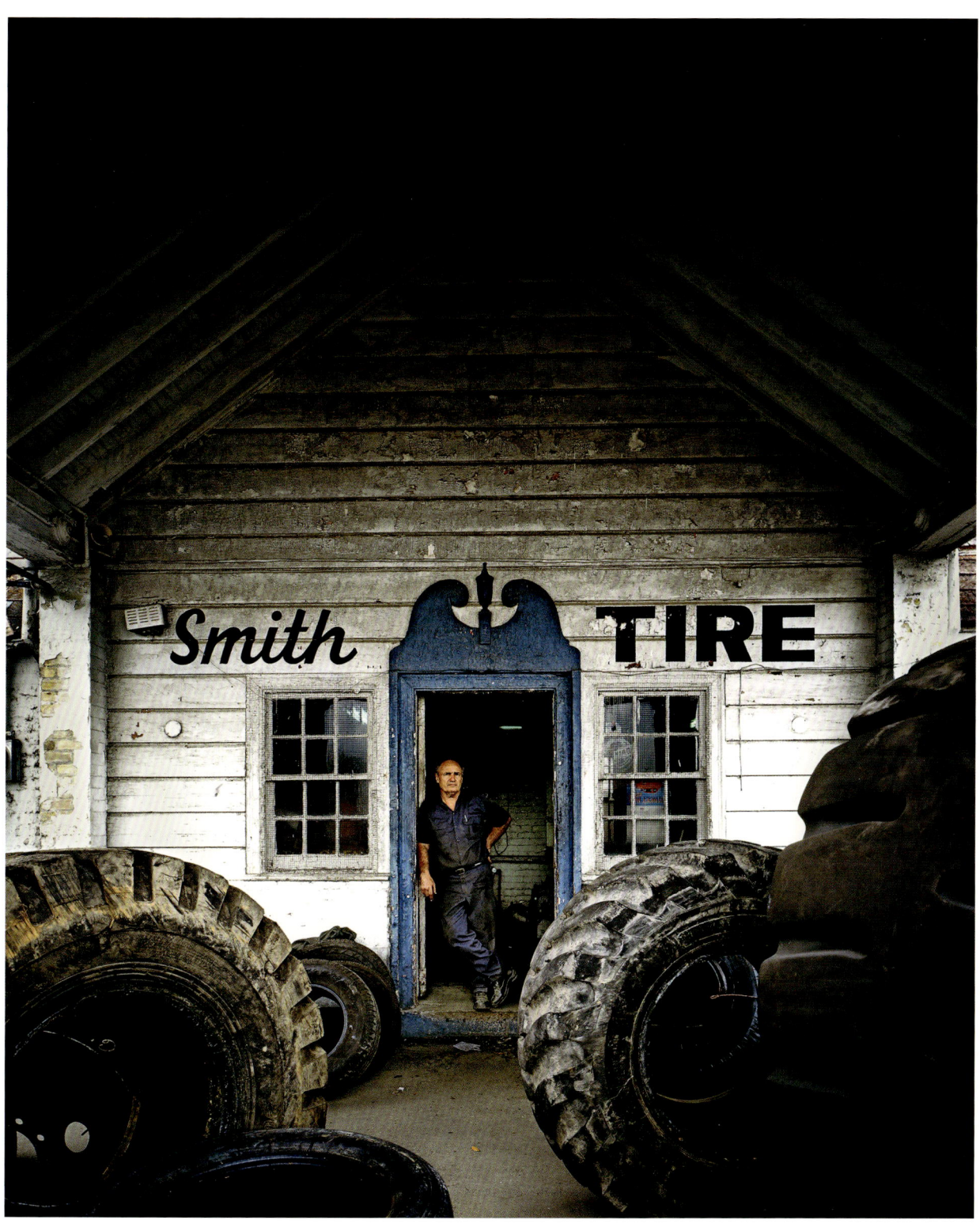

Carroll Herbert at Smith Tire, 2006

by Stephen Wilkes
inkjet print, face mounted, 40 × 31 in.
gift of Stephen and Bette Wilkes, 2011.0195.5, © Stephen Wilkes,
www.stephenwilkes.com

William K. Greiner (b. 1957)

Photographs of Hurricane Katrina's aftermath possess different characteristics, especially in how the photographers making them chose and reacted to the scene each recorded. Many pictures are gripping or terrifying in the destruction they show, while others are full of pathos for the human lives that were uprooted or ended. Some find humor in a macabre situation, focusing on grafitti and other messages that people wrote on their homes and discarded possessions. Other pictures seem to pose the question "How could this have happened?" William K. Greiner's example seen here rests in that latter category, though it contains elements of the others.

Boats perched on dry land, carpets spread across a parking lot and draped over handrails, and a sign heralding "renaissance" form a set for a theater of the absurd. Adding an enigmatic quality is the highway ramp that leads up and away, but to no clear destination. Such unusual juxtapositions were common in the aftermath of the hurricane, and the wry understatement with which Greiner composed this picture has been a part of his photography for nearly four decades. He has worked almost exclusively in color materials since the 1970s, when color photography was only beginning to be recognized as legitimate artistic expression. Though this photograph is in color, its muted tones capture the feeling of drabness that dominated the region prior to the reentry of the population and rebuilding of lives and structures.

The picture is a document of a scene, but it also alludes to an attitude about the world. Greiner's work in photography is ongoing, but in recent years his artwork has taken the form of collage, construction, painting, and assemblage. Language—often referencing the current political climate—figures prominently in Greiner's recent works.

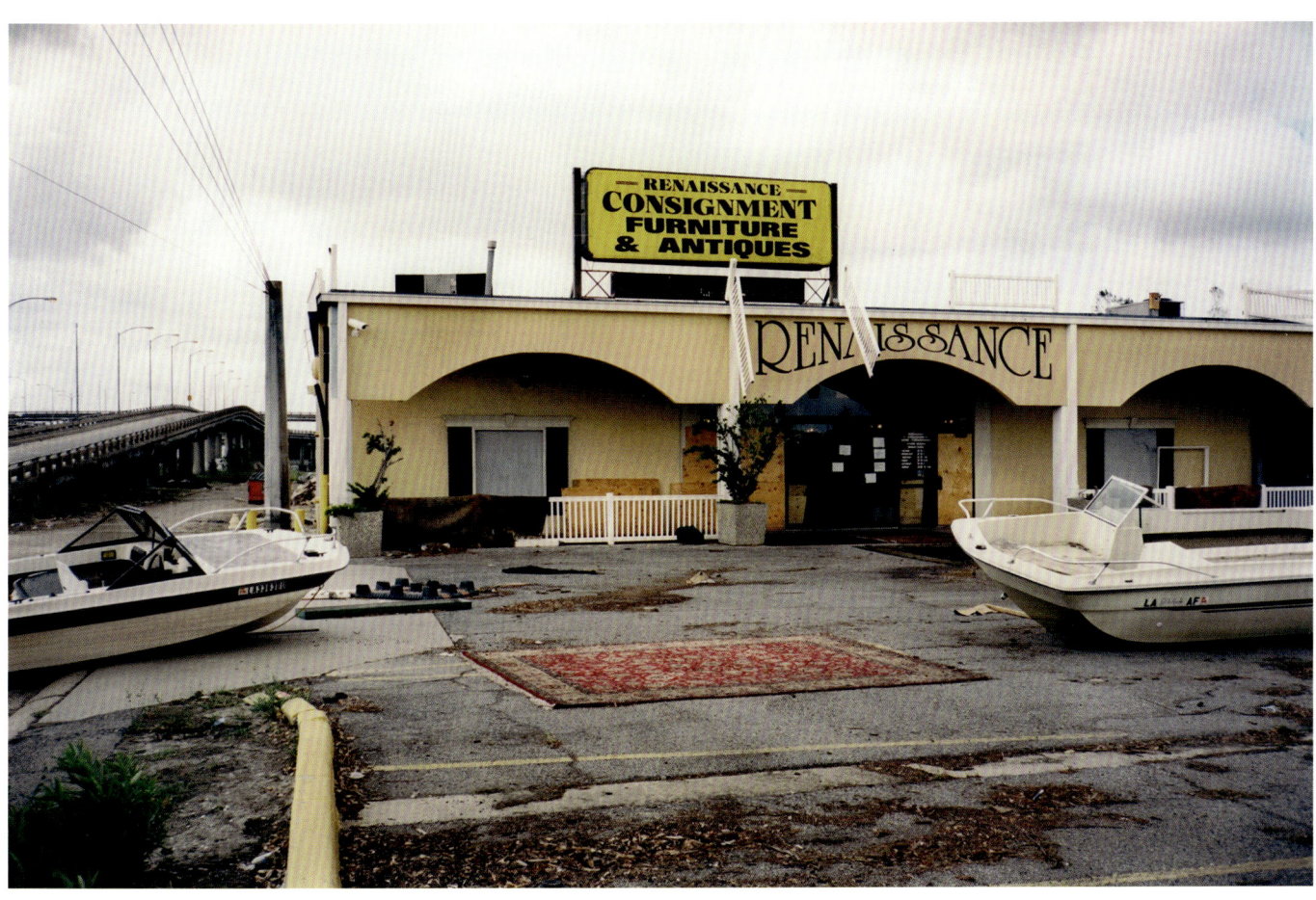

Oriental Rug, Airline Dr., Met. LA 10-13-05, 2005

by William K. Greiner
chromogenic print, 11 × 14 in.
gift of John F. Fraiche, 2012.0003.27, © William K. Greiner

Nine photographs from FEMA documentation

Much of New Orleans's housing stock is old, or at the very least, not modern. This condition is double-edged. On one hand, the older architecture that exists in many of the city's neighborhoods provides an intimate scale to these areas as well as undefinable qualities of established history, generational occupancy, and quaintness. On the other hand, older structures may not inherently offer the secure amenities of modern life like structural integrity required by current building codes, improved environmental systems, weather resistance, increased electrical capacity, and building tightness. Whichever side of this dichotomy one lands upon, the character of that building inventory in some neighborhoods changed dramatically after Hurricane Katrina and the subsequent floodwaters swept through the city in late August 2005.

A few years after the hurricane, the Federal Emergency Management Agency (FEMA) commissioned photographers to survey neighborhoods throughout New Orleans to identify which buildings were total losses and would not be repaired or rebuilt. Between 2006 and 2009, more than 1,600 such residences were demolished, paid for with funds from FEMA. A part of the demolition agreement was documenting the buildings' conditions prior to their removal. Photographers commissioned by FEMA made general views of each structure, as well as of salient architectural details. The nine photographs included here were taken by E. Amisson, B. Badinger, J. Cramer, T. Hahn, A. McCarthy, and A. Seward.

Though the photographs can never make up for the material loss, they are valuable as testament to the houses and streetscapes that are no longer present.

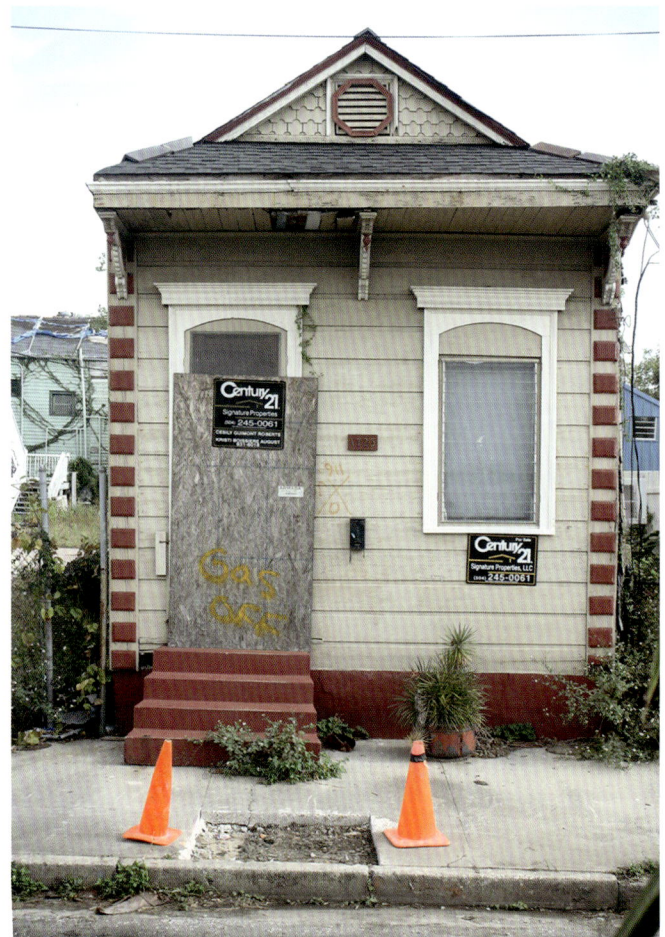

Photographs from FEMA documentation:
2013.0274.1.217.4; 2013.0274.1.9.6; 2013.0274.1.67.3; 2013.0274.1.36.3; 2013.0274.1.17.7; 2013.0274.1.63.2; 2013.0274.1.26.2; 2013.0274.1.290.1; 2013.0274.1.65.5

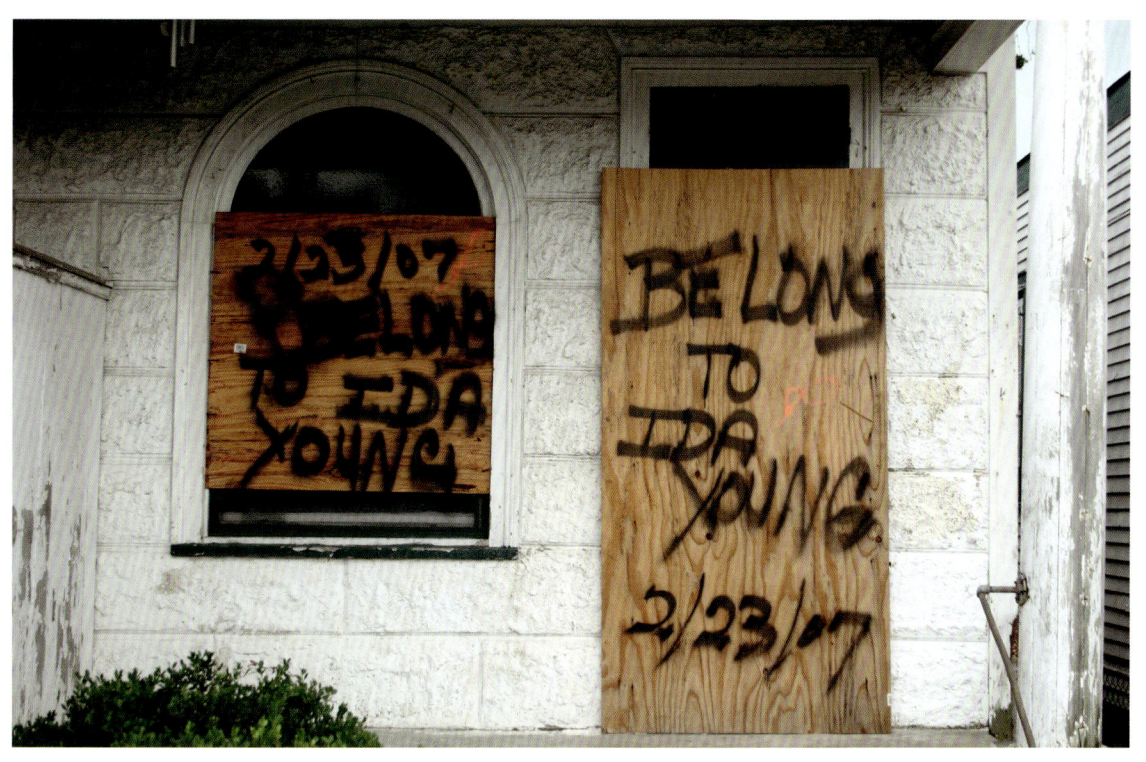

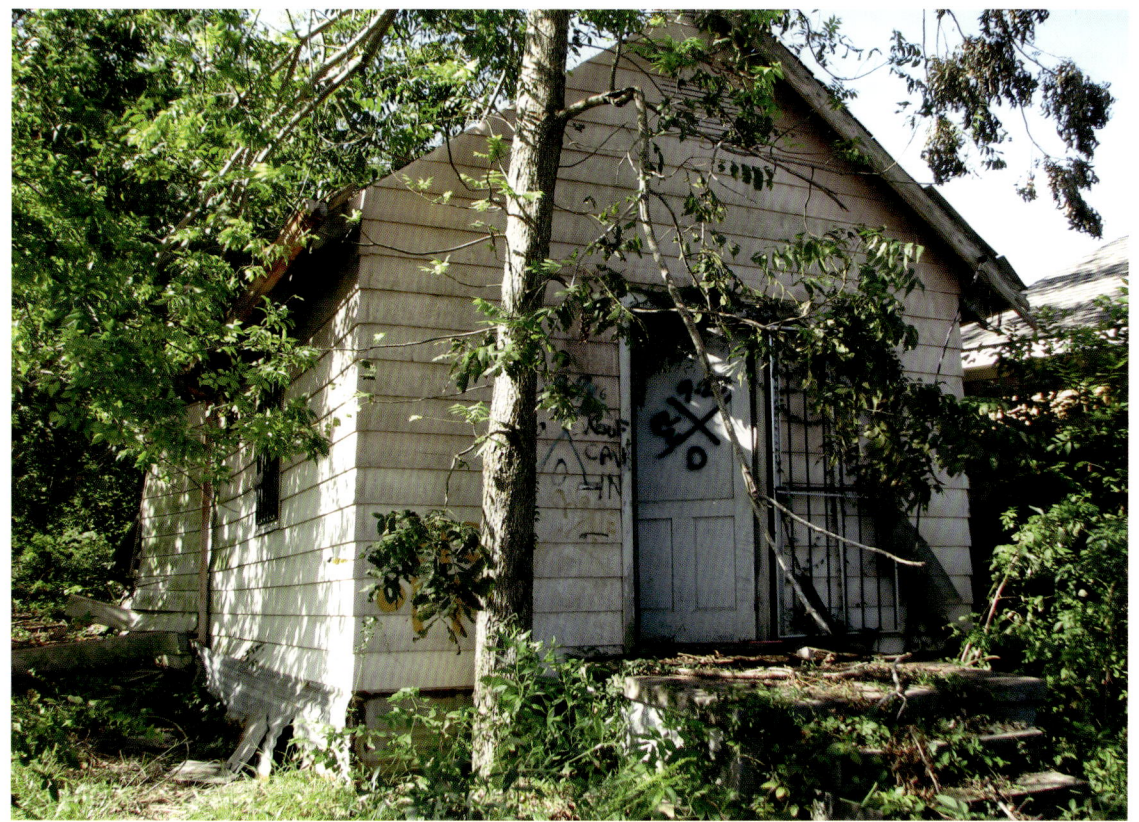

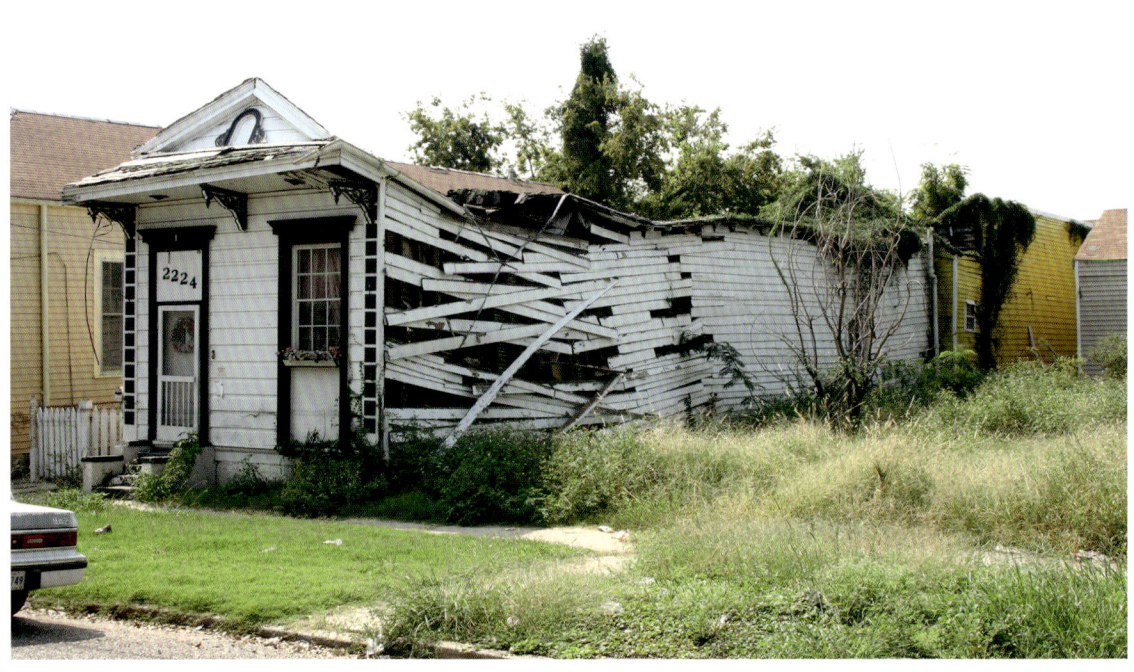

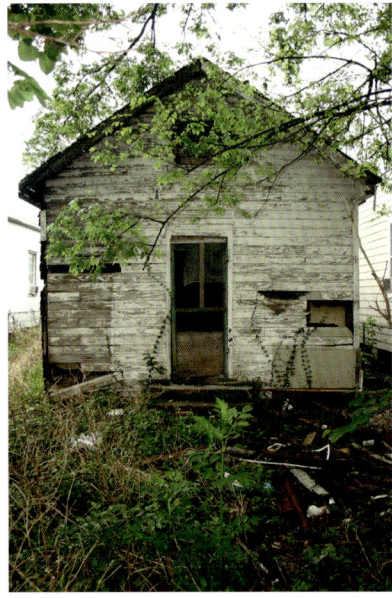

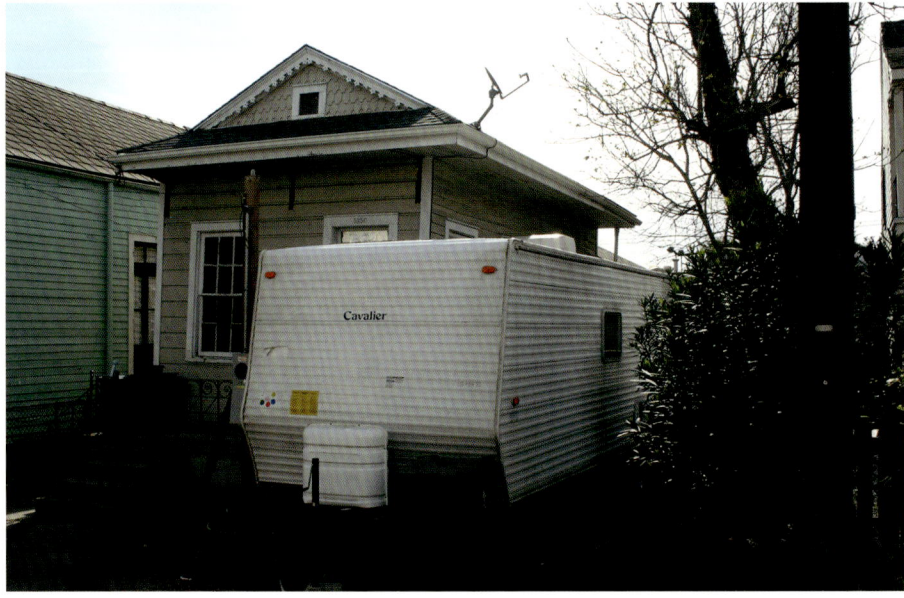

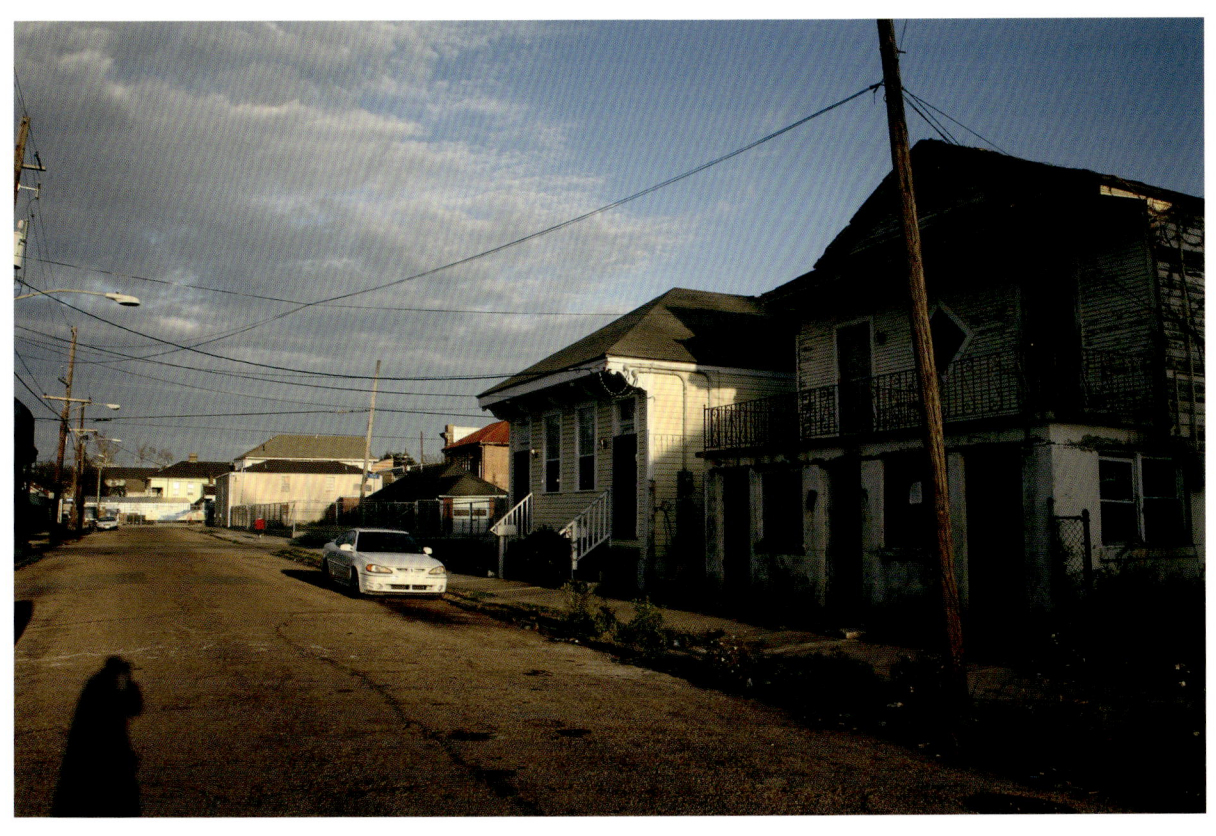

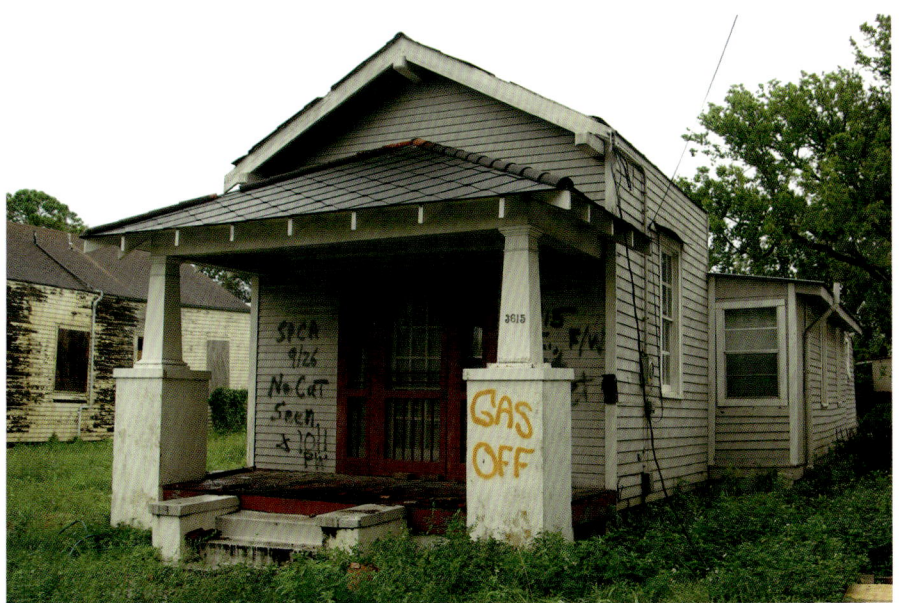

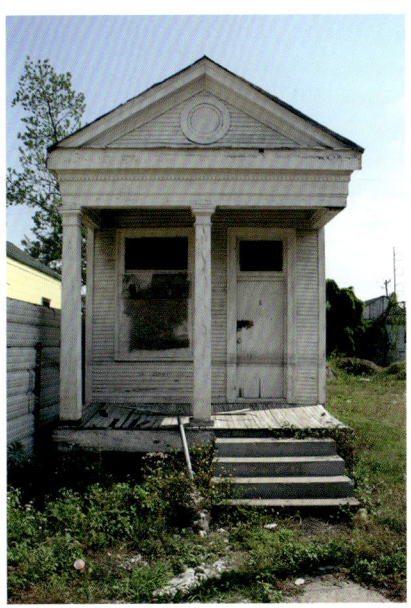

David G. Spielman (b. 1950)

Hurricane Katrina affected New Orleans–based photographer David G. Spielman profoundly. His experience during the storm and its aftermath has resulted in two books: *Katrinaville Chronicles* (2007), and *The Katrina Decade: Images of an Altered City* (2015). The first book was based on Spielman's experiences staying through the storm and sticking around afterward, witnessing the destruction when it was still fresh: sailboats piled like jackstraws in the marina, a community of nuns continuing their devotions amid disaster, and pleas for help daubed on rooftops, aimed at helicopter pilots, as people sought refuge from rising waters.

The photographs seen here are from the latter project and were acquired as part of The Historic New Orleans Collection's efforts to document the event and aftermath of Hurricane Katrina across different media. *The Katrina Decade* poses its visual question with incredulity: how are these conditions still unaddressed nearly a decade following the storm's arrival? Before Spielman's lens, the lingering destruction of the storm and its persistent presence in the city's neighborhoods hang like a question mark in the air. The answer is complicated, as many answers often are. The infusion of money from governmental and charitable agencies that followed Katrina helped, but it could not in and of itself solve problems of displacement, fix bureaucracies in chaos, compel insurance companies to pay for claims, and restore the heavily damaged infrastructure.

Spielman, a native of Tulsa, Oklahoma, has been a resident of New Orleans for more than five decades. Though he describes his approach to photography as documentary, his selection of subjects for this project in his adopted city is personal and deeply felt.

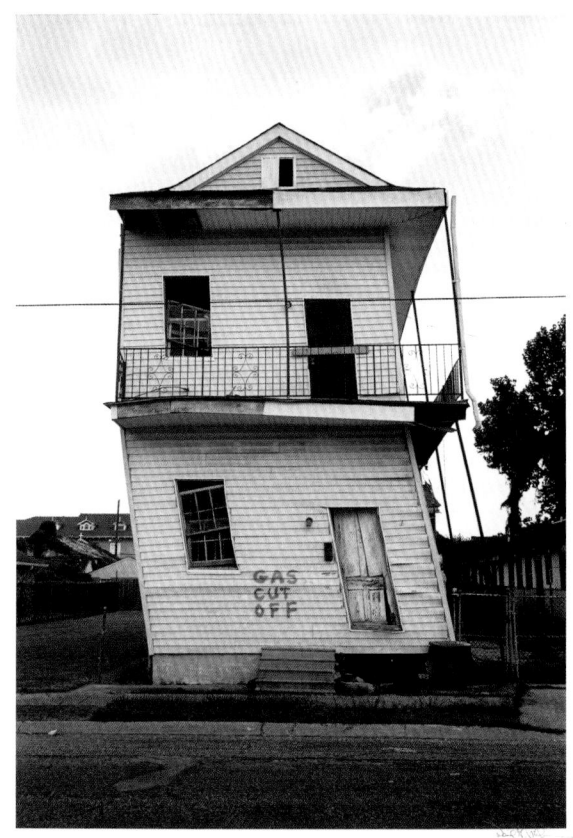

***Central City*, 2012**
by David G. Spielman
inkjet print, 37¼ × 24 in.
2015.0225.16, © David G. Spielman

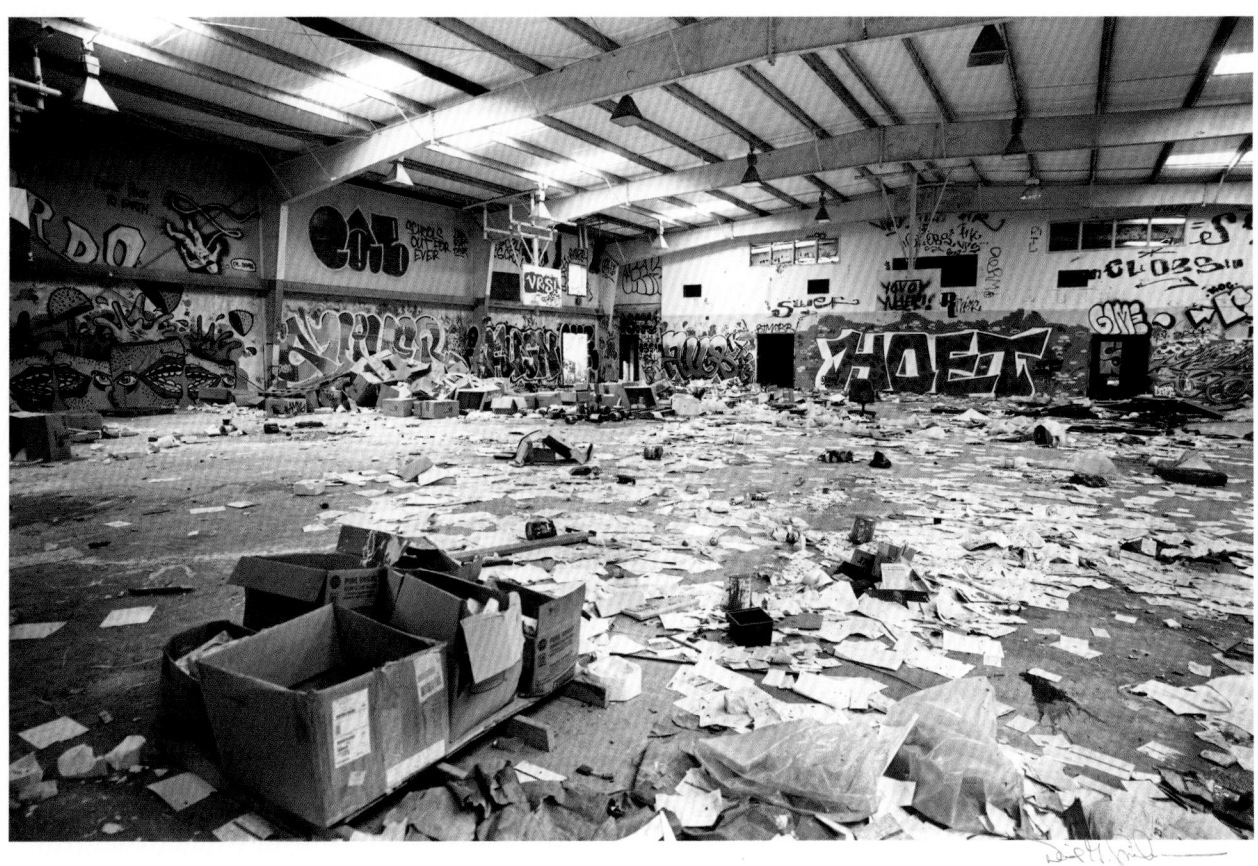

Press Park, 2014
by David G. Spielman
inkjet print, 17⅛ × 22 in.
2015.0225.15, © David G. Spielman

Carl Bergman (b. 1948)

After Hurricane Katrina, debates raged about whether certain damaged neighborhoods should be reinvested in and restored, or cleared to make way for parkland or redevelopment. These images by Carl Bergman document a neighborhood whose demolition may have been catalyzed by Katrina but whose fate was sealed by state and local government plans to create a new medical district in New Orleans.

When Charity Hospital in downtown New Orleans was damaged in 2005, some advocated for the renovation of the art deco building into a state-of-the-art modern hospital; others sought to abandon it and construct a completely new medical district in nearby Mid-City. The latter group prevailed, and in 2010, the state government claimed a twenty-seven-block residential area, via negotiated buyouts and eminent domain, to make way for the Veterans Affairs Medical Center and University Medical Center. Bergman and his wife lived within this footprint, and when the block where their house stood was claimed for the project, they were forced to move. Carl Bergman is better known as a photographic printer than as a photographer, but using a primitive and flimsy, almost toylike camera with a rudimentary lens, he chronicled the fate of his family's home and neighborhood before leaving the city. These small and meticulously printed photographs are a very personal account of Katrina's effects on the neighborhood, bridging the realms of dream, diary, and document.

The poignancy of some of the photographs is inescapable. Bergman's isolation of personal possessions—a single shoe, a candlestick, a broken record album, a comb—is imbued with the sadness of their context. Other photographs from the series feature closed small businesses—corner stores, barbershops, barrooms, and other establishments—describing a layered and varied economy soon to be replaced by a monolithic one. One may wonder about the lives of those who used the possessions and worked in the businesses, or whether the people associated

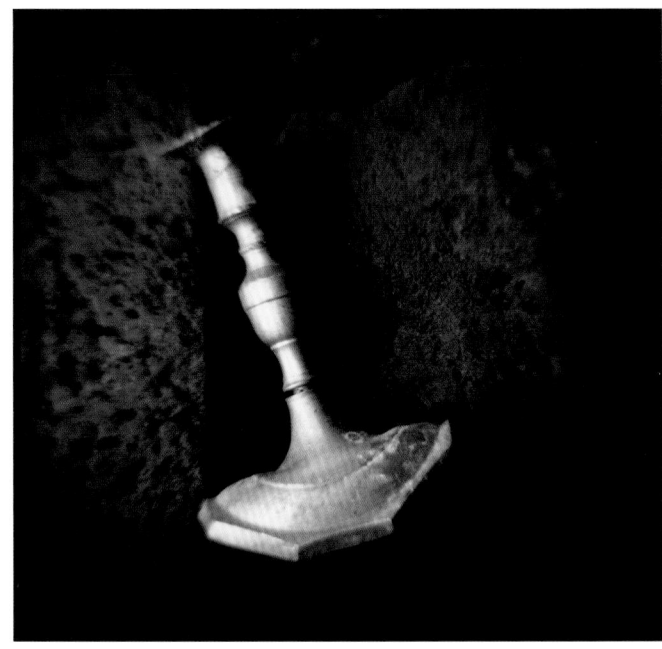

with these objects and places survived, and if so, what their current circumstances are.

The "Save Charity Hospital" yard sign in Bergman's photograph represents the campaign opposed to the wholesale redevelopment of the neighborhood. As of 2023, it appears that the former Charity Hospital complex will be redeveloped as a mixed-use facility, and not demolished as many had feared. The University Medical Center began operations in 2015.

Candlestick Holder, Katrina Street Debris (Arrangement), 2006
by Carl Bergman
gelatin silver print, 8 × 10 in.
gift of Carl Bergman, 2018.0211.75

The gelatin silver print was made in 2017.

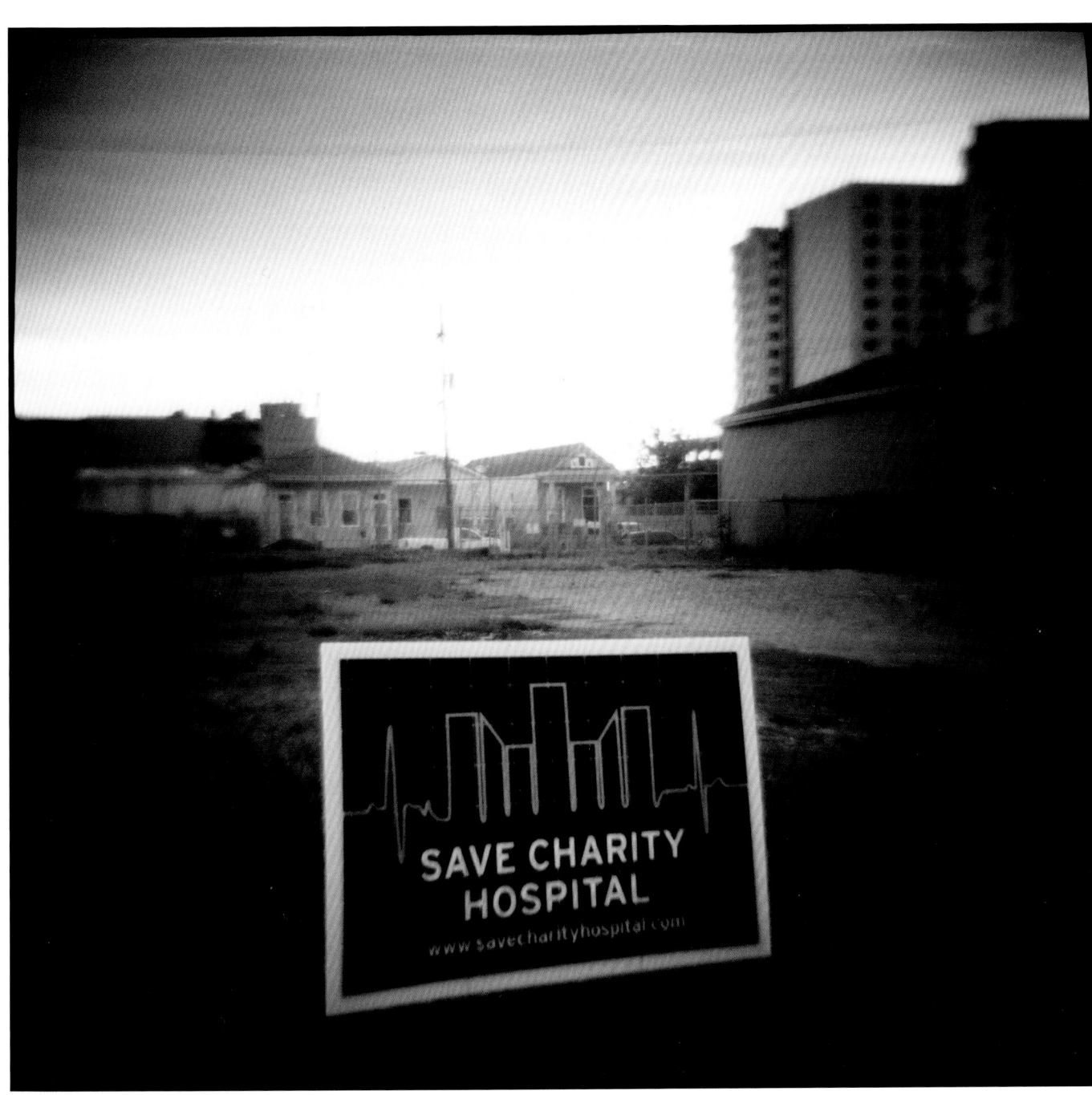

Save Charity Hospital Poster, 2009
by Carl Bergman
gelatin silver print, 8 × 10 in.
gift of Carl Bergman, 2018.0211.5

The gelatin silver print was made in 2016.

George Dureau (1930–2014)

This color self-portrait is markedly different from what a George Dureau photograph typically presents: a black-and-white, richly toned gelatin silver print with a rigorously constructed composition. Dureau's paintings are based on working out ideas in sketch form—some are visible pinned to the wall in this photograph, which was made in his studio. This photograph also represents an exploration rather than a finished work.

Though nominally a self-portrait, the image is on the brink of being a still life. The portion of Dureau's face seen in the reflection suggests he is aiming the camera without looking through the viewfinder, employing the mirror as a surrogate. The off-kilter composition of converging vertical elements adds to this teetering effect, and the reddish-orange light may be from an external source such as a sunset or sunrise, or it may have been caused by light striking the film after exposure and before development. It is another element of mystery.

George Dureau's artwork had an unmistakable look and defined iconographical components, but this is not to say he shied away from experimentation. His comfort zone (in painting or photography) rarely extended beyond the studio, and his approach to painting reflected his formal training in the discipline at Louisiana State University. Dureau's paintings often employed characters of mythology and religion—satyrs and angels, for example—and these works were uncontroversial. But when he began exhibiting photographs of nude men—often African American, sometimes amputees or people with dwarfism—the public reaction was mixed, and some expressed shock at the photographs' content. However, the dignity that Dureau saw in his sitters and the taut elegance of his compositions suggest that he celebrated his subjects' physical appearances.

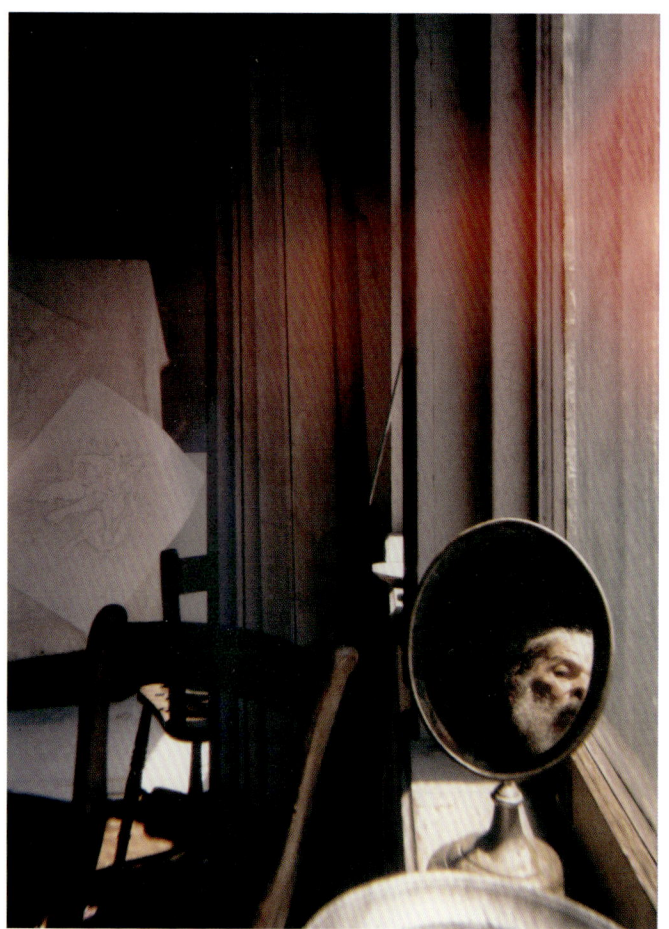

Self-portrait, 2011
by George Dureau
chromogenic print, 6 × 4 in.
gift of Donald Dureau, 2015.0293.1.30

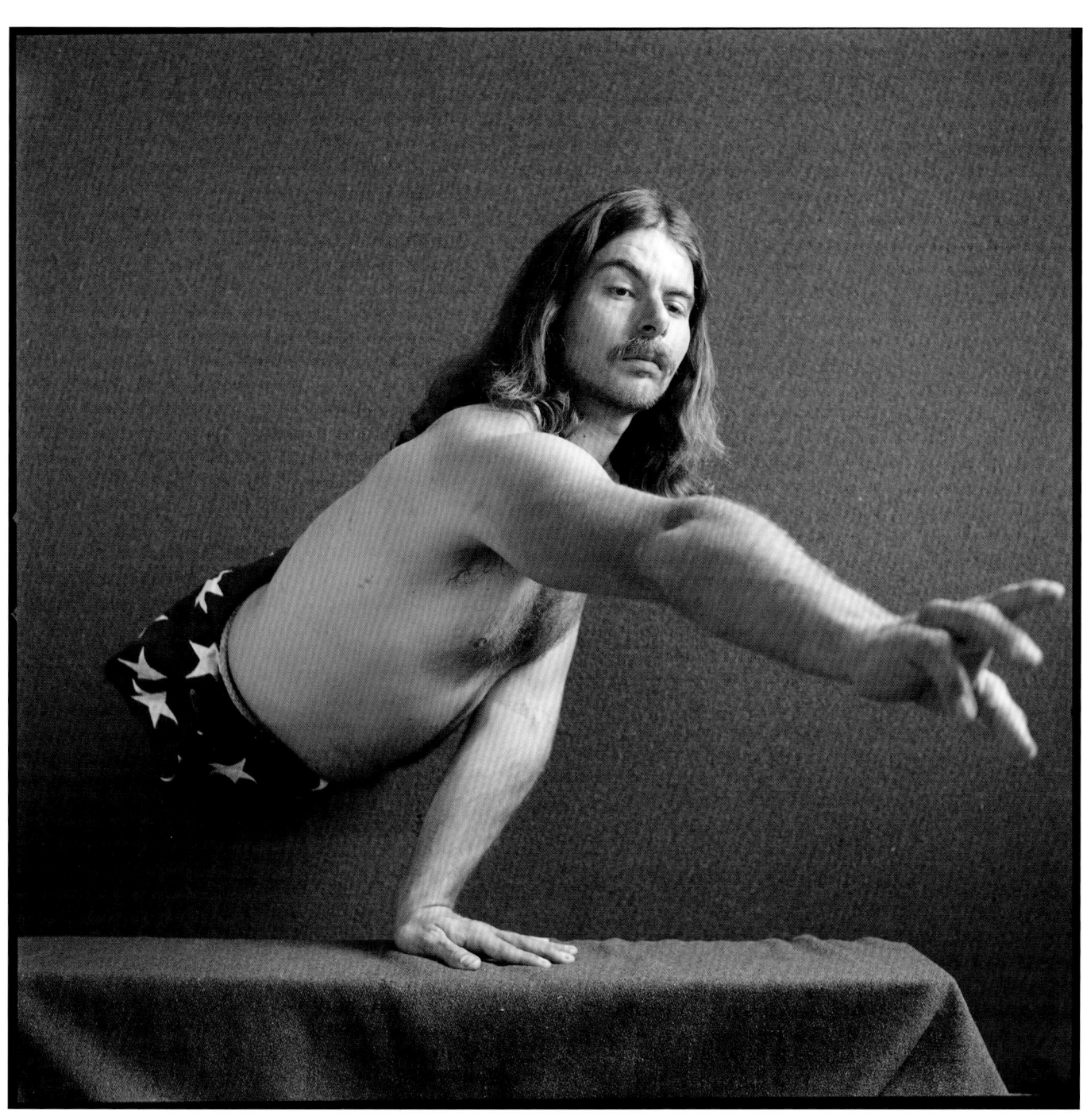

B. J. Robinson, 1983
by George Dureau
gelatin silver negative, 2¼ × 2¼ in.
gift of Donald Dureau, 2015.0293.2.19.2.4

Charles Martin (b. 1961)

Perique tobacco grows on thirty square miles of land in St. James Parish, Louisiana, along the Mississippi River between New Orleans and Baton Rouge. Its culture and processing are in keeping with over two and a half centuries of agricultural and industrial practices. Its very existence is testimony to original colonial designs (quickly abandoned) for French Louisiana to be a tobacco colony.

Perique's finished character is very pungent, and its physical properties include dampness rather than dryness. These qualities make it a tobacco to be blended with other varieties, rather than consumed on its own. Over the centuries, some tools of production have changed. Plastic barrels have, in part, replaced wooden ones, and mechanization has crept into some aspects of cultivation and manufacturing that earlier had been the domain of farm animals. But the process itself has been as durable as the arpent lines on the landscape whose alluvial soil gives the leaf its special characteristics.

Charles Martin's pact with perique is ancestral. For generations, his family has grown, harvested, cured, and marketed perique. His access to the day-to-day and season-to-season ebb and flow of the agricultural year lets him observe and photograph at leisure. Aided with this accumulation of experience, he knows when to record the "just right" human moments in the process or how to capture the quintessential elements of the barns and equipment. The push and pull of the season, from outside to indoors, from bustling activity to quietly biding time—all are present in this series of forty photographs. Those who worked the perique fields long before Martin's appearance in the world inform his photography.

Martin's photographs show two faces. They are documentary in content and style, and they are also expressions of their maker's personal history. In the parlance promoted by the late John Szarkowski, they are both a mirror and a

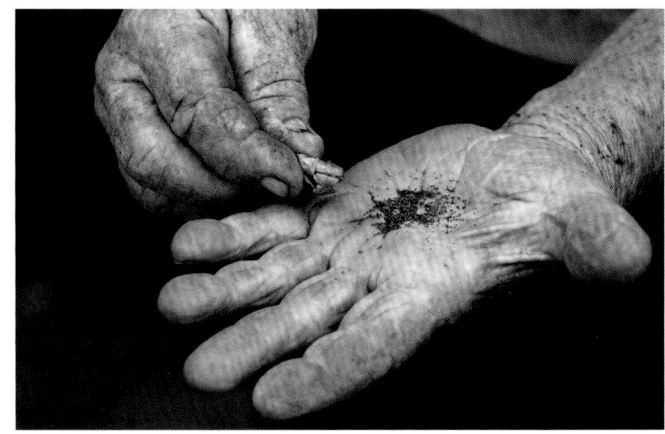

window. In the aggregate, Martin's work may look like an extended photographic essay, which in a way it is, but one without deadline.

Perique seeds, 2012
by Charles Martin
inkjet prints, 10½ × 15½ in.
gift of Charles Martin, 2013.0408.4, © Charles Martin

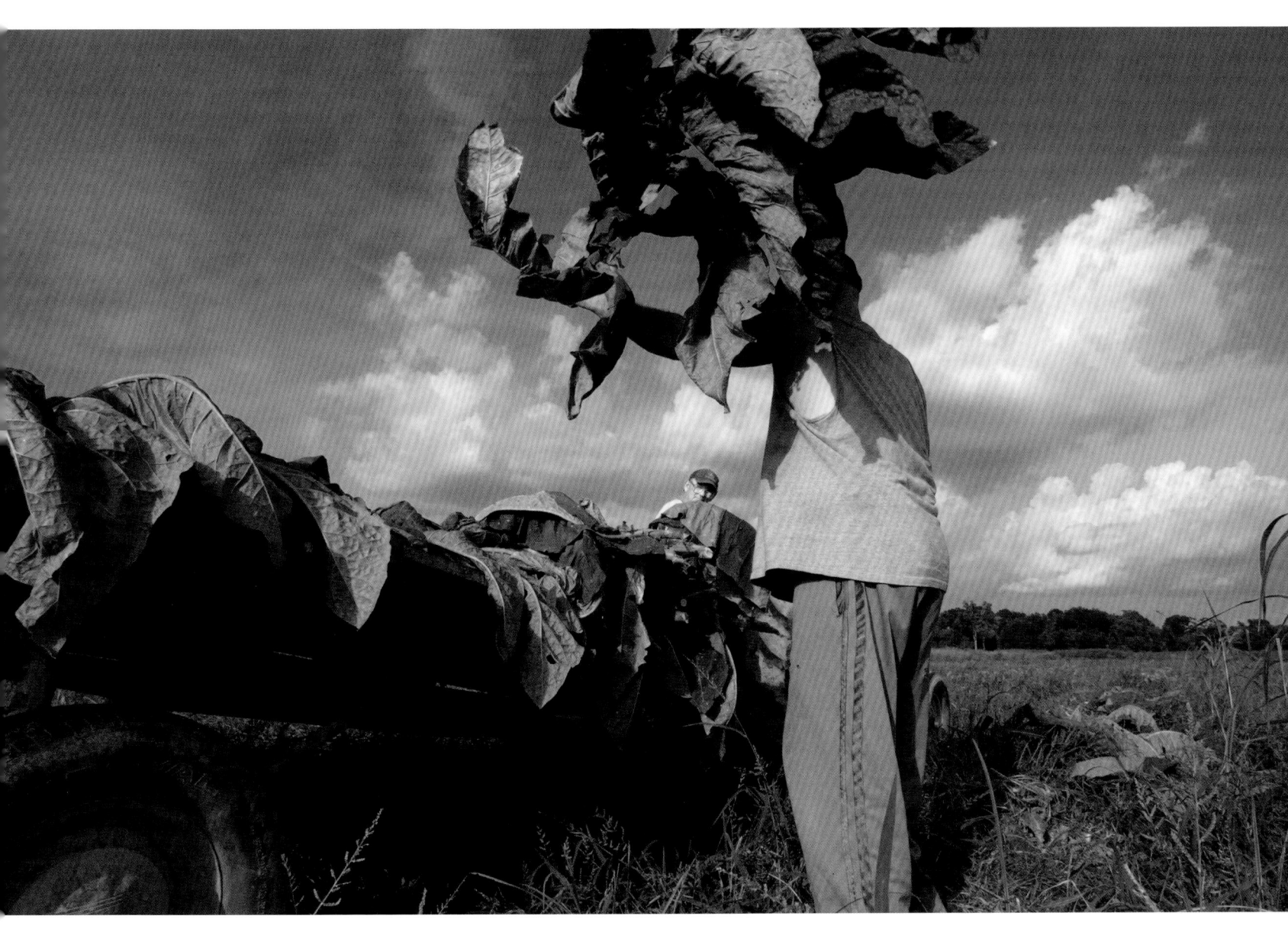

Harvesting perique stalks, 2012

by Charles Martin
inkjet prints, 10½ × 15½ in.
gift of Charles Martin, 2013.0408.16, © Charles Martin

Robert S. Brantley (b. 1948)

The design of this double house by Irish-born architect Henry Howard is as much an economic statement as an architectural one. Though Howard's decades-long practice (based in New Orleans but with selected projects scattered throughout the Deep South) included both grand and modest structures, the watershed years of the American Civil War (1861–65) tend to separate the former from the latter. The building contract for this structure dates from 1866, when Howard designed it for shipping clerk Martin O. Larsen. Larsen died the following year, which may have had something to do with the Howard family moving into the left side of the double before the 1868 birth of their tenth child, Ida Caroline. The family seems to have remained at this location until mid-1872.

Howard's design places the building directly on the sidewalk. Narrow walkways on either side maximize the width of the building relative to the size of the lot. This tactical placement—an architectural phalanx, if you will—gives the house an importance it would not have if isolated on a larger piece of ground, bordered with lawns or gardens. Unseen from the street, however, is a small backyard with outbuildings that occupy the balance of the 150-foot-deep lot, permitting a semblance of bucolic privacy. The simplicity of the house (despite the cast iron on the second floor and a modest dentiled and bracketed cornice) reflects the atmosphere of the working class neighborhood of the city's Third District, whose residents had African, French, German, and Irish roots, and whose subdivision into building lots dates to the early nineteenth century.

New Orleans–based Robert S. Brantley and his late wife Jan White Brantley (head photographer at THNOC from 1983 until her death in 2008) partnered to photograph historic and contemporary architecture in the Gulf South for architects and preservationists, and for publication in books and magazines. Their collaboration on the book *Henry Howard: Louisiana's*

Architect (published by The Historic New Orleans Collection in 2015) records the considerable output of Howard's practice in various partnerships and as a sole practitioner. In capturing this structure, Brantley has chosen a camera position that respects the confrontational character of the building, imbuing it with a monumentality that belies its size.

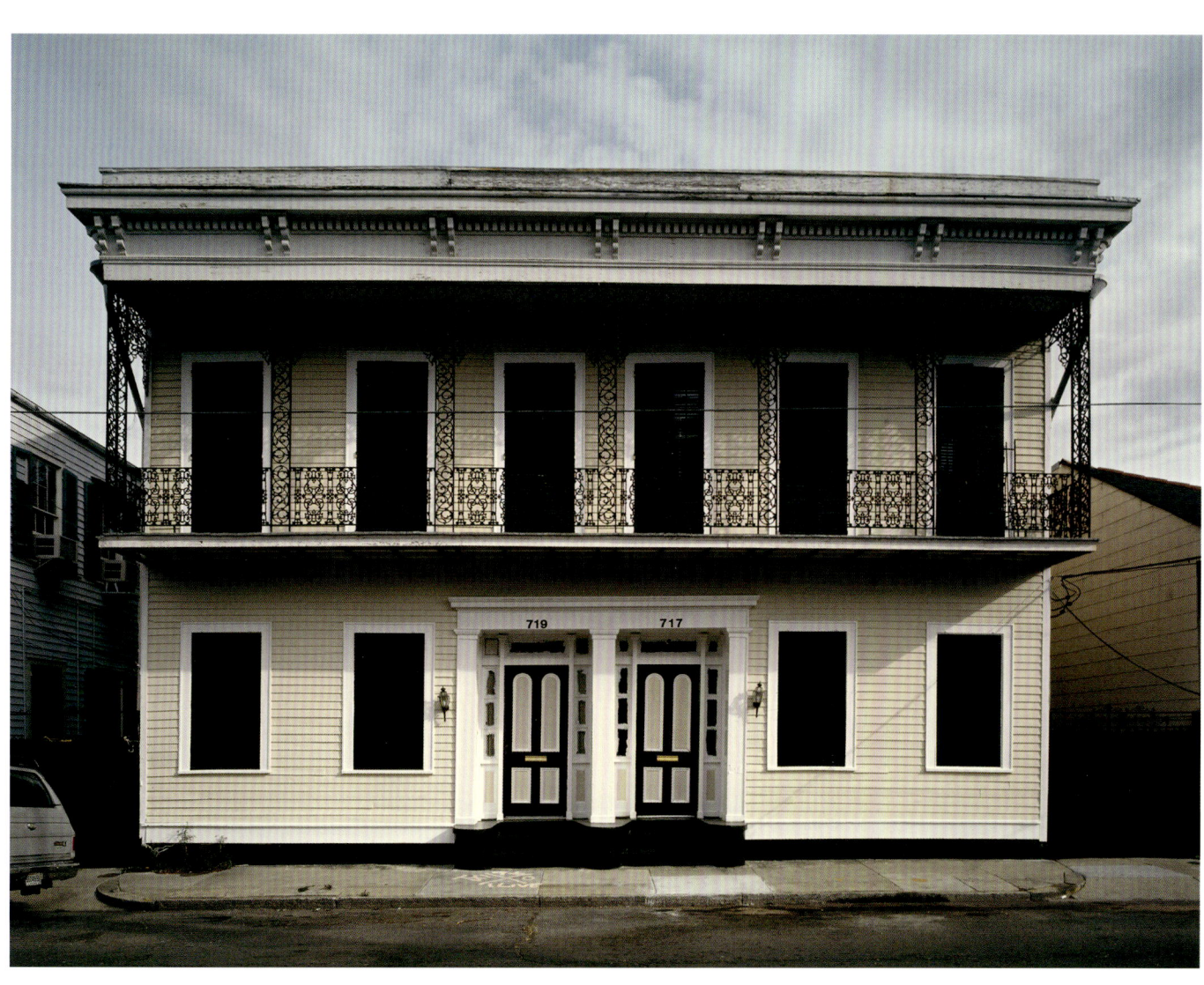

Martin O. Larsen double house, 2015
by Robert S. Brantley
digital image
gift of Jan White Brantley and Robert S. Brantley, 2015.0415.103,
© Robert S. Brantley

Richard Sexton (b. 1954)

The Mississippi River provides the lower portion of Louisiana both an identity as an industrially developed landscape and a raison d'être. A nearly unbroken "port" stretching over 140 river miles from just below New Orleans to the state capital of Baton Rouge receives and discharges inbound and outbound cargoes of coal, grain, raw materials, petrochemical products, and finished goods. Compelled by this twenty-four-hour cycle of commerce, Richard Sexton documented the lower river in a series of photographs made over the course of more than a decade. The project was published and exhibited in 2019 at The Historic New Orleans Collection under the title *Enigmatic Stream: Industrial Landscapes of the Lower Mississippi River*. The example shown here illustrates the complexities of this landscape and the issues that it raises in geographic, cultural, environmental, and social arenas.

This photograph was taken about 33 miles upriver from New Orleans, where the Mississippi meets the Bonnet Carré Spillway. The latter was constructed as part of a federally sponsored flood control system along the river following the Great Flood of 1927. The flood affected states along both sides of the waterway from Illinois to Louisiana, took 250 lives, displaced several hundred thousand people, and caused property damages with an upper estimate of $1 billion. The spillway was built between 1929 and 1932, and railroad and car bridges over it were finished in 1936. It consists of a concrete structure with 350 gates plugged by timber posts that can be opened to permit floodwater to flow into a nearly six-mile-long floodway—in effect, an artificial valley created by levees on its upriver and downiver sides—stretching between the Mississippi River and Lake Pontchartrain.

When the river's height reaches a predetermined level set by the US Army Corps of Engineers, any or all of the spillway's individual gates may be opened to allow a trickle or a torrent of the river's volume to be diverted to Lake Pontchartrain, a brackish tidal lake that lies to the north of the river's course. The diverted water of the river not only takes pressure off the levees protecting New Orleans and other downstream communities, it also carries fish with it, offering an opportunity for sport anglers to fish the Mississippi in an uncommon way—just before this relatively shallow runoff enters the spillway gates. But there is plenty of water left to float the five oceangoing bulk carriers moored in a line of the deeper channel of the river.

The spillway was first opened to alleviate flooding in 1937. The photograph on page 183 shows a satellite view of it in service in 1973. During the twentieth century, opening the spillway was a fairly rare occurrence, happening on average about once a decade. In the early twenty-first century, high water on the Mississippi has caused the Army Corps to open it more frequently, including twice in 2019. The freshwater diversion alters the salinity of Lake Ponchartrain, introducing sediment to its waters, and otherwise affecting the ecological balance of a system that extends to the coastal waters of the Mississippi Sound, part of the Gulf of Mexico.

Sexton's picture presents for consideration the often thorny conflicts that exist when humankind rubs up against nature and its forces, and the accommodations necessary to allow continued existence for both.

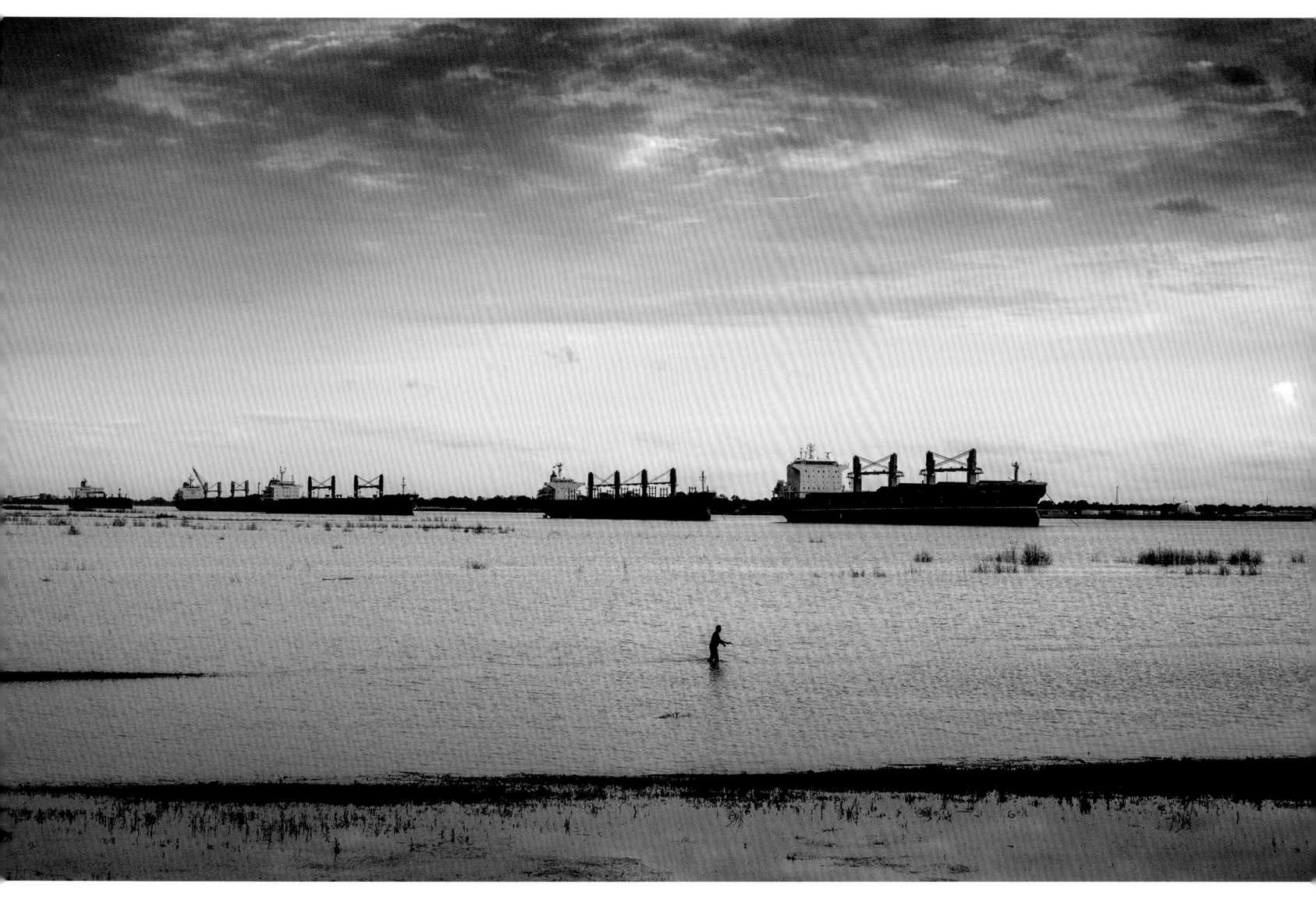

**Fishing in the Flooded Bonnet Carré Spillway with Moored
Bulk Carriers in Background, 2015**

by Richard Sexton
inkjet print, 17 × 24 in.

acquisition made possible by the G. Henry Pierson Jr. Photography
Fund, 2015.0364.51, © Richard Sexton 2015

Charles Muir Lovell (b. 1952)

The tradition of annual parades by social aid and pleasure clubs in New Orleans is more than 150 years old. The parades occur from September until late spring, only pausing during the hot summer months, and feature club members dressed in outfits designed especially for that season's outing, a brass band, and the group of followers and onlookers referred to as the second line. A second line parade is an expensive venture, so clubs sponsor events throughout the year to help defray the cost of materials, the band, and the required city permits.

Clubs with origins in the nineteenth century were often formed as mutual aid or benevolent societies to provide services like group medical benefits, financial assistance in times of need, and funeral arrangements when such things were often hard for African Americans to afford. Nearly all of today's clubs exist to promote friendship and socializing, rather than to provide financial support. Club names are both serious (Young Men Olympian Jr. Benevolent Association and Black Men of Labor, for example) and fun loving (Lady Jetsetters and the group pictured here, Money Wasters).

Charles Muir Lovell is one of several photographers who have documented the public activities of social aid and pleasure clubs over extended periods of time. His work with this subject began with his arrival in New Orleans in 2008 and builds on the visual history of earlier generations of photographers also interested in the parades, including Ralston Crawford, Jules Cahn, John Bernard, Michael P. Smith, Judy Cooper, Christopher Porché West, Eric Waters, and Bruce Sunpie Barnes. Prior to moving to New Orleans, Lovell photographed traditional public performances in Mexico and New Mexico.

Though Lovell's photographs cover nearly every aspect of clubs' parades, he is especially adept at isolating individuals, capturing in single images the exuberance, intensity, traditions, and pageantry that the parades present.

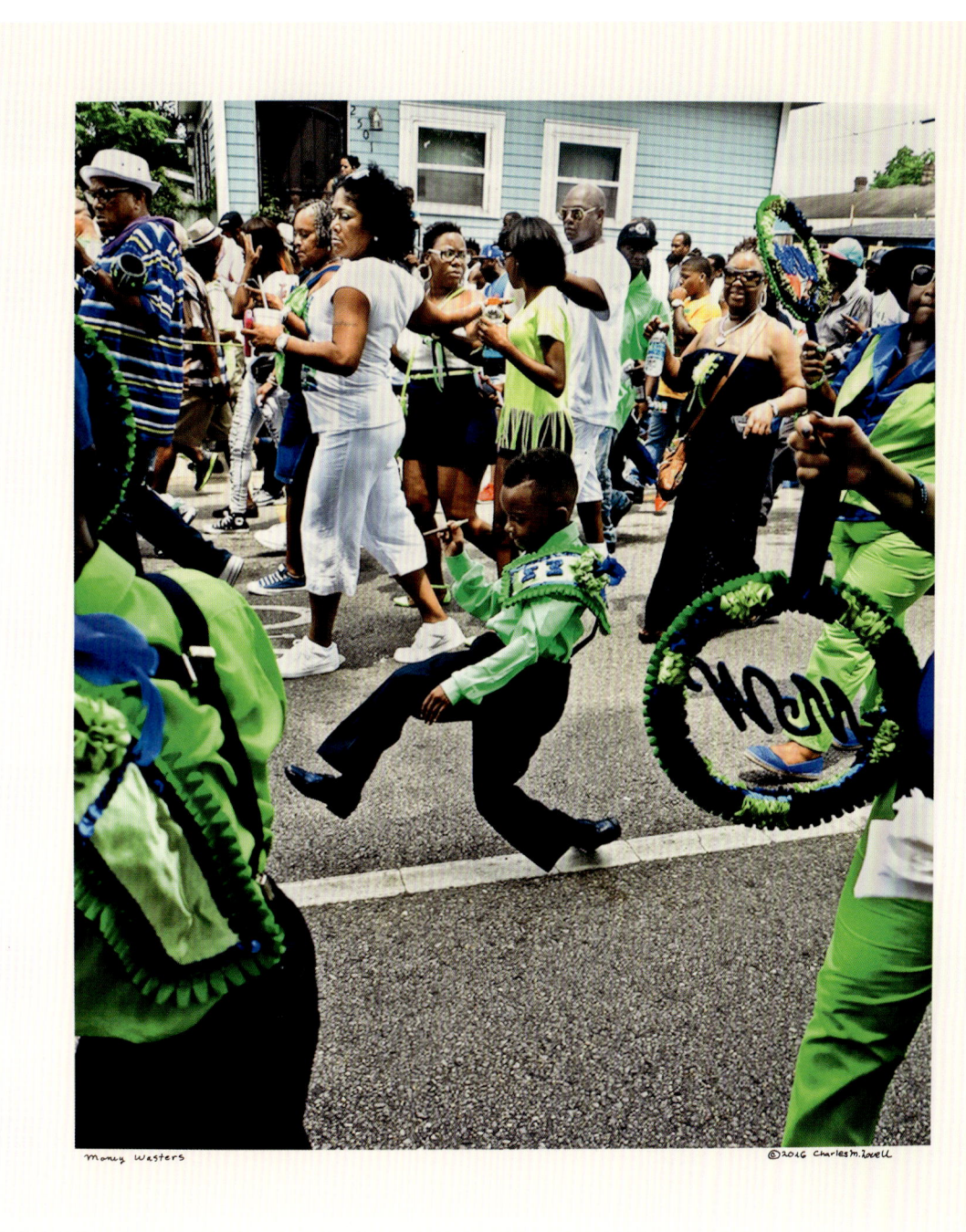

Money Wasters member Armad Rickmon, 2016
by Charles Muir Lovell
inkjet print, 24 × 20 in.
gift of Charles Muir Lovell, 2019.0393.8, © Charles Muir Lovell

Everett Kennedy Brown (b. 1959)

The filaments of history binding the city of Matsue, capital of Japan's Shimane Prefecture, and New Orleans are—like silk—thin but nonetheless strong. The thread that will always link the cities is their connection to nineteenth-century writer and cultural observer Lafcadio Hearn. In his nearly ten years in New Orleans, Hearn investigated Creole traditions of language and folklore, wrote for several newspapers, and compiled *La Cuisine Creole* (1885), considered a foundational book in the study of New Orleans cooking. He spent the final years of his life in Japan, where similar subjects—folklore, myths, traditions—with respect to that country's long history captured his attention. His writing in English about the country's people and traditions offered a glimpse of Japanese culture that had been inaccessible to westerners for centuries. Indeed, one of the books from his Japanese years is *Glimpses of Unfamiliar Japan*, published in 1894.

Like Hearn, Everett Kennedy Brown is a foreigner in Japan (an American living in Kyoto) and is drawn to the country's cultural traditions, people, and physical setting. The asymmetrical tree in Brown's photograph is evidence of its geographic setting, one where a steady force of wind from one direction literally bends the tree to its will. One may wonder if Hearn, while a resident of Matsue, on Honshu Island's west coast, saw such trees and recalled the wind-bent oaks of Louisiana's coastal *cheniers*, shaped by the incessant flow of wind from the Gulf of Mexico. The powerful effects of such wind and water were immortalized by Hearn in the novella *Chita: A Memory of Last Island*, published in 1888.

Brown's photographs are printed using a method that was the ne plus ultra of reproduction during Hearn's time, reserved for the finest reproductions in books and portfolios. The finished print—a collotype—begins with a wet-plate collodion negative that is reproduced as a hardened gelatin matrix. This becomes a printing plate of a sort, one that can be manually manipulated to change details and tonality. The gelatin matrix is inked and then printed under pressure on a sheet of paper; in Brown's case, a rice fiber paper. Over the decades, the process died off, and the atelier in Japan that prints Brown's work is the only commercially operating collotype printer in the world.

The specific nature of most photographs notwithstanding, correspondences may arise. A photograph of a Japanese landscape may spark thoughts of similar scenes in Louisiana, both of which may have been experienced by Lafcadio Hearn. Geographic boundaries are far less porous than those of the imagination, and when crossing the latter, a world based on common experiences and circumstances can shrink dramatically.

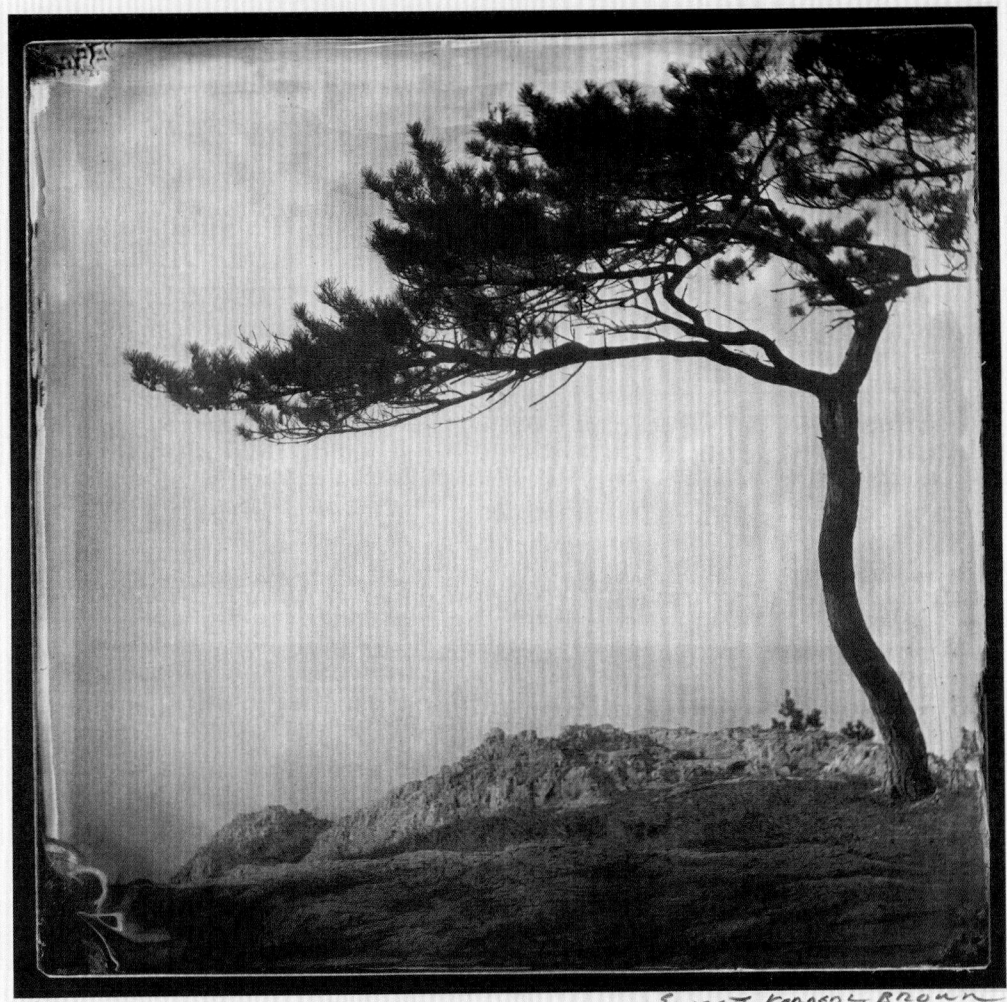

1/8

Everett Kennedy Brown

Shimane Peninsula Pine Tree, 2018
by Everett Kennedy Brown
collotype, 14 × 14 in.
acquisition made possible by Donna and John Fraiche and John
Turner and Jerry Fischer, 2020.0142.8, © Everett Kennedy Brown

ACKNOWLEDGMENTS

Having a decades-long career in a museum and authoring a book like this one are not solo enterprises. More people than I could ever hope to recognize individually are responsible in ways large and small for whatever success the career or the book may have and for the joy I experienced in each endeavor. The acknowledgements to those whose material and moral participation in seeing this book to print should take both a wide-angle approach as well as a close-up one. Any list thanking people will be incomplete, but the following have had a significant share in achieving whatever successes are identified.

At the start of my career, curator John A. Mahé II helped me to understand the important work that a curator does and made me see that a story told through historical objects is a different and often richer one told only with words alone. Mrs. Ralph V. "Dode" Platou, first as chief curator and later as executive director, championed the idea of photographic items as an essential part of the historical record and strongly supported their acquisition. Her vision and encouragement were critical elements of any success my work had.

As photographic holdings grew, certain staff members not only brought knowledge but continually gained it to ensure that photographs were inventoried, cataloged, housed, and made available to the public. For much of the time I spent at THNOC, Jude Solomon provided those skills, along with an eye for identifying photographs and photographers whose reputations and work were not widely known but are nonetheless significant in the region's history. Cath Cain, Mallory Taylor, and Catie Sampson worked with Jude and contributed in their unique ways to understanding the large and complex subject that is Louisiana photography. Catie played a particularly significant role as *Louisiana Lens* took shape.

It seemed that no matter how minimally informative a photograph seemed to be or obscure its maker was, John T.

Magill, longtime THNOC curator and head of the reading room, could almost magically uncover more about the subject or photographer. Rebecca Smith, as associate director of THNOC's Williams Research Center (WRC), continues in that role, and she and the talented reference staff who strive mightily to make the facility a pleasure to use have my sincere thanks. Special efforts in ferreting out numerous issues of fact for this book were made by M. L. Eichhorn, Jari Honora, Robert Ticknor, Heather Green, Kristin Hébert Veit, and Jennifer Navarre. Over decades of our overlapping careers, Senior Curator Judith H. Bonner employed her extensive knowledge of Louisiana's art history to ensure that the symbiosis of photographs with paintings, prints, drawings, and sculpture was both understood and revealing.

The Photography Department at THNOC, headed by Keely Merritt, relentlessly and happily produced the digital files for *Louisiana Lens*, striving for results that faithfully reproduced the objects in our collection. Responsible for the overwhelming share of this arduous work is the department's Tere Kirkland. Careful tracking of this process not only involved the photography department but the Registration Department and its head Jennifer Ghabrial. Susan Eberle and Rachel Ford were key in this work, and in checking the accession files for correspondence and other paper trails that ensured the accuracy of entries in this book.

Through many years, exhibitions, and programs, Alfred E. Lemmon, Director of the WRC, and Amanda McFillen, Director of Public Programs and Interpretive Services, offered willing support, sincere encouragement, and sound advice. The preparation and mounting of these exhibitions has been ably conducted by Tom Staples, Doug MacCash, Steve Sweet, Terry Weldon, Scott Ratterree, Dale Gunnoe, and Joseph Shores. They have my appreciation for the creative and difficult work that exhibitions involve.

That *Louisiana Lens* exists at all is due to the long-suffering and professional efforts of THNOC's Publications Department, headed for nearly two decades by Dr. Jessica Dorman. Her steady hand on a talented department of employees and independent contractors, as well as her philosophy and insight about publishing in a history museum, has served this project, and dozens of others, with excellence. Cathe Mizell-Nelson served as the principal editor for *Louisiana Lens*, and along with her colleagues Dorothy Ball, Siobhán McKiernan, and Margit Longbrake, ensured its accuracy and readability. Siobhán also indexed the book, and Dorothy chased down thousands of details about dates, dimensions, mediums, and rights. The original manuscript is far better for the thoughtfulness and industry of this special team. Any shortcomings that a reader may find are my responsibility alone. Alison Cody's design is elegant and smart, allowing every picture to have its own spotlight in the context of an extended narrative of Louisiana's photographic history.

Working in a museum has the happy circumstance of sparking connections with curators employed in others. Over the years, the conversations and engagement with such fellow travelers has enriched my experience, sharpened my thinking, and made me consider different ways of approaching photographs that without such interactions may never have happened. Among the longstanding and significant members of this cohort are Nancy C. Barrett, Keith F. Davis, Roy Flukinger, Harris Fogel, Tina Freeman, Adrian-Silvan Ionescu, Anthony Lewis, Russell Lord, Steve Maklansky, Alison Nordström, Anne E. Peterson, Françoise Reynaud, John Rohrbach, Mary Louise Tucker, William Earle Williams, and Steve Yates. I owe special thanks in this regard to Jeff L. Rosenheim for his introductory essay to *Louisiana Lens*, and for his friendship, collegiality, advice, and insights over the forty years and many conversations about photographs, photographers, and photography that we've enjoyed as friends.

My sincere thanks is extended to all photographers of Louisiana, living and deceased, included in this volume or not, for their active dedication to the medium, whether for vocation or pure enjoyment. It has been my great fortune to know many of the photographers represented in this volume. Whether over years of longstanding communication or through specific conversations about a picture in this book, their knowledge and generosity have positively affected my career as a curator as well as the character of this book.

Members of this group include Matt Anderson, Harold Baquet, Douglas Baz, Carl Bergman, George D. Berkett, John Bernard, Al Bertacci Sr., Lyle Bongé, G. Andrew Boyd, Donald Muir Bradburn, Robert S. Brantley and Jan White Brantley, Everett Kennedy Brown, Debbie Fleming Caffery, Jules Cahn, Sandra Russell Clark, Stephanie B. Dinkins, Johnny Donnels, Tina Freeman, Abbye A. Gorin, William K. Greiner, Christopher R. Harris, Allen Hess, William Karam Jr., Alan Karchmer, Stuart Klipper, Clarence John Laughlin, Charles Muir Lovell, Charles Martin, Maurice Martinez, A. J. Meek, Milton Melton, Girard Mouton,III, Owen F. Murphy, Rick Olivier, Mitchel Osborne, Josephine Sacabo, Richard Sexton, Howard Philips Smith, Michael A. Smith, Michael P. Smith, David G. Spielman, Stan Strembicki, Sam R. Sutton, Betsy Swanson, Roy Octave Trahan, Charles H. Traub, Jonathan Traviesa, John Uhl, Randell Brent Vidrine, Christopher Porché West, Stephen Wilkes, and Jim Zietz.

During my employment at THNOC, from October 1975 through December 2020, I worked with all of The Collection's executive directors except Mark McKiernan. Stanton M. Frazar, Dode Platou, Jon Kukla, Priscilla Lawrence, and Daniel Hammer all provided leadership, encouragement, and counsel as THNOC's photography collections achieved growth and prominence, qualities that continue today. The longest of these tenures occurred with Priscilla Lawrence (1999–2019), who is also my spouse, and whose guidance, support, and confidence in this book and its author have sustained its writing and completion. Her contributions, both obvious and invisible, to *Louisiana Lens* are significant factors in its realization.

INDEX

Abbeville (town), 138, **139**, 142, **143**
Adams and Hofeline, 58, **59**
aerial photography, 12, 122, 166, **167**, 170, **171**
albumen prints, 50, **50**, **51**, **53**, **55**, **61**, **66–67**
Alfieri, Richard, 200
Algiers neighborhood, 186
ambrotypes, **39**, 40
American Institute of Architects (AIA), 102, 114
American Society of Magazine Photographers, 162
Anderson, Matt, 154, 174, **175**
Andrews, James, 38, **39**
Angelo Brocato's Italian Ice Cream Parlor, 158, **159**
Angola Prison, 122, **123**
architecture
    commercial, 134, 218
    documentation, 16, 134, 170
    of French Quarter, 88, 114, 192, 228
    of New Orleans, 74, 132, 170, 260
    of plantations, 34, 110, 134
    postmodern, 220
Arts and Crafts Club of New Orleans, 104
Associated Artists Gallery, 157, **156–57**
Auden, W. H., 20–21
Audubon Park, 54
autochromes, 92, **93**

Baquet, Harold, 12, 154, 206, 238, **239**
barbershops, 194, **197**, 214, **215**, 266
Barker, Danny, 194, **196**
Barnes, Bruce Sunpie, 276
Barnes, Paul D. "Polo," 156, **157**
Bartels, William, 72
Barthelemy, Sidney, 238
Bayou Barataria, 216, **217**
Bayou Bonfouca, 96, **97**
Bayou Lafourche, 114, 134, 230, 234
Baz, Douglas, 188, **189**, 282
Bedou, Arthur P., 78, **79**, 90, **90–91**
Belle Grove plantation, 134, **135**, **137**
Bellocq, Ernest J., 12, 76, **77**
Bergman, Carl, **266–67**
Berkett, George D., 172
Bernard, Guy, 140, **141**
Bernard, John, 154, **155**
Bernard, Marie Bousquet, 160, **161**
Black newspapers, 40, 238
Black-owned businesses, 130, 194, 206, 214
Black photographers, 130, 238
Bongé, Lyle, 156, **156–57**
Bonnet Carré Spillway, 11, 182, **183**, 274, **275**
Bookhardt, D. Eric, 206
Borenstein, Larry, 76, 157
Bourbon Street, 112, **113**, 152, **153**, 156, 162, **163**
boxing, 11, 52, **53**

Boyd, G. Andrew, 222, **225**, 242
Bradburn, Anne Strickland, 176
Bradburn, Donald Muir, 176, **177**
Brantley, Jan White, 272
Brantley, Robert S., 272, **273**
Brown, Everett Kennedy, 278, **279**
Broyard, Charlotte Armantine, 30
Brulatour building, 104
Brunet, Jett, 230, **231**
Brylski, Cheron, 238
Bywater neighborhood, 198, **199**, 244, **245**

C. Bennette Moore Studio, 106–7, **107**
Cable, George Washington, 100
Caffery, Debbie Fleming, 190, **191**
Cahn, Jules, 12, 178, **179**
Cajuns, 188, 202
Calhoun, Keith, 206
Cancienne, Cleveland, 234
Cancienne Broom and Mop Factory, 234, **235**
Carnival. *See* Mardi Gras
Cartier-Bresson, Henri, 20
Castrillo, Luis, 206
Causeway bridge, 222, **223**
cemeteries
    discussion, 146, 210, 216, 246
    images of, **147**, **210–11**, **216–17**, **247**
Chandler, David, 200
Charity Hospital, 266, **267**
Charles L. Franck Photographers, 17, 86, **86–87**, 94, 96, **97**, 226. *See also* Franck-Bertacci Photographers
Chartres Street, 72, **73**, **89**
Chighizola (Chickazola) family, 122, **123**
child labor, 80, **81**
chromogenic negative, **243**
chromogenic prints, **183**, **227**, **259**, **268**
Cirkut camera, 82
City Park (New Orleans), 94
Civil War, 40, 42, 46, 48
Clark, Sandra Russell, 206, 246, **247**
Cleveland, Grover, 124
climate change, 176, 182
Cline, Isaac Monroe, 128, **129**
Coleman, Cecil R., 124
Collins, Florestine Perrault, 130, **131**
Collins C. Diboll Vieux Carré Digital Survey, 110
color transparencies, **152**
color transparencies (35 mm), **149**
contact prints, 156, **156–57**, 212, **213**, **229**
Cooper, Judy, 276
corner stores, 160, 186, **187**, 194, 266
Costanza, Rusty, 242, **242–43**
Crawford, Ralston, 146, **147**, 148, 154

Creole String Beans, 234
Creoles
    Black, 130
    history, 38, 56, **57**, 206
    identity, 18, 56
    traditions, 56, 130, 160, 278
    white, 56
Cruise, Alvyk Boyd, 10, 38, 89, 124
cyanotypes, 58, **59**, 72, **73**

daguerreotypes, 26, **27**, 28, **29**, 30, **31**, **33**, 36, **37**, 40, **41**, 48, 256
Dauphine Street, 11, **121**, 124
Davis, Arthur Quentin "Quint" Jr., **173**
de Caro, Frank, 18
de la St. Croix, Mother Marie, 12, 66, **66–67**
de la Villebeuvre, Anna Jeanne, 32, **33**
de la Villebeuvre, Jeanne Roman, 32, **33**
Decatur Street, 172
Dejan, Harold, 232
Delcroix, Eugene A., 126, **127**
digital chromogenic prints, **255**
digital images, 19–20, **253**, **273**
Dinkins, Stephanie B., 208, **209**
Donaldsonville (town), 62
Donnels, Johnny, 192, **193**
duck decoys, 230, **231**
Duke, David, 242, **242–43**
Dureau, George, 268, **268–69**
Durr, George Ernst, 116, **117**
Dyer, Chester "Chet," 166

Edwards, Edwin, 242, **242–43**
Edwards, Jay Dearborn, 16, 42, **43**
Esplanade Avenue, 42, **43**
Evan Hall plantation, 62, **63**
Evans, James Guy, 28, **29**
Evans, Walker, 11, 12, 28, 112, **113**, 120

Farm Security Administration, 120
Faulkner, William, 88
Faureaud, Marie, 12, 66, **66–67**
Federal Emergency Management Agency (FEMA), 13, 256, 260, **260–63**
ferrotyping, 132
Filipino immigrants, 70, **71**
Flaherty, Robert, 138, 142
flooding
    after Hurricane Katrina, 244, 252, 254, 256, 260
    images of, **224**, **225**, **274**
    of Mississippi River, 182, 274
    prevention, 222
Fontenot, James, 236, **237**
football, 168, 242

Franck-Bertacci Photographers, 226, **227**. *See also* Charles L. Franck Photographers
free people of color, 11, 30, 40, 214
Freed, Leonard, 164, **165**
Freeman, Tina, 230, **231**
French Quarter
    architecture, 88, 114, 192, 228
    artistic circle in, 88, 124, 128, 192
    Collins C. Diboll Vieux Carré Digital Survey, 110
    images of, **8**, **10**, **73**, **89**, **107**, **121**, **125**, **205**, **229**
    neighborhood, 72, 100, 106, 110, 126, 192, 204, 228
    Vieux Carré Courier newspaper, 172
French Quarter Festival, 228, **229**
Friedlander, Lee, 76, **77**, 156

Garrison, Jim, 184, **185**
gelatin dry plate negatives, **85**, **111**, **127**
gelatin silver negatives, **145**, **155**, **156–57**, **185**, **195**, **219**, **269**
gelatin silver prints, **8**, **63**, **77**, **79**, **81**, **83**, **86–87**, **89**, **90–91**, **95**, **97**, **99**, **100–101**, **103**, **105**, **107**, **111**, **113**, **115**, **117**, **121**, **123**, **125**, **127**, **129**, **131**, **133**, **135–37**, **139**, **141**, **143**, **147**, **151**, **159**, **163**, **165**, **167**, **169**, **171**, **173**, **175**, **177**, **187**, **191**, **193**, **196**, **199**, **201**, **207**, **209**, **210–11**, **213**, **217**, **221**, **223–25**, **229**, **235**, **237**, **239**, **241**, **247**, **249**, **266–67**, 268
Genthe, Arnold, 100, **100–101**
Gentilly neighborhood, 13
Girod Street Cemetery, 16
glass negatives, 48, 66, 76, **77**, 84, 96, 126
Goldston, Christopher "Happy," 154, **155**
Gorin, Abbye, 158, **159**
grain elevators, 86, **87**
Grand Isle, 70, **70–71**, 122, **123**
Gravois, Warren, **210–11**
Great Depression, 112, 114, 138
Greiner, William K., 258, **259**
Guesnon, George, 156
Gulf Islands National Seashore, 176

Haller, John L., 70, **70–71**
Harmony Circle, 140
Harris, Christopher R., 200, **201**
Harrison, Benjamin, 124
Hearn, Lafcadio, 100
Henry, Cammie G., 108
Herbert, Carroll, 256, **257**
Hess, Allen, 216, **217**
Hine, Lewis Wickes, 80, **81**
Historic American Buildings Survey (HABS), 102, 114, 124, 202, 218
Historic New Orleans Collection, The
    campus, 11, 104, 198, 200
    cemetery preservation, 210
    founders, 15, 16, 136, 200
    history, 15, 136
    Louisiana World Exhibition (1984), 222, 228
    non-photographic holdings, 146, 148, 150, **150**, 252
    photographic holdings, 12–17, 19, 20, 26, 30, 32, 48, 66, 74, 76, 84, 88, 107, 136, 146, 148, 150, 158, 162, 166, 176, 178, 198, 208, 238, 242, 264
    publications, 188, 194, 210, 272, 274
Hitchler, Anthony H., 126
Hofeline and Adams, 58, **59**
Holy Family Spiritual Church, 194, **195**
Horn Island, 176, **177**
Howard, Henry, 272

Huber, Leonard, 16, 17, 143
Hullaballoo (Tulane newspaper), 144, 174
Hurricane Ida, 188
Hurricane Katrina
    documentation, 12–13, 17, 166, 242, 252–253, 254, **255**, **257**, 258, 259, **259**, 260, **260–63**, 264, **264**, **265**, 266, **266**
    fires, 252, **253**
    flooding, 244, 252
    rescue effort, 256, **256**
Hymel plantation, 202, **203**

immigrants, 60, 70, **71**, 80, 158, 162, 188, 202, 220, 272
Industrial Canal, 166, **167**, 254
infrared film, 246
inkjet prints, **153**, **161**, **179**, **181**, **189**, **203**, **205**, **215**, **245**, **256–57**, **264–65**, **270–71**, **275**, **277**
Isaac Delgado Museum of Art, 74, 134
Ivy, Ernest Doty, 92, **93**

Jackson, Jesse, 238, **239**
Jackson Square, 228, **229**
Japan, 18, 98, 278, **279**
Jazz Fest, 178, **179**, 180, 194, 228
jazz funerals, 12, 146, 154, 194
jazz musicians, 12, 146, 232
Jeff, Morris F. X. Sr., 180
Jefferson, Thomas (trumpeter), 154, **155**
Jefferson Parish, 126, 170
Jewell's Crescent City Illustrated, 46, 58, 80
Jim Crow laws, 12, 90, 144, 154. *See also* racism; segregation
Johnston, Frances Benjamin, 124, **125**
Julia Street, 218, **219**

Kaiser, Barry, 206
Kane, Harnett T., 142
Karam, William Jr., 204, **205**
Karchmer, Alan, 218, **219**
K-Doe, Antoinette, 248
K-Doe, Ernie, 248, **249**
Kenison, H., 124
Kilburn, Samuel S., 38, **39**
King, Grace, 100
Klipper, Stuart, 198, 244, **245**
Koch, Richard, 110, 114, **115**
Kodachrome, 92
Kodak No. 1 camera, 62
Kohlman, Freddie, 154, **155**
Krewe of Proteus, 98, **98–99**, 106
Kuyck-Hechtermans, Beatrijs, 150, **151**

Lake Pontchartrain, 12, 166, **167**, 182, **183**, 222, **223**, 274
Lane Cotton Mill, 80, 81, **81**
Laughlin, Clarence John, 12, **14**, 15, 16, 17, 23, 134–136, **135–37**, 236, 282
Lawrence, John H., 11–13, 288, **288**
Le Pretre mansion, 124, **125**
Lee Circle, 140
Leeson, David, 222, **223**
Leyrer, Dan, 110, **111**
Lilienthal, Theodore, 46, **47**, 58
Linnenkohl Photographs, 94, **95**
Lion, Jules, 22, 30, **31**
L'Observateur newspaper, 144
Louisiana Forestry Association, 142
Louisiana Press Association, 144
Louisiana Shipbuilding Corporation, 96, **97**
Louisiana State Museum, 56
Louisiana State University, 122, 146, 202, 268

Louisiana Story (film), 138, 142, **143**
Louisiana Superdome, 166, 242, **243**
Louisiana World Exhibition (1984), 218, 220, 222, 228, 232
Lovell, Charles Muir, 276, **277**
Lower Ninth Ward (neighborhood), 13, 194, 254
Loyola University, 140, 238
Lu, Blue, 194, **196**
Lucia, Joseph Anthony Sr., 144, **145**
Lutcher (town), 144
Lynn, Stuart M., 132, **133**

Maddux, Emory N., 124
Mardi Gras
    Cajun, 202
    flambeaux carriers, 240, **241**
    krewes, 90, **93**, 98, **98–99**, 106, **117**, 128, 232
    revelers, 12, 84, **85**, **152**, **153**
Mardi Gras Indians, **117**, 194
Marigny neighborhood, 198, **199**, 244, **245**
Martin, Charles, 270, **270–71**
Martinez, Maurice, 160, **161**, 282
McCormick, Chandra, 206
McFadden mansion, 94, **95**
McKinley, William, 124
Mechanics' Institute, 46, **47**
Meek, A. J., 212, **213**
Melton, Milton, 152, **152**
Mendes, John Tibule, 84, **85**
Mickal, Chris E., 13, 252, **253**
Miner, Nancy Ewing, 17, 96, 99
Mississippi River
    bridges, 204, 226, **227**
    connection to Lake Pontchartrain, 38, 182, **183**, 274, **275**
    flooding, 182, **183**, 274, **275**
    industry on, 102, 170, **171**, 204, 226, 274
    New Orleans riverfront, 204, **205**, 222
    plantations on, 102, **103**, 110, **111**, 170, **171**, 202, **203**
    quarantine control, **82–83**, 83
Mississippi River Gulf Outlet, 166, **167**
Moissenet, Felix, 32, **33**
Money Wasters, 276, **277**
Moonwalk, 204, **205**
Moore, Charles (architect), 220
Moore, Charles Bennette, 106, **107**, 126
Morgan, Andrew, 154, **155**
Morgan, Elemore Madison Sr., 142, **143**
Morgan, Sr. Gertrude, 178, **179**, 192
Morial, Ernest N. "Dutch," 238, **239**
Moses, Gustave A., 52, **53**
Mouton, III, Girard, 180, **181**
Mugnier, George François, 60, **61**, 212
Murphy, Owen F. Jr., 206, **207**, 282
Mutchler, Kurt, 222, **224**

Napoleon Avenue, 252, **253**
NASA, 12, 182, **183**, 204
NASA Michoud Assembly Facility, 166, **167**, 204, 254
New Deal, 120, 218
New Orleans East (neighborhood), 166, **167**, 254
New Orleans Horticultural Society, 70
New Orleans Jazz and Heritage Festival, 20, 178, **179**, 180, 194, 228
New Orleans Museum of Art, 74, 134
New Orleans Recreation Department, 180, **181**
New Orleans Saints, 168, **169**, 242
New Roads (town), 208, **209**
Newton, E. H. Jr., 42

Ninas, Jane Smith, 112
North, Central, and South American Exposition (1885–1886), 54, **55**, 56, **57**, 60

Odiorne, William C., **10**, 15, 16, 88, **89**
oil and gas industries, 102, 122, 138, 142, 176, 188, 274
Olivier, Rick, 234, **235**, 282
Orleans Parish Prison, 164, **165**
Osborne, Mitchel, 232, **233**, 282
oystering, 12, 70, **71**, 80

Pailet, Joshua Mann, 206
paintings, 28, **29**, **148**, 192, 252
Palumbo, Vincent, 236, **237**
panoramic photographs, 17, 82, **82–83**, 98, **99**, **216–17**, 244, **244–45**
Parlange plantation, 208
perique tobacco, 202, 270, **270–71**
Petit Bois Island, 176
photograph albums, 11, 18, 50, 66, **66–67**, 68, **69**, 70, **71**, 86, 116, **117**
Piazza D'Italia, 220, **221**
Pichot, Adolphe Wenceslas, 56
Pichot, Clementine de Morant, 56
Pichot, H. Leonie, 56
Pickett, Jack, 206
Piron, Armand J., 90, **90–91**
plantations
    architecture, 34, 102, 110, 134
    artists at, 108, 208
    documentation, 114, 170, 202
    images of, **61**, **63**, **103**, **111**, **115**, **135**, **137**, **171**, **203**
    slavery, 42, 60, 62, 102
Plaquemines Parish, **82–83**
platinum prints, **70–71**, 74, **75**, 109
Platou, Joanne "Dode," 17
Plauché, Léda Hincks, 98
Polidori, Robert, 13, 254, **255**
politicians, 46, 184, **185**, 204, 238, 242, **242–43**
Port Fourchon (town), 188, **189**
Preservation Hall, 157
Preservation Resource Center of New Orleans, 218
prisons, 122, **123**, 164, **165**
Professional Photographers of America, 107
prostitutes. *See* sex workers
Pryer, Wilbert, 212, **213**

race, 90, 138, 144, 154, 164, 214. *See also* Black photographers; free people of color
racism, 138, 164, 180. *See also* Jim Crow laws; segregation
Reconstruction, 36, 46
record stores, 194, **197**
Red River, 50, **50–51**
religion, 136, **136** 146, 160, 178, **179**, 194, **195**, 216, 268
Resettlement Administration, 112, 120
Rex Organization, 92, **93**, **179**
Richmond, David, 206
Rickmon, Armad, **277**
River Parishes, 144, 226
Robertson, Bruce, 234
Robinson, B. J., **269**
Robinson, Jack, 152, **153**
Robinson, Jim, 156, **157**
Rockmore, Noel, 178, **179**, 192, **193**
Roosevelt, Franklin D., 120
Roosevelt, Theodore, 124
Rosenheim, Jeff L., 11–13, 19

Roudanez, Dr. Louis Charles, 40, **41**
Ruffins, Kermit, 248

Sacabo, Josephine, 17, 198, **199**, 206
salted paper prints, 16, **35**, **43**
Sampson, Mary Ann (Sister), 108, **109**
Sandmel, Ben, 234
Sarrazin, Louis Jr., 124
satellite photography, 182, **183**
Save Our Cemeteries, 210
Savoy, Rob, 234
Sayles, Emmanuel "Manny," 156, **156**
second line parades, 276, **277**
segregation, 36, 138, 144, 154, 168, 180. *See also* Jim Crow laws
Sekaer, Peter, 120, **121**
Seven Oaks plantation, 170, **171**
Seventh Ward (neighborhood), 160, **161**
sex workers, 76
Sexton, Richard, 17, 182, 274, **275**
Shakespeare, **49**
Shaw, Clay, 184, **185**
Sherwood Anderson and Other Famous Creoles, 88, 128
shipbuilding, 96, **96–97**
Sisters of the Holy Family, 108, **109**
slavery, 42, 60, 62, 102
Smith, Howard Philips, 220, **221**
Smith, Michael A., 228, **229**
Smith, Michael P., 17, 154, 194, **195–97**, 206, 276
Souby, Edward J., 52, **53**
Spielman, David G., 264, **264–65**, 282
Spratling, William, 88, 128
St. Bernard Parish, 254
St. John's Church (New Orleans), 140, **141**
St. Louis Cathedral, 126, **127**, 228
St. Patrick's Church, 26, **27**
St. Roch Cemetery, 246, **247**
St. Roch Market, 198, **199**, 244, **244–45**
Standard Oil Company, 138, 142
stereographs, 16, 46, **47**, 54, 60
Stewart, J. A., 82, **83**
Storyville, 76
Strembicki, Stan, 240, **241**
sugar farming, 102, 190, 202
Sutton, Sam R., 166, **167**
Swanson, Betsy, 16–17, 166, 170, **171**, 282
Swinney, N. M., 104, **105**

Talfor, Robert B., 50, **50**, **51**
Tebbs, Robert W., 102, **103**, 114
Temple Sinai (New Orleans), 140, **141**
Teunisson, John Norris, 68, **69**
Theriot, Uriel J., 124
Third District (neighborhood), 272
Thomas, Norman, 162, **163**
Times-Picayune newspaper, 130, 144, 222, 242
Tinker, Edward Larocque, 100
tintypes, 16, 40, 48, **49**
Tipitina's, 194
Tivoli Circle, 140
tobacco, 202, 270, **270–71**
Toulouse Street, 200, **201**
Trahan, Roy Octave, 168, **169**, 282
trappers, 126, **127**
Traub, Charles H., 188, **189**, 282
Traviesa, Jonathan, 248, **249**, 282
Tremé neighborhood, 206, **207**, 214, **215**
Tulane University, 46, 100, 144, 168, 170, 174, 208
Turner, Homer Emory, 148, **149**

Uhl, John, 186, **187**, 282
Ulmann, Doris, 12, 108, **109**
United Fruit Company, 68, **69**
United States Army Corp of Engineers, 50, 134, 274
United States Housing Authority, 120
University Medical Center, 266
University of New Orleans, 166, 210
Upper Ninth Ward neighborhood, 244, **245**
Ursuline nuns, 66, **66–67**, 108
Ursulines Street, **89**

Veterans Affairs Medical Center, 266
Vidrine, Randell Brent, 236, **237**, 282
Vietnam War, 174, **175**
Vieux Carré. *See* French Quarter
Vieux Carré Courier newspaper, 172

Waldo, James Curtis, 36, **37**
Washington, Booker T., 78, **79**
Washington, Tuts, 194, **196**
Waters, Eric, 276
Waud, Alfred R., 15, 48
WDSU, 104
Webb, Louise "Gypsy Lou," 192
Webb, Todd, 138, **139**
Weber, Charles F., 184, **185**
wedding portraits, 36, **36–37**, **145**
Weingart, George Washington, 72
West, Christopher Porché, 12, 154, 214, **215**, 276, 282
white photographers, 144, 150
Whitesell, Joseph Woodson "Pops," 94, 128, **129**
Whitney, Morgan, 74, **75**
Wicker, Chester H., 124
Wilkes, Stephen, 256, **256–57**, 282
Williams, Clarence, 90, **90**
Williams, Lewis Kemper and Leila Hardie Moore, 12, 15, 16, 136, 200
Williams, Tennessee, 200, **201**
Wilson, Edward L., 54, **55**
Winans, Fonville, 122, **123**
Winogrand, Garry, 22
Wittgenstein, Ludwig, 21
women photographers, 104, 130, 150, 158
Woods, Margaret Mary, 36, **37**
Woodward, William, 100
World War I, 96
World War II, 134
World's Industrial and Cotton Centennial Exhibition (1885), 54, **55**, 56, **57**, 60, 218

Xiques House, 11

yellow fever, 68, 83
Young Men Olympian Jr. Benevolent Association, 210, **210**, 276

Zietz, Jim, 202, **203**, 282
Zulu Social Aid and Pleasure Club, 232, **233**

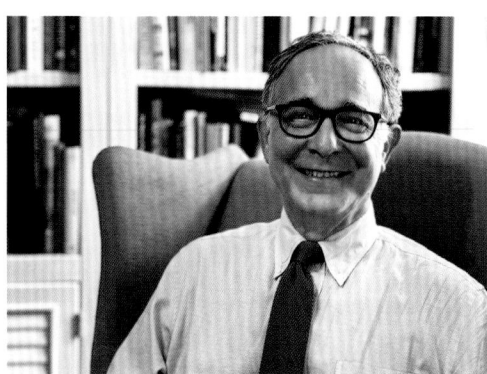

A New Orleans native, **John H. Lawrence** worked at
The Historic New Orleans Collection for forty-six years
before retiring as director of museum programs at the
end of 2020. As THNOC's head of curatorial collections, Lawrence had oversight of holdings numbering in
excess of five hundred thousand items. He has written
and lectured widely about aspects of contemporary
and historic photography, and the administration and
preservation of pictorial collections. He has also served
as principal or guest curator for dozens of exhibitions on
a variety of photographic, artistic, and general historical
topics. Lawrence holds degrees in literature and art
history from Vassar College and a certificate in museum
management from the Getty Leadership Institute,
formerly the Museum Management Institute.

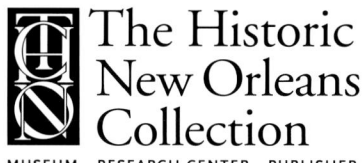

The Historic
New Orleans
Collection
MUSEUM • RESEARCH CENTER • PUBLISHER

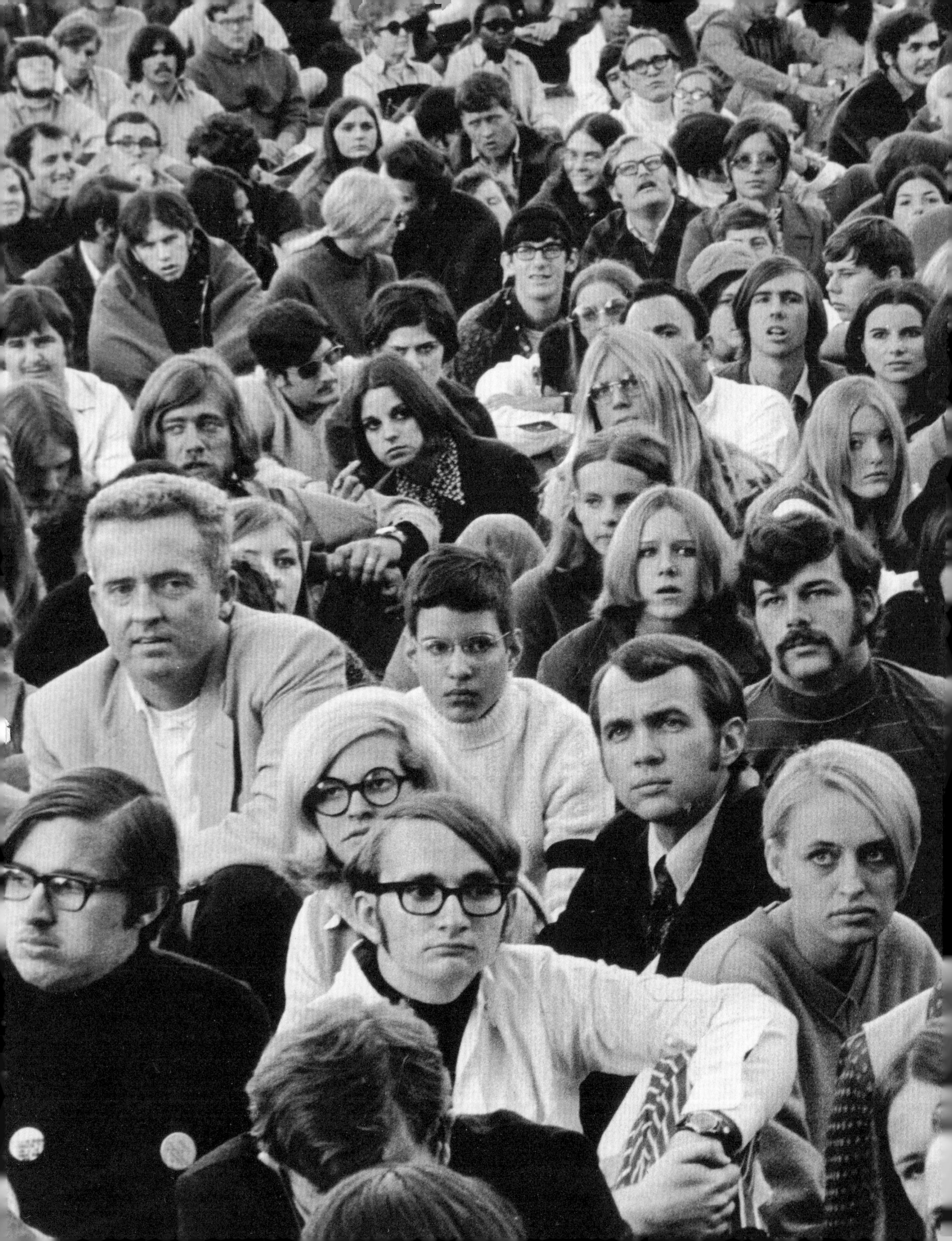